'LONGINUS'
ON THE SUBLIME

'LONGINUS'

ON THE SUBLIME

EDITED WITH
INTRODUCTION AND COMMENTARY

BY

D. A. RUSSELL

FELLOW OF ST. JOHN'S COLLEGE
OXFORD

169639

OXFORD
AT THE CLARENDON PRESS

Oxford University Press, Ely House, London W. 1

GLASGOW NEW YORK TORONTO MELBOURNE WELLINGTON
CAPE TOWN SALISBURY IBADAN NAIROBI DAR ES SALAAM LUSAKA ADDIS ABABA
BOMBAY CALCUTTA MADRAS KARACHI LAHORE DACCA
KUALA LUMPUR SINGAPORE HONG KONG TOKYO

© *Oxford University Press 1964*

FIRST PUBLISHED 1964
REPRINTED LITHOGRAPHICALLY IN GREAT BRITAIN
FROM CORRECTED SHEETS OF THE FIRST EDITION
AT THE UNIVERSITY PRESS, OXFORD
BY VIVIAN RIDLER
PRINTER TO THE UNIVERSITY
1970

PREFACE

MY object in this edition has been to make it easier for students to read a book which is certainly difficult and is generally thought important. I shall be content if I have given the beginner some help and encouraged others to attack the innumerable problems of this text with more success than has attended me.

The errors are mine, but they would have been much more numerous had it not been for the unselfishness and learning of many friends. Professor E. R. Dodds, Miss M. E. Hubbard, and Mr. A. E. Douglas have read the whole book, in typescript or in proof, and benefited it immensely. Professor Eduard Fraenkel in his unfailing kindness both read part and lent me a copy of Jahn–Vahlen in which notes from one of Wilamowitz's seminars are recorded. Professor H. Lloyd-Jones introduced me to the correspondence and acquaintance of Dr. W. Bühler, from whom I have learnt much and ought to have learnt more; he in turn enabled me to see Dr. H. Selb's typescript dissertation. Dr. H. D. Blume generously sent me his recent valuable thesis on the style of 'Longinus', to which I have been able to refer briefly in the Addenda. Mr. J. G. Griffith, Mr. A. N. Sherwin-White, Mr. E. K. Borthwick, and the late Mr. J. B. Leishman put me in their debt by answering questions and making suggestions. Finally, Mr. M. L. West read through the revises making very many saving corrections and acute remarks. To these, to the staff of the Clarendon Press, and to all others from whom I have had help, I give heartfelt thanks.

D. A. R.

I HAVE taken the opportunity of a second impression to correct some misprints and small errors, but have not made any changes of substance.

December 1969   D. A. R.

CONTENTS

INTRODUCTION	ix
I. Analysis	x
II. Date and Authorship	xxii
III. Ὕψος	xxx
IV. Influence	xlii
V. Text	xlix
SELECT BIBLIOGRAPHY	li
TEXT	1
COMMENTARY	57
ADDENDA	193
APPENDIX: LANGUAGE AND STYLE	194
INDEXES	199

INTRODUCTION

EUROPEAN literary criticism owes most, among Greek writers, to Aristotle. Its next biggest creditor it knows as Longinus. Simpler in thought and very much more colourful in expression than the *Poetics*, the treatise περὶ ὕψους had an immense influence on critical thinking from the time of Boileau to the early nineteenth century. It retains a power of immediate attraction which it is common experience to feel; yet it is a perplexing book and gives rise to many problems. Its style is difficult and often involved, its origin is a mystery, and its scope and plan are a good deal obscured by accidental losses amounting to about a third of its original length.

The subject of the book is what the author calls ὕψος, 'height'. This is a specific quality in writing, but its importance makes it in some sense of a different order from any other; it is 'that by which the greatest poets and prose-writers have won their fame'. The treatise—which is very definitely a book on 'how to write'—is concerned with how this quality is to be achieved. It treats 'height' as a product not of technique but of character. It shows how it is of practical use to people who have to influence opinions and actions by their words, and it illustrates it from the greatest literature of the Hellenic past—with one excursion into the Hebraic world and an incidental glance at Cicero.

I shall begin by giving (I) an analysis of the treatise, paying particular attention to its structure. This will be followed by (II) a general account of the evidence concerning its date and authorship, and (III) an essay on the concept of ὕψος—'ce que Longin entend par le sublime', as Boileau puts it—and its place in the history of ancient criticism. These questions of provenance and milieu admit only of approximate answers, and I have been content to handle them with broad strokes. It will be natural then to add (IV) some remarks on the nature and extent of the book's influence in the seventeenth and eighteenth centuries, and finally (V) a short note on the tradition of the text. Some comments on the language and style are reserved for an Appendix.

I shall refer to the author normally by the non-committal symbol L.

I. ANALYSIS

A. PREFACE (1–2)

L begins with an elegant and courteous address to Postumius Terentianus, his studious young friend and (presumably) patron. They have been reading together Caecilius of Calacte's treatise περὶ ὕψους and have found it inadequate and unsatisfactory in method. Terentianus has asked L to fill the gap, and L now submits his attempt to his friend's candid scrutiny. In the first few sentences we are made aware of three points which it is important to hold in mind: the author's concern for method,[1] his desire to be useful to πολιτικοὶ ἄνδρες, that is to say to all who have to use the art of speaking in public life,[2] and (most important of all) the essentially moral and psychological basis of the problem which he has set himself: how can we develop our natural capacities to some degree of greatness?

There is no need, he continues, to dwell on definitions; Terentianus knows perfectly well that ὕψος is a kind of excellence or distinction of speech and the principal quality to which the greatest poets and prose-writers owe their eternal renown. For ὕψος does not persuade, it carries us

---

[1] This characteristic is strongly emphasized by E. Olsen, *MP* xxxix (1942) 225 ff., in an interesting but not always reliable analysis (also in *Critics and Criticism* 232–59). See, for example, 5, 6, 8, 10. 1, 15. 12, 29. 2, 36. 4.

[2] See on 1. 2. Mlle Guillemin (*REL* xxxii (1954) 259 ff.) thinks that L 'legislates for epidictic oratory' and prepares the way for the Second Sophistic. But he clearly has practical ends in view: cf. the worldly advice in 17. 1.

away irresistibly, and there is no question of our choosing whether to let it affect us or not. Moreover, unlike excellence of 'invention'[1] or arrangement, it can be seen on occasion in the single blinding phrase which discloses genius.

But, it may be asked, is there really a τέχνη of which this quality is the subject? There are those who deny this outright, on the ground that it is a gift of nature and not reducible to rule. If this contention were right, L's investigation could not begin. He therefore counters it by two arguments. The first states that nature needs the help of method to control the exercise of a potentially dangerous impulse; art is to nature what good counsel is to good fortune. The second is that it is not even possible to judge some literary qualities to be gifts of nature without admitting the existence of a τέχνη which can teach us to make this discrimination.[2]

B. FURTHER PRELIMINARIES (3-8)

(a) *Faults incident to the effort to achieve ὕψος (3-5)*

The first lacuna[3]—equivalent in length to about three printed pages—deprives us of the beginning of this discussion. It seems natural to suppose that L passed straight from his demonstration that a τέχνη of ὕψος was possible to some illustrations of what may happen without it, and drew the contrast between passages of acknowledged sublimity and failures. The manuscript resumes in the course of a long quotation from tragedy which exemplifies confused and turgid imagery. The faults which are discussed in 3—turgidity, puerility, and unseasonable emotional effects—seem to be species of some generic bad quality, the name of

---

[1] i.e. the 'finding out' of suitable material. *Inventio* and εὕρεσις have nothing to do with 'invention' in the sense in which we speak of poets or novelists 'inventing' fictitious situations or characters.

[2] For the question of the authenticity of the latter part of this passage—'fragmentum Tollianum'—see on 2. 3.

[3] On the lacunae, see below, xlix.

which was given in the lost passage; the next chapter (4) at any rate begins as though its subject—frigidity—were a second main heading.¹ L gives a number of examples of frigidity, some from despised Hellenistic historians, some from Plato and Xenophon themselves. The cause of all such lapses from σεμνότης, he alleges, is the passion for novelty of thought.² How then are we to avoid them?

(b) *Some marks of the true ὑψηλόν* (6–7)

There is only one safe procedure: learning by long experience to recognize the genuine article. General advice, however, can help to some extent. As in the moral world, so in that of literature: there are some things, apparently great and desirable, which we see to be of an inferior grade as soon as we observe that it shows greater nobility to despise them than to possess them. Real ὕψος does not have this effect on us. Instead, it makes us proud and joyful, as though we had ourselves created it. It stands the test of repeated reading and reflection by experienced critics. It is irresistible and memorable. It pleases all conditions of men.

(c) *The five sources of ὕψος and the plan of the book* (8)

The five principal sources of ὑψηγορία are:

(i) The power of conceiving impressive thoughts.
(ii) Strong emotion.
(iii) Certain kinds of figures of thought and speech.

---

¹ See Philippson, *Rh. Mus.* lxxiv (1925) 267 ff. and Grube *AJP* lxxviii (1957) 362 ff. for discussions of this rather difficult and delicate problem. On the whole, I think it safer to follow the clear formal indication of θατέρου (4. 1), despite the difficulty of putting a name to the γένος of which τὸ οἰδοῦν, τὸ μειρακιῶδες, and τὸ παρένθυρσον are species: was it perhaps τὸ ἀπρεπές? The alternative view is that ψυχρός and μειρακιώδης are the same, and θατέρου signifies 'other than τὰ παθητικά'. All these words are derogatory and lack precision and consistent relationships among themselves; their use by other writers therefore has only limited value for this question.

² See, however, notes on 5 for some doubts about this view.

INTRODUCTION

(iv) Nobility of diction, including a proper choice of words and handling of metaphor and artificial language.

(v) Composition (i.e. word-order and considerations of rhythm and euphony) of a suitably elevated kind.

The first two of these sources depend on nature, the rest involve art.

This scheme is based on elements traditional in the ordering of the subject-matter of treatises on rhetoric;[1] but as a whole it is L's own and invented for the occasion. It serves as a table of contents for the rest of the book. We find that (iii) occupies 16–29, (iv) 30–38, and (v) 39–42; 43 looks like a misplaced subdivision of (iv). Further, (i) is announced in 9. 1, and apparently concluded at the end of 15. What then has happened to (ii)? We are told at the very end of the book that πάθη are to be the subject of a separate essay (ἴδιον ὑπόμνημα) and it has therefore generally been assumed that one of the two long lacunae, probably that at 9. 4, contained an indication of a change of plan.[2] This theory needs to be formulated with care, for it must not be supposed that L really changed his mind after his careful enumeration of sources; what we expect is rather an announcement that, despite καθ' ἑκάστην ἰδέαν (8. 1), the plan is to be modified and the book is not to include a separate treatment of this πηγή, because it is best handled, for the present purpose, actually in the course of the discussion of τὸ περὶ τὰς νοήσεις ἁδρεπήβολον.[3] It is noticeable that 'emotions' do in fact play a part in the following chapters.[4] At the same time, L must also have made the promise referred to in 44. 12 of a separate treatise of which the primary subject is to be πάθη. The lacuna is much too long for any further reconstruction of its contents than this. So far as length goes, indeed, it could perfectly well contain the entire

[1] See notes on 8.

[2] See, for example, Mutschmann, *TAQ* 16 ff.

[3] At 3. 5, L, having strayed into the subject, dismisses πάθη to an ἄλλος τόπος. This allusion does not help us much.

[4] As in the chapters on figures also: see below on 29.

discussion of πάθη; but Philippson's ingenious view[1] that it did do so, and that the whole passage from 9. 4 to 15. 11 falls under the head of σχήματα διανοίας, is ruled out by the form of the transition at 16. 1: αὐτόθι μέντοι καὶ ὁ περὶ σχημάτων ἐφεξῆς τέτακται τόπος. Nor is it plausible to assign the entire section from 9. 4 to 15. 11 to πάθη. It is, indeed, true that certain πάθη, fear in particular, are prominent in this section; it is also true that 9. 15 pointedly discusses the decline of πάθος into ἦθος, and that Quintilian's chapter *de affectibus* (6. 2) has much in common with 15. But the summary given at 15. 11 omits πάθη altogether; and even if we were to assume a serious corruption here, we could not conceivably give any account of the passage summarized which did not admit τὸ περὶ τὰς νοήσεις ὑψηλόν to be its principal subject.

In 8. 1–4, L offers some polemical arguments against Caecilius, who had said nothing about πάθη. πάθος, we are told, deserves to rank as a separate source; it is undoubtedly a very potent inspirer of μεγαληγορία, but τὸ ὑψηλόν and τὸ παθητικόν are not co-extensive, since some emotions, such as pity, grief, and fear, are incapable of producing ὕψος and some topics which are ὑψηλά have no emotional element. These are revealing remarks; we shall return to them.

C. THE FIRST TWO SOURCES: HIGH THINKING AND HIGH FEELING (9–15)

(a) *The beginning of the discussion* (9. 1–4)

We have only a fragment of the initial stages of L's argument here. He begins with the question, How are we to make ourselves capable of great thoughts and feelings? His answer, in brief, is that it is all a matter of mind and character.

[1] Loc. cit. 269 ff. The 'cornerstone' of Philippson's argument is Longinus, Τέχνη, p. 194 Hammer (p. 567 Walz): ὅσα δὲ σχήματα τῶν ἐννοιῶν ὠνόμασται . . . οὔ μοι δοκεῖ δικαίως σχήματα καλεῖσθαι, ἀλλ' ἔννοιαι καὶ ἐνθυμήματα καὶ λογισμοί. But L could not consistently accept this doctrine while at the same time treating figures, both of thought and of speech, as a separate πηγή.

INTRODUCTION

Words are not even necessary for the expression of ὕψος; though Ajax's indignant ghost said nothing to Odysseus in Hades, his silence is παντὸς ὑψηλότερον λόγου. It is the man of pride and greatness of mind who can alone give birth to greatness ἐν λόγοις. Alexander the Great is an example.

At this point the manuscript fails us. The equivalent of about nine printed pages is lost. Where we pick up the thread again, the discussion is running on

(b) *successful and unsuccessful ways of representing supernatural beings and of exciting awe* (9. 4–11).

Homer's Eris is a success, Hesiod's Achlys a failure; Homer's horses of the gods seem on the point of striding out of this world, his theomachy irresistibly depicts universal confusion.[1] However, the theomachy would be impious if taken literally. Homer does better where he treats of divine power with no anthropomorphic admixture of unworthy strife or unhappiness, as in the description of Poseidon's chariot speeding across the sea—a description comparable as an expression of divine grandeur with the account of creation in the first chapter of Genesis.[2]

With this surprising comparison, the argument seems at an end, and L continues with a slight apology: οὐκ ὀχληρὸς ἂν ἴσως, ἑταῖρε, δόξαιμι . . . . In fact, however, what follows is a wholly natural extension of the critique from the treatment of gods to that of heroes.[3] L quotes Ajax's prayer, ἐν δὲ φάει καὶ ὄλεσσον, as an example of the power shown by Homer in the *Iliad* (not in the *Odyssey*) of entering into the grandeur of a truly heroic character.

(c) *Comparison between the* Iliad *and the* Odyssey (9. 11–15)

The famous σύγκρισις which these remarks suggest expresses the view that the *Odyssey* was written to be a sequel

[1] I assume here that διὰ τὴν ὑπερβολὴν τοῦ μεγέθους and ὑπερφυᾶ are expressions of praise: but see notes on 9. 5–6.
[2] 9. 9: see notes.
[3] Cf. Pl. *Rep.* 3. 386 A, D ff.

and in Homer's old age. It is, of course, something of a digression, but it would be a mistake—and one against which L warns us by saying ταῦτα πολλῶν ἕνεκα προσεπιθεωρητέον—to suppose that its *raison d'être* is simply the association of ideas. Its relevance to the main theme is in fact made clear in 9. 14–15; the *Odyssey* shows how failure of power produces the absurd in place of the sublime, and incidentally how writers who in their prime were masters of πάθος descend in their old age to the humbler achievement of depicting character and atmosphere. Thus L in effect tells us a little more about the crucial difference between the genuine article and degenerate forms of it.

(d) Another road to ὕψος; proper selection and organization of material (10)

L proceeds to a new point. He quotes and comments on Sappho's φαίνεταί μοι κῆνος ἴσος θέοισιν. This poem, he says, illustrates the successful analysis of an emotion into a σύνοδος of emotions, so that the choice and combination of the right details produce an overwhelming general effect. Were it not for this we might well be tempted to take a narrower view of L's tastes than would be justified, for it is the only illustration which he draws from purely personal poetry, entirely free of heroic grandeur and magnificence.[1] He follows it up with more contrasts between Homer's successes and the failures of others, taking his examples this time from descriptions of storms.

(e) Amplification (11–12. 2)

This question of the selection and enumeration of details leads naturally to a consideration of αὔξησις (*amplificatio*), which L defines as 'an aggregation of details and topics

[1] Just for this reason, some English classical critics (Hugh Blair in his influential *Lectures on Rhetoric*, published in 1783 but written much earlier, and Vicesimus Knox (1826)) blamed L for including it. They had come to associate 'the sublime' exclusively with 'awful' and 'magnificent' subjects. Cf. Introd. IV.

INTRODUCTION

relevant to a matter, giving strength to the argument by dwelling on it'. This discussion also is a fragment, and we are left guessing about some of the differences between αὔξησις and the quality described in 10. αὔξησις, however, is much more of a technical trick; it consists simply in elaborating a statement by piling up all kinds of attendant circumstances; it does not involve the suppression of the insignificant and distracting which was an essential part of the quality described in 10, and it depends for success on the presence of ὕψος in much the same way as do the figures.

The lacuna which interrupts this discussion robs us of about three more printed pages of text. It appears, however, as if no fresh topic was begun in this interval; what we find next is a natural sequel to an account of αὔξησις.

(f) *Plato and Demosthenes, with a word on Cicero* (12. 2–13. 1)

This is a comparison between the exuberance of Plato and the thunderbolts of Demosthenes. Plato is a great hero to L, both as a philosopher and as a writer. Caecilius' criticism of him is later made the occasion of the famous passage on genius and mediocrity (33–36). L clearly feels some special need to come to his defence; current criticisms of his outrageous metaphors could not be neglected, and it had to be admitted that he sometimes fell into the faults incidental to his greatness. The passing note on Cicero is perhaps part of the defence: L, as I conceive it, cunningly invites his Roman readers to regard Plato and Cicero as both standing in the same relationship to Demosthenes.

(g) *Imitation as a means to ὕψος* (13. 2–14)

Mention of Plato leads to ἄλλη ὁδὸς ἐπὶ τὰ ὑψηλά.[1] This is μίμησις, imitation, profitable competition with the great men of old, who have power to inspire us as the gods inspire their prophets. Plato himself, and indeed other great writers

[1] Cf. 10. 1: εἴ τι καὶ ἕτερον ἔχοιμεν ὑψηλοὺς ποιεῖν τοὺς λόγους δυνάμενον. The statement of the plan to be followed which L gives in 8 does not forecast μίμησις or the subject of 10.

of old, imitated Homer; let us in our turn imitate Plato and Demosthenes and endeavour always to ask ourselves how they would have expressed our thought and judged our words. The consciousness of a responsibility to the past and to the future is the best stimulus to work of high quality.

(*h*) Φαντασία (15)

Finally, L discusses the power of vivid description—'conjuring up a scene'—to produce an impressive and impassioned effect. He distinguishes rhetorical from poetical φαντασία and illustrates the latter from Euripides and the former from Demosthenes and Hyperides.

D. THE THIRD SOURCE: FIGURES (16–29)

This part of the book is largely dependent on traditional rhetorical doctrine, but L has selected rigorously and arranged his material with some care, at least to begin with.

(*a*) He starts by giving a detailed analysis of one highly successful figure—the oath by the men of Marathon in *de corona* 208 (16). This discussion serves as a paradigm of method.

(*b*) The artificiality of figures should be concealed; they may rouse suspicion and anger. The best method of concealment is to set the figures in a context striking enough to make them seem natural (17).

(*c*) Rhetorical questions (18). This section is interrupted by one of the lacunae; the equivalent of about three printed pages is lost.

(*d*) Asyndeton (19).

(*e*) Asyndeton combined with anaphora (20).

(*f*) Polysyndeton as destructive of intensity (21).

(*g*) Hyperbaton (22).

(*h*) Various figures involving changes of case, tense, person, number. Plural for singular (23).

INTRODUCTION

(*i*) Singular where plural is expected (24).

(*j*) Vivid present (25).

(*k*) Imaginary second person (26).

(*l*) Unexpected lapse into *oratio recta* (27).

(*m*) Periphrasis and its dangers (28–29. 1).

(*n*) All these figures assist ὕψος because they express emotion (29. 2). (Thus the third source is in a sense subordinate to the missing second, and we have perhaps another clue to the way in which the programme outlined in 8 is in fact worked out.)

E. THE FOURTH SOURCE: NOBLE DICTION (30–38)

(*a*) Diction and thought are closely related. Inappropriate magnificence of diction may give rise to absurdities (30). Another lacuna follows here, again of about the length of three printed pages.

(*b*) The use of words of everyday or even vulgar vigour may occasionally be effective (31).

(*c*) *Metaphor* (32)

Caecilius has been too rigid in his rules; he seems to be of the same mind as those who forbid more than two or three metaphors on the same point. But the right guide is the practice of Demosthenes, not any rule of thumb. It is true that to apologize for a metaphor often makes its boldness more tolerable, but the best help, as with figures,[1] is given by the context; for in strong emotion audacity of expression is natural. Another use for metaphors is in descriptions (here, of course, πάθος is absent), as in the elaborate physiological passages of the *Timaeus*. Even Plato, however, can err, and his errors have given Caecilius a handle for his

---

[1] Metaphor is, of course, a trope, not a figure; hence it comes under the φραστικὸν μέρος. See on 16. 1.

unfair attacks. Caecilius in fact hates Plato even more intensely than he loves his favourite Lysias.

(d) *Digression: genius versus flawless mediocrity* (33–36)

This digression arises out of the problem of Plato, though like the earlier ones it makes a positive contribution to the main subject.

Let us consider a flawless writer and ask in general terms whether excellences are to be counted or weighed. This is particularly relevant to an inquiry about ὕψος because the endeavour to reach great heights is particularly dangerous. Even Homer errs, as we saw (9. 7), but his excellences far outweigh his faults. No one would rather be Apollonius than Homer.

Actually, if one were to count good qualities, Hyperides would prove superior to Demosthenes (34), for he has all the Attic graces. These, however, are as nothing compared with the vehemence and grandeur of Demosthenes. And the difference between Plato and Lysias is more significant even than that between Demosthenes and Hyperides.[1]

What then is the source of the greatness of the real genius? Among other things, it is his understanding of the place of man in the universe. We are endowed by nature with thought that can even pass beyond the bounds of the κόσμος and with an admiration for the grand and wonderful, both in the works of nature and in literature. A single success of a Homer, a Plato, or a Demosthenes redeems all his failures, which in any case amount only to a minute fraction of his triumphs. The fame of such men is assured for all time.

L concludes (36. 3–4) with some curious polemical arguments and with a reminder of the need for co-operation between art and nature—a corrective, we may suppose, in case the enthusiasm of 33–36 has revived in the reader's mind the suspicion which was refuted in 2, that there cannot be a τέχνη of ὕψος at all.

[1] See note on 35. 1.

INTRODUCTION

(e) *Similes* (37)

Only a few words of this section survive. There follows a lacuna of the same length as that in 30.

(f) *Hyperbole* (38)

We have only the concluding part of this section. L gives some examples of unsuccessful hyperbole and reiterates the principle that actions and emotions which come near to ἔκστασις are the cure and justification of every stylistic audacity.

F. THE FIFTH SOURCE: ΣΥΝΘΕΣΙΣ (39–42)

σύνθεσις includes word-order, rhythm, and euphony. Since L has (so he tells us) written two books on this rather technical subject, he does not here go into much detail.

(a) Psychological effect of rhythm; an example from Demosthenes showing how slight changes can ruin rhythm (39).

(b) Effect of periodic structure in securing μέγεθος (40. 1).

(c) Structure can give even common words ὄγκον καὶ διάστημα (40. 2–4).

(d) Conversely, bad and affected rhythm has a weakening effect (41).

(e) Excessive brevity is also bad (42).

G. LOW AND UNDIGNIFIED VOCABULARY (43)

This chapter is not where we should expect it. It belongs rather with φράσις (30 ff.). It does, however, cohere with 41 and 42 to form a group of sections dealing with features destructive of ὕψος. Most of the chapter is taken up by the discussion of a long example from Theopompus. Finally, L excuses himself from enumerating μικροποιά, since what they are may be inferred from the list of qualities which have the opposite effect.

Although these last few chapters are signposted in the usual pedagogic way (40. 1, 41. 1, 42. 1, 43. 1, 43. 6), their brevity and lack of connexion suggest that L is in a hurry to get to the end and somewhat indifferent to the technical details.

H. CONCLUSION: CAUSES OF THE DECLINE OF LITERATURE (44)

He inserts, however, a rather unexpected dialogue, in which he reports a recent conversation with 'one of the philosophers'. This person advanced the theory that the current λόγων ἀπορία was the result of despotism and peace; the breeding ground of eloquence is the stormy life of a free republic. L disagrees; he thinks it much more probable that the true cause is moral decline, love of gain and what we should loosely call materialism—valuing τὰ θνητὰ αὐτῶν μέρη at the expense of τὰ ἀθάνατα. The topic, as we shall see, is something of a commonplace in the literature of the first century A.D., and indeed goes back, in a sense, to the age of Plato. It is by no means irrelevant to L's theme; he has throughout the book insisted on the necessity for possessing ψυχικὸν μέγεθος before we can hope to achieve μεγάλοι λόγοι.

A short passage—perhaps only a few lines—is lost at the end of the chapter.

II. DATE AND AUTHORSHIP

The manuscript tradition of περὶ ὕψους gives no certain testimony concerning the author. In Parisinus 2036 (P), the tenth-century manuscript from which all other extant manuscripts descend,[1] we find Διονυσίου Λογγίνου in the title of the book, but Διονυσίου ἢ Λογγίνου in a table of contents (fo. 1ᵛ). This fact was noticed by F. Rostgaard in the early eighteenth century, and again brought to notice by Weiske

[1] See below, xlix.

in 1809, after Amati had warned him that one of the Renaissance manuscripts—the miscellany Vaticanus 285—actually has ἤ in the title of the extract which it contains.[1] It has been generally held since Weiske's time that the version given in P's table of contents is the correct tradition; and that we are in fact presented simply with a pair of plausible guesses on the part of some Byzantine scholar. It is not that the name Dionysius Longinus is an impossible one,[2] but that Dionysius and Longinus are exactly the names which we should expect to be attached to an anonymous work of criticism in the late empire and in Byzantine times. Dionysius will naturally be Dionysius of Halicarnassus, who wrote under Augustus and of whom we possess many works; Longinus will be the distinguished third-century scholar, the acquaintance of Plotinus, who bore the venerable name of the Cassii Longini.[3] The two are coupled, e.g. by Eunapius, who describes Longinus as 'a living library and walking university' (βιβλιοθήκη ἔμψυχος καὶ περιπατοῦν μουσεῖον) and goes on to compare him with 'others, of whom the most distinguished was Dionysius from Caria'.[4]

There is, therefore, a strong likelihood that we have two

[1] To judge from a photograph, this ἤ may be a later addition. In any case, it stems ultimately from P's table of contents. Par. 985, apparently an ancestor of Vat. 285, has ἤ on fo. 79ᵛ in its table of contents, but no ἤ where the extract begins, fo. 222ᵛ.

[2] Boyd (*CQ* N.S. vii (1957) 46) quotes Cassius Dionysius Uticensis, C. Apollonius Priscus, and similar forms.

[3] Born early in the century, this Longinus learnt rhetoric from an uncle who taught it at Athens, but travel and the friendship of Ammonius Saccas diverted him to philosophy—though he always remained in Plotinus' eyes φιλόλογος, οὐ φιλόσοφος. His later life was spent as a teacher and minister in Palmyra (his mother was from Emesa) under Odenathus (murdered A.D. 267/8) and subsequently Zenobia. He persuaded Zenobia to break with Rome and was captured and put to death on the fall of Palmyra in A.D. 273. Ancient sources: Porph. *Vita Plotini*; SHA *Aurelianus* 30; Zosimus 1. 56. The classic account in English is Gibbon, *Decline and Fall*, chap. xi.

[4] Eunapius, *Vitae Sophistarum* 4. 1. 3 (p. 6 Giangrande; p. 352 Wright). Cf. Cramer, *An. Ox.* iii. 159 and Lachares, ed. Graeven, in *Hermes* xxx (1895) 292 (Boyd, p. 43).

guesses. Could either be right? The claims of Dionysius are occasionally put forward—most recently by D. Marin[1]—but for most readers they do not survive a consecutive reading of περὶ ὕψους and any considerable part of that competent and facile critic; the whole impression of mind and style is quite different. Some specific arguments can also be brought. L, for instance, holds a favourable view of Plato's merits as a writer which closely resembles not Dionysius' own opinion but that which he criticizes in his correspondent Pompeius. Again, L refers (8. 1) to a book of his on Xenophon and (39. 1) to two books on σύνθεσις; Dionysius' περὶ συνθέσεως ὀνομάτων is in a single long book and he is not credited with anything on Xenophon.[2]

Cassius Longinus' claim was almost universally admitted until 1809.[3] The eighteenth century saw in his brilliant career and heroic death an appropriate setting for the noble and liberty-loving mind revealed in περὶ ὕψους.[4] We do, however, possess some extracts from the rhetorical works of Cassius Longinus, and they do not encourage the identification.

[1] *Studi Calderini–Paribeni* i. 157 ff. (1956).

[2] P has a marginal note on 39. 1: σημ (i.e. σημείωσαι, 'n.b.') περὶ συνθέσεως ἔγραψε Διονύσιος. This is just a cross-reference to the standard work on the subject; but it could well have given rise to the speculation that Dionysius was the author.

[3] Thus the sixteenth-century writer of the marginal note ἠπάτησαι ὦ κριτικώτατε on 4. 4 in Par. 2974 accepted it. For this stock epithet, cf. Porph. *Vita Plotini* 20 and *Scholium Moscuense*, A 3 Prickard.[2] (Both editions of Prickard's O.C.T. of περὶ ὕψους contain the *rhetorical* fragments of Cassius Longinus, but I refer to the second because the pages are lettered conveniently for reference.) Nevertheless, a Renaissance scholar wrote on a parchment attached to the cover of the Laurentianus ἀνωνύμου περὶ ὕψους—*de altitudine incerti authoris*.

[4] Zosimus, l.c.: θανάτου ζημίαν . . . οὕτω γενναίως ἤνεγκεν ὁ Λογγῖνος ὥστε καὶ τοὺς σχετλιάζοντας ἐπὶ τῷ πάθει παραμυθεῖσθαι. Boileau, *Préface*: 'On peut voir que Longin n'estoit pas seulement un habile Rhéteur . . . mais un Philosophe digne d'estre mis en parallèle avec les Socrates et avec les Catons. Son livre n'a rien qui démente ce que je dis. Le caractère d'honneste homme y paroist par tout; et ses sentimens ont je ne scay quoy qui marque non seulement un esprit sublime mais une âme fort élevée au dessus du commun.'

It is, indeed, not possible to say *for certain* that the fragment of the *ars rhetorica* could not have been written by L, though it wholly lacks the abundant metaphor and pregnant sententiousness which are his two main characteristics.[1] There are also one or two apparent parallels, but not more than can be accounted for by similarity of subject and by the fact that Longinus, too, seems to have used Caecilius as an authority.[2] There are also differences: not only does Longinus, if we may trust his epitomator, have a somewhat harsh view of Plato's style, but he also takes Aristides into account, as indeed we should expect any writer of the third century to do.[3] However, the main—I think incontrovertible—argument against the identification of L with Cassius Longinus rests on the discussion of *corrupta eloquentia* in 44. This whole topic is a commonplace in the first century, the mention of world peace is inconceivable in a writer of the middle of the third century (44. 6), and— a subordinate point—after the rise of the Second Sophistic Greek literary men were no longer as modest as is L about the achievements of their own age.[4]

There is, however, one puzzling piece of external evidence which has sometimes been used to support Longinus'

[1] One small point: L almost makes a mannerism of πάντες ἑξῆς and the like (4. 4, 9. 14, 33. 5, 34. 3): Longinus (fr. VII Toup) has πάντες ἐφεξῆς. This is the sort of detail which makes good evidence for a difference of author.

[2] For supposed parallels, see notes on 10. 7, 13. 3, 30. 1. For Longinus and Caecilius, Aulitzky, P–W, s.v. 'Longinos', col. 1406.

[3] Plato: *Scholium Moscuense*, D 7 Prickard²; Aristides: epit. Laur., E 22 and F 25.

[4] See notes on 44. Weiske saw that this was the crucial point: 'explicent quaeso si qui posthac erunt Longini sectatores pulcerrimam illam conquestionem de oratorum defectu.' 44, however, does not offer any clue to a precise dating. The outside limits are the reigns of Augustus and Antoninus Pius. For a recent attempt to establish a later date, see G. Marenghi, *Rend. Ist. Lomb.* lxxxix (1956) 485 ff. He would not support Longinus' claim, but dates the treatise in the late second or early third century, thinking its taste for 'baroque richness' a stage on the way to medieval taste. His arguments are of a very general kind.

xxvi INTRODUCTION

candidature. The eleventh-century rhetorician John of Sicily twice alludes or seems to allude to περὶ ὕψους.[1]

(i) In one passage John is discussing the meaning of στομφάζειν. He quotes Aristophanes' criticism of Aeschylus as στόμφακα κρημνοποιόν, and then goes on as follows to a somewhat different point: 'The poet's strangeness is even more apparent in the play *Orithyia*, where Boreas blows with both cheeks and disturbs the sea (I have forgotten the verses and have not got them in my head);[2] Sophocles imitates this. Longinus discusses these things more accurately ἐν τῷ κα' τῶν φιλολόγων.' If this explicit reference to Book XXI of Longinus' φιλόλογοι ὁμιλίαι (a title incidentally not found in the Suda list of Longinus' works[3]) unambiguously referred to περὶ ὕψους, we should have to adopt one of two hypotheses: either Cassius Longinus wrote our book and was, indeed, a magnificent anachronism; or else John was in error in attributing the book he has read to Longinus. Boyd contends for the second. He believes in a first-century Dionysius Longinus and thinks the intrusive ἤ in parts of the tradition of the title may be due to the speculations of a copyist who identified his author with ὁ κριτικώτατος, knew that his name should then be Cassius Longinus, and so concluded that the two names must be offered as alternatives.[4] This cannot be disproved; but it involves us not only in believing in this ingenious copyist but in a writer on literary criticism whose name luckily combined those of the two greatest critics known in late antiquity. Boyd's view, however, is not the only one possible on the assumption that John knew L; either the whole collection of φιλόλογοι ὁμιλίαι or Book XXI alone may perfectly well have been falsely attributed to the great Longinus even without any helpful coincidence in the name of its real author.[5]

[1] For text and references see notes on 3. 1, 9. 9: Boyd, pp. 39 ff.
[2] For this—perhaps imaginary—situation, cf. A. Gell. 12. 11, 19. 13.
[3] See Aulitzky, l.c., col. 1406.
[4] Euseb. *PE* 15. 20: τῷ καθ' ἡμᾶς Λογγίνῳ is not evidence for an earlier literary Longinus.
[5] In Lachares (*ap*. Graeven, *Hermes* xxx (1895) 292) we hear of ten

And in fact, the chance that John really means περὶ ὕψους is very far short of certainty. He clearly has some recollection and knowledge of a discussion of Aeschylus' and Sophocles' excesses on the theme of Boreas' threats. But in view of the way in which the same examples are copied and re-handled over and over again in Greek rhetoric, it is exceedingly unlikely that only one book ever contained such a discussion. Those 21 or more books of scholarly miscellanea must have swept up a lot of earlier learning—and might even have swept up L.[1]

(ii) But what of the other coincidence? In this passage (see on 9. 9) John is contrasting Hyperides' treatment of the divine in his *Deliacus*[2] with the account of the creation in Genesis. ' "God said: Let this be. And it was." Thus spake Moses, whom not only the Christians but the best of the pagan Greeks—Longinus and Demetrius of Phalerum—deify.' Thus John's Longinus praised the passage of Genesis which L deals with in 9. 9, though John's quotation of it is not verbally the same as L's. There is no mention here of the Philological Discourses, so that it is only an inference that John is again drawing on Book XXI of that collection. He does, however, clearly think that his source is the famous Longinus. The allusion to Demetrius is not surprising, though we do not know precisely to what it refers; Demetrius was said to have written on Jewish antiquities and to have had some connexion with the LXX translation.[3] It is not, however, very likely that a late rhetor like John should know both these authorities at first hand. If his source for both references were Longinus, this Longinus would not be L, for L makes no mention of Demetrius. We may think this

books only as the extent of Longinus' φιλόλογοι ὁμιλίαι. Either this or John's κα' is corrupt.

[1] Cf. Wilamowitz, *Hermes* x (1876) 334: 'nec videtur absurde conici Longinum Orithyiae Aeschyleae notitiam huic scriptori ipsi debere.'

[2] This is *not* a significant coincidence with L 34, for Hyperides' *Deliacus* was evidently a recognized model of poetical, non-philosophical treatment of myth; see Hermogenes περὶ ἰδεῶν 1. 6 (Spengel ii. 288).

[3] See fr. 66, 201 Wehrli.

probable, and it would be very welcome; but of course proof is out of the question.

Taken by itself, this allusion to Genesis affords no more, perhaps even less, ground for believing that John knew L than does the allusion to the *Orithyia*. The question we have to ask ourselves is whether the fact that there are *two* coincidences decisively increases the probability. Even if we hold that it does, we are still, as we have seen, not bound to identify L either with the famous Longinus or with Boyd's more obscure one. My own feeling at least is that the effect of cumulation does not make much difference. I should be inclined to proceed on the hypothesis that John cannot be shown to have known our book.

As to what really happened, we can only speculate. Perhaps there were three stages: (i) the discussions of the *Orithyia* and Genesis passages came to Cassius Longinus from L or from some other work in the same rhetorical tradition; (ii) later rhetores, including John, drew on Longinus, and it became common knowledge among them that Longinus had handled these points; (iii) the guess made in late antiquity that περὶ ὕψους was the work of Longinus followed from this knowledge—just as the guess about Dionysius may have come from L's allusion to his book on σύνθεσις. At all events, some such chain of events seems to contain less coincidence and improbability than Boyd's.[1]

Apart from 44, the text has little in the way of contemporary reference. Terentianus is unknown, and there were men of distinction with this name at any rate from Flavian times.[2] Caecilius gives us only an obvious *terminus post quem*; we have no right to suppose that his book was new when L set out to refute it. The single reference to Theodorus of Gadara tells us nothing except that this very famous teacher was well known by repute to L and to his pupil Terentianus.[3] The very general criticism of orators in 5 and

[1] Cf. Kaibel, *Hermes* xxxiv (1899), especially 114. John is probably later than P, and so cannot be said to be the source of the manuscript attribution.   [2] See on 1. 1.   [3] See on 3. 5.

41 would be in place in many periods, certainly throughout the first century A.D.¹ No contemporary events are mentioned; few will subscribe to the notion that the absence of any mention of Vesuvius among the grandeurs of nature in 35. 4 raises a presumption that the work was written before the great eruption of A.D. 79.²

In these conditions guesses at authorship based on one detail or another are shots in the dark. Such is Christ's conjecture, recently revived by Lana, that L is the rhetor Aelius Theon whose *Progymnasmata* are extant and who also wrote on Xenophon.³ Such, too, are Richards's suggestion of Pompeius Geminus,⁴ the correspondent of Dionysius of Halicarnassus, and Rostagni's⁵ of the Theodorean Hermagoras, known personally as an old man to some of Quintilian's contemporaries.⁶ The most fruitful approach is perhaps to concentrate on what may be called L's Jewish connexion; this, if it yields no local habitation or name, yet helps significantly to characterize his work. Norden⁷ and Rostagni⁸ have strongly stressed this aspect. The most conspicuous piece of evidence is, of course, the quotation from Genesis, almost unique in ancient pagan literature. Less obvious, but cumulatively important, are certain resemblances in diction and subject with Philo.⁹ A few rare

---

¹ Cf. Demetrius 287; Theon, *Progymn.* ad init.; Dio Chrysostom quoted on 41. 2; Aristides, κατὰ τῶν ἐξορχουμένων (xxxiv Keil). However, L's general contrast between πολιτικοὶ ἄνδρες and σοφισταί (see on 1. 2, 4. 2) suggests a period before the triumph of the Second Sophistic, i.e. before the middle of the second century. Cf. Rohde, *Der griechische Roman* 293, n. 2. But we knew *these* limits anyway.

² Schmid, *Gesch. gr. Lit.* II. i. 476 n. 1.

³ I. Lana, *Quintiliano, Il sublime e gli esercizi preparatori di Elio Teone*, 1951.

⁴ *CQ* xxxii (1938) 133.   ⁵ Introduzione, pp. x ff.

⁶ Quint. 3. 1. 17. There are many other suggestions: see D. Marin's article in *Studi Urbinati*, 1955. The numerous Dionysii have been exploited ever since Weiske.

⁷ 'Das Genesiszitat . . .', *Abh. D. Ak. W. Berlin* (kl. Spracheliteratur), 1954, 1.   ⁸ Introduzione, pp. xxv ff.

⁹ See on 3. 4, 44. 3, 44. 6, 44. 8.

expressions are common to the two writers, and Philo's treatment of the problems of moral decline and degeneration is very reminiscent of 44. He also uses ὑψηγορία of literary effect very much in L's sense.[1] Rostagni builds on such coincidences and on the supposed connexions of Caecilius—who was said to have been a Jew by belief—and of Theodorus—who came from Gadara—with the Jewish world, to suggest that the philosopher of 44 is Philo himself and that the date of the dialogue and therefore of the work is about the time of Philo's visit to Rome in the time of Gaius. We need not accept this reconstruction to admit, as we must, that, though Philo yields no clue to L's identity, he has undoubtedly preserved traces of the same way of thinking, both about contemporary social problems and about ὕψος itself. Mommsen thought that L was a Hellenized Jew; this cannot be proved, but it cannot be disproved either.[2]

III. ῎ΥΨΟΣ

The first work in which we hear of 'height of speech' in Greek is the *Odyssey*. Here in four almost identical passages —in other words in a single motif—Antinous calls young Telemachus ὑψαγόρης.[3] This is not a criticism of style but of the royal pride and spirit which the boy's words disclose. We should do well to remember this simple point. At no time in their history did ὕψος and its cognates quite lose their moral and social connexions; they are never entirely at home in literary criticism. Whereas many words—ἁδρός and ἰσχνός, 'fat' and 'thin', for example—appear to be transferred directly from their literal and physical uses to

[1] See p. xli below.
[2] But observe that he uses νὴ Δία and the like without inhibition (11. 2, 33. 1, 35. 4, 43. 1, 44. 2). Philo avoids this, Josephus has it only once (*contra Apionem* 1. 255). It was evidently regarded by stricter Greek-speaking Jews as a compromise with polytheism.
[3] α 385, β 85, 303, ρ 406. These examples are quoted by F. Quadlbauer in his very useful article on '*genera dicendi*', *Wien. Stud.* lxxi (1958) 55–111.

serve as descriptions of speech,[1] ὑψηλός (like its near synonym μεγαλοπρεπής) is applied to moral character and social status before it is applied to λόγοι.[2] What we may call the primary metaphorical extension of ὕψος, whereby it suggests godlike or kinglike qualities, involves two main notions: that of pride and haughty anger, as in Telemachus, and that of pomp and circumstance. This, too, it carries over into the realm of speech. When Plato[3] reaches the solemn moment when the first decline from the perfect state must be explained, inexplicable as it is, Socrates proposes to ask the Muses, as Homer did, ὅπως δὴ πρῶτον στάσις ἔμπεσε. 'And shall we say', he goes on, 'that they speak to us in tragic tones, making fun and mockery of us as though we were children, ὑψηλολογουμένας as if what they said were in earnest?' Then follows the grandiose scientific mystification of the nuptial number.

In fact the ὕψος words do not commonly occur in literary criticism until the second half of the first century B.C.[4] Dionysius uses ὑψηλός often, but generally with some other adjective to help to define it.[5] Demetrius (whatever his date) does not use it at all. Cicero does not use *sublimis* as a literary term, nor *excelsus*, *altus*, and *elatus* very often.[6] But these words had many approximate synonyms—notably the μέγας group[7]—and their intrusion, when at last it came,

---

[1] Ancient theorists understood that ἁδρός and ἰσχνός were so derived, and that χαρακτήρ meant 'bodily habit' before it meant 'style': Phoebammon in *Rhet. Gr.* xiv. 383–4 Rabe.

[2] *SVF* i. 216 (p. 52, 34). Quadlbauer, p. 71.   [3] *Rep.* 8. 545D.

[4] When they occur earlier, it is sometimes in association with Aeschylus: Dioscorides (third century B.C.), *Anth. Pal.* 7. 411. Cf. *Frogs* (see below), especially 1056 f.

[5] *ad Pomp.* 2. 2 (μῖγμα ... τοῦ τε ὑψηλοῦ καὶ ἰσχνοῦ) and 2. 16 are exceptions; but see *Lysias* 13; *Dem.* 28, 34, 39; *CV* 4, 17, 18 (= §§ 29, 107, 115).

[6] Not at all in *de oratore*: but see *Brutus* 66, *orator* 119, 124, *de opt. gen. orat.* 10. His need of a developed descriptive vocabulary for style is greater in these later works.

[7] A notion of value as well as mere size goes with μέγας; it is 'great' rather than 'big'. In L μέγεθος and its cognates are often simply

did little more than give a fresh nuance to existing theories. It did, however, inspire Caecilius and, through him, L.

If we look back to the beginnings of Greek criticism in the fifth century, we see that already a considerable vocabulary existed for describing various deviations from the norm of ordinary discourse. Any given λόγος may depart from this assumed standard in one or more different ways—in quality of diction, in magnitude of subject, in the personal dignity of the speaker, or in the intensity of his feeling. For example, tragic language was clearly abnormal in all these respects. Its diction abounded in σεμνὰ and ξενικὰ ὀνόματα, γλῶσσαι and new coinages. Its characters were the kings and queens of an age nearer to the gods, and they were frequently represented in situations of devastating emotional violence. Thus Aeschylus in the *Frogs* defends himself (1058–61) on the principle that grand personages and grand thoughts demand grand words:

ἀνάγκη
μεγάλων γνωμῶν καὶ διανοιῶν ἴσα καὶ τὰ ῥήματα τίκτειν.[1]
κἄλλως εἰκὸς τοὺς ἡμιθέους τοῖς ῥήμασι μείζοσι χρῆσθαι·
καὶ γὰρ τοῖς ἱματίοις ἡμῶν χρῶνται πολὺ σεμνοτέροισιν.

Now the common Greek idea of poetry—if we may talk in such very general terms—involved not only the notion of the skill to produce a performance appropriate to some festival or other special occasion, but also that of composition under strong emotional compulsion or inspiration. That these should be combined in one person—a Homer in splendid costume pouring forth the elaborate glories of epic diction, and all the while under the god's spell and not his own master—gave the Greeks no sense of incongruity. This may seem strange; generations of thinking in terms of a sharp antithesis between something like court poetry, on the one hand, and outbursts of lyrical passion, on the other,

synonyms of the ὕψος words (e.g. 3. 4, 8. 4, 15. 1) but in some contexts (11. 2, 12 on αὔξησις) they represent a wider concept.

[1] Cf. L 9. 3: μεγάλοι δὲ οἱ λόγοι τούτων, κατὰ τὸ εἰκός, ὧν ἂν ἐμβριθεῖς ὦσιν αἱ ἔννοιαι.

INTRODUCTION xxxiii

have made it hard work for our imaginations to re-make this synthesis. It is only to translate this two-sided conception of the poet into terms applicable to the product of his art to say that these two things, passion and splendour, are the marks that distinguish poetry from prose, and indeed— a short further step—elevated prose from ordinary speech; for in Greek literature the orator came in for much of the poet's inheritance.

Yet when we come to the criticism of oratory, this association of passion and splendour reveals itself as a source of conflict. Aristotle,[1] looking back in his dry and dispassionate way on the history of poetry and oratory saw that the comparatively new practice of writing to be read privately had introduced a fundamental difference between the style of writing and that of the law courts and real life. He called the former λέξις γραφική and the latter λέξις ἀγωνιστική.[2] Written style is exact (ἀκριβής, a good piece of craftsmanship), 'agonistic' depends for success very much on delivery and acting; hence, for example, asyndeta are an agonistic feature, and any ambiguity they cause can be cleared up in the actual delivery, while to fill in all the conjunctions is a mark of the written manner.[3] Neither type of style does well on the other's ground: οἱ μὲν τῶν γραφικῶν ⟨λόγοι⟩ ἐν τοῖς ἀγῶσι στενοὶ φαίνονται, οἱ δὲ τῶν ῥητόρων, εὖ λεχθέντες, ἰδιωτικοὶ ἐν ταῖς χερσίν.

Aristotle's analysis came after a period of controversy. Isocrates was the model of ἀκρίβεια;[4] Alcidamas' περὶ τῶν σοφιστῶν[5] gives an idea of the arguments of the practical men who lived by their own impromptu facility. The latent conflict at which I hinted appears when we observe the

[1] See *Rhet.* 3. 12. 1413ᵇ3 ff.
[2] Λέξις involves order and 'figures' as well as choice of words.
[3] Cf. L 19–21.
[4] The point made at his expense in L (4. 2) may be from an early source.
[5] Radermacher, *Artium Scriptores* 135. Cf. also Isocr. *Philippus* 25. Yet the same Alcidamas was criticized by Aristotle for frigid and farfetched metaphors (*Rhet.* 3. 1406ᵃ).

obvious fact that Isocratean prose both conceals the writer's feelings and fails to rouse any in the reader,[1] while it is the real conflict in court, with its urgency and brutality, that produces real emotion. Isocratean prose, mere parade without intensity, was impossible to defend as a complete oratorical ideal. It was therefore in Demosthenes, who first presented τὸ ἐναγώνιον with literary perfection, that Hellenistic and later critics saw a resolution of the dilemma.

Meanwhile, soon after Aristotle's time, more complex and scholastic theories of style were developed. To this period belong the beginnings of the doctrine of 'the three styles' (χαρακτῆρες λόγου, *genera dicendi*), the origin of which has been much discussed. I shall confine myself to a few general remarks.[2]

Aristotle and Theophrastus seem to have worked with a theory according to which there was such a thing as a perfect style, which was a mean between extremes. The extremes were the ἁδρὸς χαρακτήρ and the ἰσχνὸς χαρακτήρ, defined by the contrast of Aeschylus with Euripides and Gorgias with Lysias.[3] The mean had been achieved in practice, they thought, by Thrasymachus. It was a style neither too exuberant nor too plain. It might contain some poetical words but not too many. It should possess rhythm but this must not be too marked—it should be paeonic rather than dactylic. At a later period—when and by whom is unknown —the terminology and categories of this normative doctrine were adapted for a wholly different purpose, namely to describe existing styles of various kinds. It is natural to connect this with the scholarly interests of the later Peripatos and the Alexandrians. The μέσος χαρακτήρ which Isocrates had often been thought to exemplify, was now

[1] So the Peripatetics Demetrius and Hieronymus. See Hieronymus, fr. 52 (Dion. Hal. *Isocr.* 13) with Wehrli's note.

[2] The question of the origin does not much affect interpretation of L; it is the existence and popularity of the developed doctrine of which we have to take notice. But see Hendrickson, *AJP* xxv (1904) 129 ff., xxvi (1905) 249 ff.; Austin on Quint. 12. 10. 58; G. A. Kennedy, *The Art of Persuasion*, 278 ff.   [3] Cf. Dem. περὶ ἑρμ. 36.

defined in terms of specific qualities which both friends and enemies could see in him—τὸ ἀνθηρὸν καὶ γλαφυρόν. We thus have three qualitatively distinct *genera*—the plain, the smooth or florid, and the grand or magnificent. There is still room for a normative μεσότης within each genus, and, of course, we find this.[1] But there is no longer any reason, apart from superstition, why there should be three *genera* and three only. Quintilian (12. 10. 66) is clear about this, and we find the better later critics using for their own independent purposes both the vocabulary generated by the classification and the bare notion of working with some such convenient scheme. For example, Dionysius in *de compositione verborum* invents a system of three ἁρμονίαι, analogous to the three χαρακτῆρες, in order to classify writers according to their habits of word-order, euphony, and so on. Again, Demetrius, who may well be considerably earlier than Dionysius, works with a scheme of four χαρακτῆρες, which fall into two pairs—ἰσχνός and γλαφυρός, μεγαλοπρεπής and δεινός: this arrangement recognizes a specific difference between the forcible and the magnificent. Yet again, Cicero in the *Orator* uses the three-style system to describe the perfect orator; he must excel in all three, but the grand style reveals his greatness most clearly. Grube[2] has rightly played down both the value and the influence of the classic form of the doctrine of *tria genera*; it was at best a widely accepted pedagogic convenience, descriptive in purpose and according well with the comparative study of the masters of the various genres which is common in Alexandrian and later scholarship. We first meet the full-blown doctrine in the *ad Herennium*—250 years or so after Aristotle.[3] Quintilian uses it,[4] and we see a naïve version in the Stoic *de vita et poesi Homeri* attributed to Plutarch. Marcellinus' life of Thucydides shows it mechanically applied to the criticism

[1] Cf. L 3. 4.   [2] *AJP* lxxiii (1952) 251 ff.
[3] Caplan's notes in the Loeb edition are valuable. The book is commonly dated 86–82 B.C., but this is not certain.
[4] 12. 10. 58 ff., with Austin's notes.

of the historians. The following simplified summary is based mainly on Quintilian and pseudo-Plutarch.[1] It should be clearly understood that no single extant author presents the scheme just like this.

GENUS	SUBTILE, TENUE	MEDIUM, FLORIDUM	GRANDE, ROBUSTUM, SUBLIME
χαρακτήρ	ἰσχνός, λιτός	μέσος, μικτός, ἀνθηρός, γλαφυρός	μεγαλοπρεπής, ἁδρός, ὑψηλός
OFFICIUM[2]	docendi	delectandi vel conciliandi	movendi
Typical exponents	Lysias, Xenophon	Isocrates, Herodotus	Gorgias, Thucydides
Homeric prototypes[3]	Menelaus	Nestor	Ulysses
Corresponding faults[4] (παρακείμενα ἁμαρτήματα)	Aridum et exsangue: τὸ ξηρὸν καὶ ταπεινόν	Dissolutum: τὸ διαλελυμένον	Sufflatum, tumidum, frigidum: τὸ οἰδοῦν, ψυχρόν, σκληρόν

What then is the relation of L's subject to this scheme of things? There are one or two points which at first sight might lead us to think that he is in fact writing about the ὑψηλὸς χαρακτήρ and treating it, as Cicero appears to do in

[1] See also Cic. *de oratore* 3. 177, 199, 212, *orator* 20 ff., 75 ff.; Varro *ap.* Gell. 6. 14.

[2] Hellenistic theory recognized that the orator must 'prove', 'please' or 'conciliate', and 'move'. Cicero (*orator* 69 ff.) associates these *officia* with the *genera* which specially subserve them. This may well be Cicero's own contribution; so A. E. Douglas, *Eranos* lv (1957) 18 ff. From another standpoint, the *genera* can be associated with the different functions of narrative, proof, and epilogue.

[3] See Radermacher, *Artium Scriptores* 6–9; G. A. Kennedy, *AJP* lxxviii (1957) 26 ff. The lines are: (i) Γ 214 ἐπιτροχάδην ἀγόρευε, παῦρα μέν, ἀλλὰ μάλα λιγέως, (ii) Α 249 τοῦ καὶ ἀπὸ γλώσσης μέλιτος γλυκίων ῥέεν αὐδή, (iii) Γ 221 ἔπεα νιφάδεσσιν ἐοικότα χειμερίῃσιν. Note that Nestor had to be imported from another context—just as the ἀνθηρὸς χαρακτήρ was an intruder in the scheme. This is perhaps an indication of the history of the affair. Odysseus in Tryphiodorus (118–19) contrives to combine Nestor's virtues with his own: δεινὸν ἀνεβρόντησε καὶ ἠερίης ἅτε πηγῆς ἐξέχεεν μέγα λαῖτμα μελισταγέος νιφετοῖο.

[4] See especially *ad Herennium* iv.

INTRODUCTION xxxvii

the *orator*, simply as the most important of the three and the most praiseworthy achievement of the art. Thus ὕψος, just like the ὑψηλὸς χαρακτήρ, astounds the hearer; and when Dionysius says of Thucydides' style (*Dem.* 2) that καταπλήξασθαι δύναται τὴν διάνοιαν ... συστρέψαι καὶ συντεῖναι τὸν νοῦν ... εἰς πάθος προαγαγεῖν, we seem to hear L speaking. Again, the special figures and rhythms which are recommended as ὑψηγορίας ἀποτελεστικά come naturally from analyses of the high style, as does the conception and treatment of faults corresponding to ὕψος, by means of which L leads into his main subject (3–5).

Nevertheless, these similarities are superficial; Boileau[1] was right: 'Par Sublime', he said, 'Longin n'entend pas ce que les Orateurs [i.e. the rhetoricians] appellent le stile sublime. ... Une chose peut estre dans le stile sublime et n'estre pourtant pas sublime. ...' He instances the quotation from Genesis (9. 9); whereas 'God said, Let there be light, and there was light' is truly sublime, the periphrasis 'Le souverain arbitre de la nature d'une seule parole forma la lumiere' is very far from being so. The point he makes is perfectly just. L's ὕψος has nothing specially to do with grandiose diction. It could, however, so far as this goes still be a *genus dicendi*, rather like the δεινὸς χαρακτήρ of Demetrius, the development of which may also be due to the same Hellenistic interest in pregnant grandeur which L's book reflects. However, it is pretty clear that it is nothing of the sort. L's ὕψος reveals itself not in a whole context but in a single word or phrase (1. 3). It is, therefore, a special effect, not a special style. Hence it is found not only in authors distinguished for the high style but in many others—in Xenophon,[2] for example, and, still more remarkably, in Sappho—though naturally there are great ranges of literature which are poor soil for it; comedy of manners is an obvious example of this, and L clearly puts the βιολογούμενα of

---

[1] *Préface*, p. 45 Boudhors.
[2] See 8. 1. Contrast Dion. Hal. π. μιμ., p. 208 U–R: ὕψους δὲ καὶ μεγαλοπρεπείας καὶ καθόλου τοῦ ἱστορικοῦ πλάσματος οὐκ ἐπέτυχεν.

the *Odyssey* in the same category (9. 15). Again, the positive things said about ὕψος, especially the far-reaching suggestions of 6 and 7, do not apply to any one kind of style. To say that ὕψος is that which fills us with joy and pride, stays in the mind, and pleases universally, is to go much deeper into the essential qualities of greatness in literature than any stylistic description can do. Again, when L passes to his main subject—how is ὕψος to be produced?—the more important part of his answer is not to be found in the enumeration of figures or advice about σύνθεσις and ἐκλογή. All he can do here is to modify what he would have written in a treatise on the ὑψηλὸς χαρακτήρ. It lies rather in the first two sources, high thinking and strong passion. Both of these are functions of qualities of character and mind in the writer. He is to be μεγαλόψυχος; he is also (8. 4) to be on occasion beside himself and possessed, in accordance with the old but still not banal Platonic and Democritean notion of the inspired poet or writer.[1] We notice also two other points: on the one hand there are apparently differences of value between πάθη, pity, grief, and fear (8. 2) being evidently ταπεινά; on the other hand ὕψος is attainable sometimes without πάθος, namely where the subject is 'cosmic' or very grand, and in encomia or other epideictic subjects. We must remember that L admired the *Timaeus* (32). Both these judgements are strange: the first, though it accords with a precept of Aristotle, may well strike us as an unlucky limitation; would it not exclude tragedy? The second seems to open the door to mere pomposity, perhaps even to 'le souverain Arbitre de la Nature'. The cause of both opinions is the same; it is L's notion of μεγαλοφροσύνη, in other words his moral outlook. It is not that he shows clear signs of allegiance to any philosophical school; he is familiar with Plato, Aristotle, the Stoics, and the Epicureans, and his ethical views derive from all. He is not, of course, a professional philosopher; τις τῶν φιλοσόφων (44. 1) is a colleague in another faculty. His ideal—and it is more Stoic

[1] See on 13. 2.

than anything, an eclectic Stoicism like Seneca's—is the man who rises superior to weaknesses such as pity, fear, and pain, and to current trends of materialism, luxury, and idleness, and who at the same time ennobles himself by contemplation of the works of God in the universe (35, 44). This is the kind of man who will produce ὑψηλά; nobody else will. It is perhaps not unfair to call him an idealization of Pericles, of whose oratory, none of which was preserved, three characteristics were remembered: that he thundered and lightened, that he left his sting behind him in his hearers' minds, and that he acquired τὸ ὑψηλόνουν . . . καὶ πάντη τελεσιουργόν from his studies of μετεωρολογία under Anaxagoras.[1]

It is not difficult to say in broad outline how such an ideal of ὑψηγορία arose. L is naturally under pressure from fashion—philosophical and educational as well as literary. For one thing, admiration of Plato had revived among the more liberal Stoics of the second and first centuries B.C., especially with Panaetius and Posidonius, and imaginations had been fired by the great Platonic descriptions of the philosophical life and of the ascent of the soul from the material to the ideal world. With this new interest had come also a taste for Plato's style, with all its abundance and poetic features. There was evidently a lively discussion about Plato as a writer, and L's polemic against Caecilius is more vigorous and heated on this point than on any other. During the same period also, and in the same Platonizing Stoic milieu of Panaetius and his successors and their Roman friends and pupils, there arose the educational ideal which we know best in Roman dress, from Cicero's *Orator* and *de oratore*—the ideal of the orator whose achievement in his art is the fine flower of an education grounded in philosophy, and who comes into the world *non ex rhetorum officinis sed ex*

[1] (i) ἤστραπτ' ἐβρόντα, Aristoph. *Acharn.* 531. Cf. L 1. 4, δίκην σκηπτοῦ. Aristophanes intended no *stylistic* characterization: but cf. Plin. *Ep.* 1. 20. 17. For *fulmen eloquentiae*, &c.. cf. Cic. *Orator* 234, *ad Att.* 15. 1a. 2; Quint. 2. 16. 19, 12. 10. 24, 65. (ii) Μόνος τῶν ῥητόρων τὸ κέντρον ἐγκατέλειπε τοῖς ἀκροωμένοις, Eupolis, fr. 94: cf. Plin. l.c., L 7. 3. (iii) Pl. *Phaedr.* 270A, with Hackforth's note, pp. 149 ff. See also Plu. *Per.* 5, 8.

Academiae spatiis.[1] To these powerful influences was added the inheritance of Hellenistic literary taste—a liking for brevity and pungency and a distaste for the full and grandiose. In their different ways, Alexandrian poetry and the philosophical diatribe both show this trend. Often, as in the Hellenistic historians ridiculed by L in 3, the desire for point[2] produced only frivolous or inappropriate wit; but there was another side to it, to be seen in the Stoic concern for 'words dipped in sense',[3] and ultimately in the *graves sententiae* of the Roman orators and historians. A critic who both admired Plato, style as well as thought, and was conditioned to enjoy the *sententiae* of the rhetorical schools —and this was L's position—could only make his tastes consistent by trying to abstract the common quality of excellence from these very different objects of admiration. We may think of ὕψος as L's attempted answer to this problem. It is perhaps not fantastic to see a further reflection of the same ambivalence in his own style—on the one hand, lavish metaphor and immense richness, on the other, a marked fondness for *graves sententiae* of a Tacitean ring.[4]

Where else can we find similar tastes? I conclude with two examples:

(i) We have seen that the critical use of the word ὕψος and its cognates dates probably from the latter part of the first century B.C. Both this and its moral use as a term of praise, which is probably Stoic, occur in Philo.[5] He speaks, for

---

[1] See especially J. von Arnim, *Dio von Prusa*, ch. i, particularly pp. 97 ff.

[2] See in general Norden, *AK* 277 ff.; W. C. Summers, *Select Letters of Seneca*, Introduction xl–xli.

[3] Zeno: see Plu. *Phocion* 5; Quint. 4. 2. 117.

[4] Norden ('Das Genesiszitat') and Kaibel both remark on this. Cf., for example, 2. 1 μία τέχνη πρὸς αὐτὰ τὸ πεφυκέναι; 2. 3 εἶναί τινα . . . ἐπὶ μόνῃ τῇ φύσει οὐκ ἄλλοθεν ἡμᾶς ἢ παρὰ τῆς τέχνης ἐκμαθεῖν δεῖ; 4. 7 οὐ . . . καλὸν ἀσχημονεῖν πρὸς τὸν αἰῶνα; 9. 2 ὕψος μεγαλοφροσύνης ἀπήχημα; 9. 14 γῆρας διηγοῦμαι, γῆρας δ' ὅμως 'Ομήρου; 20. 3 ἡ τάξις ἄτακτον καὶ . . . ἡ ἀταξία ποιὰν περιλαμβάνει τάξιν. See Appendix, p. 194.

[5] Moral use: *de Abrahamo* 199, cf. *somn*. 1. 115. More usually ὑψηλός

INTRODUCTION

example, of μέγεθος καὶ ὕψος ψυχῆς. In two particularly interesting passages he applies this term to speech. In one place,[1] it is Moses' divine inspiration which gives him εὔτροχος καὶ ὑψήγορος δύναμις; in another,[2] Jehovah's words (Genesis iv. 10) φωνὴ αἵματος τοῦ ἀδελφοῦ σου βοᾷ πρός με ἐκ τῆς γῆς are described as possessing κατὰ τὴν φράσιν ὑψηγορία which all but the uneducated (τοῖς μὴ λόγων ἀμυήτοις) will recognize. This implies not only that the ὕψος words are recognized terms, but that the quality they describe is seen just in the sort of simplicity of diction and boldness of image (φαντασία) which L would particularly appreciate. Of the many connexions between L and Philo which have been adduced this is the one that most nearly touches L's central concept.

(ii) It is, however, a later text which most clearly gives the impression of leading us into the discussion of which L's book is a part. This is a letter of Pliny to Lupercus.[3] Pliny begins by remarking of a correct but plain writer: *nihil peccat nisi quod nihil peccat*. Attempting the heights, boiling with passion, running risks—these are the things which make for eloquence of the highest order. Pliny claims—and he thinks his friend has not sufficiently noticed this—that he has courted such risks himself. It is a difficult business to distinguish *immodicum* from *grande*, *enorme* from *altum*; even Homer fails sometimes. Like L (9. 6), Pliny quotes ἀμφὶ δὲ σάλπιγξεν. He then turns to the orators, more particularly to Demosthenes, and gives a series of examples of which one (*de corona* 296) occurs also in L, and several in other rhetoricians. He concludes by asking pardon for his own audacities. The two main points of all this—the desirability of aiming high even at the risk of a fall, and the difficulty of distinguishing successes from failures—are

means 'arrogant'. The 'good' sense is also rare in early Christian literature: v. Arndt–Gingrich s.v.   [1] *Quis rerum divinarum heres* 4.
[2] *Quod deterius* 79. The turn which Philo admires would please a Hellenic taste also: cf. Dem. 19. 81 ἡ γὰρ ἀλήθεια καὶ τὰ πεπραγμένα αὐτὰ βοᾷ.
[3] Plin. *ep.* 9. 26.

central also to L's treatment of ὕψος. We can hardly doubt that there is a common source in some rhetorical teaching.[1]

Between Philo and Pliny lies the best part of a century. L may have been a contemporary of either.

To sum up, L describes not a manner of writing but an effect. He admires, on the one hand, pungent gravity, on the other, Platonic richness and solemnity. He unites his stylistic ideals under a moral ideal—the man of dignity and integrity who does his duty in human society and understands his station as a citizen of the cosmos. By doing this he evades the purely stylistic issues important in the age— the conflict between restraint and indulgence in regard to intellectual ingenuity, the debates about periods and short sentences, archaism and modernity, Atticists and Asianists. Personality and feeling justify or ruin in his eyes any stylistic means. He does, indeed, give some practical advice of a rhetorical kind; but the sum of his approach is an appeal to moral pride. This sets him apart from that main tradition of Greek rhetoric which runs from Aristotle's non-moral analysis of the factors of success to the aesthetic discriminations of styles and qualities which are the triumph of Hermogenes. It links him rather with Plato, but also with Cicero and Seneca and Quintilian and the essentially Roman ideal of the *vir bonus dicendi peritus*.

IV. INFLUENCE

> Thee, bold Longinus, all the Nine inspire,
> And bless their critic with a poet's fire.
> An ardent judge, who, zealous in his trust,
> With warmth gives sentence, yet is always just;
> Whose own example strengthens all his laws,
> And is himself the great Sublime he draws.[2]
>
> POPE, *Essay on Criticism* (1709)

---

[1] Mr. A. N. Sherwin-White suggests that Pliny's source for Greek rhetoric may be Nicetes (*ep.* 6. 6. 3, cf. Philostr. *VS* 1. 18).

[2] Pope took the *sententia* in the last line from Boileau, but it goes

A forward critic often dupes us
With sham quotations *Peri Hupsous*;
And if we have not read Longinus
Will magisterially outshine us.
Then, lest with Greek he overrun ye,
Procure the book for love or money,
Translated[1] from Boileau's translation,
And quote quotation on quotation.
   SWIFT, *On Poetry: a Rhapsody* (1733)

We do not know precisely when P was first copied in the Renaissance; probably it was in the latter part of the fifteenth century. Nearly a dozen Renaissance manuscripts are known; and before the end of the sixteenth century there were three printed editions and translations into Latin and Italian.[2] But, whereas a Latin version of Aphthonius was much used in schools and Hermogenes was studied by more advanced students of rhetoric,[3] L's difficulty and the fact that he gives few practical rules of a teachable kind debarred him from any great educational influence. The practice of poets and prose-writers in the Elizabethan age, in so far as it was affected by the rhetorical teaching of the time, was therefore influenced by others. It is true that Milton, whom the eighteenth century rightly judged to have above all men a genius 'happily form'd for the sublime',[4] does indeed mention 'Longinus' among authors from whom

---

back at any rate to a letter from Stephanus de Castrobello printed by Petra (1612): 'Quid enim praeter ipsam sublimitatem ipso Longino sublimius? ... ipsum typum atque exemplar sublimis et grandis orationis expressissimum.'

[1] i.e. by Leonard Welsted (1712).
[2] Editions of Robortelli (1554), Manutius (1555), Portus (1569): Latin translations of Pizzimenti (1566) and Pagano (1572), both reprinted with Petra's in 1644. Another Latin translation in cod. Vat. Lat. 3441; Italian translation by Giovanni di Niccolo da Falgano (1575) in a manuscript of the Biblioteca Nazionale, Florence. See B. Weinberg, *MP* xlviii (1950) 145 ff.
[3] M. L. Clarke, *Classical Education in Britain* 16, 31-32.
[4] See Welsted's translation (1712) 156.

rhetoric may be taught;[1] but his whole scheme seems well above ordinary practice, and we have no means of telling even how much attention he had himself paid to L.

Boileau's translation was published in 1674. It produced a spectacular reaction. For the next 150 years Longinus was a household name. Identified with the learned secretary of Zenobia, the writer of περὶ ὕψους was admired not only as a great critic but as a hero in the tradition of Socrates and Cato.[2] The short vivid book, available to all in elegant translations, had an influence independent of, if not disproportionate to, its merits. The story of this has been well told; and all I shall attempt here is to name a few landmarks and draw a short moral.[3] Within two or three years of the publication of Boileau's version Dryden is familiar with the book and retails it at length.[4] John Dennis's important critical works which appeared just after the turn of the century are full of it.[5] Addison popularized it in some *Spectator*s of 1711–12 on *Paradise Lost* and on the 'Pleasures of the Imagination'.[6] In the farce *Three Hours after Marriage* (1717) Dennis appears as Sir Tremendous Longinus, and the fashionable audience is evidently expected to understand the caricature. Pope's *Martinus Scriblerus* περὶ βάθους or *Of the Art of Sinking in Poetry* (1728) is a shrewd parody.[7] And not only the literature of criticism but polite letters generally display the wide diffusion of L's ideas and phraseology. Sir Joshua Reynolds's *Discourses on Painting* show

[1] *Tractate of Education* (1644): 'Plato, Aristotle, Phalereus, Cicero, Hermogenes, Longinus.'
[2] See above, p. xxiv, n. 4.
[3] See especially the works by Abrams, Brody, Churton Collins, Henn, Monk, and Rosenberg listed in the Bibliography: and note the criticisms of the arrangement of Rosenberg's book by Hecht, *Anglia*, Beiblatt xxxi (1920) 167 ff. I have confined myself to English; in any case, L's influence was particularly strong in England.
[4] *Essays* (Everyman ed.) 109, 113, 129, 138.
[5] *Advancement and Reformation of Poetry*, 1701; *Grounds of Criticism in Poetry*, 1704. Both edited by E. N. Hooker, Baltimore, 1939.
[6] See especially *Spectator* 223, 229, 253, 279, 321, 339.
[7] See note on 2. 1.

how Longinian motifs could be turned to use in criticizing another art.¹ Casual allusions in the poets and novelists bring home to us how far L was fashionable reading for the ordinary educated man.² Apart from all this, 'the Sublime' became a focus of philosophical inquiry, though much of this—for example, the main contentions of Burke's essay on 'The Sublime and Beautiful'—owes little or nothing to L or even to Boileau except the initial impetus to discussion.

Thus L played a distinctive and important part in the development of taste in the eighteenth century and the beginnings of the Romantic movement. Some of his precepts naturally accorded with the classical poetics and liking for positive rules which prevailed in the earlier part of the period—his prescription of certain figures as conducive to ὕψος, his warning against the use of vulgar words, his advocacy of imitation. This association with the 'rules', however, brought L into contempt with the Romantics, who threw him over with the rest of their predecessors' poetical and critical apparatus. There is a touch of irony in this; the very features of eighteenth-century criticism which seem most clearly to herald the great changes were either learned from L or at least echoed and amplified by him. Thus no critic widely read before L came into fashion laid as much emphasis as he does on the personality of the poet; more important herein than his stress on moral excellence as a prerequisite of great writing is his frequent use of the metaphors of inspiration and enthusiasm. By this he certainly contributed to the diffusion of the concept of the

¹ See notes on 14. 2, 34. 2: also E. Olson, *Longinus . . . and Sir Joshua Reynolds*, '*Discourses on Art*', University Classics, 1945, pp. vii–xxi.

² See notes on 4. 4 (Fielding), 9. 4 (Sterne), 35 (Akenside). A good illustration of how ὕψος καὶ πάθος became a cliché is in Burns's epistle to Dr. Blacklock:

> To make a happy fireside clime
> To weans and wife,
> That's the true pathos and sublime
> Of human life.

inspired bard as the Romantics knew him. Again, L's insistence on the concentration of ὕψος in the lonely phrase helped to prepare the way for another characteristically Romantic point of view—that it is the short lyric, expressing a single moment of passion, which is poetry *par excellence*.

The most famous part of the book in the eighteenth century was 'the ninth chapter'.[1] Foremost in appeal was the quotation from Genesis. From this, men learned the merits of 'noble simplicity'; Boileau's defence of L's point here against Huet,[2] and his praise of the simplicity of Corneille and Racine, were much pondered. Englishmen now learned to look at the Bible, and especially the Old Testament, with whose idiom and cadences they had been familiar for a century, as a subject for literary criticism.[3] Again, what is said in 9 about the treatment of cosmic or divine subjects, together with L's remarks in 35 about man's natural inclination to admire the grander works of nature—Nile, Danube, Rhine, Ocean, Etna—nourished the notion that there were certain topics in themselves sublime. L was indeed not the only source of this; Hermogenes' list of σεμναὶ ἔννοιαι in περὶ ἰδεῶν 1. 6 may well have been even more influential. In essentials, the taste for the 'awful' is already to be found in Dennis, who wrote home from Italy in the autumn of 1688 of the 'transporting pleasures' which 'followed the sight of the Alps—the transports mingled with horrours and sometimes almost with despair'. A defender of poetry against the attacks of the Puritans, Dennis believed that its proper subject was religion and that 'enthusiastick passion' was an essential ingredient. In particular, he believed that the poet should seek to excite

[1] See Gibbon's Journal for 3 Sept. 1762, quoted on 9. 1.

[2] *Réflexion X* (1710): also *Préface*.

[3] See especially Robert Lowth's Oxford poetry lectures *De Sacra Poesi Hebraeorum*, 1753 (extracts in Prickard's translation), and the contemporary *Adventurer*, 51 and 57, 1753, where a new work by Longinus is supposed to have been discovered in which he comments on various passages of the O.T., having read this since he wrote περὶ ὕψους.

a sort of terror, and he tried to list the ideas which are capable of provoking this: 'Gods, Daemons, Hell, Spirits and Souls of Men, Miracles, Prodigies, Enchantments, Witchcraft, Volcanoes, Monsters, Serpents, Lions, Tygers, Fire, War, Pestilence, Famine, &c.'[1] The doctrine that only this kind of topic could be treated in a genuinely poetical or sublime manner was, of course, an exaggeration of L's attitude, and L naturally is not speaking specifically or even primarily of poetry; but it was made plausible by the passages in 9 and 35 and also by the depreciation of the realism of the *Odyssey* at the end of 9. It is in such contexts—particularly in places where L contrasts the awe-inspiring with the merely elegant (10. 4–6) or the vehemence of πάθος with the milder tones of ἦθος (9. 15)—that are to be found the germs of the important distinction between 'sublime' and 'beautiful' that dominates the more theoretical kind of criticism in the century between Addison and Dugald Stewart's *Essay on the Sublime* of 1810.

Nineteenth-century critics, however, with some exceptions, neglected or despised L. There is, for instance, a clear sign of this in Matthew Arnold's speculations about the grand style. Here there is no mention of L, nothing about the 'sublime'. Yet the 'grand style' which 'arises in poetry when a noble nature poetically gifted treats with simplicity or severity a serious subject' has clearly a good deal in common with ὕψος, certainly more than Arnold or his successors admitted.[2] What was the cause of this neglect? Quiller-Couch[3] suggested two reasons: that the tone of acceptance of authority in 44 was uncongenial to an age which gloried in revolutionary liberty, and that L is not the sort of writer who provokes discussion—one feels that what is said is well said and that is the end of the matter. There is

[1] i. 361 Hooker.

[2] *On Translating Homer*, Lecture II; *Last Words on Translating Homer*. I quote from p. 399, Oxford Standard Authors edition. Cf. L. Trilling, *Matthew Arnold* 173: 'in many respects the grand style *is* the Sublime.'

[3] 'A Note on Longinus', in *Studies in Literature* iii. 141 ff. (1929).

something at least in the second of these reasons; but there is surely a third, at once more obvious and more fundamental: what L says about inspiration, about the liberties allowed to genius, about genuine passion and so on, though novel and liberating to eighteenth-century writers, was commonplace to their nineteenth-century successors. To put it crudely, L gave the generations from Boileau to Burke the sense that they could indulge a natural pride in being bold, lawless, and original without making fools of themselves and on reputable, civilized authority. The special piquancy of this appeal belongs to the particular conditions of taste then prevailing; it is too much to expect later ages to feel the same.

Yet in the last 150 years, too, readers who find Aristotle and Dionysius unsympathetic have instinctively warmed to L. This is not only because our long-ingrained and often unthinking romanticism takes pleasure in the uplift of the passages on inspiration and genius. Nor is it only the freshness and vigour of the writing. It is rather the pervading sense that L loves literature and wants to communicate his love to others. Dr. Johnson put his finger on the passage which remains the best single illustration of the qualities which give L a permanent appeal.[1] It is the discussion of the Marathon oath in 16. Here L shows how one should analyse one's feelings and knowledge about a really great passage. He explains first how Demosthenes has diverged from normal usage; secondly, the effect of this both on his subject and on his hearers; thirdly, how the context and situation make the effect totally different from that of the passage of Eupolis which is its 'source'; and finally how sound sense and regard for the needs of the ἀγών have saved the orator from any absurdity. The whole treatment, for all its dependence on a school tradition, is imaginative, methodical, learned, and illuminating. This, we feel, is how we ought to read Demosthenes.

[1] *Life of Dryden* 299 (World's Classics edition).

V. TEXT[1]

The text depends almost entirely on Parisinus 2036 (P), a tenth-century manuscript containing also portions of Aristotle's *Problemata*. Περὶ ὕψους occupies fos. 178–207. The following parts of this portion of the codex have been lost:

(i) The two centre leaves of quaternion 24: 100 lines.
(ii) The whole of quaternion 25: 400 lines.
(iii) The two centre leaves of quaternion 26: 100 lines.
(iv) The two centre leaves of quaternion 27: 100 lines.
(v) The four centre leaves of quaternion 28: 200 lines.
(vi) The two centre leaves of quaternion 29: 100 lines.
(vii) The last leaf of the group of four (205–8) with which the treatise ended.

There are therefore six long lacunae. One is in 2, one in 8–9, one in 12, one in 18, one in 30, and one in 37. At the end of 44 a later hand has added a few words (not a complete sentence) of the closing section. Whether or not this addition is genuine, it is very unlikely that there is much missing at the end.[2]

Of the other ten extant manuscripts, eight are derived directly or indirectly from P. They show the same lacunae, except that they all preserve the contents of the two outside leaves of quaternion 25 of P—i.e. the two passages ὡς κἂν (8. 1)—ἠρκέσθην (9. 4) and τὸ ἐπ' οὐρανόν (9. 4)—ἰδέσθαι (9. 10). We do not know when P suffered the further loss which reduced it to its present condition, except that it was before Victorius made his collation, and this was, anyway, earlier than 1568.[3] It is not clear, therefore, whether the archetype of these eight manuscripts is P itself or a copy of P, and I have not investigated this nor attempted to establish the affiliations of the apographa among themselves. The earliest are probably Marcianus 522 (before 1468) and Parisinus 2960

[1] Rhys Roberts, Prickard, Jahn–Vahlen⁴, Lebègue, and Rostagni all give useful information in their introductions.
[2] See notes on 44. 12.
[3] The date of the first edition of his *Variae Lectiones*.

(dated 1491). Two miscellanies (Parisinus 985 (B) and its copy Vaticanus 285 (A)) contain, among various other works, the preface of περὶ ὕψους, including the passage φύσις—θεωρίαν (2. 3), which is not preserved elsewhere and was first published by Toll in 1694. Both manuscripts insert after τῶν ἀγαθῶν (2. 3) a passage from Aristotle's *Problemata* (879ᵃ27–ᵇ35). The authenticity of this 'fragmentum Tollianum' has been disputed.[1]

The apographa therefore are of critical use only where P fails. All differences from P are either error or conjecture; right or probable readings in the apographa should be treated as conjectures just as much as those in the printed editions. The manuscript on which Robortelli based the editio princeps of 1554 has not been identified, but was certainly a descendant of P. Manutius (1555) worked independently of Robortelli and used the Venice manuscript, making a large number of corrections on his own.

L's quotations from earlier writers are numerous. Like those in other rhetores and critics, they are often very free, especially the prose ones (13. 1, 15. 9, 18. 1, 22. 1, 32. 2, 32. 5 ff., 38. 3). Those from the poets are not always metrically complete (e.g. 26. 1, 27. 4, 40. 4). In general I have refrained from accommodating the tradition of L to that of the authors concerned, except where his text as it stands gives nonsense or spoils his point (e.g. 24. 1, 27. 2 (?), 31. 1, 38. 4, 38. 5(?)). Thus I have left ταὐτὸ at 23. 3, though I think Jebb was right to read ταὐτοῦ by conjecture in Sophocles, and δύο at 26. 2, though the tradition of Herodotus says δώδεκα rightly, and L's text is factually wrong. Decision is often difficult: see 15. 3 (οὐρῇ [δέ]), 27. 4 (εἰπεμέναι), and the Theopompus quotation in 43. 2. I have treated the poem of Sappho (10. 2) as a case by itself, not attempting to distinguish L's errors from those of his copyists (see notes ad loc.).

---

[1] See notes on 2. 3. A contains all B's errors and some of its own; since both omit πάντως (2. 3) and leave a lacuna, there was at least one intermediate copy between B and P—perhaps a codex with the first pages of L wrongly bound in the middle of the *Problemata*.

SELECT BIBLIOGRAPHY

THIS is not a complete list of works about L, though I have included most of the major contributions after 1900. For the earlier period, Rhys Roberts's Bibliography should be consulted. Works particularly useful to the student are marked with an asterisk.

1. *Editions*

Editions including translations are indicated by the note (Lat.), (Eng.), &c.

F. ROBORTELLI, Basle, 1554.
P. MANUTIUS, Venice, 1555.
F. PORTUS, Geneva, 1569.
G. DE PETRA, Geneva, 1612 (Lat.).
G. LANGBAINE, Oxford, 1636 (Lat.).
C. MANOLESIUS, Bologna, 1644 (Lat.: Petra, Pizzimenti, and Pagano).
T. FABER, Saumur, 1663.
J. TOLL, Utrecht, 1694 (Lat., Fr.).
J. HUDSON, Oxford, 1710 (Lat.).
Z. PEARCE, London, 1724; Amsterdam, 1733 (with Portus' notes) (Lat.).
S. F. N. MORUS, Leipzig, 1769 (Lat.).
*J. TOUP, Oxford, 1778 (Lat.).
*B. WEISKE, Leipzig, 1809 (Lat.). Valuable as a variorum edition. (Note review by 'Cl.-Slm.', *Jenäer allg. lit. Zeit.* 1810 (= *censor Jenensis*).)
D. B. HICKIE, London, 1838. A school edition, based on Pearce, Toup, and Weiske.
L. SPENGEL in *Rhetores Graeci* i, Leipzig, 1853.
L. VAUCHER, *Études critiques sur le Traité du Sublime*, Geneva, 1854.
O. JAHN, Bonn, 1867 (revised later by J. Vahlen, *ed. 4, 1910).
C. HAMMER, in *Rhetores Graeci* i. 2, Leipzig, 1894.
*W. RHYS ROBERTS, Cambridge, 1899, 1907 (Eng.).
*A. O. PRICKARD, Oxford, 1906, revised ed. 1946 (see Introduction xxiv, n. 3).
*P. S. PHOTIADES, Athens, 1927.
*W. H. FYFE, London, 1927 (Eng.). (Loeb Classical Library.)
R. VON SCHELIHA, Berlin, 1938 (Germ.).
*H. LEBÈGUE, Paris, 1939 (Fr.).
*A. ROSTAGNI, Milan, 1945 (Ital.).

II. *Vernacular translations without Greek text*

J. HALL, London, 1652.
*N. BOILEAU-DESPRÉAUX, Paris, 1674, &c. (ed. C.-H. Boudhors, Paris, 1942).
L. WELSTED, London, 1712.
A. F. GORI, Florence, 1737, &c.
W. SMITH, London, 1739, &c.
H. L. HAVELL, London, 1890.
*A. O. PRICKARD, Oxford, 1906.
F. GRANGER, London, 1935.
T. G. TUCKER, Melbourne, 1935.
J. HOOGLAND, Groningen, 1936 (with valuable linguistic and textual commentary).
*G. M. A. GRUBE, New York, 1957.

III. *Some editions of other authors on rhetoric and criticism*

Caecilii Calactini fragmenta, ed. E. Ofenloch, 1907.
*[Cicero] *ad Herennium*, ed. H. Caplan, 1954 (Loeb).
Cicero, *De Oratore*, ed. A. S. Wilkins (i³, 1893; ii, 1881; iii, 1882).
—— *Orator*, ed. W. Kroll, 1913.
*Demetrius, περὶ ἑρμηνείας, ed. L. Radermacher, 1901.
*—— —— —— ed. W. Rhys Roberts, 1902 (also in Loeb, 1927).
*—— —— —— trans. by G. M. A. Grube, 1961.
Dionysius of Halicarnassus, *Opuscula*, ed. H. Usener–L. Radermacher, 2 vols., 1899–1929.(= U–R).
*—— —— *de Compositione Verborum*, ed. W. Rhys Roberts, 1910.
*—— —— *Three Literary Letters*, ed. W. Rhys Roberts, 1901.
Quintilian, ed. L. Radermacher, with addenda by V. Buchheit, 1959.
*Quintilian, *XII*, ed. R. G. Austin, 1948.
Rhetores Graeci, ed. C. Walz, 1832–6 (= Walz).
*—— —— ed. L. Spengel, 1854 (= Spengel). (Vol. I. ii revised by C. Hammer, 1894.)
—— —— ed. H. Rabe and others (1913– , incomplete).
Theophrasti περὶ λέξεως *fragmenta*, ed. H. Mayer, 1910.

IV. *Other books and articles*

*M. H. ABRAMS, *The Mirror and the Lamp*. New York and London, 1953.
G. AMMON, *De Dionysii Hal. librorum rhetoricorum fontibus*. Munich, 1889.
H. V. APFEL, *Literary Quotation in Demetrius and Longinus*. New York, 1935.

SELECT BIBLIOGRAPHY

J. W. H. ATKINS, *Literary Criticism in Antiquity*, ii. Cambridge, 1934.
C. S. BALDWIN, *Ancient Rhetoric and Poetic*. New York, 1924.
*S. F. BONNER, *The Literary Treatises of Dionysius of Halicarnassus*. Cambridge, 1939.
—— *Roman Declamation*. Liverpool, 1949.
A. BOULANGER, *Aelius Aristide*, Paris, 1923.
*M. J. BOYD, 'Longinus, the Philological Discourses and the Essay on the Sublime', *CQ*, N.S. vii (1957) 39 ff. (= Boyd).
J. BRODY, *Boileau and Longinus*. Geneva, 1958.
V. BUCHHEIT, *Untersuchungen zur Theorie des Genos Epideiktikon*. Munich, 1960.
R. CANTARELLA, in *REG* xxxviii (1925) 137 ff. (critical notes).
Q. CATAUDELLA, 'Intorno al περὶ ὕψους', *REG* xliii (1930) 160 ff.
C. CAUSERET, *Étude sur la langue de la rhétorique et de la critique littéraire dans Cicéron*. Paris, 1886.
M. L. CLARKE, *Rhetoric at Rome*. London, 1953.
J. CHURTON COLLINS, *Studies in Poetry and Criticism*. London, 1905.
J. COUSIN, *Études sur Quintilien*. Paris, 1936– .
*J. F. D'ALTON, *Roman Literary Theory and Criticism*. London, 1931.
J. D. DENNISTON, *Greek Prose Style*. Oxford, 1952.
F. FOCKE, 'Synkrisis', *Hermes* lviii (1923) 327 ff.
C. GALLAVOTTI, 'Pensiero e fonti dottrinari nel Dialogo degli Oratori' *Athenaeum*, N.S. ix (1931) 35 ff.
G. M. A. GRUBE, 'Notes on περὶ ὕψους', *AJP* lxxviii (1957) 355 ff.
—— 'Theodorus of Gadara', *AJP* lxxx (1959) 337 ff.
—— 'Thrasymachus, Theophrastus and Dionysius of Halicarnassus', *AJP* lxxiii (1952) 251 ff.
—— 'Theophrastus as a literary critic', *TAPA* lxxxiii (1952) 172 ff.
M. HAUPT, *Index lectionum hibernarum*, 1870 = *Opuscula* ii. 428 ff.
G. L. HENDRICKSON, 'The Peripatetic Mean of Style and the Three Stylistic Characters', *AJP* xxv (1904) 125 ff.
—— 'The Origin and Meaning of the Ancient Characters of Style', *AJP* xxvi (1905) 249 ff.
T. R. HENN, *Longinus and English Criticism*. Cambridge, 1934.
O. IMMISCH, 'Bemerkungen zur Schrift vom Erhabenen', *Sitzungsb. Akad. Wiss. Heidelberg*, Phil.-hist. Klasse, 1924–5, ii.
G. KAIBEL, 'Cassius Longinus und die Schrift περὶ ὕψους', *Hermes* xxxiv (1899) 107 ff.
G. A. KENNEDY, 'Theophrastus on Stylistic Distinction', *Harvard Studies in Classical Philology* lxii (1957) 93 ff.
*—— *The Art of Persuasion in Greece*, 1963.
W. KROLL, *Studien zum Verständnis der römischen Literatur*. Stuttgart, 1924.
LA RUE VAN HOOK, *The Metaphorical Terminology of Greek Rhetoric and Literary Criticism*. Chicago, 1905.

SELECT BIBLIOGRAPHY

- H. LACKENBACHER, 'Die Behandlung des πάθος in περὶ ὕψους', *Wien. Stud.* xxxiii (1911) 213 ff.
- I. LANA, *Quintiliano, Il Sublime e gli esercizi preparatori di Elio Teone*. Turin, 1951.
- R. MCKEON, 'Literary Criticism and the Concept of Imitation in Antiquity', *MP* xxxiv (1936) 1 ff.
- G. MARENGHI, '*Περὶ ὕψους* nell'evoluzione del gusto post-classico', *Rend. Ist. Lomb.* lxxxix (1956) 485 ff.
- D. MARIN, 'L'opposizione sotto Augusto e la datazione del saggio del Sublime', *Studi Calderini–Paribeni*, i (1956) 157 ff.
- L. MARTENS, *De libello περὶ ὕψους*. Bonn, 1877.
- S. H. MONK, *The Sublime*. New York, 1935 (paperback reprint, Ann Arbor, 1960).
- *H. MUTSCHMANN, 'Tendenz, Aufbau und Quellen der Schrift vom Erhabenen', 1912 (*TAQ*).
- —— 'Das Genesiszitat . . .', *Hermes* lii (1917) 161 ff.
- E. NORDEN, *Antike Kunstprosa* (*AK*).
- —— 'Das Genesiszitat . . .', *Abh. deutsch. Akad. Wiss. Berlin* (Klasse Spr.-Lit.), 1954, i.
- H. NORTH, 'The Use of Poetry in the Training of the Ancient Orator', *Traditio* viii (1952) 1 ff.
- E. OLSON, 'The Argument of Longinus "On the Sublime"', *MP* xxxix (1942) 225 ff.
- P. OTTO, *Quaestiones selectae ad librum περὶ ὕψους spectantes*. Fulda, 1906.
- *R. PHILIPPSON, 'Zu περὶ ὕψους', *Rh. Mus.* lxxiv (1925) 267 ff.
- P. S. PHOTIADES, in *Ἀθηνᾶ* xxxii (1920) 1 ff. (critical notes).
- G. PUTTENHAM, *The Arte of English Poesie*, 1588; ed. Willcock and Walter, 1936.
- *F. QUADLBAUER, 'Die *genera dicendi* bis auf Plinius', *Wien. Stud.* lxxi (1958) 55 ff.
- L. RADERMACHER, *Artium Scriptores*. Vienna, 1954.
- C. REHDANTZ, *Demosthenes' Neun Philippische Reden*, Indices, ed. 4. Leipzig, 1886.
- W. RHYS ROBERTS, 'Caecilius of Caleacte', *AJP* xviii (1897) 302–12.
- —— 'Longinus on the Sublime', *Philol. Quart.* (1928) 299 ff.
- —— 'The Cambridge Manuscript of De Sublimitate', *CR* xii (1898) 299.
- *H. RICHARDS, 'Critical Notes on the De Sublimitate', *CR* xvi (1902) 160 ff.
- H. VON ROHDEN, 'Quas rationes in hiatu vitando scriptor de sublimitate et Onesander secuti sint', in *Comm. in hon. Buecheleri et Useneri*. Bonn, 1873.
- H. ROSENBERG, *Longinus in England*, 1918.
- A. ROSTAGNI, 'Il Sublime nella storia dell'estetica antica', *Annali della reale scuola normale di Pisa*, 1933, 99–120, 175–202.

SELECT BIBLIOGRAPHY

M. ROTHSTEIN, 'In libellum de sublimitate coniectanea critica', *Hermes* xxii (1887) 535 ff.

M. ROTHSTEIN, 'Caecilius von Caleacte', *Hermes* xxiii (1888) 1 ff.

W. G. RUTHERFORD, *A Chapter in the History of Greek Annotation*, 1905.

G. SAINTSBURY, *History of Criticism*, 1900, i. 152–73.

*M. SCHANZ, 'Die Apollodoreer und die Theodoreer', *Hermes* xxv (1890) 36 ff.

W. SCHMID, 'Antike Stillehre', *Rh. Mus.* xlix (1894) 133 ff.

—— *Der Atticismus*. Stuttgart, 1887–97.

H. SCHRADER, 'σχῆμα und τρόπος in den Homerscholien', *Hermes* xxxix (1904) 563 ff.

H. S. SCHULTZ, *Der Aufbau der Schrift περὶ ὕψους*. Berlin, 1936.

T. SCHWAB, 'Alexander Numeniu, περὶ σχημάτων', *Rhet. Stud.* 5, Paderborn.

C. P. SEGAL, "Ὕψος and the problem of cultural decline . . .', *Harv. St. Class. Phil.* lxiv (1959) 121 ff.

F. SOLMSEN, 'The Aristotelian Tradition in Ancient Rhetoric', *AJP* lxii (1941) 35 ff.

N. TERZAGHI, 'Marginalia al trattato περὶ ὕψους', *Athenaeum* vi (1918) 146 ff.

*J. VAHLEN, 'Libellus de sublimitate emendatur', *Opuscula* i. 121 ff.

*R. VOLKMANN, *Die Rhetorik der Griechen und Römer*. Ed. 2, Leipzig, 1885.

*G. J. DE VRIES, 'Notes on Longinus περὶ ὕψους', *Mnem.* s. iv. xii (1959) 54 ff.

*F. WEHRLI, 'Der schlichte und der erhabene Stil', in *Phyllobolia für P. von der Mühll*. Basel, 1946.

B. WEINBERG, 'Translations and Commentaries of Longinus up to 1600', *MP* xlvii (1950) 145 ff.

E. WENKEBACH, 'Textkritische Bemerkungen zur Schrift vom Erhabenen', *Hermes* lxxxii (1954) 477 ff.

*U. VON WILAMOWITZ-MÖLLENDORF, 'In libellum περὶ ὕψους coniectanea', *Hermes* x (1876) 334 ff.

*—— 'Atticismus und Asianismus', *Hermes* xxxv (1900) 1 ff.

*—— *Griechisches Lesebuch*. Berlin, 1904.

E. ZIEGLER, 'Das Genesiszitat . . .', *Hermes* l (1915) 572 ff.

ABBREVIATIONS FOR WORKS OF REFERENCE

Arndt–Gingrich	*A Greek–English Lexicon of the New Testament*, Chicago, 1957.
B–D	F. Blass–A. Debrunner, *Grammatik des neutestamentlichen Griechisch*, ed. 8, 1949.
D–K	H. Diels–W. Kranz, *Die Fragmente der Vorsokratiker* ed. 6.
Denniston	J. D. Denniston, *Greek Particles*, ed. 2, 1954.
Ernesti	J. C. G. Ernesti, *Lexicon Technologiae Graecorum Rhetoricae*, and *Lexicon Technologiae Latinorum Rhetoricae*, 1795–7.
FGrHist	F. Jacoby, *Fragmente der griechischen Historiker*.
GMT	W. W. Goodwin, *Syntax of the Moods and Tenses of the Greek Verb*, 1897.
K–B	R. Kühner–F. Blass, *Ausführliche Grammatik der griechischen Sprache* I, 1890.
K–G	R. Kühner–B. Gerth, *Ausf. Gramm.* . . . II, (Satzlehre), 1898.
LSJ	Liddell–Scott–Jones, *Greek–English Lexicon*, 1925–40.
P–W	Pauly–Wissowa, *Realenzyklopädie der klassischen Altertumswissenschaft*.
OCD	*Oxford Classical Dictionary*.
Schwyzer	E. Schwyzer–A. Debrunner, *Griechische Grammatik*, 1939–40.

SIGLA

P Parisinus gr. 2036, saec. X.
p eiusdem manus recentior.
A Vaticanus 285, saec. XV–XVI.
B Parisinus 985, saec. XV.
K Cantabrigiensis KK vi. 34: v. Rhys Roberts, *CR* xii (1898) 299 sqq.
Marcianus 522 saec. XV.
Ambrosianus B 144 sup., saec. XV–XVI.
Laurentianus xxviii. 30, saec. XV.
Vaticanus 194, saec. XV–XVI.
Vaticanus 1417, saec. XV–XVI.
Parisinus gr. 2960, a. 1491.
Parisinus gr. 2974, saec. XVI.

apogr. unus vel plures codicum recentiorum.
marg.   in margine adscriptum.
Rob.   editio Fr. Robortelli, Basileae, 1554.
Man.   editio P. Manutii, Venetiis, 1555.

ΠΕΡΙ ΥΨΟΥΣ

Τὸ μὲν τοῦ Καικιλίου συγγραμμάτιον, ὃ περὶ ὕψους συνετάξατο, **1** ἀνασκοπουμένοις ἡμῖν ὡς οἶσθα κοινῇ, Ποστούμιε Τερεντιανὲ φίλτατε, ταπεινότερον ἐφάνη τῆς ὅλης ὑποθέσεως καὶ ἥκιστα τῶν καιρίων ἐφαπτόμενον, οὐ πολλήν τε ὠφέλειαν, ἧς μάλιστα δεῖ 5 στοχάζεσθαι τὸν γράφοντα, περιποιοῦν τοῖς ἐντυγχάνουσιν, εἴγ᾿ ἐπὶ πάσης τεχνολογίας δυεῖν ἀπαιτουμένων, προτέρου μὲν τοῦ δεῖξαι τί τὸ ὑποκείμενον, δευτέρου δὲ τῇ τάξει, τῇ δυνάμει δὲ κυριωτέρου, πῶς ἂν ἡμῖν αὐτὸ τοῦτο καὶ δι᾿ ὧν τινων μεθόδων κτητὸν γένοιτο, ὅμως ὁ Καικίλιος ποῖον μέν τι ὑπάρχει τὸ 10 ὑψηλὸν διὰ μυρίων ὅσων ὡς ἀγνοοῦσι πειρᾶται δεικνύναι, τὸ δὲ δι᾿ ὅτου τρόπου τὰς ἑαυτῶν φύσεις προάγειν ἰσχύοιμεν ἂν εἰς ποσὴν μεγέθους ἐπίδοσιν οὐκ οἶδ᾿ ὅπως ὡς οὐκ ἀναγκαῖον παρέλιπεν· πλὴν ἴσως τουτονὶ μὲν τὸν ἄνδρα οὐχ οὕτως αἰτιᾶσθαι τῶν **2** ἐκλελειμμένων ὡς αὐτῆς τῆς ἐπινοίας καὶ σπουδῆς ἄξιον ἐπαινεῖν. 15 ἐπεὶ δὲ ἐνεκελεύσω καὶ ἡμᾶς τι περὶ ὕψους πάντως εἰς σὴν ὑπομνηματίσασθαι χάριν, φέρε, εἴ τι δὴ δοκοῦμεν ἀνδράσι πολιτικοῖς τεθεωρηκέναι χρήσιμον ἐπισκεψώμεθα. αὐτὸς δ᾿ ἡμῖν, ἑταῖρε, τὰ ἐπὶ μέρους, ὡς πέφυκας καὶ καθήκει, συνεπικρινεῖς ἀληθέστατα· εὖ γὰρ δὴ ὁ ἀποφηνάμενος τί θεοῖς ὅμοιον ἔχομεν 20 "εὐεργεσίαν" εἶπας "καὶ ἀλήθειαν." γράφων δὲ πρὸς σέ, **3** φίλτατε, τὸν παιδείας ἐπιστήμονα, σχεδὸν ἀπήλλαγμαι καὶ τοῦ διὰ πλειόνων προϋποτίθεσθαι ὡς ἀκρότης καὶ ἐξοχή τις λόγων

---

20 Arsen. *Viol.*, p. 189: Δημοσθένης ἐρωτηθεὶς τί ἄνθρωπος ἔχει ὅμοιον θεῷ, ἔφη, Τὸ εὐεργετεῖν καὶ ἀληθεύειν. Cf. Ael. *VH* 12. 59

Tit. Διονυσίου Λογγίνου περὶ ὕψους P: Διονυσίου ἢ Λογγίνου περὶ ὕψους P in indice (fol. 1ᵛ), etiam A   1 Κεκιλίου ubique P   2 Τερεντιανὲ Man.: Φλώρεντιανε P: Μαῦρε Τερεντιανὲ Roberts: Φλ. Τερεντιανὲ Schurzfleisch: Φλῶρε Τερεντιανὲ Reifferscheid   4 τε] γε Reiske   5 εἴγ᾿ Spengel: εἴτ᾿ P: εἶτ᾿ Man.   10 ὅσων ⟨παραδειγμάτων⟩ Rothstein   18 πέφυκᾶς P: πέφυκε vel -ες apogr.   20 εἶπας] εἶπε Rob.

ἐστὶ τὰ ὕψη, καὶ ποιητῶν τε οἱ μέγιστοι καὶ συγγραφέων οὐκ ἄλλοθεν ἢ ἐνθένδε ποθὲν ἐπρώτευσαν καὶ ταῖς ἑαυτῶν περιέβαλον 4 εὐκλείαις τὸν αἰῶνα. οὐ γὰρ εἰς πειθὼ τοὺς ἀκροωμένους ἀλλ' εἰς ἔκστασιν ἄγει τὰ ὑπερφυᾶ· πάντη δέ γε σὺν ἐκπλήξει τοῦ πιθανοῦ καὶ τοῦ πρὸς χάριν ἀεὶ κρατεῖ τὸ θαυμάσιον, εἴγε τὸ μὲν 5 πιθανὸν ὡς τὰ πολλὰ ἐφ' ἡμῖν, ταῦτα δὲ δυναστείαν καὶ βίαν ἄμαχον προσφέροντα παντὸς ἐπάνω τοῦ ἀκροωμένου καθίσταται. καὶ τὴν μὲν ἐμπειρίαν τῆς εὑρέσεως καὶ τὴν τῶν πραγμάτων τάξιν καὶ οἰκονομίαν οὐκ ἐξ ἑνὸς οὐδ' ἐκ δυεῖν, ἐκ δὲ τοῦ ὅλου τῶν λόγων ὕφους μόλις ἐκφαινομένην ὁρῶμεν, ὕψος δέ που 10 καιρίως ἐξενεχθὲν τά τε πράγματα δίκην σκηπτοῦ πάντα διεφόρησε καὶ τὴν τοῦ ῥήτορος εὐθὺς ἀθρόαν ἐνεδείξατο δύναμιν. ταῦτα γὰρ οἶμαι καὶ τὰ παραπλήσια, Τερεντιανὲ ἥδιστε, κἂν αὐτὸς ἐκ πείρας ὑφηγήσαιο.

2 Ἡμῖν δ' ἐκεῖνο διαπορητέον ἐν ἀρχῇ, εἰ ἔστιν ὕψους τις ἢ 15 βάθους τέχνη, ἐπεί τινες ὅλως οἴονται διηπατῆσθαι τοὺς τὰ τοιαῦτα ἄγοντας εἰς τεχνικὰ παραγγέλματα. γεννᾶται γάρ, φησί, τὰ μεγαλοφυῆ καὶ οὐ διδακτὰ παραγίνεται, καὶ μία τέχνη πρὸς αὐτὰ τὸ πεφυκέναι· χείρω τε τὰ φυσικὰ ἔργα, ὡς οἴονται, καὶ τῷ παντὶ δειλότερα καθίσταται ταῖς τεχνολογίαις κατασκελετευό- 20 2 μενα. ἐγὼ δὲ ἐλεγχθήσεσθαι τοῦθ' ἑτέρως ἔχον φημί, εἰ ἐπισκέψαιτό τις ὅτι ἡ φύσις, ὥσπερ τὰ πολλὰ ἐν τοῖς παθητικοῖς καὶ διηρμένοις αὐτόνομον, οὕτως οὐκ εἰκαῖόν τι κἀκ παντὸς ἀμέθοδον εἶναι φιλεῖ, καὶ ὅτι αὐτὴ μὲν πρῶτόν τι καὶ ἀρχέτυπον γενέσεως στοιχεῖον ἐπὶ πάντων ὑφέστηκεν, τὰς δὲ ποσότητας καὶ τὸν 25 ἐφ' ἑκάστου καιρὸν ἔτι δὲ τὴν ἀπλανεστάτην ἄσκησίν τε καὶ χρῆσιν ἱκανὴ πορίσαι καὶ συνενεγκεῖν ἡ μέθοδος, καὶ ὡς ἐπικινδυνότερα αὐτὰ ἐφ' αὑτῶν δίχα ἐπιστήμης ἀστήρικτα καὶ

1 οὐκ ἄλλοθέν ποθεν ἢ ἐνθένδε ἐπρώτευσαν Weiske   2 περιέβαλον] περιεβάλοντο Weiske   4 ⟨τὸ⟩ σὺν ἐκπλήξει Langbaine; quod si acceperis, delendum erit τὸ post κρατεῖ (5)   16 βάθους] πάθους Upton (?), fortasse recte: βάρους Schmid: μεγέθους Diels: ἢ βάθους del. Jahn (omiserat in versione Boilavius)   17 φησί] φασί Man. 24 αὐτὴ scripsi: αὕτη P   27 πορίσαι P marg., apogr.: παρορίσαι P 27–28 ἐπικινδυνότερα ⟨τὰ πλοῖα⟩ τὰ ἐφ' Tollius

ἀνερμάτιστα ἐαθέντα τὰ μεγάλα, ἐπὶ μόνῃ τῇ φορᾷ καὶ ἀμαθεῖ τόλμῃ λειπόμενα· δεῖ γὰρ αὐτοῖς ὡς κέντρου πολλάκις οὕτω δὲ καὶ χαλινοῦ. ὅπερ γὰρ ὁ Δημοσθένης ἐπὶ τοῦ κοινοῦ τῶν ἀνθρώ- 3 πων ἀποφαίνεται βίου, μέγιστον μὲν εἶναι τῶν ἀγαθῶν τὸ εὐτυχεῖν,
5 δεύτερον δὲ καὶ οὐκ ἔλαττον τὸ εὖ βουλεύεσθαι, ὅπερ οἷς ἂν μὴ παρῇ συναναιρεῖ πάντως καὶ θάτερον, τοῦτ' ἂν καὶ ἐπὶ τῶν λόγων εἴποιμεν, ὡς ἡ μὲν φύσις τὴν τῆς εὐτυχίας τάξιν ἐπέχει, ἡ τέχνη δὲ τὴν τῆς εὐβουλίας. τὸ δὲ κυριώτατον, ὅτι καὶ αὐτὸ τὸ εἶναί τινα τῶν ἐν λόγοις ἐπὶ μόνῃ τῇ φύσει οὐκ ἄλλοθεν ἡμᾶς ἢ
10 παρὰ τῆς τέχνης ἐκμαθεῖν δεῖ. εἰ ταῦθ', ὡς ἔφην, ἐπιλογίσαιτο καθ' ἑαυτὸν ὁ τοῖς χρηστομαθοῦσιν ἐπιτιμῶν, οὐκ ἂν ἔτι, μοι δοκῶ, περιττὴν καὶ ἄχρηστον τὴν ἐπὶ τῶν προκειμένων ⟨ἡγή⟩σαιτο θεωρίαν.

. . . .

15 . . . καὶ καμίνου σχῶσι μάκιστον σέλας. 3

εἰ γάρ τιν' ἑστιοῦχον ὄψομαι μόνον,
μίαν παρείρας πλεκτάνην χειμάρροον,
στέγην πυρώσω καὶ κατανθρακώσομαι·
νῦν δ' οὐ κέκραγά πω τὸ γενναῖον μέλος.

20 οὐ τραγικὰ ἔτι ταῦτα, ἀλλὰ παρατράγῳδα, αἱ πλεκτάναι, καὶ τὸ πρὸς οὐρανὸν ἐξεμεῖν, καὶ τὸ τὸν Βορέαν αὐλητὴν ποιεῖν, καὶ τὰ ἄλλα ἑξῆς· τεθόλωται γὰρ τῇ φράσει καὶ τεθορύβηται ταῖς φαντασίαις μᾶλλον ἢ δεδείνωται, κἂν ἕκαστον αὐτῶν πρὸς αὐγὰς ἀνασκοπῇς, ἐκ τοῦ φοβεροῦ κατ' ὀλίγον ὑπονοστεῖ πρὸς τὸ

3 Dem. 23. 113 δυοῖν ἀγαθοῖν ὄντοιν πᾶσιν ἀνθρώποις, τοῦ μὲν ἡγουμένου καὶ μεγίστου πάντων, τοῦ εὐτυχεῖν, τοῦ δ' ἐλάττονος ... τοῦ καλῶς βουλεύεσθαι. Cf. etiam [Isocr.] 1. 34   15 Aesch. fr. 281 Nauck[2]

---

1 μεγάλα] μεγαλοφυᾶ Wilamowitz   2 δὲ] δὴ Rob.   4 inter ἀγαθῶν et ἐντυχεῖν (sic) locum ex Arist. *Problem*. 879[a]27–[b]35 inserunt AB   7–13 post ἡ μὲν desunt in P duo folia: φύσις ... θεωρίαν in solis AB servantur   8 ὅτι Pearce: τε AB   11–12 μοιδοκῶ AB: ἐμοὶ δοκεῖ Spengel   12 ⟨ἡγή⟩σαιτο Boivin: ... σαιτο B: κομίσαιτο A   15 ⟨ἦν⟩ καὶ vel similia edd. Sed ipsum καί dubium   16 τιν'] τὸν Toup   μόνον] δόμων Dobree   24 ἀντὶ τοῦ χωρισθῆναι δυνήσεταί σοι, P marg. (vocis ὑπονοστεῖ interpretatio)

ΠΕΡΙ ΥΨΟΥΣ [3. 1-

εὐκαταφρόνητον. ὅπου δ' ἐν τραγῳδίᾳ, πράγματι ὀγκηρῷ φύσει καὶ ἐπιδεχομένῳ στόμφον, ὅμως τὸ παρὰ μέλος οἰδεῖν ἀσύγγνωστον, σχολῇ γ' ἂν οἶμαι λόγοις ἀληθινοῖς ἁρμόσειεν. ταύτῃ καὶ τὰ τοῦ Λεοντίνου Γοργίου γελᾶται γράφοντος "Ξέρξης ὁ τῶν Περσῶν Ζεύς," καὶ "γῦπες ἔμψυχοι τάφοι," καί τινα τῶν Καλλισθένους ὄντα οὐχ ὑψηλά, ἀλλὰ μετέωρα, καὶ ἔτι μᾶλλον τὰ Κλειτάρχου· φλοιώδης γὰρ ἀνὴρ καὶ φυσῶν κατὰ τὸν Σοφοκλέα

μικροῖς μὲν αὐλίσκοισι, φορβειᾶς δ' ἄτερ.

τά γε μὴν Ἀμφικράτους τοιαῦτα καὶ Ἡγησίου καὶ Μάτριδος· πολλαχοῦ γὰρ ἐνθουσιᾶν ἑαυτοῖς δοκοῦντες οὐ βακχεύουσιν, ἀλλὰ παίζουσιν. ὅλως δ' ἔοικεν εἶναι τὸ οἰδεῖν ἐν τοῖς μάλιστα δυσφυλακτότατον. φύσει γὰρ ἅπαντες οἱ μεγέθους ἐφιέμενοι, φεύγοντες ἀσθενείας καὶ ξηρότητος κατάγνωσιν, οὐκ οἶδ' ὅπως ἐπὶ τοῦθ' ὑποφέρονται, πειθόμενοι τῷ "μεγάλων ἀπολισθαίνειν ὅμως εὐγενὲς ἁμάρτημα". κακοὶ δὲ ὄγκοι καὶ ἐπὶ σωμάτων καὶ λόγων οἱ χαῦνοι καὶ ἀναλήθεις καὶ μήποτε περιστάντες ἡμᾶς εἰς τοὐναντίον· οὐδὲν γάρ φασι ξηρότερον ὑδρωπικοῦ. ἀλλὰ τὸ μὲν οἰδοῦν ὑπεραίρειν βούλεται τὰ ὕψη, τὸ δὲ μειρακιῶδες ἄντικρυς ὑπεναντίον τοῖς μεγέθεσι· ταπεινὸν γὰρ ἐξ ὅλου καὶ μικρόψυχον καὶ τῷ ὄντι κακὸν ἀγεννέστατον. τί ποτ' οὖν τὸ μειρακιῶδές ἐστιν; ἢ δῆλον ὡς σχολαστικὴ νόησις, ὑπὸ περιεργασίας λήγουσα εἰς ψυχρότητα; ὀλισθαίνουσι δ' εἰς τοῦτο τὸ γένος ὀρεγόμενοι μὲν τοῦ περιττοῦ καὶ πεποιημένου καὶ μάλιστα τοῦ ἡδέος, ἐξοκέλλοντες δὲ εἰς τὸ ῥωπικὸν καὶ κακόζηλον. τούτῳ παράκειται τρίτον τι κακίας εἶδος ἐν τοῖς παθητικοῖς, ὅπερ ὁ Θεόδωρος παρένθυρσον ἐκάλει. ἔστι δὲ πάθος ἄκαιρον καὶ κενὸν ἔνθα μὴ

4 Gorgias B 5a D-K   7-8 Soph. fr. 701 Nauck²

---

7 ἀνήρ] ἀνὴρ Man.   14 μεγάλων Columbus: μεγάλῳ P: μεγάλως Man.   ἀπολισθάνειν Ruhnken   16 ⟨ἐπὶ⟩ λόγων Wilamowitz   οἱ ... ἀναλήθεις del. Vaucher   καὶ² fort. secludendum   περιστάντες apogr.: ... ιστάντες P   23 ἐξοκέλλοντες Wilamowitz: ἐποκέλλοντες P   24 ῥωπικὸν I. Vossius: ῥοπικὸν P: τροπικὸν apogr.   26 ἄκαιρον καὶ del. Weiske   καὶ κενὸν] καὶ ἐνὸν Vahlen: κείμενον Wilamowitz

ΠΕΡΙ ΥΨΟΥΣ

δεῖ πάθους, ἢ ἄμετρον ἔνθα μετρίου δεῖ. πολλὰ γὰρ ὥσπερ ἐκ μέθης τινὲς εἰς τὰ μηκέτι τοῦ πράγματος ἴδια ⟨δ'⟩ ἑαυτῶν καὶ σχολικὰ παραφέρονται πάθη, εἶτα πρὸς οὐδὲν πεπονθότας ἀκροατὰς ἀσχημονοῦσιν εἰκότως, ἐξεστηκότες πρὸς οὐκ ἐξεστηκότας· πλὴν περὶ μὲν τῶν παθητικῶν ἄλλος ἡμῖν ἀπόκειται τόπος.

Θατέρου δὲ ὧν εἴπομεν, λέγω δὲ τοῦ ψυχροῦ, πλήρης ὁ Τίμαιος, 4 ἀνὴρ τὰ μὲν ἄλλα ἱκανὸς καὶ πρὸς λόγων ἐνίοτε μέγεθος οὐκ ἄφορος, πολυΐστωρ, ἐπινοητικός, πλὴν ἀλλοτρίων μὲν ἐλεγκτικώτατος ἁμαρτημάτων ἀνεπαίσθητος δὲ ἰδίων, ὑπὸ δὲ ἔρωτος τοῦ ξένας νοήσεις ἀεὶ κινεῖν πολλάκις ἐκπίπτων εἰς τὸ παιδαριωδέστατον. παραθήσομαι δὲ τἀνδρὸς ἓν ἢ δύο, ἐπειδὴ τὰ πλείω 2 προέλαβεν ὁ Καικίλιος. ἐπαινῶν Ἀλέξανδρον τὸν μέγαν, "ὃς τὴν Ἀσίαν ὅλην" φησίν "ἐν ἐλάττοσι⟨ν ἔτεσι⟩ παρέλαβεν ἢ ὅσοις τὸν ὑπὲρ τοῦ πρὸς Πέρσας πολέμου πανηγυρικὸν λόγον Ἰσοκράτης ἔγραψεν." θαυμαστή γε τοῦ Μακεδόνος ἡ πρὸς τὸν σοφιστὴν σύγκρισις· δῆλον γάρ, ὦ Τίμαιε, ὡς οἱ Λακεδαιμόνιοι διὰ τοῦτο πολὺ τοῦ Ἰσοκράτους κατ' ἀνδρείαν ἐλείποντο, ἐπειδὴ οἱ μὲν ⟨ἐν⟩ τριάκοντα ἔτεσι Μεσσήνην παρέλαβον, ὁ δὲ τὸν πανηγυρικὸν ἐν μόνοις δέκα συνετάξατο. τοῖς δὲ Ἀθηναίοις 3 ἁλοῦσι περὶ Σικελίαν τίνα τρόπον ἐπιφωνεῖ; ὅτι "εἰς τὸν Ἑρμῆν ἀσεβήσαντες καὶ περικόψαντες αὐτοῦ τὰ ἀγάλματα, διὰ τοῦτ' ἔδωκαν δίκην, οὐχ ἥκιστα δι' ἕνα ἄνδρα, ὃς ἀπὸ τοῦ παρανομηθέντος διὰ πατέρων ἦν, Ἑρμοκράτη τὸν Ἕρμωνος". ὥστε θαυμάζειν με, Τερεντιανὲ ἥδιστε, πῶς οὐ καὶ εἰς Διονύσιον γράφει τὸν τύραννον· "ἐπεὶ γὰρ εἰς τὸν Δία καὶ τὸν Ἡρακλέα δυσσεβὴς ἐγένετο, διὰ τοῦτ' αὐτὸν Δίων καὶ Ἡρακλείδης τῆς τυραννίδος ἀφείλοντο." ⟨καὶ⟩ τί δεῖ περὶ Τιμαίου λέγειν, ὅπου 4 γε καὶ οἱ ἥρωες ἐκεῖνοι, Ξενοφῶντα λέγω καὶ Πλάτωνα, καίτοιγε ἐκ τῆς Σωκράτους ὄντες παλαίστρας, ὅμως διὰ τὰ οὕτως

6 Timaeus T 23 *FGrHist* 566   12 ibid. F 139   20 ibid. F 102a

2 ⟨δ'⟩ add. Faber   13 ἐλάττοσι⟨ν ἔτεσι⟩ Spengel   18 μὲν ⟨ἐν⟩ Cobet   τριάκοντα] εἴκοσι Faber   23 ἦν Man.: ἂν P   27 ⟨καὶ⟩ τί δεῖ Toup: τί ⟨δὲ⟩ δεῖ Schurzfleisch: ⟨καίτοι⟩ τί δεῖ Man.

μικροχαρῆ ποτε ἑαυτῶν ἐπιλανθάνονται; ὁ μέν γε ἐν τῇ Λακεδαιμονίων γράφει πολιτείᾳ· "ἐκείνων [μὲν] γοῦν ἧττον μὲν ἂν φωνὴν ἀκούσαις ἢ τῶν λιθίνων, ἧττον δ' ἂν ὄμματα στρέψαις ἢ τῶν χαλκῶν, αἰδημονεστέρους δ' ἂν αὐτοὺς ἡγήσαιο καὶ αὐτῶν τῶν ἐν τοῖς ὀφθαλμοῖς παρθένων." Ἀμφικράτει καὶ οὐ Ξενοφῶντι ἔπρεπε τὰς ἐν τοῖς ὀφθαλμοῖς ἡμῶν κόρας λέγειν παρθένους αἰδήμονας· οἷον δὲ Ἡράκλεις τὸ τὰς ἁπάντων ἑξῆς κόρας αἰσχυντηλὰς εἶναι πεπεῖσθαι, ὅπου φασὶν οὐδενὶ οὕτως ἐνσημαίνεσθαι τήν τινων ἀναίδειαν ὡς ἐν τοῖς ὀφθαλμοῖς, ⟨ὡς καὶ ὁ Ἀχιλλεὺς τοῦ Ἀγαμέμνονος ὀνειδίζων τὸ ἐν τοῖς ὀφθαλμοῖς⟩ ἰταμὸν "οἰνοβαρές, κυνὸς ὄμματ' ἔχων" φησίν. ὁ μέντοι Τίμαιος, ὡς φωρίου τινὸς ἐφαπτόμενος, οὐδὲ τοῦτο Ξενοφῶντι τὸ ψυχρὸν κατέλιπεν. φησὶ γοῦν ἐπὶ τοῦ Ἀγαθοκλέους †καὶ τὸ† τὴν ἀνεψιὰν ἑτέρῳ δεδομένην ἐκ τῶν ἀνακαλυπτηρίων ἁρπάσαντα ἀπελθεῖν· "ὃ τίς ἂν ἐποίησεν ἐν ὀφθαλμοῖς κόρας, μὴ πόρνας ἔχων;" τί δέ; ὁ τἆλλα θεῖος Πλάτων τὰς δέλτους θέλων εἰπεῖν "γράψαντες" φησίν "ἐν τοῖς ἱεροῖς θήσουσι κυπαριττίνας μνήμας". καὶ πάλιν "περὶ δὲ τειχῶν, ὦ Μέγιλλε, ἐγὼ ξυμφεροίμην ἂν τῇ Σπάρτῃ τὸ καθεύδειν ἐᾶν ἐν τῇ γῇ κατακείμενα τὰ τείχη καὶ μὴ ἐπανίστασθαι". καὶ τὸ Ἡροδότειον οὐ πόρρω, τὸ φάναι τὰς καλὰς γυναῖκας "ἀλγηδόνας ὀφθαλμῶν." καίτοιγε ἔχει τινὰ παραμυθίαν, οἱ γὰρ παρ' αὐτῷ ταυτὶ λέγοντές εἰσι[ν οἱ] βάρβαροι καὶ ἐν

2 Xen. *Resp. Lac.* 3. 5   11 Hom. *A* 225   11 sqq. Timaeus, F 122 *FGrHist* 566   16 sqq. Pl. *Leges* 741C: γράψαντες δ' ἐν τοῖς ἱεροῖς θήσουσι κυπαριττίνας μνήμας εἰς τὸν ἔπειτα χρόνον καταγεγραμμένας : ibid. 778D : περὶ δὲ τειχῶν, ὦ Μέγιλλε, ἔγωγ' ἂν τῇ Σπάρτῃ συμφεροίμην τὸ καθεύδειν ἐᾶν ἐν τῇ γῇ κατακείμενα τὰ τείχη καὶ μὴ ἐπανιστάναι   20 Her. 5. 18.

2 [μὲν] om. codd. Xen., Stob. *Ecl.* 4. 2. 23 (iv, p. 145 Hense) 3 στρέψαις] μεταστρέψαις codd. Xen.   4 ὀφθαλμοῖς etiam Stob. l.c.: θαλάμοις codd. Xen.   7 αἰδήμονας del. Wilamowitz 8 οὐδενὶ] οὐδὲν Immisch   9–10 ⟨ὡς καὶ ... ὀφθαλμοῖς⟩ ex. gr. supplevi: similia Cobet, Rothstein   11 ἰταμὸν ... φησίν del. Kayser: ὡς ⟨τὸ⟩ ἐν τοῖς ὀφθαλμοῖς ἰταμόν· Immisch   12 φωρίου] φὼρ ἰοῦ Rohde : φωτίου Meerwaldt   13 †καὶ τὸ†] κατὰ τὸ vel καὶ τοῦ Reiske; plura deesse crediderim   22 [οἱ] secl. Wilamowitz

ΠΕΡΙ ΥΨΟΥΣ

μέθῃ, ἀλλ' οὐδ' ἐκ τοιούτων προσώπων διὰ μικροψυχίαν καλὸν ἀσχημονεῖν πρὸς τὸν αἰῶνα.

Ἅπαντα μέντοι τὰ οὕτως ἄσεμνα διὰ μίαν ἐμφύεται τοῖς λόγοις αἰτίαν, διὰ τὸ περὶ τὰς νοήσεις καινόσπουδον, περὶ ὃ δὴ μάλιστα κορυβαντιῶσιν οἱ νῦν· ἀφ' ὧν γὰρ ἡμῖν τἀγαθά, σχεδὸν ἀπ' αὐτῶν τούτων καὶ τὰ κακὰ γεννᾶσθαι φιλεῖ. ὅθεν, ἐπεὶ φορὸν εἰς συνταγμάτων κατόρθωσιν τά τε κάλλη τῆς ἑρμηνείας καὶ τὰ ὕψη καὶ πρὸς τούτοις αἱ ἡδοναί, καὶ αὐτὰ ταῦτα, καθάπερ τῆς ἐπιτυχίας, οὕτως ἀρχαὶ καὶ ὑποθέσεις καὶ τῶν ἐναντίων καθίστανται. τοιοῦτόν πως καὶ αἱ μεταβολαὶ καὶ ὑπερβολαὶ καὶ τὰ πληθυντικά· δείξομεν δ' ἐν τοῖς ἔπειτα τὸν κίνδυνον, ὃν ἔχειν ἐοίκασι. διόπερ ἀναγκαῖον ἤδη διαπορεῖν καὶ ὑποτίθεσθαι δι' ὅτου τρόπου τὰς ἀνακεκραμένας κακίας τοῖς ὑψηλοῖς ἐκφεύγειν δυνάμεθα. ἔστι δέ, ὦ φίλος, εἴ τινα περιποιησαίμεθ' ἐν πρώτοις καθαρὰν τοῦ κατ' ἀλήθειαν ὕψους ἐπιστήμην καὶ ἐπίκρισιν. καίτοι τὸ πρᾶγμα δύσληπτον· ἡ γὰρ τῶν λόγων κρίσις πολλῆς ἐστι πείρας τελευταῖον ἐπιγέννημα· οὐ μὴν ἀλλ', ὡς εἰπεῖν ἐν παραγγέλματι, ἐντεῦθέν ποθεν ἴσως τὴν διάγνωσιν αὐτῶν οὐκ ἀδύνατον πορίζεσθαι.

Εἰδέναι χρή, φίλτατε, διότι, καθάπερ κἀν τῷ κοινῷ βίῳ οὐδὲν ὑπάρχει μέγα οὗ τὸ καταφρονεῖν ἐστι μέγα, οἷον πλοῦτοι τιμαὶ δόξαι τυραννίδες καὶ ὅσα δὴ ἄλλα ἔχει πολὺ τὸ ἔξωθεν προστραγῳδούμενον οὐκ ἂν τῷ γε φρονίμῳ δόξειεν ἀγαθὰ ὑπερβάλλοντα ὧν αὐτὸ τὸ περιφρονεῖν ἀγαθὸν οὐ μέτριον—θαυμάζουσι γοῦν τῶν ἐχόντων αὐτὰ μᾶλλον τοὺς δυναμένους ἔχειν καὶ διὰ μεγαλοψυχίαν ὑπερορῶντας—τῇδέ που καὶ ἐπὶ τῶν διῃρημένων ἐν ποιήμασι καὶ λόγοις ἐπισκεπτέον, μή τινα μεγέθους φαντασίαν ἔχοι τοιαύτην, ᾗ πολὺ πρόσκειται τὸ εἰκῇ προσαναπλαττόμενον, ἀναπτυττόμενα δὲ ἄλλως εὑρίσκοιτο χαῦνα, ὧν τοῦ θαυμάζειν τὸ περιφρονεῖν εὐγενέστερον. φύσει γάρ πως ὑπὸ τἀληθοῦς ὕψους ἐπαίρεταί τε ἡμῶν ἡ ψυχὴ καὶ γαῦρόν τι ἀνάστημα λαμβάνουσα πληροῦται

---

4 καινόσπουδον] κενόσπουδον Vaucher   6 ἐπεὶ φορὸν von Arnim: ἐπίφορον P   8 καὶ post ἡδοναί del. von Arnim   10 ⟨αἱ⟩ ὑπερβολαὶ Morus   31 ἀνάστημα apogr.: ἀνάθημα P: παράστημα Man.

3 χαρᾶς καὶ μεγαλαυχίας, ὡς αὐτὴ γεννήσασα ὅπερ ἤκουσεν. ὅταν οὖν ὑπ' ἀνδρὸς ἔμφρονος καὶ ἐμπείρου λόγων πολλάκις ἀκουόμενόν τι πρὸς μεγαλοφροσύνην τὴν ψυχὴν μὴ συνδιατιθῇ μηδ' ἐγκαταλείπῃ τῇ διανοίᾳ πλεῖον τοῦ λεγομένου τὸ ἀναθεωρούμενον, πίπτῃ δέ, ἂν αὐτὸ συνεχὲς ἐπισκοπῇς, εἰς ἀπαύξησιν, οὐκ ἂν ἔτ' ἀληθὲς ὕψος εἴη μέχρι μόνης τῆς ἀκοῆς σῳζόμενον. τοῦτο γὰρ τῷ ὄντι μέγα, οὗ πολλὴ μὲν ἡ ἀναθεώρησις, δύσκολος δὲ μᾶλλον δ' ἀδύνατος ἡ κατεξανάστασις, ἰσχυρὰ δὲ ἡ μνήμη καὶ δυσεξάλει-
4 πτος. ὅλως δὲ καλὰ νόμιζε ὕψη καὶ ἀληθινὰ τὰ διὰ παντὸς ἀρέσκοντα καὶ πᾶσιν. ὅταν γὰρ τοῖς ἀπὸ διαφόρων ἐπιτηδευμάτων βίων ζήλων ἡλικιῶν λόγων ἕν τι καὶ ταὐτὸν ἅμα περὶ τῶν αὐτῶν ἅπασι δοκῇ, τόθ' ἡ ἐξ ἀσυμφώνων ὡς κρίσις καὶ συγκατάθεσις τὴν ἐπὶ τῷ θαυμαζομένῳ πίστιν ἰσχυρὰν λαμβάνει καὶ ἀναμφίλεκτον.

8 Ἐπεὶ δὲ πέντε, ὡς ἂν εἴποι τις, πηγαί τινές εἰσιν αἱ τῆς ὑψηγορίας γονιμώταται, προϋποκειμένης ὥσπερ ἐδάφους τινὸς κοινοῦ ταῖς πέντε ταύταις ἰδέαις τῆς ἐν τῷ λέγειν δυνάμεως, ἧς ὅλως χωρὶς οὐδέν, πρῶτον μὲν καὶ κράτιστον τὸ περὶ τὰς νοήσεις ἁδρεπήβολον, ὡς κἀν τοῖς περὶ Ξενοφῶντος ὡρισάμεθα· δεύτερον δὲ τὸ σφοδρὸν καὶ ἐνθουσιαστικὸν πάθος· ἀλλ' αἱ μὲν δύο αὗται τοῦ ὕψους κατὰ τὸ πλέον αὐθιγενεῖς συστάσεις, αἱ λοιπαὶ δ' ἤδη καὶ διὰ τέχνης, ἥ τε ποιὰ τῶν σχημάτων πλάσις (δισσὰ δέ που ταῦτα, τὰ μὲν νοήσεως, θάτερα δὲ λέξεως), ἐπὶ δὲ τούτοις ἡ γενναία φράσις, ἧς μέρη πάλιν ὀνομάτων τε ἐκλογὴ καὶ ἡ τροπικὴ καὶ πεποιημένη λέξις· πέμπτη δὲ μεγέθους αἰτία καὶ συγκλείουσα τὰ πρὸ αὐτῆς ἅπαντα, ἡ ἐν ἀξιώματι καὶ διάρσει σύνθεσις· φέρε δὴ τὰ ἐμπεριεχόμενα καθ' ἑκάστην ἰδέαν τούτων ἐπισκεψώμεθα, τοσοῦτον προειπόντες, ὅτι τῶν πέντε μορίων ὁ Καικίλιος ἔστιν

5 ἂν αὐτὸ Pearce: ἄνευ τὸ P: ἂν τὸ apogr.: ἂν εὖ τὸ Reiske   συνεχὲς] συνεχῶς Wakefield: 'fortasse ἂν εὖ τε καὶ συνεχῶς' Photiades: ἂν κατὰ τὸ συνεχὲς Wilamowitz   11 λόγων suspectum: χρόνων Richards: τρόπων Dodds   12 κρίσις] κρᾶσις Pearce   18 ὡς κἀν ... ἐν δὲ φάει καὶ ὄλεσσον (9. 10 = p. 12, 10) desunt in P, octo foliis deperditis: ὡς κἀν ... ἠρκέσθην et τὸ ἐπ' οὐρανὸν ... ὀφθαλμοῖσιν ἰδέσθαι servant apographa, duobus scilicet exterioribus quaternionis foliis nondum amissis descripta   27 πέντε del. Immisch

ἃ παρέλιπεν, ὡς καὶ τὸ πάθος ἀμέλει. ἀλλ' εἰ μὲν ὡς ἕν τι ταῦτ' 2
ἄμφω, τό τε ὕψος καὶ τὸ παθητικόν, [καὶ] ἔδοξεν αὐτῷ πάντη
συνυπάρχειν τε ἀλλήλοις καὶ συμπεφυκέναι, διαμαρτάνει· καὶ γὰρ
πάθη τινὰ διεστῶτα ὕψους καὶ ταπεινὰ εὑρίσκεται, καθάπερ
οἶκτοι λῦπαι φόβοι, καὶ ἔμπαλιν πολλὰ ὕψη δίχα πάθους, ὡς πρὸς
μυρίοις ἄλλοις καὶ τὰ περὶ τοὺς Ἀλῳάδας τῷ ποιητῇ παρατετολ-
μημένα,

"Οσσαν ἐπ' Οὐλύμπῳ μέμασαν θέμεν· αὐτὰρ ἐπ' Ὄσσῃ
Πήλιον εἰνοσίφυλλον, ἵν' οὐρανὸς ἄμβατος εἴη·
καὶ τὸ τούτοις ἔτι μεῖζον ἐπιφερόμενον,
καί νύ κεν ἐξετέλεσσαν.

παρά γε μὴν τοῖς ῥήτορσι τὰ ἐγκώμια καὶ τὰ πομπικὰ καὶ 3
ἐπιδεικτικὰ τὸν μὲν ὄγκον καὶ τὸ ὑψηλὸν ἐξ ἅπαντος περιέχει,
πάθους δὲ χηρεύει κατὰ τὸ πλεῖστον, ὅθεν ἥκιστα τῶν ῥητόρων
οἱ περιπαθεῖς ἐγκωμιαστικοὶ ἢ ἔμπαλιν οἱ ἐπαινετικοὶ περιπαθεῖς. εἰ δ' αὖ πάλιν ἐξ ὅλου μὴ ἐνόμισεν ὁ Καικίλιος τὸ 4
ἐμπαθὲς ⟨εἰς⟩ τὰ ὕψη ποτὲ συντελεῖν καὶ διὰ τοῦτ' οὐχ ἡγήσατο
μνήμης ἄξιον, πάνυ διηπάτηται· θαρρῶν γὰρ ἀφορισαίμην ἂν
ὡς οὐδὲν οὕτως ὡς τὸ γενναῖον πάθος, ἔνθα χρή, μεγαλήγορον,
ὥσπερ ὑπὸ μανίας τινὸς καὶ πνεύματος ἐνθουσιαστικῶς ἐκπνέον
καὶ οἱονεὶ φοιβάζον τοὺς λόγους.

Οὐ μὴν ἀλλ' ἐπεὶ τὴν κρατίστην μοῖραν ἐπέχει τῶν ἄλλων τὸ 9
πρῶτον, λέγω δὲ τὸ μεγαλοφυές, χρὴ κἀνταῦθα, καὶ εἰ δωρητὸν
τὸ πρᾶγμα μᾶλλον ἢ κτητόν, ὅμως καθ' ὅσον οἷόν τε τὰς ψυχὰς
ἀνατρέφειν πρὸς τὰ μεγέθη καὶ ὥσπερ ἐγκύμονας ἀεὶ ποιεῖν
γενναίου παραστήματος. τίνα, φήσεις, τρόπον; γέγραφά που 2
καὶ ἑτέρωθι τὸ τοιοῦτον· ὕψος μεγαλοφροσύνης ἀπήχημα. ὅθεν
καὶ φωνῆς δίχα θαυμάζεταί ποτε ψιλὴ καθ' ἑαυτὴν ἡ ἔννοια

8–11 Hom. λ 315–17

1 ὡς ἕν τι] ἤνωσέν τι van Groningen   2 [καὶ] secl. Pearce
17 ⟨εἰς⟩ add. Faber (ἐς)   20 ἐνθουσιαστικῶς] ἐνθουσιαστικοῦ Faber
ἐκπνέον] ἐπιπνέον vel ἐμπνέον Morus   26 φήσεις Vaticani 194 et 1417:
φήσει vel φήσει τις cett.   27 num ἑτέρωθί τι?

ΠΕΡΙ ΥΨΟΥΣ [9. 2–

δι' αὐτὸ τὸ μεγαλόφρον, ὡς ἡ τοῦ Αἴαντος ἐν Νεκυίᾳ σιωπὴ
3 μέγα καὶ παντὸς ὑψηλότερον λόγου. πρῶτον οὖν τὸ ἐξ οὗ γίνεται
προϋποτίθεσθαι πάντως ἀναγκαῖον, ὡς ἔχειν δεῖ τὸν ἀληθῆ
ῥήτορα μὴ ταπεινὸν φρόνημα καὶ ἀγεννές. οὐδὲ γὰρ οἷόν τε
μικρὰ καὶ δουλοπρεπῆ φρονοῦντας καὶ ἐπιτηδεύοντας παρ' ὅλον 5
τὸν βίον θαυμαστόν τι καὶ τοῦ παντὸς αἰῶνος ἐξενεγκεῖν ἄξιον·
μεγάλοι δὲ οἱ λόγοι τούτων, κατὰ τὸ εἰκός, ὧν ἂν ἐμβριθεῖς
ὦσιν αἱ ἔννοιαι. ταύτῃ καὶ εἰς τοὺς μάλιστα φρονηματίας
4 ἐμπίπτει τὰ ὑπερφυᾶ· ὁ γὰρ τῷ Παρμενίωνι φήσαντι "ἐγὼ μὲν
ἠρκέσθην ... 10
. . . .
5 ... τὸ ἐπ' οὐρανὸν ἀπὸ γῆς διάστημα· καὶ τοῦτ' ἂν εἴποι τις οὐ
μᾶλλον τῆς Ἔριδος ἢ Ὁμήρου μέτρον. ᾧ ἀνόμοιόν γε τὸ Ἡσι-
όδειον ἐπὶ τῆς Ἀχλύος, εἴγε Ἡσιόδου καὶ τὴν Ἀσπίδα θετέον·

τῆς ἐκ μὲν ῥινῶν μύξαι ῥέον· 15

οὐ γὰρ δεινὸν ἐποίησε τὸ εἴδωλον, ἀλλὰ μισητόν. ὁ δὲ πῶς μεγε-
θύνει τὰ δαιμόνια;

ὅσσον δ' ἠεροειδὲς ἀνὴρ ἴδεν ὀφθαλμοῖσιν,
ἥμενος ἐν σκοπιῇ, λεύσσων ἐπὶ οἴνοπα πόντον,
τόσσον ἐπιθρώσκουσι θεῶν ὑψηχέες ἵπποι. 20

τὴν ὁρμὴν αὐτῶν κοσμικῷ διαστήματι καταμετρεῖ. τίς οὖν οὐκ
ἂν εἰκότως διὰ τὴν ὑπερβολὴν τοῦ μεγέθους ἐπιφθέγξαιτο, ὅτι
ἂν δὶς ἑξῆς ἐφορμήσωσιν οἱ τῶν θεῶν ἵπποι, οὐκέθ' εὑρήσουσιν ἐν
κόσμῳ τόπον; ὑπερφυᾶ καὶ τὰ ἐπὶ τῆς θεομαχίας φαντάσματα·

6 ἀμφὶ δ' ἐσάλπιγξεν μέγας οὐρανὸς Οὔλυμπός τε. 25

1 Hom. λ 563   9 v. Arrian. Anab. 2. 25. 2, Plu. Alex. 29   11 Hom.
Δ 442 : ἥ τ' ὀλίγη μὲν πρῶτα κορύσσεται, αὐτὰρ ἔπειτα οὐρανῷ ἐστήριξε κάρη
καὶ ἐπὶ χθονὶ βαίνει   15 Hes. Scutum 267   18–20 Hom. E 770–2

12 εἴποι Man. : εἰπεῖν codd.   20 ὑψηχέες] ὑψαύχενες K marg., Man.
23–24 ἐν ⟨τῷ⟩ κόσμῳ 'vel potius ὑπὸ κόσμῳ' Photiades   24 καὶ τὰ
Man. : codicum alii καὶ, alii τὰ   25 Οὔλυμπός τε del. Immisch
⟨καὶ⟩ inter primum et secundum versuum Homericorum add. K supra
lineam, Portus, Immisch

ἔδδεισεν δ' ὑπένερθεν ἄναξ ἐνέρων Ἀιδωνεύς,
δείσας δ' ἐκ θρόνου ἆλτο καὶ ἴαχε, μή οἱ ἔπειτα
γαῖαν ἀναρρήξειε Ποσειδάων ἐνοσίχθων,
οἰκία δὲ θνητοῖσι καὶ ἀθανάτοισι φανείη
σμερδαλέ' εὐρώεντα, τά τε στυγέουσι θεοί περ.

ἐπιβλέπεις, ἑταῖρε, ὡς ἀναρρηγνυμένης μὲν ἐκ βάθρων γῆς, αὐτοῦ δὲ γυμνουμένου ταρτάρου, ἀνατροπὴν δὲ ὅλου καὶ διάστασιν τοῦ κόσμου λαμβάνοντος, πάνθ' ἅμα, οὐρανὸς ᾅδης, τὰ θνητὰ τὰ ἀθάνατα, ἅμα τῇ τότε συμπολεμεῖ καὶ συγκινδυνεύει μάχῃ; ἀλλὰ ταῦτα φοβερὰ μέν, πλὴν ἄλλως, εἰ μὴ κατ' ἀλληγορίαν 7 λαμβάνοιτο, παντάπασιν ἄθεα καὶ οὐ σώζοντα τὸ πρέπον. Ὅμηρος γάρ μοι δοκεῖ παραδιδοὺς τραύματα θεῶν στάσεις τιμωρίας δάκρυα δεσμὰ πάθη πάμφυρτα τοὺς μὲν ἐπὶ τῶν Ἰλιακῶν ἀνθρώπους ὅσον ἐπὶ τῇ δυνάμει θεοὺς πεποιηκέναι, τοὺς θεοὺς δὲ ἀνθρώπους. ἀλλ' ἡμῖν μὲν δυσδαιμονοῦσιν ἀπόκειται λιμὴν κακῶν ὁ θάνατος, τῶν θεῶν δ' οὐ τὴν φύσιν, ἀλλὰ τὴν ἀτυχίαν ἐποίησεν αἰώνιον. πολὺ δὲ τῶν περὶ τὴν θεομαχίαν ἀμείνω τὰ ὅσα ἄχραντόν 8 τι καὶ μέγα τὸ δαιμόνιον ὡς ἀληθῶς καὶ ἄκρατον παρίστησιν, οἷα (πολλοῖς δὲ πρὸ ἡμῶν ὁ τόπος ἐξείργασται) τὰ ἐπὶ τοῦ Ποσειδῶνος,

τρέμε δ' οὔρεα μακρὰ καὶ ὕλη
καὶ κορυφαὶ Τρώων τε πόλις καὶ νῆες Ἀχαιῶν
ποσσὶν ὑπ' ἀθανάτοισι Ποσειδάωνος ἰόντος.

βῆ δ' ἐλάαν ἐπὶ κύματ', ἄταλλε δὲ κήτε' ὑπ' αὐτοῦ
πάντοθεν ἐκ κευθμῶν, οὐδ' ἠγνοίησεν ἄνακτα·
γηθοσύνῃ δὲ θάλασσα διίστατο, τοὶ δὲ πέτοντο.

ταύτῃ καὶ ὁ τῶν Ἰουδαίων θεσμοθέτης, οὐχ ὁ τυχὼν ἀνήρ, ἐπειδὴ 9

p. 10, 25–5 Hom. Φ 388 (ἀμφὶ ... οὐρανός)+E 750 (Οὔλυμπός τε) +Υ 61–65   20–25 Hom. N 18 +Y 60+N 19+N 27–29

2 ἔπειτα] ὕπερθε Hom.   7 ὅλου] δι' ὅλου Rothstein   16 ἀλλὰ ⟨καὶ⟩ G. S. A. (*Class. J.* 3. 5, p. 65)   18 ἄκρατον] ἴσως ἀκήρατον K marg., Portus   26–p. 12, 3 ταύτῃ ... ἐγένετο spuria iudicaverunt Portus, Spengel, alii

τὴν τοῦ θείου δύναμιν κατὰ τὴν ἀξίαν ἐχώρησε κἀξέφηνεν, εὐθὺς
ἐν τῇ εἰσβολῇ γράψας τῶν νόμων "εἶπεν ὁ Θεός", φησί,—τί;
"γενέσθω φῶς, καὶ ἐγένετο· γενέσθω γῆ, καὶ ἐγένετο." οὐκ
ὀχληρὸς ἂν ἴσως, ἑταῖρε, δόξαιμι, ἓν ἔτι τοῦ ποιητοῦ καὶ τῶν
ἀνθρωπίνων παραθέμενος τοῦ μαθεῖν χάριν ὡς εἰς τὰ ἡρωικὰ
μεγέθη συνεμβαίνειν ἐθίζει. ἀχλὺς ἄφνω καὶ νὺξ ἄπορος αὐτῷ
τὴν τῶν Ἑλλήνων ἐπέχει μάχην· ἔνθα δὴ ὁ Αἴας ἀμηχανῶν

Ζεῦ πάτερ (φησίν), ἀλλὰ σὺ ῥῦσαι ὑπ' ἠέρος υἷας Ἀχαιῶν,
ποίησον δ' αἴθρην, δὸς δ' ὀφθαλμοῖσιν ἰδέσθαι·
ἐν δὲ φάει καὶ ὄλεσσον.

ἔστιν ὡς ἀληθῶς τὸ πάθος Αἴαντος, οὐ γὰρ ζῆν εὔχεται (ἦν
γὰρ τὸ αἴτημα τοῦ ἥρωος ταπεινότερον), ἀλλ' ἐπειδὴ ἐν ἀπράκτῳ
σκότει τὴν ἀνδρείαν εἰς οὐδὲν γενναῖον εἶχε διαθέσθαι, διὰ ταῦτ'
ἀγανακτῶν ὅτι πρὸς τὴν μάχην ἀργεῖ, φῶς ὅτι τάχιστα αἰτεῖται,
ὡς πάντως τῆς ἀρετῆς εὑρήσων ἐντάφιον ἄξιον, κἂν αὐτῷ Ζεὺς
ἀντιτάττηται. ἀλλὰ γὰρ Ὅμηρος μὲν ἐνθάδε οὔριος συνεμπνεῖ
τοῖς ἀγῶσι, καὶ οὐκ ἄλλο τι αὐτὸς πέπονθεν ἢ

μαίνεται, ὡς ὅτ' Ἄρης ἐγχέσπαλος ἢ ὀλοὸν πῦρ
οὔρεσι μαίνηται, βαθέης ἐν τάρφεσιν ὕλης,
ἀφλοισμὸς δὲ περὶ στόμα γίγνεται.

δείκνυσι δ' ὅμως διὰ τῆς Ὀδυσσείας (καὶ γὰρ ταῦτα πολλῶν
ἕνεκα προσεπιθεωρητέον), ὅτι μεγάλης φύσεως ὑποφερομένης
ἤδη ἴδιόν ἐστιν ἐν γήρᾳ τὸ φιλόμυθον. δῆλος γὰρ ἐκ πολλῶν τε
ἄλλων συντεθεικὼς ταύτην δευτέραν τὴν ὑπόθεσιν, ἀτὰρ δὴ κἀκ
τοῦ λείψανα τῶν Ἰλιακῶν παθημάτων διὰ τῆς Ὀδυσσείας
ὡς ἐπεισόδιά τινα [τοῦ Τρωικοῦ πολέμου] προσεπεισφέρειν, καὶ
νὴ Δί' ἐκ τοῦ τὰς ὀλοφύρσεις καὶ τοὺς οἴκτους ὡς πάλαι που

2–3 cf. Genesis i. 3–9   8–10 Hom. P 645–7   18–20 Hom. O 605–7

1 ἐχώρησε] ἐγνώρισε Man.   4 καὶ] κἀκ Wilamowitz : κἀπὶ Hammer   16 Ὅμηρος ἐνθάδε μὲν Hefermehl : ἐνθάδε μὲν Ὅμηρος Richards   ἐνθάδε] ἐν Ἰλιάδι Wilamowitz   18 μαίνεται] μαίνετο δ' Hom.   20 γίγνεται] γίγνετο Hom.   23 ἐν γήρᾳ secl. Hefermehl   26 [τοῦ ... πολέμου] post Wilamowitzium seclusi

προεγνωσμένοις τοῖς ἥρωσιν ἐνταῦθα προσαποδιδόναι. οὐ γὰρ ἀλλ' ἢ τῆς Ἰλιάδος ἐπίλογός ἐστιν ἡ Ὀδύσσεια·

ἔνθα μὲν Αἴας κεῖται ἀρήιος, ἔνθα δ' Ἀχιλλεύς,
ἔνθα δὲ Πάτροκλος, θεόφιν μήστωρ ἀτάλαντος·
5   ἔνθα δ' ἐμὸς φίλος υἱός.

ἀπὸ δὲ τῆς αὐτῆς αἰτίας, οἶμαι, τῆς μὲν Ἰλιάδος γραφομένης 13 ἐν ἀκμῇ πνεύματος ὅλον τὸ σωμάτιον δραματικὸν ὑπεστήσατο καὶ ἐναγώνιον, τῆς δὲ Ὀδυσσείας τὸ πλέον διηγηματικόν, ὅπερ ἴδιον γήρως. ὅθεν ἐν τῇ Ὀδυσσείᾳ παρεικάσαι τις ἂν καταδυο-
10 μένῳ τὸν Ὅμηρον ἡλίῳ, οὗ δίχα τῆς σφοδρότητος παραμένει τὸ μέγεθος. οὐ γὰρ ἔτι τοῖς Ἰλιακοῖς ἐκείνοις ποιήμασιν ἴσον ἐνταῦθα σῴζει τὸν τόνον, οὐδ' ἐξωμαλισμένα τὰ ὕψη καὶ ἰζήματα μηδαμοῦ λαμβάνοντα, οὐδὲ τὴν πρόχυσιν ὁμοίαν τῶν ἐπαλλήλων παθῶν, οὐδὲ τὸ ἀγχίστροφον καὶ πολιτικὸν καὶ ταῖς ἐκ τῆς
15 ἀληθείας φαντασίαις καταπεπυκνωμένον· ἀλλ' οἷον ὑποχωροῦντος εἰς ἑαυτὸν Ὠκεανοῦ καὶ περὶ τὰ ἴδια μέτρα †ἐρημουμένου τὸ λοιπὸν φαίνονται τοῦ μεγέθους ἀμπώτιδες κἀν τοῖς μυθώδεσι καὶ ἀπίστοις πλάνος. λέγων δὲ ταῦτ' οὐκ ἐπιλέλησμαι τῶν ἐν τῇ 14 Ὀδυσσείᾳ χειμώνων καὶ τῶν περὶ τὸν Κύκλωπα καί τινων ἄλλων,
20 ἀλλὰ γῆρας διηγοῦμαι, γῆρας δ' ὅμως Ὁμήρου· πλὴν ἐν ἅπασι τούτοις ἑξῆς τοῦ πρακτικοῦ κρατεῖ τὸ μυθικόν. παρεξέβην δ' εἰς ταῦθ', ὡς ἔφην, ἵνα δείξαιμι ὡς εἰς λῆρον ἐνίοτε ῥᾷστον κατὰ τὴν ἀπακμὴν τὰ μεγαλοφυῆ παρατρέπεται, οἷα τὰ περὶ τὸν ἀσκὸν καὶ τοὺς ἐν Κίρκης συοφορβουμένους, οὓς ὁ Ζωίλος ἔφη

3–5 Hom. γ 109–11   18–19 Hom. ε 291 sqq., ι 181 sqq.   23–24 Hom. κ 17 sqq., κ 237 sqq.   24 Zoilus F 3 FGrHist 71

1 προεγνωσμένοις Reiske : προεγνωσμένους P   1–2 οὐ ...
Ὀδύσσεια post υἱός (5) traicienda censebat Jahn   11 ποιήμασιν fortasse secludendum : παθήμασιν Wilamowitz   16 μέτρα] τέρματα Man. : τέλματα Tollius   †ἐρημουμένου corruptum : ex. gr. ἠρέμ⟨α κεχυμένου⟩ latere crediderim : ἠπειρουμένου Toup : ἡμερουμένου Ruhnken   18 πλάνος] πλάνοις Pearce : πλάτος Lebègue : πλάδος Immisch   22 ῥᾷστον] τεράστιον Richards   23 ἀπακμὴν Man. : παρακμὴν K marg., Portus : ἀκμὴν P   24 ἐν Faber ; ἐκ P   συοφορβουμένους] συομορφουμένους Valckenaer

χοιρίδια κλαίοντα, καὶ τὸν ὑπὸ τῶν πελειάδων ὡς νεοσσὸν
παρατρεφόμενον Δία καὶ τὸν ἐπὶ τοῦ ναυαγίου δέχ' ἡμέρας ἄσιτον
τά τε περὶ τὴν μνηστηροφονίαν ἀπίθανα. τί γὰρ ἂν ἄλλο φήσαιμεν
ταῦτα ἢ τῷ ὄντι τοῦ Διὸς ἐνύπνια; δευτέρου δὲ εἵνεκα προσιστορήσθω τὰ κατὰ τὴν Ὀδύσσειαν, ὅπως ᾖ σοι γνώριμον ὡς ἡ ἀπακμὴ
τοῦ πάθους ἐν τοῖς μεγάλοις συγγραφεῦσι καὶ ποιηταῖς εἰς ἦθος
ἐκλύεται. τοιαῦτα γάρ που τὰ περὶ τὴν τοῦ Ὀδυσσέως ἠθικῶς
αὐτῷ βιολογούμενα οἰκίαν οἱονεὶ κωμῳδία τίς ἐστιν ἠθολογουμένη.

10 Φέρε νῦν, εἴ τι καὶ ἕτερον ἔχοιμεν ὑψηλοὺς ποιεῖν τοὺς λόγους
δυνάμενον, ἐπισκεψώμεθα. οὐκοῦν ἐπειδὴ πᾶσι τοῖς πράγμασι
φύσει συνεδρεύει τινὰ μόρια ταῖς ὕλαις συνυπάρχοντα, ἐξ ἀνάγκης
γένοιτ' ἂν ἡμῖν ὕψους αἴτιον τὸ τῶν ἐμφερομένων ἐκλέγειν ἀεὶ τὰ
καιριώτατα καὶ ταῦτα τῇ πρὸς ἄλληλα ἐπισυνθέσει καθάπερ ἕν τι
σῶμα ποιεῖν δύνασθαι· ὃ μὲν γὰρ τῇ ἐκλογῇ τὸν ἀκροατὴν τῶν
λημμάτων, ὃ δὲ τῇ πυκνώσει τῶν ἐκλελεγμένων προσάγεται.
οἷον ἡ Σαπφὼ τὰ συμβαίνοντα ταῖς ἐρωτικαῖς μανίαις παθήματα
ἐκ τῶν παρεπομένων καὶ ἐκ τῆς ἀληθείας αὐτῆς ἑκάστοτε λαμβάνει. ποῦ δὲ τὴν ἀρετὴν ἀποδείκνυται; ὅτι τὰ ἄκρα αὐτῶν καὶ
ὑπερτεταμένα δεινὴ καὶ ἐκλέξαι καὶ εἰς ἄλληλα συνδῆσαι·

2 φαίνεταί μοι κῆνος ἴσος θέοισιν
ἔμμεν' ὤνηρ, ὄττις ἐνάντιός τοι
ἰσδάνει καὶ πλάσιον ἆδυ φωνεί-
    σας ὑπακούει
καὶ γελαίσας ἰμέροεν, τό μ' ἦ μὰν
καρδίαν ἐν στήθεσιν ἐπτόαισεν.
ὠς γὰρ ἔς σ' ἴδω βρόχε', ὤς με φώναισ'
οὐδὲν ἔτ' εἴκει·

1-3 μ 62 sq., 447 sqq., χ 79 sqq.   20-p. 15, 9 Sappho, fr. 31 *Poet.
Lesb. Fragm.*, ed. Lobel-Page

2 ἄσιτον ⟨ὄντα⟩ Groeneboom: τὸ ... ἀσιτεῖν Photiades   4 τοῦ
Διὸς] οὐχ ὑγιοῦς Haupt: τοῦ secl. Wilamowitz   προσιστορήσθω Weiske:
προσιστορείσθω P   9 ἔχοιμεν] ἔχομεν Man.   14-15 ὃ μὲν ... ὃ δὲ
Pearce: ὁ μὲν ... ὁ δὲ P   18 ὅτι Wifstrand: ὅτε P   20-p. 15, 9
leviores correctiones non notavi   21-22 τοι ἰζάνει apogr.: τοιζάνει P
24 τό μ' ἦ μὰν Lobel: τὸ μὴ ἐμὰν P   26 ὠς γὰρ ἔς σ' ἴδω Lobel: ὡς γὰρ
σίδω P   βρόχεώς P: distinxit Tollius   φώναισ' Danielsson: φωνὰς P

ἀλλὰ κὰμ μὲν γλῶσσα †ἔαγε· λέπτον δ'
αὔτικα χρῷ πῦρ ὑπαδεδρόμακεν·
ὀππάτεσσι δ' οὐδὲν ὄρημμ', ἐπιρρόμ-
βεισι δ' ἄκουαι·
†ἐκαδε μ' ἵδρως ψυχρός† κακχέεται, τρόμος δὲ
παῖσαν ἄγρει, χλωροτέρα δὲ ποίας
ἔμμι· τεθνάκην δ' ὀλίγω 'πιδεύης
φαίνομαι . . .
ἀλλὰ πᾶν τόλματον, †ἐπεὶ καὶ πένητα†

οὐ θαυμάζεις ὡς ὑπὸ τὸ αὐτὸ τὴν ψυχὴν τὸ σῶμα, τὰς ἀκοὰς τὴν 3 γλῶσσαν, τὰς ὄψεις τὴν χρόαν, πάνθ' ὡς ἀλλότρια διοιχόμενα ἐπιζητεῖ, καὶ καθ' ὑπεναντιώσεις ἅμα ψύχεται καίεται, ἀλογιστεῖ φρονεῖ †ἢ γὰρ† φοβεῖται †ἢ παρ' ὀλίγον τέθνηκεν ἵνα μὴ ἕν τι περὶ αὐτὴν πάθος φαίνηται, παθῶν δὲ σύνοδος; πάντα μὲν τοιαῦτα γίνεται περὶ τοὺς ἐρῶντας, ἡ λῆψις δ' ὡς ἔφην τῶν ἄκρων καὶ ἡ εἰς ταὐτὸ συναίρεσις ἀπειργάσατο τὴν ἐξοχήν. ὅνπερ οἶμαι καὶ ἐπὶ τῶν χειμώνων τρόπον ὁ ποιητὴς ἐκλαμβάνει τῶν παρακολουθούντων τὰ χαλεπώτατα. ὁ μὲν γὰρ τὰ Ἀριμάσπεια 4 ποιήσας ἐκεῖνα οἴεται δεινά·

θαῦμ' ἡμῖν καὶ τοῦτο μέγα φρεσὶν ἡμετέρῃσιν.
ἄνδρες ὕδωρ ναίουσιν ἀπὸ χθονὸς ἐν πελάγεσσι·
δύστηνοί τινές εἰσιν, ἔχουσι γὰρ ἔργα πονηρά·
ὄμματ' ἐν ἄστροισι, ψυχὴν δ' ἐνὶ πόντῳ ἔχουσιν.
ἦ που πολλὰ θεοῖσι φίλας ἀνὰ χεῖρας ἔχοντες
εὔχονται σπλάγχνοισι κακῶς ἀναβαλλομένοισι.

20-25 Arimaspea, fr. 1 Kinkel = fr. 7 Bolton

1 ἀλλὰ κὰμ apogr.: ἀλλὰ κᾶν P: ἀλλὰ κατὰ Plu. *Mor.* 81D: ἀλλ' ἄκαν Lobel–Page †ἔαγε] 'fortasse γέγακε' Page 5 ἀδεμ' ἵδρὼς κακὸς χέεται *An. Ox.* Cramer i. 208: κὰδ δέ μ' ἵδρως κακχέεται Ahrens: κὰδ δέ μ' ἵδρως ψῦχρος ἔχει Page 7 'πιδεύης Hermann: πιδεύσην P: 'πιδεύην Ahrens 8-9 nondum sanata 10 θαυμάζεις Rob.: θαυμάζοις P 12 ἀλογιστεῖ Man.: ἀλογιστί P 13 †ἢ γὰρ† . . . †ἢ obelo notanda an potius secludenda? et haec et φρονεῖ secl. Hermann φοβεῖται] πτοεῖται Ruhnken: φοιβᾶται Rothstein 16 ὅνπερ Man.: ὅπερ P 20 ἡμῖν] ἦ μὴν Faber 25 ἀναβαλλομένοισι] ἀναπαλλομένοισι Wilamowitz

παντὶ οἶμαι δῆλον, ὡς πλέον ἄνθος ἔχει τὰ λεγόμενα ἢ δέος. ὁ δὲ
5 Ὅμηρος πῶς; ἓν γὰρ ἀπὸ πολλῶν λεγέσθω·

> ἐν δ᾽ ἔπεσ᾽, ὡς ὅτε κῦμα θοῇ ἐν νηὶ πέσῃσι
> λάβρον ὑπαὶ νεφέων ἀνεμοτρεφές, ἡ δέ τε πᾶσα
> ἄχνῃ ὑπεκρύφθη, ἀνέμοιο δὲ δεινὸς ἀήτης   5
> ἱστίῳ ἐμβρέμεται, τρομέουσι δέ τε φρένα ναῦται
> δειδιότες· τυτθὸν γὰρ ὑπὲκ θανάτοιο φέρονται.

6 ἐπεχείρησε καὶ ὁ Ἄρατος τὸ αὐτὸ τοῦτο μετενεγκεῖν,

> ὀλίγον δὲ διὰ ξύλον ἄιδ᾽ ἐρύκει·

πλὴν μικρὸν αὐτὸ καὶ γλαφυρὸν ἐποίησεν ἀντὶ φοβεροῦ· ἔτι δὲ 10
παρώρισε τὸν κίνδυνον εἰπών "ξύλον ἄιδ᾽ ἐρύκει". οὐκοῦν
ἀπείργει. ὁ δὲ ποιητὴς οὐκ εἰς ἅπαξ παρορίζει τὸ δεινόν, ἀλλὰ
τοὺς ἀεὶ καὶ μόνον οὐχὶ κατὰ πᾶν κῦμα πολλάκις ἀπολλυμένους
εἰκονογραφεῖ. καὶ μὴν τὰς προθέσεις ἀσυνθέτους οὔσας συναναγκάσας παρὰ φύσιν καὶ εἰς ἀλλήλας συμβιασάμενος, [ὑπὲκ θανά- 15
τοιο] τῷ μὲν συνεμπίπτοντι πάθει τὸ ἔπος ὁμοίως ἐβασάνισε, τῇ
δὲ τοῦ ἔπους συνθλίψει τὸ πάθος ἄκρως ἀπεπλάσατο καὶ μόνον
οὐκ ἐνετύπωσε τῇ λέξει τοῦ κινδύνου τὸ ἰδίωμα· " ὑπὲκ θανάτοιο
7 φέρονται." οὐκ ἄλλως ὁ Ἀρχίλοχος ἐπὶ τοῦ ναυαγίου, καὶ ἐπὶ
τῇ προσαγγελίᾳ ὁ Δημοσθένης· " ἑσπέρα μὲν γὰρ ἦν " φησίν. 20
ἀλλὰ τὰς ἐξοχάς, ὡς ⟨ἂν⟩ εἴποι τις, ἀριστίνδην ἐκκαθήραντες
ἐπισυνέθηκαν, οὐδὲν φλοιῶδες ἢ ἄσεμνον ἢ σχολικὸν ἐγκατατάττοντες διὰ μέσου. λυμαίνεται γὰρ ταῦτα τὸ ὅλον, ὡσανεὶ ψύγματα

3–7 Hom. O 624 sqq.   9 Aratus, Phaen. 299   19 Archilochus,
10, 12, 21, 56 A Diehl (?)   20 Dem. 18. 169

---

1 παντὶ ⟨δ᾽⟩ Richards : παντί ⟨γ᾽⟩ Rohden   ἢ δέος Victorius : ἡδέως
P   11 ἐρύκει Man. : ἀπείργει P   11–12 οὐκοῦν ἀπείργει om. Rob., del.
Ruhnken   12–13 ἀλλὰ τοὺς] ἀλλ᾽ αὐτοὺς Lebègue   πολλάκις] an
secludendum?   15–16 [ὑπὲκ θανάτοιο] secl. G. S. A. (v. ad 9. 7)
19 φέρονται Man. : φέροντα P   21 ⟨ἂν⟩ add. Ruhnken   ἐκκαθήραντες] ἐπικρίναντες Ruhnken   23 ψύγματα] ψήγματα Man.

ἢ ἀραιώματα ἐμποιοῦντα μεγέθη συνοικοδομούμενα τῇ πρὸς ἄλληλα σχέσει συντετειχισμένα.

Σύνεδρός ἐστι ταῖς προεκκειμέναις ἀρετὴ καὶ ἣν καλοῦσιν 11 αὔξησιν, ὅταν δεχομένων τῶν πραγμάτων καὶ ἀγώνων κατὰ
5 περιόδους ἀρχάς τε πολλὰς καὶ ἀναπαύλας ἕτερα ἑτέροις ἐπεισκυκλούμενα μεγέθη συνεχῶς ἐπεισάγηται κατ' ἐπίτασιν. τοῦτο δὲ εἴτε διὰ τοπηγορίαν, εἴτε δείνωσιν ἢ πραγμάτων ἢ κατασκευῶν ἐπίρρωσιν, εἴτ' ἐποικοδομίαν ἔργων ἢ παθῶν (μυρίαι γὰρ ἰδέαι τῶν αὐξήσεων) γίνοιτο, χρὴ γινώσκειν ὅμως τὸν ῥήτορα, ὡς οὐδὲν ἂν
10 τούτων καθ' αὑτὸ συσταίη χωρὶς ὕψους τέλειον, πλὴν εἰ μὴ ἐν οἴκτοις ἄρ' ἢ νὴ Δία ἐν εὐτελισμοῖς, τῶν δ' ἄλλων αὐξητικῶν ὅτου περ ἂν τὸ ὑψηλὸν ἀφέλῃς, ὡς ψυχὴν ἐξαιρήσεις σώματος· εὐθὺς γὰρ ἀτονεῖ καὶ κενοῦται τὸ ἔμπρακτον αὐτῶν μὴ τοῖς ὕψεσι συνεπιρρωννύμενον. ᾗ μέντοι διαφέρει τοῦ ἀρτίως εἰρη- 3
15 μένου τὰ νῦν παραγγελλόμενα—περιγραφὴ γάρ τις ἦν ἐκεῖνο τῶν ἄκρων λημμάτων καὶ εἰς ἑνότητα σύνταξις—καὶ τίνι καθόλου τῶν αὐξήσεων παραλλάττει τὰ ὕψη, τῆς σαφηνείας αὐτῆς ἕνεκα συντόμως διοριστέον.

Ὁ μὲν οὖν τῶν τεχνογράφων ὅρος ἔμοιγ' οὐκ ἀρεστός. αὔξησίς 12
20 ἐστι, φασί, λόγος μέγεθος περιτιθεὶς τοῖς ὑποκειμένοις. δύναται γὰρ ἀμέλει καὶ ὕψους καὶ πάθους καὶ τρόπων εἶναι κοινὸς οὗτος ὅρος, ἐπειδὴ κἀκεῖνα τῷ λόγῳ περιτίθησι ποιόν τι μέγεθος. ἐμοὶ δὲ φαίνεται ταῦτα ἀλλήλων παραλλάττειν, ᾗ κεῖται τὸ μὲν ὕψος ἐν διάρματι, ἡ δ' αὔξησις καὶ ἐν πλήθει· διὸ κεῖνο μὲν κἂν νοήματι
25 ἑνὶ πολλάκις, ἡ δὲ πάντως μετὰ ποσότητος καὶ περιουσίας τινὸς ὑφίσταται. καὶ ἔστιν ἡ αὔξησις, ὡς τύπῳ περιλαβεῖν, συμπλήρωσις 2

---

1 ἐμποιοῦντα ⟨ἐς⟩ Roberts, fortasse recte: ἐμποιοῦν τὰ Vahlen: ἐμποιοῦντα ⟨τὰ⟩ Wendland: ἐμποδιοῦντα dubitanter Prickard   ἢ...
μεγέθη] ἃ εἰς ἀραιώματα ἐμβύεται, τὰ μεγέθη Ruhnken   συνοικοδομούμενα Man.: συνοικονομούμενα P del. Pearce   τῇ ⟨τε⟩ Tollius   συντετειχισμένα] συνεστοιχισμένα Ellis   3 καὶ del. Tollius   5 ἀρχάς] ἀργίας Rothstein   6 ἐπίτασιν Wilamowitz: ἐπίβασιν P   7 prius ἢ secl. Portus   8 ἐποικοδομίαν K marg.: ἐποικονομίαν P   9 γίνοιτο Morus: γίνοιντο P   11 ἄρ' ἢ νὴ Δία scripsi: ἄρα νὴ Δία ἢ P   13 κενοῦται] σβέννυται Ruhnken: μειοῦται Wenkebach   22 ⟨ὁ⟩ ὅρος Man.

18   ΠΕΡΙ ΥΨΟΥΣ   [12. 3–

ἀπὸ πάντων τῶν ἐμφερομένων τοῖς πράγμασι μορίων καὶ τόπων, ἰσχυροποιοῦσα τῇ ἐπιμονῇ τὸ κατεσκευασμένον, ταύτῃ τῆς πίστεως διεστῶσα, ὅτι ἡ μὲν τὸ ζητούμενον ἀποδεί⟨κνυσιν⟩...

. . . πλουσιώτατα, καθάπερ τι πέλαγος, εἰς ἀναπεπταμένον 5 κέχυται πολλαχῇ μέγεθος. ὅθεν, οἶμαι, κατὰ λόγον ὁ μὲν ῥήτωρ ἅτε παθητικώτερος πολὺ τὸ διάπυρον ἔχει καὶ θυμικῶς ἐκφλεγόμενον, ὁ δέ, καθεστὼς ἐν ὄγκῳ καὶ μεγαλοπρεπεῖ σεμνότητι, οὐκ 4 ἔψυκται μέν, ἀλλ' οὐχ οὕτως ἐπέστραπται. οὐ κατ' ἄλλα δέ τινα ἢ ταῦτα, ἐμοὶ δοκεῖ, φίλτατε Τερεντιανέ, (λέγω δέ, ⟨εἰ⟩ καὶ ἡμῖν 10 ὡς Ἕλλησιν ἐφεῖταί τι γινώσκειν) καὶ ὁ Κικέρων τοῦ Δημοσθένους ἐν τοῖς μεγέθεσι παραλλάττει. ὁ μὲν γὰρ ἐν ὕψει τὸ πλέον ἀποτόμῳ, ὁ δὲ Κικέρων ἐν χύσει, καὶ ὁ μὲν ἡμέτερος διὰ τὸ μετὰ βίας ἕκαστα, ἔτι δὲ τάχους ῥώμης δεινότητος, οἷον καίειν τε ἅμα καὶ διαρπάζειν σκηπτῷ τινι παρεικάζοιτ' ἂν ἢ κεραυνῷ, ὁ δὲ 15 Κικέρων ὡς ἀμφιλαφής τις ἐμπρησμός, οἶμαι, πάντῃ νέμεται καὶ ἀνειλεῖται, πολὺ ἔχων καὶ ἐπίμονον ἀεὶ τὸ καῖον καὶ διακληρονομούμενον ἄλλοτ' ἀλλοίως ἐν αὐτῷ καὶ κατὰ διαδοχὰς ἀνα- 5 τρεφόμενον. ἀλλὰ ταῦτα μὲν ὑμεῖς ἂν ἄμεινον ἐπικρίνοιτε, καιρὸς δὲ τοῦ Δημοσθενικοῦ μὲν ὕψους καὶ ὑπερτεταμένου ἔν τε ταῖς 20 δεινώσεσι καὶ τοῖς σφοδροῖς πάθεσι καὶ ἔνθα δεῖ τὸν ἀκροατὴν τὸ σύνολον ἐκπλῆξαι, τῆς δὲ χύσεως ὅπου χρὴ καταντλῆσαι· τοπηγορίαις τε γὰρ καὶ ἐπιλόγοις κατὰ τὸ πλέον καὶ παρεκβάσεσι καὶ τοῖς φραστικοῖς ἅπασι καὶ ἐπιδεικτικοῖς, ἱστορίαις τε καὶ φυσιολογίαις, καὶ οὐκ ὀλίγοις ἄλλοις μέρεσιν ἁρμόδιος.   25
13   Ὅτι μέντοι ὁ Πλάτων (ἐπάνειμι γάρ) τοιούτῳ τινὶ χεύματι ἀψοφητὶ ῥέων οὐδὲν ἧττον μεγεθύνεται, ἀνεγνωκὼς τὰ ἐν τῇ Πολιτείᾳ τὸν τύπον οὐκ ἀγνοεῖς. "οἱ ἄρα φρονήσεως" φησί
28 et sqq. Pl. Resp. 9. 586A : omittuntur nonnulla

---

1 πράγμασι μορίων apogr. : πράγμασιν ὁρίων P   3 ἀποδεί⟨κνυσιν⟩ Man.
9 ἐπέστραπται] ἀπαστράπτει Bentley   10 ⟨εἰ⟩ add. Man.   14 ῥώμης] ῥύμης Lebègue   17 καὶ post καῖον del. Wilamowitz   18 αὐτῷ] αὑτῷ?
23 ἐπιλόγοις] ἀπολόγοις apogr.   παρεκβάσεσι scripsi : παραβάσεσι P
27 lacunam post μεγεθύνεται statuit Lebègue sic fere supplendam : ⟨ἐν ἑνὶ παραδείγματι ἀρκέσει σοὶ δεικνύναι ὅτι⟩   28 τὸν τύπον del. Faber

"καὶ ἀρετῆς ἄπειροι, εὐωχίαις δὲ καὶ τοῖς τοιούτοις ἀεὶ συνόντες, κάτω ὡς ἔοικε φέρονται καὶ ταύτῃ πλανῶνται διὰ βίου, πρὸς δὲ τὸ ἀληθὲς ἄνω οὔτ' ἀνέβλεψαν πώποτε οὔτ' ἀνηνέχθησαν οὐδὲ βεβαίου τε καὶ καθαρᾶς ἡδονῆς ἐγεύσαντο, ἀλλὰ βοσκημάτων δίκην κάτω ἀεὶ βλέποντες καὶ κεκυφότες εἰς γῆν καὶ εἰς τραπέζας βόσκονται χορταζόμενοι καὶ ὀχεύοντες, καὶ ἕνεκα τῆς τούτων πλεονεξίας λακτίζοντες καὶ κυρίττοντες ἀλλήλους σιδηροῖς κέρασι καὶ ὁπλαῖς ἀποκτιννύουσι δι' ἀπληστίαν."

Ἐνδείκνυται δ' ἡμῖν οὗτος ἀνήρ, εἰ βουλοίμεθα μὴ κατολιγω- 2 ρεῖν, ὡς καὶ ἄλλη τις παρὰ τὰ εἰρημένα ὁδὸς ἐπὶ τὰ ὑψηλὰ τείνει. ποία δὲ καὶ τίς αὕτη; ⟨ἡ⟩ τῶν ἔμπροσθεν μεγάλων συγγραφέων καὶ ποιητῶν μίμησίς τε καὶ ζήλωσις. καί γε τούτου, φίλτατε, ἀπρὶξ ἐχώμεθα τοῦ σκοποῦ· πολλοὶ γὰρ ἀλλοτρίῳ θεοφοροῦνται πνεύματι τὸν αὐτὸν τρόπον ὃν καὶ τὴν Πυθίαν λόγος ἔχει τρίποδι πλησιάζουσαν, ἔνθα ῥῆγμά ἐστι γῆς ἀναπνέον, ὥς φασιν, ἀτμὸν ἔνθεον, αὐτόθεν ἐγκύμονα τῆς δαιμονίου καθισταμένην δυνάμεως παραυτίκα χρησμῳδεῖν κατ' ἐπίπνοιαν· οὕτως ἀπὸ τῆς τῶν ἀρχαίων μεγαλοφυΐας εἰς τὰς τῶν ζηλούντων ἐκείνους ψυχὰς ὡς ἀπὸ ἱερῶν στομίων ἀπόρροιαί τινες φέρονται, ὑφ' ὧν ἐπιπνε-όμενοι καὶ οἱ μὴ λίαν φοιβαστικοὶ τῷ ἑτέρων συνενθουσιῶσι μεγέθει. μόνος Ἡρόδοτος Ὁμηρικώτατος ἐγένετο; Στησίχορος 3 ἔτι πρότερον ὅ τε Ἀρχίλοχος, πάντων δὲ τούτων μάλιστα ὁ Πλάτων, ἀπὸ τοῦ Ὁμηρικοῦ κείνου νάματος εἰς αὑτὸν μυρίας ὅσας παρατροπὰς ἀποχετευσάμενος. καὶ ἴσως ἡμῖν ἀποδείξεων ἔδει, εἰ μὴ τὰ ἐπ' εἴδους καὶ οἱ περὶ Ἀμμώνιον ἐκλέξαντες ἀνέγραψαν. ἔστι δ' οὐ κλοπὴ τὸ πρᾶγμα, ἀλλ' ὡς ἀπὸ καλῶν 4 ἠθῶν ἢ πλασμάτων ἢ δημιουργημάτων ἀποτύπωσις. καὶ οὐδ'

3 ἀνηνέχθησαν] ἠνέχθησαν codd. Plat.   7 ἀλλήλοις P, corr. Man.
9 ἀνήρ] ἀνήρ Man.   11 ⟨ἡ⟩ add. Man.   15–16 ἔνθα ... ἔνθεον
del. Reiske   15 ἀναπνέον Man.: ἀναπνεῖν P   16 ⟨καὶ⟩ αὐτόθεν Man.
17 κατ' ἐπίπνοιαν secl. Wilamowitz   21 ⟨ἡ⟩ μόνος Morus: ⟨τί δέ;⟩
μόνος Photiades (cf. 23. 1, 33. 5)   22 τε Man.: γε P   23 αὑτὸν
Faber: αὐτὸν P   25 ἐπ' εἴδους Faber: ἐπ' ἴνδους P: cf. 43. 6
27 ἠθῶν] εἰδῶν Tollius: λίθων Diels: θεῶν (spectaculorum) Bury   ἡ
Buecheler: ἢ P: del. Wilamowitz   ἡ δημιουργημάτων Immisch: ἢ
δημιουργημάτων del. Jahn

ἂν ἐπακμάσαι μοι δοκεῖ τηλικαῦτά τινα τοῖς τῆς φιλοσοφίας δόγμασι καὶ εἰς ποιητικὰς ὕλας πολλαχοῦ συνεμβῆναι καὶ φράσεις, εἰ μὴ περὶ πρωτείων νὴ Δία παντὶ θυμῷ πρὸς Ὅμηρον, ὡς ἀνταγωνιστὴς νέος πρὸς ἤδη τεθαυμασμένον, ἴσως μὲν φιλονικότερον καὶ οἱονεὶ διαδορατιζόμενος, οὐκ ἀνωφελῶς δ᾽ ὅμως διηριστεύετο· "ἀγαθὴ" γὰρ κατὰ τὸν Ἡσίοδον "ἔρις ἥδε βροτοῖσι." καὶ τῷ ὄντι καλὸς οὗτος καὶ ἀξιονικότατος εὐκλείας ἀγών τε καὶ στέφανος, ἐν ᾧ καὶ τὸ ἡττᾶσθαι τῶν προγενεστέρων οὐκ ἄδοξον.

14 Οὐκοῦν καὶ ἡμᾶς, ἡνίκ᾽ ἂν διαπονῶμεν ὑψηγορίας τι καὶ μεγαλοφροσύνης δεόμενον, καλὸν ἀναπλάττεσθαι ταῖς ψυχαῖς πῶς ἂν εἰ τύχοι ταὐτὸ τοῦθ᾽ Ὅμηρος εἶπεν, πῶς δ᾽ ἂν Πλάτων ἢ Δημοσθένης ὕψωσαν ἢ ἐν ἱστορίᾳ Θουκυδίδης. προσπίπτοντα γὰρ ἡμῖν κατὰ ζῆλον ἐκεῖνα τὰ πρόσωπα καὶ οἷον διαπρέποντα **2** τὰς ψυχὰς ἀνοίσει πως πρὸς τὰ ἀνειδωλοποιούμενα μέτρα· ἔτι δὲ μᾶλλον, εἰ κἀκεῖνο τῇ διανοίᾳ προσυπογράφοιμεν, πῶς ἂν τόδε τι ὑπ᾽ ἐμοῦ λεγόμενον παρὼν Ὅμηρος ἤκουσεν ἢ Δημοσθένης, ἢ πῶς ἂν ἐπὶ τούτῳ διετέθησαν· τῷ γὰρ ὄντι μέγα τὸ ἀγώνισμα, τοιοῦτον ὑποτίθεσθαι τῶν ἰδίων λόγων δικαστήριον καὶ θέατρον, καὶ ἐν τηλικούτοις ἥρωσι κριταῖς τε καὶ μάρτυσιν **3** ὑπέχειν τῶν γραφομένων εὐθύνας πεπλάσθαι. πλέον δὲ τούτων παρορμητικόν, εἰ προστιθείης, πῶς ἂν ἐμοῦ ταῦτα γράψαντος ὁ μετ᾽ ἐμὲ πᾶς ἀκούσειεν αἰών; εἰ δέ τις αὐτόθεν φοβοῖτο, μὴ τοῦ ἰδίου βίου καὶ χρόνου φθέγξαιτό τι ὑπερήμερον, ἀνάγκη καὶ τὰ συλλαμβανόμενα ὑπὸ τῆς τούτου ψυχῆς ἀτελῆ καὶ τυφλὰ ὥσπερ ἀμβλοῦσθαι, πρὸς τὸν τῆς ὑστεροφημίας ὅλως μὴ τελεσφορούμενα χρόνον.

15 Ὄγκου καὶ μεγαληγορίας καὶ ἀγῶνος ἐπὶ τούτοις, ὦ νεανία,

6 Hes. Opera 24

---

1 ἐπακμάσαι] ἐπιπάσαι Morus: ἐμβιβάσαι Man.: ἐγκαταμίξαι Toup: ἐπακταινῶσαι Immisch   4 φιλονικότερον scripsi: φιλονεικότερον P
13 ὕψωσαν] ὕψωσεν Pearce   προσπίπτοντα Man.: προπίπτοντα P
15 μέτρα suspectum: num μεγέθη vel μεγάλα?   16 'num προϋπο-?'
M. L. West   21 πεπλάσθαι scripsi: πεπ..χθαι P, -αῖ- postea addito: πεπαῖχθαι apogr.: om. Rob.: πεπεῖσθαι Reiske

ΠΕΡΙ ΥΨΟΥΣ

καὶ αἱ φαντασίαι παρασκευαστικώταται· οὕτω γοῦν ⟨ἡμεῖς⟩, εἰδωλοποιίας ⟨δ'⟩ αὐτὰς ἔνιοι λέγουσι· καλεῖται μὲν γὰρ κοινῶς φαντασία πᾶν τὸ ὁπωσοῦν ἐννόημα γεννητικὸν λόγου παριστάμενον· ἤδη δ' ἐπὶ τούτων κεκράτηκε τοὔνομα ὅταν ἃ λέγεις ὑπ'
5 ἐνθουσιασμοῦ καὶ πάθους βλέπειν δοκῇς καὶ ὑπ' ὄψιν τιθῇς τοῖς ἀκούουσιν. ὡς δ' ἕτερόν τι ἡ ῥητορικὴ φαντασία βούλεται καὶ 2 ἕτερον ἡ παρὰ ποιηταῖς οὐκ ἂν λάθοι σε, οὐδ' ὅτι τῆς μὲν ἐν ποιήσει τέλος ἐστὶν ἔκπληξις, τῆς δ' ἐν λόγοις ἐνάργεια, ἀμφότεραι δ' ὅμως τό τε ⟨παθητικὸν⟩ ἐπιζητοῦσι καὶ τὸ συγκεκινημένον.

10   ὦ μῆτερ, ἱκετεύω σε, μὴ 'πίσειέ μοι
    τὰς αἱματωποὺς καὶ δρακοντώδεις κόρας·
    αὗται γάρ, αὗται πλησίον θρώσκουσί μου.

καὶ
    οἴμοι, κτανεῖ με· ποῖ φύγω;

15 ἐνταῦθ' ὁ ποιητὴς αὐτὸς εἶδεν Ἐρινύας· ὃ δ' ἐφαντάσθη, μικροῦ δεῖν θεάσασθαι καὶ τοὺς ἀκούοντας ἠνάγκασεν. ἔστι μὲν οὖν φιλο- 3 πονώτατος ὁ Εὐριπίδης δύο ταυτὶ πάθη, μανίας τε καὶ ἔρωτας, ἐκτραγῳδῆσαι, κἀν τούτοις ὡς οὐκ οἶδ' εἴ τισιν ἑτέροις ἐπιτυχέστατος, οὐ μὴν ἀλλὰ καὶ ταῖς ἄλλαις ἐπιτίθεσθαι φαντασί-
20 αις οὐκ ἄτολμος. ἥκιστά γέ τοι μεγαλοφυὴς ὢν ὅμως τὴν αὐτὸς αὑτοῦ φύσιν ἐν πολλοῖς γενέσθαι τραγικὴν προσηνάγκασε, καὶ παρ' ἕκαστα ἐπὶ τῶν μεγεθῶν, ὡς ὁ ποιητής,

    οὐρῇ [δὲ] πλευράς τε καὶ ἰσχίον ἀμφοτέρωθεν
    μαστίεται, ἓ δ' αὐτὸν ἐποτρύνει μαχέσασθαι.

25 τῷ γοῦν Φαέθοντι παραδιδοὺς τὰς ἡνίας ὁ Ἥλιος,   4
    ἔλα δὲ μήτε Λιβυκὸν αἰθέρ' εἰσβαλών·

10–12 Eur. *Orestes* 255–7   14 Eur. *Iph. Taur.* 291   23–24 Hom. Υ 170–1   26–p. 22, 10 Eur. *Phaethon*, fr. 779 Nauck[2]

1–2 ⟨ἡμεῖς⟩ et ⟨δ'⟩ addidi: οὕτω γοῦν ⟨ἐγώ φημι, καίτοιγ' εἰδὼς ὅτι⟩ Martens   2 ⟨τὰς⟩ εἰδωλοποιίας Dobree   αὐτὰς del. Morus   4 λέγεις Spengel : λέγῃς P   9 ⟨παθητικὸν⟩ add. Kayser : ⟨συμπαθὲς⟩ Lebègue 14 κτανεῖ] κτείνει vel κτενεῖ codd. Eur.   15 ⟨οὐκ⟩ εἶδεν Man.   18 εἴ τισιν ἑτέροις] εἴ τις ἕτερος Stanley, fortasse recte   23 [δὲ] seclusi : ἓ Vahlen   ἰσχία codd. Hom.   24 μαχέσασθαι Hom.: μάχεσθαι P

ΠΕΡΙ ΥΨΟΥΣ [15. 4-

κρᾶσιν γὰρ ὑγρὰν οὐκ ἔχων ἀψῖδα σὴν
κάτω διήσει,

φησίν, εἶθ' ἑξῆς·

"ἵει δ', ἐφ' ἑπτὰ Πλειάδων ἔχων δρόμον."
τοσαῦτ' ἀκούσας παῖς ἔμαρψεν ἡνίας·
κρούσας δὲ πλευρὰ πτεροφόρων ὀχημάτων
μεθῆκεν, αἱ δ' ἔπταντ' ἐπ' αἰθέρος πτύχας.
πατὴρ δ' ὄπισθε νῶτα Σειρίου βεβὼς
ἵππευε παῖδα νουθετῶν· "ἐκεῖσ' ἔλα,
τῇδε στρέφ' ἅρμα, τῇδε."

ἆρ' οὐκ ἂν εἴποις, ὅτι ἡ ψυχὴ τοῦ γράφοντος συνεπιβαίνει τοῦ ἅρματος καὶ συγκινδυνεύουσα τοῖς ἵπποις συνεπτέρωται; οὐ γὰρ ἄν, εἰ μὴ τοῖς οὐρανίοις ἐκείνοις ἔργοις ἰσοδρομοῦσα ἐφέρετο, τοιαῦτ' ἄν ποτε ἐφαντάσθη. ὅμοια καὶ τὰ ἐπὶ τῆς Κασσάνδρας αὐτῷ,

ἀλλ', ὦ φίλιπποι Τρῶες.

5 τοῦ δ' Αἰσχύλου φαντασίαις ἐπιτολμῶντος ἡρωικωτάταις, ὥσπερ καὶ ⟨οἱ⟩ Ἑπτὰ ἐπὶ Θήβας παρ' αὐτῷ—

ἄνδρες (φησὶν) ἑπτὰ θούριοι λοχαγέται,
ταυροσφαγοῦντες εἰς μελάνδετον σάκος,
καὶ θιγγάνοντες χερσὶ ταυρείου φόνου,
Ἄρη τ' Ἐνυὼ καὶ φιλαίματον Φόβον
ὡρκωμότησαν,

τὸν ἴδιον αὐτῶν πρὸς ἀλλήλους δίχα οἴκτου συνομνύμενοι θάνατον —ἐνίοτε μέντοι ἀκατεργάστους καὶ οἱονεὶ ποκοειδεῖς τὰς ἐννοίας καὶ ἀμαλάκτους φέροντος, ὅμως ἑαυτὸν ὁ Εὐριπίδης κἀκείνοις

15 Eur. fr. 935 Nauck² 18–22 Aesch. *Septem* 42 sqq. 23 δίχα οἴκτου] cf. ibid. 51

1 ἀψῖδας ἦν P: corr. Faber 2 κάτω] καίων Richards διήσει Faber: δίεισι P 5 παῖς K marg.: τις P 8 ὄπισθεν ὦτα P: corr. Man. Σειρίου] σειραίου Rutgers 10 ἔλα, τῇδε στρέφ' Portus: ἐλατῆρα ἔστρεφ' P 17 ⟨οἱ⟩ add. Morus 22 ὡρκωμότησαν codd. Aesch. 25 ἀναλλάκτους φέροντας P: corr. Man.

ὑπὸ φιλοτιμίας τοῖς κινδύνοις προσβιβάζει. καὶ παρὰ μὲν Αἰσχύλῳ 6
παραδόξως τὰ τοῦ Λυκούργου βασίλεια κατὰ τὴν ἐπιφάνειαν τοῦ
Διονύσου θεοφορεῖται—

ἐνθουσιᾷ δὴ δῶμα, βακχεύει στέγη·

ὁ δὲ Εὐριπίδης τὸ αὐτὸ τοῦθ᾽ ἑτέρως ἐφηδύνας ἐξεφώνησε,

πᾶν δὲ συνεβάκχευ᾽ ὄρος.

ἄκρως δὲ καὶ ὁ Σοφοκλῆς ἐπὶ τοῦ θνήσκοντος Οἰδίπου καὶ 7
ἑαυτὸν μετὰ διοσημίας τινὸς θάπτοντος πεφάνταστai, καὶ κατὰ
τὸν ἀπόπλουν τῶν Ἑλλήνων ἐπὶ τἀχιλλέως προφαινομένου τοῖς
ἀναγομένοις ὑπὲρ τοῦ τάφου, ἣν οὐκ οἶδ᾽ εἴ τις ὄψιν ἐναργέστερον
εἰδωλοποίησε Σιμωνίδου· πάντα δ᾽ ἀμήχανον παρατίθεσθαι. οὐ 8
μὴν ἀλλὰ τὰ μὲν παρὰ τοῖς ποιηταῖς μυθικωτέραν ἔχει τὴν
ὑπερέκπτωσιν, ὡς ἔφην, καὶ πάντῃ τὸ πιστὸν ὑπεραίρουσαν, τῆς
δὲ ῥητορικῆς φαντασίας κάλλιστον ἀεὶ τὸ ἔμπρακτον καὶ ἐνάληθες,
δειναὶ δὲ καὶ ἔκφυλοι αἱ παραβάσεις ἡνίκ᾽ ἂν ᾖ ποιητικὸν τοῦ
λόγου καὶ μυθῶδες τὸ πλάσμα καὶ εἰς πᾶν προεκπῖπτον [τὸ] ἀδύνατον, ὡς ἤδη νὴ Δία καὶ οἱ καθ᾽ ἡμᾶς δεινοὶ ῥήτορες, καθάπερ οἱ
τραγῳδοί, βλέπουσιν Ἐρινύας καὶ οὐδὲ ἐκεῖνο μαθεῖν οἱ γενναῖοι
δύνανται, ὅτι ὁ λέγων Ὀρέστης

μέθες· μί᾽ οὖσα τῶν ἐμῶν Ἐρινύων
μέσον μ᾽ ὀχμάζεις, ὡς βάλῃς ἐς τάρταρον,

φαντάζεται ταῦθ᾽ ὅτι μαίνεται. τί οὖν ἡ ῥητορικὴ φαντασία 9
δύναται; πολλὰ μὲν ἴσως καὶ ἄλλα τοῖς λόγοις ἐναγώνια καὶ
ἐμπαθῆ προσεισφέρειν, κατακιρναμένη μέντοι ταῖς πραγματικαῖς
ἐπιχειρήσεσιν οὐ πείθει τὸν ἀκροατὴν μόνον, ἀλλὰ καὶ δουλοῦται.

1-4 Aesch. fr. 58 Nauck²   6 Eur. *Bacch.* 726   7 Soph.
OC 1586 sqq.   9 cf. Soph. fr. 479 sqq. Nauck²   11 Simonides,
fr. 209 Bergk⁴, 52 Page   20-21 Eur. *Orestes* 264-5

6 συνεβάκχευ᾽ Porson: συνεβάκχευεν P: συνεβάκχευσ᾽ codd. Eur.
8 διοσημίας scripsi: διοσημείας P   9 ἐπὶ τἀχιλλέως Vahlen: ἔπειτ᾽
Ἀχιλλέως P   15 παραβάσεις] παρεκβάσεις Petra   16 προεκπῖπτον
Morus: προσεκπῖπτον P   [τὸ] secl. M. L. West   ἀδύνατον Man.: δυνατὸν P

"καὶ μὴν εἴ τις" φησίν "αὐτίκα δὴ μάλα κραυγῆς ἀκούσειε πρὸ τῶν δικαστηρίων, εἶτ' εἴποι τις, ὡς ἀνέῳκται τὸ δεσμωτήριον, οἱ δὲ δεσμῶται φεύγουσιν, οὐδεὶς οὕτως οὔτε γέρων οὔτε νέος ὀλίγωρός ἐστιν ὃς οὐχὶ βοηθήσει καθ' ὅσον δύναται· εἰ δὲ δή τις εἴποι παρελθὼν ὡς ὁ τούτους ἀφεὶς οὗτός ἐστιν, οὐδὲ λόγου τυχὼν παραυτίκ' ἂν ἀπόλοιτο." ὡς νὴ Δία καὶ ὁ Ὑπερείδης κατηγορούμενος, ἐπειδὴ τοὺς δούλους μετὰ τὴν ἧτταν ἐλευθέρους ἐψηφίσατο, "τοῦτο τὸ ψήφισμα" εἶπεν "οὐχ ὁ ῥήτωρ ἔγραψεν, ἀλλ' ἡ ἐν Χαιρωνείᾳ μάχη". ἅμα γὰρ τῷ πραγματικῶς ἐπιχειρεῖν ὁ ῥήτωρ πεφάνταστai, διὸ καὶ τὸν τοῦ πείθειν ὅρον ὑπερβέβηκε τῷ λήμματι. φύσει δέ πως ἐν τοῖς τοιούτοις ἅπασιν ἀεὶ τοῦ κρείττονος ἀκούομεν, ὅθεν ἀπὸ τοῦ ἀποδεικτικοῦ περιελκόμεθα εἰς τὸ κατὰ φαντασίαν ἐκπληκτικόν, ᾧ τὸ πραγματικὸν ἐγκρύπτεται περιλαμπόμενον. καὶ τοῦτ' οὐκ ἀπεικότως πάσχομεν· δυεῖν γὰρ συνταττομένων ὑφ' ἕν, ἀεὶ τὸ κρεῖττον εἰς ἑαυτὸ τὴν θατέρου δύναμιν περισπᾷ.

12 Τοσαῦτα περὶ τῶν κατὰ τὰς νοήσεις ὑψηλῶν καὶ ὑπὸ μεγαλοφροσύνης ⟨ἢ⟩ μιμήσεως ἢ φαντασίας ἀπογεννωμένων ἀρκέσει.

16 Αὐτόθι μέντοι καὶ ὁ περὶ σχημάτων ἐφεξῆς τέτακται τόπος· καὶ γὰρ ταῦτ' ἂν ὂν δεῖ σκευάζηται τρόπον, ὡς ἔφην, οὐκ ἂν ἡ τυχοῦσα μεγέθους εἴη μερίς. οὐ μὴν ἀλλ' ἐπεὶ τὸ πάντα διακριβοῦν πολὺ ἔργον ἐν τῷ παρόντι, μᾶλλον δ' ἀπεριόριστον, ὀλίγα τῶν ὅσα μεγαληγορίας ἀποτελεστικὰ τοῦ πιστώσασθαι τὸ προκείμενον ἕνεκα καὶ δὴ διέξιμεν. ἀπόδειξιν ὁ Δημοσθένης ὑπὲρ τῶν πεπολιτευμένων εἰσφέρει· τίς δ' ἦν ἡ κατὰ φύσιν χρῆσις αὐτῆς; "οὐχ ἡμάρτετε, ὦ τὸν ὑπὲρ τῆς τῶν Ἑλλήνων ἐλευθερίας

1–6 Dem. 24. 208   7–9 Hyperides, fr. 28 Kenyon   26 sqq. Dem. 18. 208

1–6 leviores discrepantias non notavi   1 κραυγῆς] κραυγὴν codd. Dem.   2 πρὸ τῶν δικαστηρίων] πρὸς τῷ δικαστηρίῳ codd. Dem.   4 βοηθήσει] βοηθήσειεν ἂν codd. Dem.   6 παραυτίκ' ἂν ἀπόλοιτο] ἂν εὐθὺς ἀπαχθεὶς θανάτῳ ζημιωθείη codd. Dem.   Ὑπερίδης ubique P: corr. Lebègue   9 πραγματικῶς K marg.: πραγματικῷ P   18 ⟨ἢ⟩ add. Man.: ⟨διὰ⟩ μιμήσεως Wilamowitz: ⟨ἢ διὰ⟩ μιμήσεως Vahlen   22 πολὺ ἔργον Bühler: πολύεργον P (ut videtur)   26 ἥμαρτε P: corr. Man.   ὦ ἄνδρες Ἀθηναῖοι codd. Dem.

ἀγῶνα ἀράμενοι· ἔχετε δὲ οἰκεῖα τούτου παραδείγματα· οὐδὲ γὰρ οἱ ἐν Μαραθῶνι ἥμαρτον οὐδ' οἱ ἐν Σαλαμῖνι οὐδ' οἱ ἐν Πλαταιαῖς." ἀλλ' ἐπειδὴ καθάπερ ἐμπνευσθεὶς ἐξαίφνης ὑπὸ θεοῦ καὶ οἱονεὶ φοιβόληπτος γενόμενος τὸν ⟨κατὰ⟩ τῶν ἀριστέων τῆς Ἑλλάδος ὅρκον ἐξεφώνησεν "οὐκ ἔστιν ὅπως ἡμάρτετε, μὰ τοὺς ἐν Μαραθῶνι προκινδυνεύσαντας", φαίνεται δι' ἑνὸς τοῦ ὀμοτικοῦ σχήματος, ὅπερ ἐνθάδε ἀποστροφὴν ἐγὼ καλῶ, τοὺς μὲν προγόνους ἀποθεώσας, ὅτι δεῖ τοὺς οὕτως ἀποθανόντας ὡς θεοὺς ὀμνύναι παριστάνων, τοῖς δὲ κρίνουσι τὸ τῶν ἐκεῖ προκινδυνευσάντων ἐντιθεὶς φρόνημα, τὴν δὲ τῆς ἀποδείξεως φύσιν μεθεστακὼς εἰς ὑπερβάλλον ὕψος καὶ πάθος καὶ ξένων καὶ ὑπερφυῶν ὅρκων ἀξιοπιστίαν, καὶ ἅμα παιώνειόν τινα καὶ ἀλεξιφάρμακον εἰς τὰς ψυχὰς τῶν ἀκουόντων καθιεὶς λόγον, ὡς κουφιζομένους ὑπὸ τῶν ἐγκωμίων μηδὲν ἔλαττον τῇ μάχῃ τῇ πρὸς Φίλιππον ἢ ἐπὶ τοῖς κατὰ Μαραθῶνα καὶ Σαλαμῖνα νικητηρίοις παρίστασθαι φρονεῖν· οἷς πᾶσι τοὺς ἀκροατὰς διὰ τοῦ σχηματισμοῦ συναρπάσας ᾤχετο.

καίτοι παρὰ τῷ Εὐπόλιδι τοῦ ὅρκου τὸ σπέρμα φασὶν εὑρῆσθαι· 3

οὐ γὰρ μὰ τὴν Μαραθῶνι τὴν ἐμὴν μάχην
χαίρων τις αὐτῶν τοὐμὸν ἀλγυνεῖ κέαρ.

ἔστι δ' οὐ τὸ ὁπωσοῦν τινα ὀμόσαι μέγα, τὸ δὲ ποῦ καὶ πῶς καὶ ἐφ' ὧν καιρῶν καὶ τίνος ἕνεκα. ἀλλ' ἐκεῖ μὲν οὐδέν ἐστ' εἰ μὴ ὅρκος, καὶ πρὸς εὐτυχοῦντας ἔτι καὶ οὐ δεομένους παρηγορίας τοὺς Ἀθηναίους, ἔτι δ' οὐχὶ τοὺς ἄνδρας ἀπαθανατίσας ὁ ποιητὴς ὤμοσεν, ἵνα τῆς ἐκείνων ἀρετῆς τοῖς ἀκούουσιν ἐντέκῃ λόγον ἄξιον, ἀλλ' ἀπὸ τῶν προκινδυνευσάντων ἐπὶ τὸ ἄψυχον ἀπεπλανήθη, τὴν μάχην. παρὰ δὲ τῷ Δημοσθένει πεπραγμάτευται πρὸς ἡττημένους ὁ ὅρκος, ὡς μὴ Χαιρώνειαν ἔτ' Ἀθηναίοις ἀτύχημα φαίνεσθαι, καὶ ταὐτόν, ὡς ἔφην, ἅμα ἀπόδειξίς ἐστι τοῦ μηδὲν ἡμαρτηκέναι, παράδειγμα, [ὅρκων] πίστις, ἐγκώμιον,

18 Eupolis, fr. 90 Kock

4 τὸν ⟨κατὰ⟩ K marg., Toup   6 ἐν om. codd. Dem.   14 ⟨ἐπὶ⟩ τῇ μάχῃ censor Jenensis   21 ἐστ' Man. : ἔτ' P   29 [ὅρκων] secl. Kayser

ΠΕΡΙ ΥΨΟΥΣ [16. 3–

4 προτροπή. κἀπειδήπερ ὑπήντα τῷ ῥήτορι, "λέγεις ἧτταν πολιτευσάμενος, εἶτα νίκας ὀμνύεις", διὰ ταῦθ' ἑξῆς κανονίζει καὶ δι' ἀσφαλείας ἄγει †καὶ ὀνόματα, διδάσκων ὅτι κἂν βακχεύμασι νήφειν ἀναγκαῖον· "τοὺς προκινδυνεύσαντας" φησί "Μαραθῶνι καὶ τοὺς Σαλαμῖνι καὶ ἐπ' Ἀρτεμισίῳ ναυμαχήσαντας καὶ τοὺς ἐν Πλαταιαῖς παραταξαμένους." οὐδαμοῦ "νικήσαντας" εἶπεν, ἀλλὰ πάντη τὸ τοῦ τέλους διακέκλοφεν ὄνομα, ἐπειδήπερ ἦν εὐτυχὲς καὶ τοῖς κατὰ Χαιρώνειαν ὑπεναντίον. διόπερ καὶ τὸν ἀκροατὴν φθάνων εὐθὺς ὑποφέρει· "οὓς ἅπαντας ἔθαψε δημοσίᾳ" φησίν "ἡ πόλις, Αἰσχίνη, οὐχὶ τοὺς κατορθώσαντας μόνους."

17 Οὐκ ἄξιον ἐπὶ τούτου τοῦ τόπου παραλιπεῖν ἕν τι τῶν ἡμῖν τεθεωρημένων, φίλτατε, ἔσται δὲ πάνυ σύντομον, ὅτι φύσει πως συμμαχεῖ τε τῷ ὕψει τὰ σχήματα καὶ πάλιν ἀντισυμμαχεῖται θαυμαστῶς ὑπ' αὐτοῦ. πῇ δὲ καὶ πῶς ἐγὼ φράσω. ὕποπτόν ἐστιν ἰδίως τὸ διὰ σχημάτων πανουργεῖν καὶ προσβάλλον ὑπόνοιαν ἐνέδρας ἐπιβουλῆς παραλογισμοῦ, †καὶ ταῦθ'† ὅταν ᾖ πρὸς κριτὴν κύριον ὁ λόγος, μάλιστα δὲ πρὸς τυράννους βασιλέας ἡγεμόνας ⟨πάντας τοὺς⟩ ἐν ὑπεροχαῖς· ἀγανακτεῖ γὰρ εὐθὺς εἰ ὡς παῖς ἄφρων ὑπὸ τεχνίτου ῥήτορος σχηματίοις κατασοφίζεται, καὶ εἰς καταφρόνησιν ἑαυτοῦ λαμβάνων τὸν παραλογισμὸν ἐνίοτε μὲν ἀποθηριοῦται τὸ σύνολον, κἂν ἐπικρατήσῃ δὲ τοῦ θυμοῦ, πρὸς τὴν πειθὼ τῶν λόγων πάντως ἀντιδιατίθεται. διόπερ καὶ τότε ἄριστον δοκεῖ τὸ σχῆμα, ὅταν αὐτὸ τοῦτο διαλανθάνῃ, ὅτι σχῆμά 2 ἐστι. τὸ τοίνυν ὕψος καὶ πάθος τῆς ἐπὶ τῷ σχηματίζειν ὑπονοίας ἀλέξημα καὶ θαυμαστή τις ἐπικουρία καθίσταται, καί πως περιλαμφθεῖσ' ἡ τοῦ πανουργεῖν τέχνη τοῖς κάλλεσι καὶ μεγέθεσι τὸ λοιπὸν δέδυκε καὶ πᾶσαν ὑποψίαν ἐκπέφευγεν. ἱκανὸν δὲ τεκμήριον τὸ προειρημένον "μὰ τοὺς ἐν Μαραθῶνι". τίνι γὰρ

1 ὑπήντα ⟨τις⟩ Faber   λέγεις λέγεις P: corr. Rob.   ⟨τί⟩ λέγεις; λέγεις Jahn, fortasse recte   3 ⟨πράγματα⟩ καὶ ὀνόματα Photiades   †καὶ] τὰ Wilamowitz : καὶ ⟨τὰ⟩ Reiske   5 καὶ τοὺς ἐπ' Ἀρτεμισίῳ codd. Dem.   13 συμμαχεῖ τε Schurzfleisch : συμμαχεῖται P   16 †καὶ ταῦθ'† in suspicionem adduxit Tucker: num καὶ ⟨φυλακτέα⟩ ταῦθ'?   18 ⟨πάντας τοὺς⟩ addidi: ⟨καὶ πάντας τοὺς⟩ Cobet: ⟨καὶ ὅλως τοὺς⟩ Terzaghi   25 περιλαμφθεῖσ' ἡ Bury : παραληφθεῖσαν P   26 κάλλεσι] πάθεσι Tollius

ἐνταῦθ' ὁ ῥήτωρ ἀπέκρυψε τὸ σχῆμα; δῆλον ὅτι τῷ φωτὶ αὐτῷ. σχεδὸν γὰρ ὥσπερ καὶ τἀμυδρὰ φέγγη ἐναφανίζεται τῷ ἡλίῳ περιαυγούμενα, οὕτω τὰ τῆς ῥητορικῆς σοφίσματα ἐξαμαυροῖ περιχυθὲν πάντοθεν τὸ μέγεθος. οὐ πόρρω δ' ἴσως τούτου καὶ ἐπὶ τῆς 3 ζωγραφίας τι συμβαίνει· ἐπὶ γὰρ τοῦ αὐτοῦ κειμένων ἐπιπέδου παραλλήλων ἐν χρώμασι τῆς σκιᾶς τε καὶ τοῦ φωτός, ὅμως προϋπαντᾷ τε τὸ φῶς ταῖς ὄψεσι καὶ οὐ μόνον ἔξοχον ἀλλὰ καὶ ἐγγυτέρω παρὰ πολὺ φαίνεται. οὐκοῦν κἀπὶ τῶν λόγων τὰ πάθη καὶ τὰ ὕψη ταῖς ψυχαῖς ἡμῶν ἐγγυτέρω κείμενα διά τε φυσικήν τινα συγγένειαν καὶ διὰ λαμπρότητα, ἀεὶ τῶν σχημάτων προεμφανίζεται καὶ τὴν τέχνην αὐτῶν ἐπισκιάζει καὶ οἷον ἐν κατακαλύψει τηρεῖ.

Τί δ' ἐκεῖνα φῶμεν, τὰς πεύσεις τε καὶ ἐρωτήσεις; ἆρα οὐκ 18 αὐταῖς ταῖς τῶν σχημάτων εἰδοποιίαις παρὰ πολὺ ἐμπρακτότερα καὶ σοβαρώτερα συντείνει τὰ λεγόμενα; "ἢ βούλεσθε, εἰπέ μοι, περιιόντες ἀλλήλων πυνθάνεσθαι· λέγεταί τι καινόν; τί γὰρ ἂν γένοιτο τούτου καινότερον ἢ Μακεδὼν ἀνὴρ καταπολεμῶν τὴν Ἑλλάδα; τέθνηκε Φίλιππος; οὐ μὰ Δί' ἀλλ' ἀσθενεῖ. τί δ' ὑμῖν διαφέρει; καὶ γὰρ ἂν οὗτός τι πάθῃ, ταχέως ὑμεῖς ἕτερον Φίλιππον ποιήσετε." καὶ πάλιν "πλέωμεν ἐπὶ Μακεδονίαν" φησί. "ποῖ δὴ προσορμιούμεθα, ἤρετό τις. εὑρήσει τὰ σαθρὰ τῶν Φιλίππου πραγμάτων αὐτὸς ὁ πόλεμος." ἦν δὲ ἁπλῶς ῥηθὲν τὸ πρᾶγμα τῷ παντὶ καταδεέστερον, νυνὶ δὲ τὸ ἔνθουν καὶ ὀξύρροπον τῆς πεύσεως καὶ ἀποκρίσεως καὶ τὸ πρὸς ἑαυτὸν ὡς πρὸς ἕτερον ἀνθυπαντᾶν οὐ μόνον ὑψηλότερον ἐποίησε τῷ σχηματισμῷ τὸ ῥηθὲν ἀλλὰ καὶ πιστότερον. ἄγει γὰρ τὰ παθητικὰ τότε μᾶλλον, 2 ὅταν αὐτὰ φαίνηται μὴ ἐπιτηδεύειν αὐτὸς ὁ λέγων ἀλλὰ γεννᾶν ὁ καιρός, ἡ δ' ἐρώτησις ἡ εἰς ἑαυτὸν καὶ ἀπόκρισις μιμεῖται τοῦ πάθους τὸ ἐπίκαιρον. σχεδὸν γὰρ ὡς οἱ ὑφ' ἑτέρων ἐρωτώμενοι παροξυνθέντες ἐκ τοῦ παραχρῆμα πρὸς τὸ λεχθὲν ἐναγωνίως καὶ

14 Dem. 4. 10   19 Dem. 4. 44

---

7 καὶ οὐ μόνον Victorius: καιόμενον P   8 κἀπὶ scripsi: καὶ P
11 ἐπισκιάζει Reiske: ἀποσκιάζει P   14–21 discrepant nonnulla a codd. Dem.   25 μᾶλλον] μάλιστα Spengel   28 ὡς οἱ Faber: ὅσον P
29 παροξυνθέντες Morus: παροξύνοντες P: παροξύνονται Lebègue

ἀπ' αὐτῆς τῆς ἀληθείας ἀνθυπαντῶσιν, οὕτως τὸ σχῆμα τῆς πεύσεως καὶ ἀποκρίσεως εἰς τὸ δοκεῖν ἕκαστον τῶν ἐσκεμμένων ἐξ ὑπογύου κεκινῆσθαί τε καὶ λέγεσθαι τὸν ἀκροατὴν ἀπάγον καὶ παραλογίζεται. ἔτι τοίνυν (ἓν γάρ τι τῶν ὑψηλοτάτων τὸ Ἡροδότειον πεπίστευται), εἰ οὕτως ἔ... 5
. . . .

19 ... ⟨ἀσύμ⟩πλοκα ἐκπίπτει καὶ οἱονεὶ προχεῖται τὰ λεγόμενα, ὀλίγου δεῖν φθάνοντα καὶ αὐτὸν τὸν λέγοντα. "καὶ συμβαλόντες" φησὶν ὁ Ξενοφῶν "τὰς ἀσπίδας ἐωθοῦντο ἐμάχοντο ἀπέκτεινον 2 ἀπέθνησκον." καὶ τὰ τοῦ Εὐρυλόχου,

ἤλθομεν ὡς ἐκέλευες ἀνὰ δρυμά, φαίδιμ' Ὀδυσσεῦ· 10
εἴδομεν ἐν βήσσῃσι τετυγμένα δώματα καλά.

τὰ γὰρ ἀλλήλων διακεκομμένα καὶ οὐδὲν ἧττον κατεσπευσμένα φέρει τῆς ἀγωνίας ἔμφασιν ἅμα καὶ ἐμποδιζούσης τι καὶ συνδιωκούσης. τοιαῦθ' ὁ ποιητὴς ἐξήνεγκε διὰ τῶν ἀσυνδέτων.

20 Ἄκρως δὲ καὶ ἡ ἐπὶ ταὐτὸ σύνοδος τῶν σχημάτων εἴωθε κινεῖν, 15 ὅταν δύο ἢ τρία οἷον κατὰ συμμορίαν ἀνακιρνάμενα ἀλλήλοις ἐρανίζῃ τὴν ἰσχὺν τὴν πειθὼ τὸ κάλλος, ὁποῖα καὶ τὰ εἰς τὸν Μειδίαν, ταῖς ἀναφοραῖς ὁμοῦ καὶ τῇ διατυπώσει συναναπεπλεγμένα ⟨ἔχοντα⟩ τὰ ἀσύνδετα. "πολλὰ γὰρ ἂν ποιήσειεν ὁ τύπτων, ὧν ὁ παθὼν ἔνια οὐδ' ἂν ἀπαγγεῖλαι δύναιτο ἑτέρῳ, τῷ σχήματι 20 2 τῷ βλέμματι τῇ φωνῇ." εἶθ' ἵνα μὴ ἐπὶ τῶν αὐτῶν ὁ λόγος ἰὼν στῇ (ἐν στάσει γὰρ τὸ ἠρεμοῦν, ἐν ἀταξίᾳ δὲ τὸ πάθος, ἐπεὶ φορὰ ψυχῆς καὶ συγκίνησίς ἐστιν), εὐθὺς ἐπ' ἄλλα μεθήλατο ἀσύνδετα καὶ ἐπαναφοράς· "τῷ σχήματι τῷ βλέμματι τῇ φωνῇ, ὅταν ὡς

5 fortasse Herod. 7. 21   7 Xen. *Hell.* 4. 3. 19 = *Ages.* 2. 12
10 Hom. κ 251–2   19 sqq. Dem. 21. 72

---

5 desunt duo folia in P   6 ⟨ἀσύμ⟩πλοκα Reiske   10 ἤλθομεν] ἤομεν codd. Hom.   11 .ίδομεν P (i.e. εἴδομεν): εὔρομεν P marg., codd. Hom.   13 συνδιωκούσης Faber: συνδιοικούσης P   16 συμμορίαν Man.: συμμορίας P   19 ⟨ἔχοντα⟩ addidi (post ἀσύνδετα add. Rothstein): τὰ del. Weiske   τύπτων, ὦ ἄνδρες Ἀθηναῖοι codd. Dem.

ὑβρίζων, ὅταν ὡς ἐχθρός, ὅταν κονδύλοις, ὅταν ἐπὶ κόρρης." οὐδὲν ἄλλο διὰ τούτων ὁ ῥήτωρ ἢ ὅπερ ὁ τύπτων ἐργάζεται· τὴν διάνοιαν τῶν δικαστῶν τῇ ἐπαλλήλῳ πλήττει φορᾷ. εἶτ' ἐντεῦθεν 3 πάλιν ὡς αἱ καταιγίδες ἄλλην ποιούμενος ἐμβολήν "ὅταν κονδύλοις, ὅταν ἐπὶ κόρρης" φησί· "ταῦτα κινεῖ, ταῦτα ἐξίστησιν ἀνθρώπους, ἀήθεις ὄντας τοῦ προπηλακίζεσθαι· οὐδεὶς ἂν ταῦτα ἀπαγγέλλων δύναιτο τὸ δεινὸν παραστῆσαι." οὐκοῦν τὴν μὲν φύσιν τῶν ἐπαναφορῶν καὶ ἀσυνδέτων πάντη φυλάττει τῇ συνεχεῖ μεταβολῇ· οὕτως αὐτῷ καὶ ἡ τάξις ἄτακτον καὶ ἔμπαλιν ἡ ἀταξία ποιὰν περιλαμβάνει τάξιν.

Φέρε οὖν, πρόσθες τοὺς συνδέσμους, εἰ θέλεις, ὡς ποιοῦσιν 21 οἱ Ἰσοκράτειοι· "καὶ μὴν οὐδὲ τοῦτο χρὴ παραλιπεῖν, ὡς πολλὰ ἂν ποιήσειεν ὁ τύπτων, πρῶτον μὲν τῷ σχήματι, εἶτα δὲ τῷ βλέμματι, εἶτά γε μὴν αὐτῇ τῇ φωνῇ," καὶ εἴσῃ κατὰ τὸ ἑξῆς οὕτως παραγράφων ὡς τοῦ πάθους τὸ συνδεδιωγμένον καὶ ἀποτραχυνόμενον, ἐὰν τοῖς συνδέσμοις ἐξομαλίσῃς εἰς λειότητα, ἄκεντρόν τε προσπίπτει καὶ εὐθὺς ἔσβεσται. ὥσπερ γὰρ εἴ τις 2 συνδήσειε τῶν θεόντων τὰ σώματα τὴν φορὰν αὐτῶν ἀφῄρηται, οὕτως καὶ τὸ πάθος ὑπὸ τῶν συνδέσμων καὶ τῶν ἄλλων προσθηκῶν ἐμποδιζόμενον ἀγανακτεῖ· τὴν γὰρ ἐλευθερίαν ἀπολλύει τοῦ δρόμου καὶ τὸ ὡς ἀπ' ὀργάνου τινὸς ἀφίεσθαι.

Τῆς δὲ αὐτῆς ἰδέας καὶ τὰ ὑπερβατὰ θετέον. ἔστι δὲ λέξεων 22 ἢ νοήσεων ἐκ τοῦ κατ' ἀκολουθίαν κεκινημένη τάξις καὶ οἱονεὶ * * * χαρακτὴρ ἐναγωνίου πάθους ἀληθέστατος. ὡς γὰρ οἱ τῷ ὄντι ὀργιζόμενοι ἢ φοβούμενοι ἢ ἀγανακτοῦντες ἢ ὑπὸ ζηλοτυπίας ἢ ὑπὸ ἄλλου τινὸς (πολλὰ γὰρ καὶ ἀναρίθμητα πάθη καὶ οὐδ' ἂν εἰπεῖν τις ὁπόσα δύναιτο) ἑκάστοτε παραπίπτοντες ἄλλα προθέμενοι πολλάκις ἐπ' ἄλλα μεταπηδῶσι, μέσα τινὰ παρεμβάλλοντες

1 ἐπὶ κόρρης Man. e Dem.: ὡς δοῦλον P: ὅταν ὡς δοῦλον secl. Radermacher   6 ἂν apogr.: om. P   7-8 μὲν φύσιν] ἔμφασιν Photiades: μεγαλοφυΐαν Vaucher   11 θέλεις apogr.: θέλοις P   20 ἀγανακτεῖ] ἀπακμάζει Richards: ἀτονεῖ Cumanudes: ἀπακταίνει Haupt   ἀπολλύει Finckh: ἀπολύει P   24 lacunam post οἱονεὶ indicavit Wilamowitz   26 ⟨τὰ⟩ πάθη Wilamowitz   28 παρεμβάλλοντες Janzon: παρεμβαλόντες P

ἀλόγως, εἶτ' αὖθις ἐπὶ τὰ πρῶτα ἀνακυκλοῦντες καὶ πάντη πρὸς τῆς ἀγωνίας, ὡς ὑπ' ἀστάτου πνεύματος, τῇδε κἀκεῖσε ἀγχιστρόφως ἀντισπώμενοι τὰς λέξεις τὰς νοήσεις τὴν ἐκ τοῦ κατὰ φύσιν εἱρμοῦ παντοίως πρὸς μυρίας τροπὰς ἐναλλάττουσι τάξιν, οὕτως παρὰ τοῖς ἀρίστοις συγγραφεῦσι διὰ τῶν ὑπερβατῶν ἡ μίμησις 5 ἐπὶ τὰ τῆς φύσεως ἔργα φέρεται. τότε γὰρ ἡ τέχνη τέλειος ἡνίκ' ἂν φύσις εἶναι δοκῇ, ἡ δ' αὖ φύσις ἐπιτυχὴς ὅταν λανθάνουσαν περιέχῃ τὴν τέχνην. ὥσπερ λέγει ὁ Φωκαεὺς Διονύσιος παρὰ τῷ Ἡροδότῳ· "ἐπὶ ξυροῦ γὰρ ἀκμῆς ἔχεται ἡμῖν τὰ πράγματα, ἄνδρες Ἴωνες, εἶναι ἐλευθέροις ἢ δούλοις, καὶ τούτοις ὡς δραπέ- 10 τῃσι. νῦν ὦν ὑμεῖς ἢν μὲν βούλησθε ταλαιπωρίας ἐνδέχεσθαι, παραχρῆμα μὲν πόνος ὑμῖν, οἷοί τε δὲ ἔσεσθε ὑπερβαλέσθαι τοὺς 2 πολεμίους." ἐνταῦθ' ἦν τὸ κατὰ τάξιν· "ὦ ἄνδρες Ἴωνες, νῦν καιρός ἐστιν ὑμῖν πόνους ἐπιδέχεσθαι· ἐπὶ ξυροῦ γὰρ ἀκμῆς ἔχεται ἡμῖν τὰ πράγματα." ὁ δὲ τὸ μὲν "ἄνδρες Ἴωνες" ὑπερ- 15 εβίβασε· προεισέβαλε γὰρ εὐθὺς ἀπὸ τοῦ φόβου, ὡς μηδ' ἀρχὴν φθάνων πρὸς τὸ ἐφεστὼς δέος προσαγορεῦσαι τοὺς ἀκούοντας· ἔπειτα δὲ τὴν τῶν νοημάτων ἀπέστρεψε τάξιν. πρὸ γὰρ τοῦ φῆσαι ὅτι αὐτοὺς δεῖ πονεῖν (τοῦτο γάρ ἐστιν ὃ παρακελεύεται) ἔμπροσθεν ἀποδίδωσι τὴν αἰτίαν δι' ἣν πονεῖν δεῖ, "ἐπὶ ξυροῦ 20 ἀκμῆς" φήσας "ἔχεται ἡμῖν τὰ πράγματα," ὡς μὴ δοκεῖν 3 ἐσκεμμένα λέγειν, ἀλλ' ἠναγκασμένα. ἔτι δὲ μᾶλλον ὁ Θουκυδίδης καὶ τὰ φύσει πάντως ἡνωμένα καὶ ἀδιανέμητα ὅμως ταῖς ὑπερβάσεσιν ἀπ' ἀλλήλων ἄγειν δεινότατος. ὁ δὲ Δημοσθένης οὐχ οὕτως μὲν αὐθάδης ὥσπερ οὗτος, πάντων δ' ἐν τῷ γένει τούτῳ 25 κατακορέστατος καὶ πολὺ τὸ ἀγωνιστικὸν ἐκ τοῦ ὑπερβιβάζειν καὶ ἔτι νὴ Δία τὸ ἐξ ὑπογύου λέγειν συνεμφαίνων, καὶ πρὸς τούτοις εἰς τὸν κίνδυνον τῶν μακρῶν ὑπερβατῶν τοὺς ἀκούον- 4 τας συνεπισπώμενος· πολλάκις γὰρ τὸν νοῦν ὃν ὥρμησεν εἰπεῖν

9 sqq. Herod. 6. 11

9 sqq. discrepant nonnulla a codd. Her.   11 ταλαιπωρίαις P: corr. Man.   16 γὰρ Man.: ἂν P, suprascripto οὖν: γοῦν Morus 16 ἀρχὴ P: corr. Rob.   17 ἐφεστὼς] ἐφεστὸς Spengel   18 ἀπέστρεψε] ἀνέστρεψε Finckh   29 ὄν] ὦν Nolte

ἀνακρεμάσας, καὶ μεταξύ πως εἰς ἀλλόφυλον καὶ ἀπεοικυῖαν τάξιν
ἀλλ' ἐπ' ἄλλοις διὰ μέσου καὶ ἔξωθέν ποθεν ἐπεισκυκλῶν, εἰς
φόβον ἐμβαλὼν τὸν ἀκροατὴν ὡς ἐπὶ παντελεῖ τοῦ λόγου διαπτώ-
σει, καὶ συναποκινδυνεύειν ὑπ' ἀγωνίας τῷ λέγοντι συναναγκά-
5 σας, εἶτα παραλόγως διὰ μακροῦ τὸ πάλαι ζητούμενον εὐκαίρως
ἐπὶ τέλει που προσαποδούς, αὐτῷ τῷ κατὰ τὰς ὑπερβάσεις παραβόλῳ καὶ ἀκροσφαλεῖ πολὺ μᾶλλον ἐκπλήττει. φειδὼ δὲ τῶν
παραδειγμάτων ἔστω διὰ τὸ πλῆθος.

Τά γε μὴν πολύπτωτα λεγόμενα, ἀθροισμοὶ καὶ μεταβολαὶ καὶ 23
10 κλίμακες, πάνυ ἀγωνιστικά, ὡς οἶσθα, κόσμου τε καὶ παντὸς ὕψους
καὶ πάθους συνεργά. τί δέ; αἱ τῶν πτώσεων χρόνων προσώπων
ἀριθμῶν γενῶν ἐναλλάξεις, πῶς ποτε καταποικίλλουσι καὶ ἐπεγεί-
ρουσι τὰ ἑρμηνευτικά; φημὶ δὴ τῶν κατὰ τοὺς ἀριθμοὺς οὐ μόνα 2
ταῦτα κοσμεῖν ὁπόσα τοῖς τύποις ἑνικὰ ὄντα τῇ δυνάμει κατὰ τὴν
15 ἀναθεώρησιν πληθυντικὰ εὑρίσκεται·

αὐτίκα (φησὶ) λαὸς ἀπείρων
θύννον ἐπ' ἠιόνεσσι διιστάμενοι κελάδησαν·

ἀλλ' ἐκεῖνα μᾶλλον παρατηρήσεως ἄξια, ὅτι ἔσθ' ὅπου προσπίπτει
τὰ πληθυντικὰ μεγαλορρημονέστερα καὶ αὐτῷ δοξοκοποῦντα
20 τῷ ὄχλῳ τοῦ ἀριθμοῦ. τοιαῦτα παρὰ τῷ Σοφοκλεῖ τὰ ἐπὶ τοῦ 3
Οἰδίπου·

ὦ γάμοι, γάμοι,
ἐφύσαθ' ἡμᾶς καὶ φυτεύσαντες πάλιν
ἀνεῖτε ταὐτὸ σπέρμα κἀπεδείξατε
25   πατέρας ἀδελφοὺς παῖδας, αἷμ' ἐμφύλιον,
νύμφας γυναῖκας μητέρας τε χὠπόσα
αἴσχιστ' ἐν ἀνθρώποισιν ἔργα γίγνεται.

16–17 poeta incertus   22–27 Soph. *OT* 1403 sqq.

---

1 μεταξύ πως Wilamowitz: μεταξὺ ὡς P   4 ὑπ' ἀγωνίας p
marg.: ὑπογωνία P: ὑπαγωνιῶντα Immisch   9 ἀθροισμοὶ] κάθροι
σμοὶ Martens   μεταβολαί] ἀντιμεταβολαί Man.   13 δὴ edd. vett.:
δὲ P   17 θύννον Vahlen: θύννων P: θινῶν [ἐπ'] M. L. West   ἐπ' del.
Wyttenbach: ἐπ' olim Vahlen   20 ὄχλῳ] ὄγκῳ Wilamowitz   24
ταὐτὸ] ταὐτὸν codd. Soph.: ταὐτοῦ Jebb

ΠΕΡΙ ΥΨΟΥΣ [23. 3–

πάντα γὰρ ταῦτα ἓν ὄνομά ἐστιν, Οἰδίπους, ἐπὶ δὲ θατέρου
Ἰοκάστη, ἀλλ' ὅμως χυθεὶς εἰς τὰ πληθυντικὰ ὁ ἀριθμὸς συν-
επλήθυσε καὶ τὰς ἀτυχίας· καὶ ὡς ἐκεῖνα πεπλεόνασται

ἐξῆλθον Ἕκτορές τε καὶ Σαρπηδόνες·

καὶ τὸ Πλατωνικόν, ὃ καὶ ἑτέρωθι παρετεθείμεθα, ἐπὶ τῶν
Ἀθηναίων· "οὐ γὰρ Πέλοπες οὐδὲ Κάδμοι οὐδ' Αἰγυπτοί τε καὶ
Δαναοὶ οὐδ' ἄλλοι πολλοὶ φύσει βάρβαροι συνοικοῦσιν ἡμῖν, ἀλλ'
αὐτοὶ Ἕλληνες οὐ μιξοβάρβαροι οἰκοῦμεν" καὶ τὰ ἑξῆς. φύσει
γὰρ ἐξακούεται τὰ πράγματα κομπωδέστερα ἀγεληδὸν οὕτως τῶν
ὀνομάτων ἐπισυντιθεμένων. οὐ μέντοι δεῖ ποιεῖν αὐτὸ ἐπ' ἄλλων,
εἰ μὴ ἐφ' ὧν δέχεται τὰ ὑποκείμενα αὔξησιν ἢ πληθὺν ἢ ὑπερβολὴν ἢ πάθος, ἕν τι τούτων ἢ [τὰ] πλείονα, ἐπεί τοι τὸ πανταχοῦ κώδωνας ἐξῆφθαι λίαν σοφιστικόν. ἀλλὰ μὴν καὶ τοὐναντίον
τὰ ἐκ τῶν πληθυντικῶν εἰς τὰ ἑνικὰ ἐπισυναγόμενα ἐνίοτε ὑψηλο-
φανέστατα. "ἔπειθ' ἡ Πελοπόννησος ἅπασα διειστήκει" φησί.
"καὶ δὴ Φρυνίχῳ δρᾶμα Μιλήτου ἅλωσιν διδάξαντι εἰς δάκρυα
⟨ἔπεσε τὸ θέατρον", ἀντὶ τοῦ⟩ "ἔπεσον οἱ θεώμενοι"· τὸ ἐκ τῶν
διῃρημένων εἰς τὰ ἡνωμένα ἐπισυστρέψαι τὸν ἀριθμὸν σωματο-
ειδέστερον. αἴτιον δ' ἐπ' ἀμφοῖν τοῦ κόσμου ταὐτὸν οἶμαι· ὅπου
τε γὰρ ἑνικὰ ὑπάρχει τὰ ὀνόματα, τὸ πολλὰ ποιεῖν αὐτὰ παρὰ
δόξαν ἐμπαθοῦς· ὅπου τε πληθυντικά, τὸ εἰς ἕν τι εὔηχον συγ-
κορυφοῦν τὰ πλείονα διὰ τὴν εἰς τοὐναντίον μεταμόρφωσιν τῶν
πραγμάτων ἐν τῷ παραλόγῳ.

4 Trag. adesp. fr. 289 Nauck²   6 sqq. Pl. *Menex.* 245D
15 Dem. 18. 18   16 Herod. 6. 21

1–2 ἐπὶ ... Ἰοκάστῃ secl. Rohden   7–8 φύσει μὲν βάρβαροι
ὄντες νόμῳ δὲ Ἕλληνες codd. Pl.   9 ἐξακούεται] num ἐξογκοῦται?
11 ὑπερκείμενα P: corr. Petra   αὔξησιν Rob.: αὔχησιν P   12 [τὰ]
secl. Faber: καὶ Steinheil   15 ἔπειθ' ἡ Man. e Dem.: ἐπειδὴ P   17
⟨ἔπεσε τὸ θέητρον ἀντὶ τοῦ⟩ suppl. Vahlen; at non est cur Ionice θέητρον
scribas, cf. 22. 1: ⟨ἔπεσε τὸ θέητρον. τοῦ γὰρ⟩ Wilamowitz, sublata post
θεώμενοι interpunctione   ἔπεσον οἱ θεώμενοι] ἔπεσε τὸ θέατρον Tollius
20 τε Rob.: τὰ P   21 ἐμπαθοῦς vel ἐκπαθοῦς Faber   εὐπαθοῦς P
ὅπουτε ὁπότε P: corr. Man.   23 ἐν τῷ παραλόγῳ] ἓν τῶν παραλόγων
Richards: ἐν τῷ παραλόγῳ ⟨τὸ ὑψηλοποιὸν ἔχει⟩ Rothstein

"Όταν γε μὴν τὰ παρεληλυθότα τοῖς χρόνοις εἰσάγῃς ὡς γινό- 25
μενα καὶ παρόντα, οὐ διήγησιν ἔτι τὸν λόγον ἀλλ' ἐναγώνιον
πρᾶγμα ποιήσεις. "πεπτωκὼς δέ τις" φησὶν ὁ Ξενοφῶν "ὑπὸ
τῷ Κύρου ἵππῳ καὶ πατούμενος παίει τῇ μαχαίρᾳ εἰς τὴν
γαστέρα τὸν ἵππον· ὁ δὲ σφαδᾴζων ἀποσείεται τὸν Κῦρον, ὁ δὲ
πίπτει." τοιοῦτος ἐν τοῖς πλείστοις ὁ Θουκυδίδης.

Ἐναγώνιος δ' ὁμοίως καὶ ἡ τῶν προσώπων ἀντιμετάθεσις, 26
[καὶ] πολλάκις ἐν μέσοις τοῖς κινδύνοις ποιοῦσα τὸν ἀκροατὴν
δοκεῖν στρέφεσθαι·

      φαίης κ' ἀκμῆτας καὶ ἀτειρέας . . .
      ἄντεσθ' ἐν πολέμῳ· ὡς ἐσσυμένως ἐμάχοντο.

καὶ ὁ Ἄρατος·

      μὴ κείνῳ ἐνὶ μηνὶ περικλύζοιο θαλάσσῃ.

ὡδέ που καὶ ὁ Ἡρόδοτος· "ἀπὸ δὲ Ἐλεφαντίνης πόλεως ἄνω 2
πλεύσεαι, καὶ ἔπειτα ἀφίξῃ ἐς πεδίον λεῖον· διεξελθὼν δὲ τοῦτο
τὸ χωρίον αὖθις εἰς ἕτερον πλοῖον ἐμβὰς πλεύσεαι δύ' ἡμέρας,
ἔπειτα ἥξεις ἐς πόλιν μεγάλην, ᾗ ὄνομα Μερόη." ὁρᾷς, ὦ ἑταῖρε,
ὡς παραλαβών σου τὴν ψυχὴν διὰ τῶν τόπων ἄγει τὴν ἀκοὴν
ὄψιν ποιῶν; πάντα δὲ τὰ τοιαῦτα πρὸς αὐτὰ ἀπερειδόμενα τὰ
πρόσωπα ἐπ' αὐτῶν ἵστησι τὸν ἀκροατὴν τῶν ἐνεργουμένων. καὶ 3
ὅταν ὡς οὐ πρὸς ἅπαντας, ἀλλ' ὡς πρὸς μόνον τινὰ λαλῇς—

      Τυδείδην δ' οὐκ ἂν γνοίης ποτέροισι μετείη—

ἐμπαθέστερόν τε αὐτὸν ἅμα καὶ προσεκτικώτερον καὶ ἀγῶνος
ἔμπλεων ἀποτελέσεις, ταῖς εἰς ἑαυτὸν προσφωνήσεσιν ἐξεγειρόμενον.

Ἔτι γε μὴν ἔσθ' ὅτε περὶ προσώπου διηγούμενος ὁ συγγραφεὺς 27

---

3 Xen. *Cyr.* 7. 1. 37   10 Hom. *O* 697   13 Aratus, *Phaen.*
287   14 Herod. 2. 29. 2-6: sed et multa omisit noster et pleraque
ad Attici sermonis normam accommodavit   22 Hom. *E* 85

5–6 ὁ δὲ πίπτει om. codd. Xen.   8 [καὶ] seclusi   10 ἀτείρεας
ἀλλήλοισιν Hom.: ἀλλήλοις add. K marg.   16 δύ'] δυώδεκα Man.
24 ἐξεγειρόμενον Faber: ἐξεγειρόμενος P

ἐξαίφνης παρενεχθεὶς εἰς τὸ αὐτὸ πρόσωπον ἀντιμεθίσταται, καὶ ἔστι τὸ τοιοῦτον εἶδος ἐκβολή τις πάθους·

"Ἕκτωρ δὲ Τρώεσσιν ἐκέκλετο μακρὸν ἀύσας
νηυσὶν ἐπισσεύεσθαι, ἐᾶν δ' ἔναρα βροτόεντα·
"ὃν δ' ἂν ἐγὼν ἀπάνευθε νεῶν ἐθέλοντα νοήσω, 5
αὐτοῦ οἱ θάνατον μητίσομαι."

οὐκοῦν τὴν μὲν διήγησιν ἅτε πρέπουσαν ὁ ποιητὴς προσῆψεν ἑαυτῷ, τὴν δ' ἀπότομον ἀπειλὴν τῷ θυμῷ τοῦ ἡγεμόνος ἐξαπίνης οὐδὲν προδηλώσας περιέθηκεν· ἐψύχετο γὰρ εἰ παρενετίθει· "ἔλεγε δὲ τοῖά τινα καὶ τοῖα ὁ Ἕκτωρ," νυνὶ δ' ἔφθακεν ἄφνω τὸν 10
2 μεταβαίνοντα ἡ τοῦ λόγου μετάβασις. διὸ καὶ ἡ πρόσχρησις τοῦ σχήματος τότε ἡνίκ' ἂν ὀξὺς ὁ καιρὸς ὢν διαμέλλειν τῷ γράφοντι μὴ διδῷ, ἀλλ' εὐθὺς ἐπαναγκάζῃ μεταβαίνειν ἐκ προσώπων εἰς πρόσωπα, ὡς καὶ παρὰ τῷ Ἑκαταίῳ· "Κῆυξ δὲ ταῦτα δεινὰ ποιούμενος αὐτίκα ἐκέλευε τοὺς [Ἡρακλείδας] ἐπιγόνους ἐκ- 15
χωρεῖν· οὐ γὰρ ὑμῖν δυνατός εἰμι ἀρήγειν. ὡς μὴ ὦν αὐτοί τε
3 ἀπόλησθε κἀμὲ τρώσητε, ἐς ἄλλον τινὰ δῆμον ἀποίχεσθε." ὁ μὲν γὰρ Δημοσθένης κατ' ἄλλον τινὰ τρόπον ἐπὶ τοῦ Ἀριστογείτονος ἐμπαθὲς τὸ πολυπρόσωπον καὶ ἀγχίστροφον παρέστακεν. "καὶ οὐδεὶς ὑμῶν χολήν" φησίν "οὐδ' ὀργὴν ἔχων εὑρεθήσεται ἐφ' οἷς 20
ὁ βδελυρὸς οὗτος καὶ ἀναιδὴς βιάζεται; ὅς, ὦ μιαρώτατε ἁπάντων, κεκλειμένης σοι τῆς παρρησίας οὐ κιγκλίσιν οὐδὲ θύραις, ἃ καὶ παρανοίξειεν ἄν τις"—ἐν ἀτελεῖ τῷ νῷ ταχὺ διαλλάξας καὶ μόνον

3–6 Hom. O 346–9   14 Hecataeus F 30, T 20 FGrHist 1
19 sqq. [Dem.] 25. 27, cf. Alexander (Spengel iii. 33)

5 ἐθέλοντα] ἑτέρωθι Hom., sed cf. B 391   7 πρέπουσαν Rob.: τρέπουσαν P   11 πρόσχρησις Man.: πρόχρησις P   12 ἡνίκ' ἂν Jahn: ἡνίκα P   15 [Ἡρακλείδας] seclusi: Ἡρακλείους von Scheliha: ἐπιγόνους secl. Toup: ⟨καὶ τοὺς τοῦ Λικυμνίου⟩ ἐπιγόνους Morus   16 ὑμῖν Stephanus: ἡμῖν P   17 ἀπόλησθε ... τρώσητε Rob.: ἀπόλεσθε ... τρώσετε P   ἀποίχεσθε apogr.: ἀποίχεσθαι P   20 χολήν Dem.: σχολήν P   εὑρεθήσεται etiam Alexander: φανήσεται codd. Dem.   21 οὗτος etiam Alexander: om. codd. Dem.   ἀναιδὴς ἄνθρωπος codd. Dem.: ἄνθρωπος om. etiam Alexander   βιάζεται τοὺς νόμους codd. Dem.: τοὺς νόμους om. etiam Alexander

οὐ μίαν λέξιν διὰ τὸν θυμὸν εἰς δύο διασπάσας πρόσωπα "ὅς, ὢ μιαρώτατε," εἶτα [τὸν] πρὸς τὸν Ἀριστογείτονα ⟨τὸν⟩ λόγον ἀποστρέψας καὶ ἀπολιπεῖν δοκῶν, ὅμως διὰ τοῦ πάθους πολὺ πλέον ἐπέστρεψεν. οὐκ ἄλλως ἡ Πηνελόπη· 4

κῆρυξ, τίπτε δέ σε πρόεσαν μνηστῆρες ἀγανοί
εἰπέμεναι δμωῇσιν Ὀδυσσῆος θείοιο
ἔργων παύσασθαι, σφίσι δ' αὐτοῖς δαῖτα πένεσθαι;
μὴ μνηστεύσαντες μηδ' ἄλλοθ' ὁμιλήσαντες,
ὕστατα καὶ πύματα νῦν ἐνθάδε δειπνήσειαν,
οἳ θάμ' ἀγειρόμενοι βίοτον κατακείρετε πολλόν
... οὐδέ τι πατρῶν
ὑμετέρων τῶν πρόσθεν ἀκούετε παῖδες ἐόντες,
οἷος Ὀδυσσεὺς ἔσκε.

Καὶ μέντοι περίφρασις ὡς οὐχ ὑψηλοποιόν, οὐδεὶς ἂν οἶμαι 28 διστάσειεν. ὡς γὰρ ἐν μουσικῇ διὰ τῶν παραφώνων καλουμένων ὁ κύριος φθόγγος ἡδίων ἀποτελεῖται, οὕτως ἡ περίφρασις πολλάκις συμφθέγγεται τῇ κυριολογίᾳ καὶ εἰς κόσμον ἐπὶ πολὺ συνηχεῖ, καὶ μάλιστ' ἂν μὴ ἔχῃ φυσῶδές τι καὶ ἄμουσον ἀλλ' ἡδέως κεκραμένον. ἱκανὸς δὲ τοῦτο τεκμηριῶσαι καὶ Πλάτων 2 κατὰ τὴν εἰσβολὴν τοῦ Ἐπιταφίου· "ἔργῳ μὲν ἡμῖν οἶδ' ἔχουσι τὰ προσήκοντα σφίσιν αὐτοῖς, ὧν τυχόντες πορεύονται τὴν εἱμαρμένην πορείαν, προπεμφθέντες κοινῇ μὲν ὑπὸ τῆς πόλεως, ἰδίᾳ δὲ ἕκαστος ὑπὸ τῶν προσηκόντων." οὐκοῦν τὸν θάνατον εἶπεν εἱμαρμένην πορείαν, τὸ δὲ τετυχηκέναι τῶν νομιζομένων προπομπήν τινα δημοσίαν ὑπὸ τῆς πατρίδος. ἆρα δὴ τούτοις μετρίως ὤγκωσε τὴν νόησιν; ἢ ψιλὴν λαβὼν τὴν λέξιν ἐμελοποίησε, καθάπερ ἁρμονίαν τινὰ τὴν ἐκ τῆς περιφράσεως περιχεάμενος εὐμέλειαν; καὶ Ξενοφῶν· "πόνον δὲ τοῦ ζῆν ἡδέως ἡγεμόνα 3

5 sqq. Hom. δ 681 sqq.   20 sqq. Pl. *Menex.* 236D   28 Xen. *Cyr.* I. 5. 12 (πόνους ... ἡγεμόνας)

2 [τὸν] del. Tollius   ⟨τὸν⟩ add. Weiske   6 ἢ εἰπέμεναι codd. Hom.   11 κτῆσιν Τηλεμάχοιο δαΐφρονος οὐδέ Hom.   12 τῶν] τὸ Hom.   14 οὐχ del. Portus   19 ἡδέως Man.: ἀδεῶς P: ⟨ᾗ⟩ ἡδέως Wilamowitz   23 ἕκαστος om. codd. Plat.   προσηκόντων] οἰκείων codd. Plat.   26 ἢ] ᾗ (*quatenus*) Pearce: ἦν ... τῇ λέξει Morus: num καὶ?

ΠΕΡΙ ΥΨΟΥΣ

νομίζετε· κάλλιστον δὲ πάντων καὶ πολεμικώτατον κτῆμα εἰς τὰς ψυχὰς συγκεκόμισθε· ἐπαινούμενοι γὰρ μᾶλλον ἢ τοῖς ἄλλοις πᾶσι χαίρετε''· ἀντὶ τοῦ πονεῖν θέλετε ''πόνον ἡγεμόνα τοῦ ζῆν ἡδέως ποιεῖσθε'' εἰπὼν καὶ τἆλλ' ὁμοίως ἐπεκτείνας μεγάλην τινὰ
4 ἔννοιαν τῷ ἐπαίνῳ προσπεριωρίσατο. καὶ τὸ ἀμίμητον ἐκεῖνο τοῦ Ἡροδότου· ''τῶν δὲ Σκυθέων τοῖς συλήσασι τὸ ἱερὸν ἐνέβαλεν ἡ θεὸς θήλειαν νοῦσον.''

29 Ἐπίκηρον μέντοι [τὸ] πρᾶγμα ἡ περίφρασις τῶν ἄλλων πλέον, εἰ μὴ σὺν μέτρῳ τινὶ λαμβάνοιτο· εὐθὺς γὰρ ἀβλεμὲς προσπίπτει, κουφολογίας τε ὄζον καὶ παχύτητος· ὅθεν καὶ τὸν Πλάτωνα (δεινὸς γὰρ ἀεὶ περὶ ⟨τὸ⟩ σχῆμα κἄν τισιν ἀκαίρως) ἐν τοῖς Νόμοις λέγοντα ''ὡς οὔτε ἀργυροῦν δεῖ πλοῦτον οὔτε χρυσοῦν ἐν πόλει ἱδρυμένον ἐᾶν οἰκεῖν'' διαχλευάζουσιν, ὡς εἰ πρόβατα, φησίν, ἐκώλυε κεκτῆσθαι, δῆλον ὅτι προβάτειον ἂν καὶ βόειον πλοῦτον ἔλεγεν.

2 Ἀλλὰ γὰρ ἅλις ὑπὲρ τῆς εἰς τὰ ὑψηλὰ τῶν σχημάτων χρήσεως ἐκ παρενθήκης τοσαῦτα πεφιλολογῆσθαι, Τερεντιανὲ φίλτατε· πάντα γὰρ ταῦτα παθητικωτέρους καὶ συγκεκινημένους ἀποτελεῖ τοὺς λόγους· πάθος δὲ ὕψους μετέχει τοσοῦτον, ὁπόσον ἦθος ἡδονῆς.

30 Ἐπειδὴ μέντοι ἡ τοῦ λόγου νόησις ἥ τε φράσις τὰ πλείω δι' ἑκατέρου διέπτυκται, ἴθι δή, [ἂν] τοῦ φραστικοῦ μέρους εἴ τινα λοιπὰ ἔτι, προσεπιθεασώμεθα. ὅτι μὲν τοίνυν ἡ τῶν κυρίων καὶ μεγαλοπρεπῶν ὀνομάτων ἐκλογὴ θαυμαστῶς ἄγει καὶ κατακηλεῖ τοὺς ἀκούοντας καὶ ὡς πᾶσι τοῖς ῥήτορσι καὶ συγγραφεῦσι κατ' ἄκρον ἐπιτήδευμα, μέγεθος ἅμα κάλλος εὐπίνειαν βάρος ἰσχὺν κράτος, ἔτι δὲ γάνωσίν τινα, τοῖς λόγοις ὥσπερ ἀγάλμασι καλλίστοις δι' αὐτῆς ἐπανθεῖν παρασκευάζουσα, καὶ οἱονεὶ ψυχήν τινα

---

6 Herod. 1. 105   12 Pl. Leges 801B

8 [τὸ] del.Weiske, qui et glossam olere ἡ περίφρασις censet   9 σὺν μέτρῳ Morus : συμμέτρως P   10 παχύτητος Man.: παχύτατον P   11 ⟨τὸ⟩ σχῆμα Man.   ἀκαίρως] ἄκαιρος Schurzfleisch   13 φησίν] φασίν Man.   21 δι' Man.: δὲ P   22 [ἂν] seclusi: αὐτοῦ Morus   εἴ] ᾗ Spengel   25–26 κατ' ἄκρον] κατάκορον Rohde   27 γάνωσιν censor Jenensis: τὰν ὦσι P

τοῖς πράγμασι φωνητικὴν ἐντιθεῖσα, μὴ καὶ περιττὸν ᾗ πρὸς εἰδότας διεξιέναι. φῶς γὰρ τῷ ὄντι ἴδιον τοῦ νοῦ τὰ καλὰ ὀνόματα. ὁ μέντοι γε ὄγκος αὐτῶν οὐ πάντῃ χρειώδης, ἐπεὶ τοῖς 2 μικροῖς πραγματίοις περιτιθέναι μεγάλα καὶ σεμνὰ ὀνόματα ταὐτὸν ἂν φαίνοιτο ὡς εἴ τις τραγικὸν προσωπεῖον μέγα παιδὶ περιθείη νηπίῳ· πλὴν ἐν μὲν ποιήσει καὶ ἱ⟨στορίᾳ⟩ ...

... πτικώτατον καὶ γόνιμον †τὸ δ' Ἀνακρέοντος οὐκέτι† 31 "Θρηικίης ⟨πώλου⟩ ἐπιστρέφομαι." ταύτῃ καὶ τὸ τοῦ Θεοπόμπου ἐκεῖνο ἐπαινετὸν διὰ τὸ ἀνάλογον ἔμοιγε σημαντικώτατα ἔχειν δοκεῖ· ὅπερ ὁ Καικίλιος οὐκ οἶδ' ὅπως καταμέμφεται· "δεινὸς ὤν" φησίν "ὁ Φίλιππος ἀναγκοφαγῆσαι πράγματα." ἔστιν ἄρ' ὁ ἰδιωτισμὸς ἐνίοτε τοῦ κόσμου παρὰ πολὺ ἐμφανιστικώτερον· ἐπιγινώσκεται γὰρ αὐτόθεν ἐκ τοῦ κοινοῦ βίου, τὸ δὲ σύνηθες ἤδη πιστότερον. οὐκοῦν ἐπὶ τοῦ τὰ αἰσχρὰ καὶ ῥυπαρὰ τλημόνως καὶ μεθ' ἡδονῆς ἕνεκα πλεονεξίας καρτεροῦντος τὸ ἀναγκοφαγεῖν τὰ πράγματα ἐναργέστατα παρείληπται. ὡδέ πως ἔχει καὶ τὰ 2 Ἡροδότεια· "ὁ Κλεομένης" φησί "μανεὶς τὰς ἑαυτοῦ σάρκας ξιφιδίῳ κατέτεμεν εἰς λεπτά, ἕως ὅλον καταχορδεύων ἑαυτὸν διέφθειρεν" καὶ "ὁ Πύθης ἕως τοῦδε ἐπὶ τῆς νεὼς ἐμάχετο, ἕως ἅπας κατεκρεουργήθη." ταῦτα γὰρ ἐγγὺς παραξύει τὸν ἰδιώτην, ἀλλ' οὐκ ἰδιωτεύει τῷ σημαντικῶς.

Περὶ δὲ πλήθους [καὶ] μεταφορῶν ὁ μὲν Καικίλιος ἔοικε συγ- 32 κατατίθεσθαι τοῖς δύο ἢ τὸ πλεῖστον τρεῖς ἐπὶ ταὐτοῦ νομοθετοῦσι

7 Anacreon, fr. 96 Bergk   10 Theopompus F 262, FGrHist 115
17 sqq. Herod. 6. 75   19 sqq. Herod. 7. 181

1–2 πρὸς εἰδότας] πρὸς εἰδότα σε Tollius   6 ἱ⟨στορίᾳ⟩ Tollius   desunt quattuor folia in P   7 θρεπτικώτατον p   †τὸ δ' Ἀνακρέοντος] num τὸ τἀνακρέοντος?   8 ⟨πώλου⟩ add. Bergk   9 ἐκεῖνο ἐπαινετόν· Hammer: ego non ita fortiter interpungendum censeo: καὶ τὸν ἐπήνετον P: κεκαινοτομημένον Wilamowitz: καίτοι ⟨κοινὸν ὂν⟩ ἐπαινετόν (διὰ ... δοκεῖ) Wenkebach   11 ⟨τὰ⟩ πράγματα Morus   21 σημαντικῶς] σημαντικῷ Rob.   22 [καὶ] del. Rob.: καὶ ⟨τόλμης⟩ Tollius: καὶ ⟨συνεχείας⟩, ex. gr., Lebègue   23 τοῖς Rob.: τοὺς P τάττεσθαι. ὁ γὰρ Δημοσθένης ὅρος καὶ τῶν τοιούτων· ὁ τῆς χρείας δὲ καιρός, ἔνθα τὰ πάθη χειμάρρου δίκην ἐλαύνεται καὶ τὴν πολυπλήθειαν αὐτῶν ὡς ἀναγκαίαν ἐνταῦθα συνεφέλκεται.

2 "ἄνθρωποι" φησί "μιαροὶ καὶ κόλακες, ἠκρωτηριασμένοι τὰς ἑαυτῶν ἕκαστοι πατρίδας, τὴν ἐλευθερίαν προπεπωκότες πρότερον Φιλίππῳ, νυνὶ δὲ Ἀλεξάνδρῳ, τῇ γαστρὶ μετροῦντες καὶ τοῖς αἰσχίστοις τὴν εὐδαιμονίαν, τὴν δ' ἐλευθερίαν καὶ τὸ μηδένα ἔχειν δεσπότην, ἃ τοῖς πρότερον Ἕλλησιν ὅροι τῶν ἀγαθῶν ἦσαν καὶ κανόνες, ἀνατετροφότες." ἐνταῦθα τῷ πλήθει τῶν τροπικῶν 3 ὁ κατὰ τῶν προδοτῶν ἐπιπροσθεῖ τοῦ ῥήτορος θυμός. διόπερ ὁ μὲν Ἀριστοτέλης καὶ ὁ Θεόφραστος μειλίγματά φασί τινα τῶν θρασειῶν εἶναι ταῦτα μεταφορῶν, τὸ "ὡσπερεὶ" φάναι καὶ "οἱονεὶ" καὶ "εἰ χρὴ τοῦτον εἰπεῖν τὸν τρόπον" καὶ "εἰ δεῖ παρακινδυνευτικώτερον λέξαι"· ἡ γὰρ ὑποτίμησις, φασίν, ἰᾶται 4 τὰ τολμηρά. ἐγὼ δὲ καὶ ταῦτα μὲν ἀποδέχομαι, ὅμως δὲ πλήθους καὶ τόλμης μεταφορῶν, ὅπερ ἔφην κἀπὶ τῶν σχημάτων, τὰ εὔκαιρα καὶ σφοδρὰ πάθη καὶ τὸ γενναῖον ὕψος εἶναί φημι ἴδιά τινα ἀλεξιφάρμακα, ὅτι τῷ ῥοθίῳ τῆς φορᾶς ταυτὶ πέφυκεν ἅπαντα τἆλλα παρασύρειν καὶ προωθεῖν, μᾶλλον δὲ καὶ ὡς ἀναγκαῖα πάντως εἰσπράττεσθαι τὰ παράβολα, καὶ οὐκ ἐᾷ τὸν ἀκροατὴν σχολάζειν περὶ τὸν τοῦ πλήθους ἔλεγχον διὰ τὸ συνεν- 5 θουσιᾶν τῷ λέγοντι. ἀλλὰ μὴν ἔν γε ταῖς τοπηγορίαις καὶ διαγραφαῖς οὐκ ἄλλο τι οὕτως κατασημαντικὸν ὡς οἱ συνεχεῖς καὶ ἐπάλληλοι τρόποι. δι' ὧν καὶ παρὰ Ξενοφῶντι ἡ τἀνθρωπίνου σκήνους ἀνατομὴ πομπικῶς καὶ ἔτι μᾶλλον ἀναζωγραφεῖται θείως παρὰ τῷ Πλάτωνι. τὴν μὲν κεφαλὴν αὐτοῦ φησιν ἀκρόπολιν, ἰσθμὸν δὲ μέσον διῳκοδομῆσθαι μεταξὺ τοῦ στήθους τὸν αὐχένα,

4 sqq. Dem. 18. 296   11 cf. Arist. fr. 131 Rose   24 Xen. Mem. 1. 4. 5 sqq.   26–p. 39, 21 loci ex Pl. Tim. 65C–85E desumpti   26 ibid. 70A6   27 ibid. 69E1

1–2 ὁ γὰρ ... ὁ τῆς χρείας δὲ] ὁ δὲ ... ὁ τῆς χρείας γὰρ Schück, fortasse recte   4–6 discrepant nonnulla a codd. Dem.   10 ἐπιπροσθεῖ Rob.: ἐπίπροσθε P   12 θρασέων P: corr. Faber   τὸ Spengel: τὰ P   16 κἀπὶ Stephanus: κἄπειτα P   18 ἀλεξιφάρκακα P

σφονδύλους τε ὑπεστηρίχθαι φησὶν οἷον στρόφιγγας, καὶ τὴν μὲν ἡδονὴν ἀνθρώποις εἶναι κακοῦ δέλεαρ, γλῶσσαν δὲ γεύσεως δοκίμιον· ἄναμμα δὲ τῶν φλεβῶν τὴν καρδίαν καὶ πηγὴν τοῦ περιφερομένου σφοδρῶς αἵματος, εἰς τὴν δορυφορικὴν οἴκησιν
5 κατατεταγμένην· τὰς δὲ διαδρομὰς τῶν πόρων ὀνομάζει στενωπούς· "τῇ δὲ πηδήσει τῆς καρδίας ἐν τῇ τῶν δεινῶν προσδοκίᾳ καὶ τῇ τοῦ θυμοῦ ἐπεγέρσει, ἐπειδὴ διάπυρος ἦν, ἐπικουρίαν μηχανώμενοι" φησί "τὴν τοῦ πλεύμονος ἰδέαν ἐνεφύτευσαν, μαλακὴν καὶ ἄναιμον καὶ σήραγγας ἐντὸς ἔχουσαν ὁποῖον μά-
10 λαγμα, ἵν' ὁ θυμὸς ὁπότ' ἐν αὐτῇ ζέσῃ πηδῶσα εἰς ὑπεῖκον μὴ λυμαίνηται." καὶ τὴν μὲν τῶν ἐπιθυμιῶν οἴκησιν προσεῖπεν ὡς γυναικωνῖτιν, τὴν τοῦ θυμοῦ δὲ ὥσπερ ἀνδρωνῖτιν· τόν γε μὴν σπλῆνα τῶν ἐντὸς μαγεῖον, ὅθεν πληρούμενος τῶν ἀποκαθαιρομένων μέγας καὶ ὕπουλος αὔξεται. "μετὰ δὲ ταῦτα σαρξὶ πάντα"
15 φησί "κατεσκίασαν, προβολὴν τῶν ἔξωθεν τὴν σάρκα, οἷον τὰ πιλήματα, προθέμενοι·" νομὴν δὲ σαρκῶν ἔφη τὸ αἷμα· " τῆς δὲ τροφῆς ἕνεκα" φησί "διωχέτευσαν τὸ σῶμα, τέμνοντες ὥσπερ ἐν κήποις ὀχετούς, ὡς ἔκ τινος νάματος ἐπιόντος, ἀραιοῦ ὄντος αὐλῶνος τοῦ σώματος, τὰ τῶν φλεβῶν ῥέοι νάματα." ἡνίκα δὲ ἡ
20 τελευτὴ παραστῇ, λύεσθαί φησι τὰ τῆς ψυχῆς οἱονεὶ νεὼς πείσματα, μεθεῖσθαί τε αὐτὴν ἐλευθέραν. ταῦτα καὶ τὰ παραπλήσια 6 μυρί' ἄττα ἐστὶν ἑξῆς· ἀπόχρη ✳ ✳ δεδηλωμένα, ὡς μεγάλαι τε φύσιν εἰσὶν αἱ τροπικαί, καὶ ὡς ὑψηλοποιὸν αἱ μεταφοραί, καὶ

1 ibid. 74A2   2 ibid. 69D1, 65C7   3–4 ibid. 70A7–B2
5 ibid. 70B6   6–11 ibid. 70CI sqq.   11–12 cf. ibid. 69E6 sqq.
13 ibid. 72C6   14–16 ibid. 74B, 74D   16 ibid. 80E6   16–19 ibid.
77C, 79A   19–21 ibid. 85E

2 κακοῦ codd. Pl.: κακὸν P: κακῶν Man. (*malorum*, Cic. Cat.
Mai. 13. 44)   3 ἄναμμα P: ἄμμα vel ἅμα codd. Pl., Galen.
8 φησί Tollius: φασί P   ἐνεφύτευσαν Man. e Plat.: ἐνεφύτευσε P
9 ὁποῖον P: οἷον Toup   μάλαγμα] ἄλμα μαλακὸν vel ἅμμα μαλακὸν
codd. Plat.   13 μαγεῖον Vossius: μάγειον P, ρεῖ suprascr. p (i.e. *coquinam*)   15 φησί Rob.: φύσιν P   16 πιλήματα Toup: πιλητὰ
codd. Plat.: πηδήματα P   18–19 ἀραιοῦ ... αὐλῶνος] ἄρδοιτο καὶ ὡς δι'
αὐλῶνος Wilamowitz   22 ἀπόχρη ⟨δὲ τὰ⟩ p: plura deesse suspicor:
expectes 'sufficiunt autem quae enumeravi ad demonstrandum ...'
23 τροπικαί] τροπαί Man.   φύσιν] num φύσεις?

ὅτι οἱ παθητικοὶ καὶ φραστικοὶ κατὰ τὸ πλεῖστον αὐταῖς χαίρουσι
7 τόποι. ὅτι μέντοι καὶ ἡ χρῆσις τῶν τρόπων, ὥσπερ τἆλλα πάντα
καλὰ ἐν λόγοις, προαγωγὸν ἀεὶ πρὸς τὸ ἄμετρον, δῆλον ἤδη, κἂν
ἐγὼ μὴ λέγω. ἐπὶ γὰρ τούτοις καὶ τὸν Πλάτωνα οὐχ ἥκιστα
διασύρουσι, πολλάκις ὥσπερ ὑπὸ βακχείας τινὸς τῶν λόγων εἰς 5
ἀκράτους καὶ ἀπηνεῖς μεταφορὰς καὶ εἰς ἀλληγορικὸν στόμφον
ἐκφερόμενον. "οὐ γὰρ ῥᾴδιον ἐπινοεῖν" φησίν "ὅτι πόλιν εἶναι
⟨δεῖ⟩ δίκην κρατῆρος κεκερασμένην, οὗ μαινόμενος μὲν οἶνος
ἐγκεχυμένος ζεῖ, κολαζόμενος δ' ὑπὸ νήφοντος ἑτέρου θεοῦ, καλὴν
κοινωνίαν λαβών, ἀγαθὸν πόμα καὶ μέτριον ἀπεργάζεται." νήφον- 10
τα γάρ, φασί, θεὸν τὸ ὕδωρ λέγειν, κόλασιν δὲ τὴν κρᾶσιν, ποιητοῦ
8 τινος τῷ ὄντι οὐχὶ νήφοντός ἐστι. τοῖς τοιούτοις ἐλαττώμασιν
ἐπιχειρῶν †ὅμως αὐτὸ καὶ† ὁ Καικίλιος ἐν τοῖς ὑπὲρ Λυσίου
συγγράμμασιν ἀπεθάρρησε τῷ παντὶ Λυσίαν ἀμείνω Πλάτωνος
ἀποφήνασθαι, δυσὶ πάθεσι χρησάμενος ἀκρίτοις· φιλῶν γὰρ τὸν 15
Λυσίαν ὡς οὐδ' αὐτὸς αὑτόν, ὅμως μᾶλλον μισεῖ [τῷ παντὶ]
Πλάτωνα ἢ Λυσίαν φιλεῖ. πλὴν οὗτος μὲν ὑπὸ φιλονικίας, οὐδὲ
τὰ θέματα ὁμολογούμενα, καθάπερ ᾠήθη. ὡς γὰρ ἀναμάρτητον
καὶ καθαρὸν τὸν ῥήτορα προφέρει πολλαχῇ διημαρτημένου τοῦ
Πλάτωνος· τὸ δ' ἦν ἄρα οὐχὶ τοιοῦτον, οὐδὲ ὀλίγου δεῖ. 20
33 Φέρε δή, λάβωμεν τῷ ὄντι καθαρόν τινα συγγραφέα καὶ
ἀνέγκλητον. ἆρ' οὐκ ἄξιόν ἐστι διαπορῆσαι περὶ αὐτοῦ τούτου
καθολικῶς, πότερόν ποτε κρεῖττον ἐν ποιήμασι καὶ λόγοις μέγεθος
ἐν ἐνίοις διημαρτημένον ἢ τὸ σύμμετρον μὲν ἐν τοῖς κατορθώμασιν
ὑγιὲς δὲ πάντη καὶ ἀδιάπτωτον; καὶ ἔτι νὴ Δία πότερόν ποτε αἱ 25
πλείους ἀρεταὶ τὸ πρωτεῖον ἐν λόγοις ἢ αἱ μείζους δικαίως ἂν
φέροιντο; ἔστι γὰρ ταῦτ' οἰκεῖα τοῖς περὶ ὕψους σκέμματα, καὶ

7 Pl. Leges 773C-D   13 Caecilius, fr. 150 Ofenloch

7 ἐπινοεῖν] ἐννοεῖν codd. Plat.   8 ⟨δεῖ⟩ add. Man. ex Plat.
κεκερασμένην] κεκραμένην codd. Plat.   9 ἐγκεχυμένος Man. ex
Plat.: ἐκκεχυμένος P   10 πόμα] πῶμα codd. Plat.   13 †ὅμως
αὐτὸ καὶ†] ὅμως αὐτόθεν Man.   15 ἀκρίτοις suspectum: num ἀκρίτως?
16 [τῷ παντὶ] secl. Weiske   17 φιλονικίας scripsi: φιλονεικίας P
18 θέματα ⟨τίθησι⟩ Reiske   24 διημαρτημένον Man.: διημαρτημένοις P

ἐπικρίσεως ἐξ ἅπαντος δεόμενα. ἐγὼ δ' οἶδα μὲν ὡς αἱ ὑπερμεγέθεις φύσεις ἥκιστα καθαραί· ⟨τὸ⟩ γὰρ ἐν παντὶ ἀκριβὲς κίνδυνος μικρότητος, ἐν δὲ τοῖς μεγέθεσιν, ὥσπερ ἐν τοῖς ἄγαν πλούτοις, εἶναί τι χρὴ καὶ παρολιγωρούμενον· μήποτε δὲ τοῦτο καὶ ἀναγκαῖον ᾖ, τὸ τὰς μὲν ταπεινὰς καὶ μέσας φύσεις διὰ τὸ μηδαμῇ παρακινδυνεύειν μηδὲ ἐφίεσθαι τῶν ἄκρων ἀναμαρτήτους ὡς ἐπὶ τὸ πολὺ καὶ ἀσφαλεστέρας διαμένειν, τὰ δὲ μεγάλα ἐπισφαλῆ δι' αὐτὸ γίνεσθαι τὸ μέγεθος. ἀλλὰ μὴν οὐδὲ ἐκεῖνο ἀγνοῶ τὸ δεύτερον, ὅτι φύσει πάντα τὰ ἀνθρώπεια ἀπὸ τοῦ χείρονος ἀεὶ μᾶλλον ἐπιγινώσκεται καὶ τῶν μὲν ἁμαρτημάτων ἀνεξάλειπτος ἡ μνήμη παραμένει, τῶν καλῶν δὲ ταχέως ἀπορρεῖ.

παρατεθειμένος δ' οὐκ ὀλίγα καὶ αὐτὸς ἁμαρτήματα καὶ Ὁμήρου καὶ τῶν ἄλλων ὅσοι μέγιστοι, καὶ ἥκιστα τοῖς πταίσμασιν ἀρεσκόμενος, ὅμως δὲ οὐχ ἁμαρτήματα μᾶλλον αὐτὰ ἑκούσια καλῶν ἢ παροράματα δι' ἀμέλειαν εἰκῇ που καὶ ὡς ἔτυχεν ὑπὸ μεγαλοφυΐας ἀνεπιστάτως παρενηνεγμένα, οὐδὲν ἧττον οἶμαι τὰς μείζονας ἀρετάς, εἰ καὶ μὴ ἐν πᾶσι διομαλίζοιεν, τὴν τοῦ πρωτείου ψῆφον μᾶλλον ἀεὶ φέρεσθαι, κἂν εἰ μηδενὸς ἑτέρου, τῆς μεγαλοφροσύνης αὐτῆς ἕνεκα· ἐπείτοιγε καὶ ἄπτωτος ὁ Ἀπολλών⟨ιος ἐν τοῖς⟩ Ἀργοναύταις ποιητής, κἂν τοῖς βουκολικοῖς πλὴν ὀλίγων τῶν ἔξωθεν ὁ Θεόκριτος ἐπιτυχέστατος· ἆρ' οὖν Ὅμηρος ἂν μᾶλλον ἢ Ἀπολλώνιος ἐθέλοις γενέσθαι; τί δέ; Ἐρατοσθένης ἐν τῇ Ἠριγόνῃ (διὰ πάντων γὰρ ἀμώμητον τὸ ποιημάτιον) Ἀρχιλόχου πολλὰ καὶ ἀνοικονόμητα παρασύροντος, κἀκείνης τῆς ἐκβολῆς τοῦ δαιμονίου πνεύματος ἣν ὑπὸ νόμον τάξαι δύσκολον,

22–23 cf. J. U. Powell, *Collectanea Alexandrina* 64 sqq.

---

2 ⟨τὸ⟩ add. p   3 κίνδυνος Man.: κίνδυνοι P   4 τοῦτο Man.: τούτου P   7 τὰ δὲ Rob.: τὸ δὲ P   8 ἐκεῖνο Man.: ἐκείνου P   17 ἀρετάς Petra: αἰτίας P   18 μηδενὸς censor Jenensis: μὴ δι' ἑνὸς P   19–20 Ἀπολλών⟨ιος ἐν τοῖς⟩ Spengel: Ἀπολλώνιος τοῖς p, apogr.   20–21 κἂν ... εὐτυχέστατος del. Toup   21 ἆρ' οὖν] ἆρ' οὐχ Pearce   24 κἀκείνης] ἕνεκ' ἐκείνης Jannarakis: num ⟨ὑπ'⟩ ἐκείνης? lacunam post παρασύροντος statuit Vahlen ⟨τῷ ῥοθίῳ τῆς φορᾶς⟩ vel sim. intercidisse suspicatus

42 ΠΕΡΙ ΥΨΟΥΣ [33. 5-

ἆρα δὴ μείζων ποιητής; τί δέ; ἐν μέλεσι μᾶλλον ἂν εἶναι Βακχυλίδης ἕλοιο ἢ Πίνδαρος, καὶ ἐν τραγῳδίᾳ Ἴων ὁ Χῖος ἢ νὴ Δία Σοφοκλῆς; ἐπειδὴ οἱ μὲν ἀδιάπτωτοι καὶ ἐν τῷ γλαφυρῷ πάντη κεκαλλιγραφημένοι, ὁ δὲ Πίνδαρος καὶ ὁ Σοφοκλῆς ὁτὲ μὲν οἷον πάντα ἐπιφλέγουσι τῇ φορᾷ, σβέννυνται δ' ἀλόγως πολλάκις καὶ 5 πίπτουσιν ἀτυχέστατα. ἢ οὐδεὶς ἂν εὖ φρονῶν ἑνὸς δράματος, τοῦ Οἰδίποδος, εἰς ταὐτὸ συνθεὶς τὰ Ἴωνος ⟨πάντ'⟩ ἀντιτιμήσαιτο ἑξῆς.

34 Εἰ δ' ἀριθμῷ, μὴ τῷ ἀληθεῖ κρίνοιτο τὰ κατορθώματα, οὕτως ἂν καὶ Ὑπερείδης τῷ παντὶ προέχοι Δημοσθένους. ἔστι γὰρ αὐτοῦ πολυφωνότερος καὶ πλείους ἀρετὰς ἔχων, καὶ σχεδὸν ὕπακρος ἐν 10 πᾶσιν ὡς ὁ πένταθλος, ὥστε τῶν μὲν πρωτείων ἐν ἅπασι τῶν 2 ἄλλων ἀγωνιστῶν λείπεσθαι, πρωτεύειν δὲ τῶν ἰδιωτῶν. ὁ μέν γε Ὑπερείδης πρὸς τῷ πάντα, ἔξω γε τῆς συνθέσεως, μιμεῖσθαι τὰ Δημοσθένεια κατορθώματα καὶ τὰς Λυσιακὰς ἐκ περιττοῦ περιείληφεν ἀρετάς τε καὶ χάριτας. καὶ γὰρ λαλεῖ μετὰ ἀφελείας 15 ἔνθα χρή, καὶ οὐ πάντα ἑξῆς [καὶ] μονοτόνως ὡς ὁ Δημοσθένης λέγει· τό τε ἠθικὸν ἔχει μετὰ γλυκύτητος [ἡδύ,] λιτῶς ἐφηδυνόμενον· ἄφατοί τε περὶ αὐτόν εἰσιν ἀστεϊσμοί, μυκτὴρ πολιτικώτατος, εὐγένεια, τὸ κατὰ τὰς εἰρωνείας εὐπάλαιστρον, σκώμματα οὐκ ἄμουσα οὐδ' ἀνάγωγα, κατὰ τοὺς Ἀττικοὺς ἐκείνους ἅλας 20 ἐπικείμενα, διασυρμός τε ἐπιδέξιος καὶ πολὺ τὸ κωμικὸν ⟨ἔχων⟩ καὶ μετὰ παιδιᾶς εὐστόχου κέντρον, ἀμίμητον δὲ εἰπεῖν τὸ ἐν πᾶσι τούτοις ἐπαφρόδιτον· οἰκτίσασθαί τε προσφυέστατος, ἔτι δὲ μυθολογῆσαι κεχυμένως καὶ ἐν ὑγρῷ πνεύματι διεξοδεῦσαι [ἔτι] εὐκαμπὴς ἄκρως, ὥσπερ ἀμέλει τὰ μὲν περὶ τὴν Λητὼ ποιητικώ- 25 τερα, τὸν δ' Ἐπιτάφιον ἐπιδεικτικῶς, ὡς οὐκ οἶδ' εἴ τις ἄλλος,

25 Hyper. frr. 67–75 Kenyon 26 Ἐπιτάφιον] Hyper. Orat. 6

6 ἢ Radermacher: ἦ P 7 ⟨πάντ'⟩ add. Toup 8 τῷ ἀληθεῖ] τῷ μεγέθει Pearce 15 λαλεύματα P: corr. Pearce 16 [καὶ] om. apogr. 17 λέγει Man.: λέγεται P [ἡδύ] del. Weiske: νὴ Δία Richards 20 ἅλας Tucker: ἀλλὰ P: ἀλλὰ ⟨χάριν⟩ Richards 21 ἐπικείμενα] ἐπικεκριμένα Wilamowitz ⟨ἔχων⟩ add. Selb 22 ⟨ὡς⟩ εἰπεῖν apogr. 24 κεχυμένως Blass: κεχυμένος P [ἔτι] seclusi: τι Bücheler: ante ἔτι interpunxit Richards 25 ἄκρως Man.: ἄκρος P ποιητικώτερα] ποιητικώτατα Wilamowitz

ΠΕΡΙ ΥΨΟΥΣ

διέθετο. ὁ δὲ Δημοσθένης ἀνηθοποίητος, ἀδιάχυτος, ἥκιστα ὑγρὸς 3
ἢ ἐπιδεικτικός, ἁπάντων ἑξῆς τῶν προειρημένων κατὰ τὸ πλέον
ἄμοιρος· ἔνθα μέντοι γελοῖος εἶναι βιάζεται καὶ ἀστεῖος οὐ
γέλωτα κινεῖ μᾶλλον ἢ καταγελᾶται, ὅταν δὲ ἐγγίζειν θέλῃ τῷ
ἐπίχαρις εἶναι, τότε πλέον ἀφίσταται. τό γέ τοι περὶ Φρύνης ἢ
Ἀθηνογένους λογίδιον ἐπιχειρήσας γράφειν ἔτι μᾶλλον ἂν Ὑπερείδην συνέστησεν. ἀλλ' ἐπειδήπερ, οἶμαι, τὰ μὲν θατέρου καλά, 4
καὶ εἰ πολλὰ ὅμως ἀμεγέθη, "καρδίῃ νήφοντος ἀργὰ" καὶ τὸν
ἀκροατὴν ἠρεμεῖν ἐῶντα (οὐδεὶς γοῦν Ὑπερείδην ἀναγινώσκων
φοβεῖται), ὁ δὲ ἔνθεν ἑλὼν τοῦ μεγαλοφυεστάτου καὶ ἐπ' ἄκρον
ἀρετὰς συντετελεσμένας, ὑψηγορίας τόνον, ἔμψυχα πάθη, περι-
ουσίαν ἀγχίνοιαν τάχος, ἔνθα δὴ κύριον, τὴν ἅπασιν ἀπρόσιτον
δεινότητα καὶ δύναμιν—ἐπειδὴ ταῦτα, φημί, ὡς θεόπεμπτά τινα
δωρήματα (οὐ γὰρ εἰπεῖν θεμιτὸν ἀνθρώπινα) ἀθρόα εἰς ἑαυτὸν
ἔσπασε, διὰ τοῦτο οἷς ἔχει καλοῖς ἅπαντας ἀεὶ νικᾷ καὶ ὑπὲρ ὧν
οὐκ ἔχει, καὶ ὡσπερεὶ καταβροντᾷ καὶ καταφέγγει τοὺς ἀπ' αἰῶνος ῥήτορας· καὶ θᾶττον ἄν τις κεραυνοῖς φερομένοις ἀντανοῖξαι
τὰ ὄμματα δύναιτο ἢ ἀντοφθαλμῆσαι τοῖς ἐπαλλήλοις ἐκείνου
πάθεσιν. ἐπὶ μέντοι τοῦ Πλάτωνος καὶ ἄλλη τίς ἐστιν, ὡς ἔφην, 35
διαφορά· οὐ γὰρ μεγέθει τῶν ἀρετῶν, ἀλλὰ καὶ τῷ πλήθει πολὺ
λειπόμενος ὁ Λυσίας ὅμως πλεῖον ἔτι τοῖς ἁμαρτήμασι περιττεύει
ἢ ταῖς ἀρεταῖς λείπεται.

Τί ποτ' οὖν εἶδον οἱ ἰσόθεοι ἐκεῖνοι καὶ τῶν μεγίστων ἐπορεξά- 2
μενοι τῆς συγγραφῆς, τῆς δ' ἐν ἅπασιν ἀκριβείας ὑπερφρονήσαντες;
πρὸς πολλοῖς ἄλλοις ἐκεῖνο, ὅτι ἡ φύσις οὐ ταπεινὸν ἡμᾶς ζῷον
οὐδ' ἀγεννὲς †ἐ.. κρινε τὸν ἄνθρωπον, ἀλλ' ὡς εἰς μεγάλην τινὰ

5 Hyper. frr. 171–80 Kenyon   6 κατὰ Ἀθηνογένους, Hyper. Orat. 3 (5)

---

3 μέντοι] μὲν Finckh   5 ἐπίχαρις Toup: ἐπιχάρης P   Φρύνης Schurzfleisch: Φρυγίης P   11 ἀρετῆς συντετελεσμένης Wilamowitz   12 κύριον P: καίριον Richards   τὴν ⟨ἐν⟩ Rothstein   13 τινα Man.: δεινὰ P: secl. Jahn   15 ὑπὲρ] ἄτερ Gemoll   16 καταφέγγῃ P: corr. Man.   21 ὁ Λυσίας Man.: ἀπουσίας P   ὅμως Toup: ὁ μὲν P: ὅθεν Schurzfleisch   26 †ἐ.. κρινε] ἔκρινε apogr.: ἔκτισε Seager: ἐξέκρινε Selb   τὸν ἄνθρωπον secl. Wilamowitz

πανήγυριν εἰς τὸν βίον καὶ εἰς τὸν σύμπαντα κόσμον ἐπάγουσα, θεατάς τινας τῶν ἄθλων αὐτῆς ἐσομένους καὶ φιλοτιμοτάτους ἀγωνιστάς, εὐθὺς ἄμαχον ἔρωτα ἐνέφυσεν ἡμῶν ταῖς ψυχαῖς 3 παντὸς ἀεὶ τοῦ μεγάλου καὶ ὡς πρὸς ἡμᾶς δαιμονιωτέρου. διόπερ τῇ θεωρίᾳ καὶ διανοίᾳ τῆς ἀνθρωπίνης ἐπιβολῇ οὐδ' ὁ σύμπας 5 κόσμος ἀρκεῖ, ἀλλὰ καὶ τοὺς τοῦ περιέχοντος πολλάκις ὅρους ἐκβαίνουσιν αἱ ἐπίνοιαι, καὶ εἴ τις περιβλέψαιτο ἐν κύκλῳ τὸν βίον, ὅσῳ πλέον ἔχει τὸ περιττὸν ἐν πᾶσι καὶ μέγα καὶ καλόν, 4 ταχέως εἴσεται πρὸς ἃ γεγόναμεν. ἔνθεν φυσικῶς πως ἀγόμενοι μὰ Δί' οὐ τὰ μικρὰ ῥεῖθρα θαυμάζομεν, εἰ καὶ διαυγῆ καὶ χρή- 10 σιμα, ἀλλὰ τὸν Νεῖλον καὶ Ἴστρον ἢ Ῥῆνον, πολὺ δ' ἔτι μᾶλλον τὸν Ὠκεανόν· οὐδέ γε τὸ ὑφ' ἡμῶν τουτὶ φλογίον ἀνακαιόμενον, ἐπεὶ καθαρὸν σῴζει τὸ φέγγος, ἐκπληττόμεθα τῶν οὐρανίων μᾶλλον, καίτοι πολλάκις ἐπισκοτουμένων, οὐδὲ τῶν τῆς Αἴτνης κρατήρων ἀξιοθαυμαστότερον νομίζομεν, ἧς αἱ ἀναχοαὶ πέτρους 15 τε ἐκ βυθοῦ καὶ ὅλους ὄχθους ἀναφέρουσι καὶ ποταμοὺς ἐνίοτε τοῦ 5 γηγενοῦς ἐκείνου καὶ αὐτομάτου προχέουσι πυρός. ἀλλ' ἐπὶ τῶν τοιούτων ἁπάντων ἐκεῖν' ἂν εἴποιμεν, ὡς εὐπόριστον μὲν ἀνθρώποις τὸ χρειῶδες ἢ καὶ ἀναγκαῖον, θαυμαστὸν δ' ὅμως ἀεὶ τὸ παράδοξον. 20

36 Οὐκοῦν ἐπί γε τῶν ἐν λόγοις μεγαλοφυῶν, ἐφ' ὧν οὐκέτ' ἔξω τῆς χρείας καὶ ὠφελείας πίπτει τὸ μέγεθος, προσήκει συνθεωρεῖν αὐτόθεν, ὅτι τοῦ ἀναμαρτήτου πολὺ ἀφεστῶτες οἱ τηλικοῦτοι ὅμως παντὸς εἰσὶν ἐπάνω τοῦ θνητοῦ· καὶ τὰ μὲν ἄλλα τοὺς χρωμένους ἀνθρώπους ἐλέγχει, τὸ δ' ὕψος ἐγγὺς αἴρει μεγαλο- 25 φροσύνης θεοῦ· καὶ τὸ μὲν ἄπταιστον οὐ ψέγεται, τὸ μέγα δὲ καὶ 2 θαυμάζεται. τί χρὴ πρὸς τούτοις ἔτι λέγειν, ὡς ἐκείνων τῶν ἀνδρῶν ἕκαστος ἅπαντα τὰ σφάλματα ἑνὶ ἐξωνεῖται πολλάκις ὕψει καὶ κατορθώματι, καὶ τὸ κυριώτατον, ὡς, εἴ γε ἐκλέξας τὰ Ὁμήρου, τὰ Δημοσθένους, τὰ Πλάτωνος, τῶν ἄλλων ὅσοι δὴ 30

---

2 τῶν ἄθλων Reiske: τῶν ὅλων P   5 τῇ θεωρίᾳ καὶ διανοίᾳ τῆς ἀνθρωπίνης ἐπιβολῆς P: corr. Ruhnken   10 εἰ Faber: ἢ P
17 γηγενοῦς Markland: γένους P   αὐτομάτου Haupt: αὐτοῦ μόνου P
24 παντὸς Pearce: πάντες P   30 ⟨τὰ⟩ τῶν ἄλλων Lebègue

ΠΕΡΙ ΥΨΟΥΣ

μέγιστοι παραπτώματα πάντα ὁμόσε συναθροίσειεν, ἐλάχιστον ἄν τι, μᾶλλον δ' οὐδὲ πολλοστημόριον ἂν εὑρεθείη τῶν ἐκείνοις τοῖς ἥρωσι πάντη κατορθουμένων; διὰ ταῦθ' ὁ πᾶς αὐτοῖς αἰὼν καὶ βίος, οὐ δυνάμενος ὑπὸ τοῦ φθόνου παρανοίας ἁλῶναι, φέρων ἀπέδωκε τὰ νικητήρια, καὶ ἄχρι νῦν ἀναφαίρετα φυλάττει, καὶ ἔοικε τηρήσειν

ἔστ' ἂν ὕδωρ τε ῥέῃ καὶ δένδρεα μακρὰ τεθήλῃ.

πρὸς μέντοι γε τὸν γράφοντα ὡς ὁ Κολοσσὸς ὁ ἡμαρτημένος οὐ 3 κρείττων ἢ ὁ Πολυκλείτου Δορυφόρος παράκειται πρὸς πολλοῖς εἰπεῖν ὅτι ἐπὶ μὲν τέχνης θαυμάζεται τὸ ἀκριβέστατον, ἐπὶ δὲ τῶν φυσικῶν ἔργων τὸ μέγεθος, φύσει δὲ λογικὸν ὁ ἄνθρωπος· κἀπὶ μὲν ἀνδριάντων ζητεῖται τὸ ὅμοιον ἀνθρώπῳ, ἐπὶ δὲ τοῦ λόγου τὸ ὑπεραῖρον, ὡς ἔφην, τὰ ἀνθρώπινα. προσήκει δ' ὅμως (ἀνα- 4 κάμπτει γὰρ ἐπὶ τὴν ἀρχὴν ἡμῖν τοῦ ὑπομνήματος ἡ παραίνεσις), ἐπειδὴ τὸ μὲν ἀδιάπτωτον ὡς ἐπὶ τὸ πολὺ τέχνης ἐστὶ κατόρθωμα, τὸ δ' ἐν ὑπεροχῇ, πλὴν οὐχ ὁμότονον, μεγαλοφυΐας, βοήθημα τῇ φύσει πάντη πορίζεσθαι τὴν τέχνην· ἡ γὰρ ἀλληλουχία τούτων ἴσως γένοιτ' ἂν τὸ τέλειον.

Τοσαῦτα ἦν ἀναγκαῖον ὑπὲρ τῶν προτεθέντων ἐπικρῖναι σκεμμάτων· χαιρέτω δ' ἕκαστος οἷς ἥδεται.

Ταῖς δὲ μεταφοραῖς γειτνιῶσιν (ἐπανιτέον γάρ) αἱ παραβολαὶ 37 καὶ εἰκόνες, ἐκείνῃ μόνον παραλλάττουσαι . . .

. . . στοι καὶ αἱ τοιαῦται· "εἰ μὴ τὸν ἐγκέφαλον ἐν ταῖς πτέρναις 38 καταπεπατημένον φορεῖτε." διόπερ εἰδέναι χρὴ τὸ μέχρι ποῦ παρoριστέον ἕκαστον· τὸ γὰρ ἐνίοτε περαιτέρω προεκπίπτειν ἀναιρεῖ τὴν ὑπερβολὴν καὶ τὰ τοιαῦτα ὑπερτεινόμενα χαλᾶται,

7 cf. Pl. Phaedr. 264D, Anth. Pal. 7. 153, Diog. Laert. 1. 6. 89   23 sq. [Dem.] 7. 45: cf. Plu. de def. or. 425B

7 ὄφρ' ἂν . . . νάῃ Pl., Anth. Pal.   17 πάντη Tollius: παντὶ P
22 desunt duo folia in P   23 ⟨καταγέλα⟩στοι Dobree   εἴπερ ὑμεῖς τὸν ἐγκέφαλον ἐν τοῖς κροτάφοις καὶ μὴ κ.τ.λ. codd. Dem.   24 μέχρι ποῦ] num μέχρι πόσου?   25 παροριστέον suspectum: προοιστέον Seager; num προσοιστέον?

2 ἔσθ' ὅτε δὲ καὶ εἰς ὑπεναντιώσεις ἀντιπερίσταται. ὁ γοῦν Ἰσοκράτης οὐκ οἶδ' ὅπως παιδὸς πρᾶγμα ἔπαθε διὰ τὴν τοῦ πάντα αὐξητικῶς ἐθέλειν λέγειν φιλοτιμίαν. ἔστι μὲν γὰρ ὑπόθεσις αὐτῷ τοῦ Πανηγυρικοῦ λόγου ὡς ἡ Ἀθηναίων πόλις ταῖς εἰς τοὺς Ἕλληνας εὐεργεσίαις ὑπερβάλλει τὴν Λακεδαιμονίων, ὁ δ' εὐθὺς ἐν τῇ εἰσβολῇ ταῦτα τίθησιν· "ἔπειθ' οἱ λόγοι τοσαύτην ἔχουσι δύναμιν, ὥσθ' οἷόν τ' εἶναι καὶ τὰ μεγάλα ταπεινὰ ποιῆσαι καὶ τοῖς μικροῖς περιθεῖναι μέγεθος, καὶ τὰ παλαιὰ καινῶς εἰπεῖν καὶ περὶ τῶν νεωστὶ γεγενημένων ἀρχαίως διελθεῖν." οὐκοῦν, φησί τις, Ἰσόκρατες, οὕτως μέλλεις καὶ τὰ περὶ Λακεδαιμονίων καὶ Ἀθηναίων ἐναλλάττειν; σχεδὸν γὰρ τὸ τῶν λόγων ἐγκώμιον ἀπιστίας τῆς καθ' αὑτοῦ τοῖς ἀκούουσι παράγγελμα καὶ προοίμιον 3 ἐξέθηκε. μήποτ' οὖν ἄρισται τῶν ὑπερβολῶν, ὡς καὶ ἐπὶ τῶν σχημάτων προείπομεν, αἱ αὐτὸ τοῦτο διαλανθάνουσαι ὅτι εἰσὶν ὑπερβολαί. γίνεται δὲ τὸ τοιόνδε ἐπειδὰν ὑπὸ ἐκπαθείας μεγέθει τινὶ συνεκφωνῶνται περιστάσεως, ὅπερ ὁ Θουκυδίδης ἐπὶ τῶν ἐν Σικελίᾳ φθειρομένων ποιεῖ. "οἵ τε γὰρ Συρακούσιοι" φησίν "ἐπικαταβάντες τοὺς ἐν τῷ ποταμῷ μάλιστα ἔσφαζον, καὶ τὸ ὕδωρ εὐθὺς διέφθαρτο· ἀλλ' οὐδὲν ἧσσον ἐπίνετο ὁμοῦ τῷ πηλῷ ᾑματωμένον καὶ τοῖς πολλοῖς ἔτι ἦν περιμάχητον." αἷμα καὶ πηλὸν πινόμενα ὅμως εἶναι περιμάχητα ἔτι ποιεῖ πιστὸν ἡ τοῦ 4 πάθους ὑπεροχὴ καὶ περίστασις. καὶ τὸ Ἡροδότειον ἐπὶ τῶν ἐν Θερμοπύλαις ὅμοιον. "ἐν τούτῳ" φησίν "ἀλεξομένους μαχαίρῃσιν, ὅσοις αὐτῶν ἔτι ἐτύγχανον περιοῦσαι, καὶ χερσὶ καὶ στόμασι κατέχωσαν οἱ βάρβαροι ⟨βάλλοντες⟩." ἐνταῦθ' οἷόν ἐστι

6 sqq. Isocr. *Paneg.* 8: ἐπειδὴ δ' οἱ λόγοι τοιαύτην ἔχουσι τὴν φύσιν ὥσθ' οἷόν τ' εἶναι περὶ τῶν αὐτῶν πολλαχῶς ἐξηγήσασθαι καὶ τά τε μεγάλα ταπεινὰ ποιῆσαι καὶ τοῖς μικροῖς μέγεθος περιθεῖναι, καὶ τά τε παλαιὰ καινῶς διελθεῖν καὶ περὶ τῶν νεωστὶ γεγενημένων ἀρχαίως εἰπεῖν   17 sqq. Thuc. 7. 84   23 sqq. Herod. 7. 225

5 Λακεδαιμονίαν P : corr. Rob.   10 φήσει Tollius   12 ⟨πλείσ⟩της Lebègue   16 ⟨πρὸς τῆς⟩ περιστάσεως Photiades   17 οἵ τε Πελοποννήσιοι ἐπικαταβάντες codd. Thuc.   Συρακούσιοι] rectius Συρακόσιοι, cf. Meisterhans *Gramm. Att. Inschr.*, p. 21   20 καὶ περιμάχητον ἦν τοῖς πολλοῖς codd. Thuc.   25 κατέχωσαν Man. ex Her.: κατίσχυσαν P   ⟨βάλλοντες⟩ add. Man. ex Her.

τὸ καὶ στόμασι μάχεσθαι πρὸς ὡπλισμένους καὶ ὁποῖόν τι τὸ κατακεχῶσθαι βέλεσιν ἐρεῖς, πλὴν ὅμως ἔχει πίστιν· οὐ γὰρ τὸ πρᾶγμα ἕνεκα τῆς ὑπερβολῆς παραλαμβάνεσθαι δοκεῖ, ἡ ὑπερβολὴ δ᾽ εὐλόγως γεννᾶσθαι πρὸς τοῦ πράγματος. ἔστι γάρ, ὡς 5 οὐ διαλείπω λέγων, παντὸς τολμήματος λεκτικοῦ λύσις καὶ πανάκειά τις τὰ ἐγγὺς ἐκστάσεως ἔργα καὶ πάθη· ὅθεν καὶ τὰ κωμικά, καίτοιγ᾽ εἰς ἀπιστίαν ἐκπίπτοντα, πιθανὰ διὰ τὸ γελοῖον·

ἀγρὸν ἔσχ᾽ ἐλάττω γῆν ἔχοντ᾽ ἐπιστολῆς ⟨Λακωνικῆς⟩.

καὶ γὰρ ὁ γέλως πάθος ἐν ἡδονῇ. αἱ δ᾽ ὑπερβολαὶ καθάπερ ἐπὶ τὸ 6 μεῖζον οὕτως καὶ ἐπὶ τοὔλαττον, ἐπειδὴ κοινὸν ἀμφοῖν ἡ ἐπίτασις· καί πως ὁ διασυρμὸς ταπεινότητός ἐστιν αὔξησις.

Ἡ πέμπτη μοῖρα τῶν συντελουσῶν εἰς τὸ ὕψος, ὧν γε ἐν 39 ἀρχῇ προὐθέμεθα, ἔθ᾽ ἡμῖν λείπεται, κράτιστε, ἡ δὲ τῶν λόγων αὕτη ποιὰ σύνθεσις. ὑπὲρ ἧς ἐν δυσὶν ἀποχρώντως ἀποδεδωκότες συντάγμασιν, ὅσα γε τῆς θεωρίας ἦν ἡμῖν ἐφικτά, τοσοῦτον ἐξ ἀνάγκης προσθείημεν ἂν εἰς τὴν παροῦσαν ὑπόθεσιν, ὡς οὐ μόνον ἐστὶ πειθοῦς καὶ ἡδονῆς ἡ ἁρμονία φυσικὸν ἀνθρώποις, ἀλλὰ καὶ μεγαληγορίας καὶ πάθους θαυμαστόν τι ὄργανον. οὐ γὰρ αὐλὸς 2 μὲν ἐντίθησί τινα πάθη τοῖς ἀκροωμένοις καὶ οἷον ἔκφρονας καὶ κορυβαντιασμοῦ πλήρεις ἀποτελεῖ, καὶ βάσιν ἐνδούς τινα ῥυθμοῦ πρὸς ταύτην ἀναγκάζει βαίνειν ἐν ῥυθμῷ καὶ συνεξομοιοῦσθαι τῷ μέλει τὸν ἀκροατήν, "κἂν ἄμουσος ᾖ" παντάπασι, καὶ νὴ Δία φθόγγοι κιθάρας, οὐδὲν ἁπλῶς σημαίνοντες, ταῖς τῶν ἤχων μεταβολαῖς καὶ τῇ πρὸς ἀλλήλους κράσει καὶ μίξει τῆς συμφωνίας θαυμαστὸν ἐπάγουσι πολλάκις, ὡς ἐπίστασαι, θέλγητρον | (καίτοι 3

8 fr. com. adesp. 417-19 Kock   22 Eur. *Stheneboea*, fr. 663 Nauck²

---

4 εὐλόγως Rob.: εὐλόγους P   6 ἐκστάσεως Portus: ἐξετάσεως P   8 ἔχοντ᾽ ἐπιστολῆς ⟨Λακωνικῆς⟩ Valckenaer: ἔχον γὰρ στολῆς P   13 ἦν δὲ scripsi: ἡ διὰ P: διὰ del. Pearce   14 αὕτη P: αὐτὴ Spengel   18 μεγαληγορίας Tollius: μετ᾽ ἐλευθερίας P   οὐ] ὅπου Wenkebach: εἰ Photiades   20 ῥυθμοῦ del. Valckenaer   22 ἄμουσος ᾖ Boivin: ἄλλους ὅση P   24 κράσει K marg.: κρούσει P   25 ἐπίστασαι Faber: ἐπίστασιν P

48 ΠΕΡΙ ΥΨΟΥΣ [39. 3–

ταῦτα εἴδωλα καὶ μιμήματα νόθα ἐστὶ πειθοῦς, οὐχὶ τῆς ἀνθρωπείας φύσεως, ὡς ἔφην, ἐνεργήματα γνήσια), οὐκ οἰόμεθα δ' ἄρα τὴν σύνθεσιν, ἁρμονίαν τινὰ οὖσαν λόγων ἀνθρώποις ἐμφύτων καὶ τῆς ψυχῆς αὐτῆς, οὐχὶ τῆς ἀκοῆς μόνης ἐφαπτομένων, ποικίλας κινοῦσαν ἰδέας ὀνομάτων νοήσεων πραγμάτων κάλλους εὐμελείας, 5 πάντων ἡμῖν ἐντρόφων καὶ συγγενῶν, καὶ ἅμα τῇ μίξει καὶ πολυμορφίᾳ τῶν ἑαυτῆς φθόγγων τὸ παρεστὼς τῷ λέγοντι πάθος εἰς τὰς ψυχὰς τῶν πέλας παρεισάγουσαν καὶ εἰς μετουσίαν αὐτοῦ τοὺς ἀκούοντας ἀεὶ καθιστᾶσαν, τῇ τε τῶν λέξεων ἐποικοδομήσει τὰ μεγέθη συναρμόζουσαν, δι' αὐτῶν τούτων κηλεῖν τε ὁμοῦ καὶ 10 πρὸς ὄγκον τε καὶ ἀξίωμα καὶ ὕψος καὶ πᾶν ὃ ἐν αὐτῇ περιλαμβάνει καὶ ἡμᾶς ἑκάστοτε συνδιατιθέναι, παντοίως ἡμῶν τῆς διανοίας ἐπικρατοῦσαν; ἀλλ' εἰ καὶ μανία τὸ περὶ τῶν οὕτως ὁμολογου-
4 μένων διαπορεῖν, ἀποχρῶσα γὰρ ἡ πεῖρα πίστις, | ὑψηλόν γέ που δοκεῖ νόημα καὶ ἔστι τῷ ὄντι θαυμάσιον, ὃ τῷ ψηφίσματι ὁ 15 Δημοσθένης ἐπιφέρει· "τοῦτο τὸ ψήφισμα τὸν τότε τῇ πόλει περιστάντα κίνδυνον παρελθεῖν ἐποίησεν ὥσπερ νέφος·" ἀλλ' αὐτῆς τῆς διανοίας οὐκ ἔλαττον τῇ ἁρμονίᾳ πεφώνηται. ὅλον τε γὰρ ἐπὶ τῶν δακτυλικῶν εἴρηται ῥυθμῶν, εὐγενέστατοι δ' οὗτοι καὶ μεγεθοποιοί· διὸ καὶ τὸ ἡρῷον ὧν ἴσμεν κάλλιστον μέτρον 20 συνιστᾶσι· τό τε * * * ἐπείτοιγε ἐκ τῆς ἰδίας αὐτὸ χώρας μετάθες ὅποι δὴ ἐθέλεις, "τοῦτο τὸ ψήφισμα ὥσπερ νέφος ἐποίησε τὸν τότε κίνδυνον παρελθεῖν," ἢ νὴ Δία μίαν ἀπόκοψον συλλαβὴν μόνον "ἐποίησε παρελθεῖν ὡς νέφος," καὶ εἴσῃ πόσον ἡ ἁρμονία τῷ ὕψει συνηχεῖ. αὐτὸ γὰρ τὸ "ὥσπερ νέφος" ἐπὶ μακροῦ τοῦ 25 πρώτου ῥυθμοῦ βέβηκε, τέτρασι καταμετρουμένου χρόνοις· ἐξαιρεθείσης δὲ τῆς μιᾶς συλλαβῆς "ὡς νέφος" εὐθὺς ἀκρωτηριάζει

16 Dem. 18. 188

3 ἐμφύτων Man.: ἐμφύτοις P: ἔμφυτον Bake   4 ἐφαπτομένων P: ἐφαπτομένην Faber   10 κηλεῖν Rob.: καλεῖν P   11 αὐτῇ Tollius: αὐτῇ P   14–15 που δοκεῖ Reiske: τοῦ δοκεῖν P   18 πεφώνηται] πεφώτισται Rohde   21 post τό τε lacunam ind. Pearce   23 τότε Man. ex Dem.: τότ' ἐν P   26 καταμετρουμένου Tollius: καταμετρούμενον P   27 ἀκρωτηριάζει P: ἀκρωτηριάζεται Tollius: ἀκρωτηριάζεις Lebègue

τῇ συγκοπῇ τὸ μέγεθος· ὡς ἔμπαλιν, ἐὰν ἐπεκτείνῃς "παρελθεῖν ἐποίησεν ὥσπερ⟨εἰ⟩ νέφος," τὸ αὐτὸ σημαίνει, οὐ τὸ αὐτὸ δὲ ἔτι προσπίπτει, ὅτι τῷ μήκει τῶν ἄκρων χρόνων συνεκλύεται καὶ διαχαλᾶται τὸ ὕψος τὸ ἀπότομον.

5 Ἐν δὲ τοῖς μάλιστα μεγεθοποιεῖ τὰ λεγόμενα, καθάπερ τὰ **40** σώματα ἡ τῶν μελῶν ἐπισύνθεσις, ὧν ἓν μὲν οὐδὲν τμηθὲν ἀφ' ἑτέρου καθ' ἑαυτὸ ἀξιόλογον ἔχει, πάντα δὲ μετ' ἀλλήλων ἐκπληροῖ τέλειον σύστημα, οὕτως τὰ μεγάλα σκεδασθέντα μὲν ἀπ' ἀλλήλων ἄλλοσ' ἄλλῃ ἅμα ἑαυτοῖς συνδιαφορεῖ καὶ τὸ ὕψος,
10 σωματοποιούμενα δὲ τῇ κοινωνίᾳ καὶ ἔτι δεσμῷ τῆς ἁρμονίας περικλειόμενα αὐτῷ τῷ κύκλῳ φωνήεντα γίνεται· καὶ σχεδὸν ἐν ταῖς περιόδοις ἔρανός ἐστι πλήθους τὰ μεγέθη. ἀλλὰ μὴν ὅτι γε 2 πολλοὶ καὶ συγγραφέων καὶ ποιητῶν οὐκ ὄντες ὑψηλοὶ φύσει, μήποτε δὲ καὶ ἀμεγέθεις, ὅμως κοινοῖς καὶ δημώδεσι τοῖς ὀνόμασι
15 καὶ οὐδὲν ἐπαγομένοις περιττὸν ὡς τὰ πολλὰ συγχρώμενοι, διὰ μόνου τοῦ συνθεῖναι καὶ ἁρμόσαι ταῦτα †δ' ὅμως† ὄγκον καὶ διάστημα καὶ τὸ μὴ ταπεινοὶ δοκεῖν εἶναι περιεβάλοντο, καθάπερ ἄλλοι τε πολλοὶ καὶ Φίλιστος, Ἀριστοφάνης ἔν τισιν, ἐν τοῖς πλείστοις Εὐριπίδης, ἱκανῶς ἡμῖν δεδήλωται. μετά γέ τοι τὴν 3
20 τεκνοκτονίαν Ἡρακλῆς φησι

γέμω κακῶν δὴ κοὐκέτ' ἔσθ' ὅποι τεθῇ.

σφόδρα δημῶδες τὸ λεγόμενον, ἀλλὰ γέγονεν ὑψηλὸν τῇ πλάσει ἀναλογοῦν· εἰ δ' ἄλλως αὐτὸ συναρμόσεις, φανήσεταί σοι διότι τῆς συνθέσεως ποιητὴς ὁ Εὐριπίδης μᾶλλόν ἐστιν ἢ τοῦ νοῦ. ἐπὶ δὲ 4
25 τῆς συρομένης ὑπὸ τοῦ ταύρου Δίρκης,

21 Eur. *HF* 1245

---

2 ὥσπερ⟨εἰ⟩ Tollius: ὥσπερ P   4 τὸ ὕψος] τοῦ ὕψους Toup
9 ἄλλοσ' ἄλλῃ Vahlen: ἄλλοσ' P, suprascr. ἄλλῃ p   12 γε Tollius: τε P   14 ὅμως] fortasse ὅλως (cum ἀμεγέθεις coniungendum), si ὅμως (16) vera est lectio   16 ταῦτα †δ' ὅμως†] ταῦτα ὅμως Rob.: num ταῦτά γ' ὅμως?: ταῦτα δολίως Immisch   22–23 τῇ πλάσει ἀναλογοῦν] τῇ ἀνάλογον πλάσει Kayser   24 ἐπὶ Man.: ἐπεὶ P

ΠΕΡΙ ΥΨΟΥΣ

εἰ δέ που τύχοι
πέριξ ἑλίξας ... εἶλχ' ὁμοῦ λαβών,
γυναῖκα πέτραν δρῦν μεταλλάσσων ἀεί,

ἔστι μὲν γενναῖον καὶ τὸ λῆμμα, ἁδρότερον δὲ γέγονε τῷ τὴν ἁρμονίαν μὴ κατεσπεῦσθαι μηδ' οἷον ἐν ἀποκυλίσματι φέρεσθαι, ἀλλὰ στηριγμούς τε ἔχειν πρὸς ἄλληλα τὰ ὀνόματα καὶ ἐξερείσματα τῶν χρόνων πρὸς ἑδραῖον διαβεβηκότα μέγεθος.

41 Μικροποιὸν δ' οὐδὲν οὕτως ἐν τοῖς ὑψηλοῖς ὡς ῥυθμὸς κεκλασμένος λόγων καὶ σεσοβημένος, οἷον δὴ πυρρίχιοι καὶ τροχαῖοι καὶ διχόρειοι, τέλεον εἰς ὀρχηστικὸν συνεκπίπτοντες· εὐθὺς γὰρ πάντα φαίνεται τὰ κατάρρυθμα κομψὰ καὶ μικροχαρῆ, [καὶ] ἀπαθέστατα διὰ τῆς ὁμοειδείας ἐπιπολάζοντα· καὶ ἔτι τούτων τὸ χείριστον, ὅτι, ὥσπερ τὰ ᾠδάρια τοὺς ἀκροατὰς ἀπὸ τοῦ πράγματος ἀφέλκει καὶ ἐφ' αὑτὰ βιάζεται, οὕτως καὶ τὰ κατερρυθμισμένα τῶν λεγομένων οὐ τὸ τοῦ λόγου πάθος ἐνδίδωσι τοῖς ἀκούουσι, τὸ δὲ τοῦ ῥυθμοῦ, ὡς ἐνίοτε προειδότας τὰς ὀφειλομένας καταλήξεις αὐτοὺς ὑποκρούειν τοῖς λέγουσι καὶ φθάνοντας ὡς ἐν χορῷ τινι προαποδιδόναι τὴν βάσιν.

3 Ὁμοίως δὲ ἀμεγέθη καὶ τὰ λίαν συγκείμενα καὶ εἰς μικρὰ καὶ βραχυσύλλαβα συγκεκομμένα καὶ ὡσανεὶ γόμφοις τισὶν ἐπαλλήλοις κατ' ἐγκοπὰς καὶ σκληρότητας ἐπισυνδεδεμένα.

42 Ἔτι γε μὴν ὕψους μειωτικὸν καὶ ἡ ἄγαν τῆς φράσεως συγκοπή· πηροῖ γὰρ τὸ μέγεθος ὅταν εἰς λίαν συνάγηται βραχύ· ἀκουέσθω δὲ νῦν μὴ τὰ [οὐ] δεόντως συνεστραμμένα, ἀλλ' ὅσα ἄντικρυς μικρὰ καὶ κατακεκερματισμένα· συγκοπὴ μὲν γὰρ κολούει τὸν

1 sqq. Eur. *Antiope*, fr. 221 Nauck²

2 ⟨ταῦρος⟩ εἶλχ' Valckenaer: εἷλκε ⟨πάνθ'⟩ Bergk 4 λῆμμα Rob.: λῆμα P 8 μικροποιὸν Photiades: μικροποιοῦν P 11 κατάρυθμα P: corr. Schurzfleisch [καὶ] seclusi 12 ὁμοειδ.ίας P ὅτι Man.: ὅπως P 19 συγκείμενα] συνηγμένα Kayser 23 πηροῖ Man.: πληροῖ P 24 [οὐ] del. Man. 25 κολούει Faber: κωλούει P

νοῦν, συντομία δ' †ἐπ' εὐθύ†. δῆλον δ' ὡς ἔμπαλιν τὰ ἐκτάδην· ἀπόψυχα τὰ παρὰ καιρὸν μῆκος ἀνακαλούμενα.

Δεινὴ δ' αἰσχῦναι τὰ μεγέθη καὶ ἡ μικρότης τῶν ὀνομάτων. **43** παρὰ γοῦν τῷ Ἡροδότῳ κατὰ μὲν τὰ λήμματα δαιμονίως ὁ χειμὼν πέφρασται, τινὰ δὲ νὴ Δία περιέχει τῆς ὕλης ἀδοξότερα, καὶ τοῦτο μὲν ἴσως "ζεσάσης δὲ τῆς θαλάσσης," ὡς τὸ "ζεσάσης" πολὺ τὸ ὕψος περισπᾷ διὰ τὸ κακόστομον· ἀλλ' "ὁ ἄνεμος" φησίν "ἐκοπίασε", καὶ τοὺς περὶ τὸ ναυάγιον βρασσομένους ἐξεδέχετο "τέλος ἀχάριστον". ἄσεμνον γὰρ τὸ κοπιάσαι ⟨καὶ⟩ ἰδιωτικόν, τὸ δ' ἀχάριστον τηλικούτου πάθους ἀνοίκειον. ὁμοίως **2** καὶ ὁ Θεόπομπος ὑπερφυῶς σκευάσας τὴν τοῦ Πέρσου κατάβασιν ἐπ' Αἴγυπτον ὀνοματίοις τισὶ τὰ ὅλα διέβαλε. "ποία γὰρ πόλις ἢ ποῖον ἔθνος τῶν κατὰ τὴν Ἀσίαν οὐκ ἐπρεσβεύετο πρὸς βασιλέα; τί δὲ τῶν ἐκ τῆς γῆς γεννωμένων ἢ τῶν κατὰ τέχνην ἐπιτελουμένων καλῶν ἢ τιμίων οὐκ ἐκομίσθη δῶρον ὡς αὐτόν; οὐ πολλαὶ μὲν καὶ πολυτελεῖς στρωμναὶ καὶ χλανίδες (τὰ μὲν ἁλουργῆ, τὰ δὲ ποικιλτά, τὰ δὲ λευκά), πολλαὶ δὲ σκηναὶ χρυσαῖ κατεσκευασμέναι πᾶσι τοῖς χρησίμοις, πολλαὶ δὲ καὶ ξυστίδες καὶ κλῖναι πολυτελεῖς; ἔτι δὲ καὶ κοῖλος ἄργυρος καὶ χρυσὸς ἀπειργασμένος καὶ ἐκπώματα καὶ κρατῆρες, ὧν τοὺς μὲν λιθοκολλήτους, τοὺς δ' ἄλλους ἀκριβῶς καὶ πολυτελῶς εἶδες ἂν ἐκπεπονημένους. πρὸς δὲ τούτοις ἀναρίθμητοι μὲν ὅπλων μυριάδες τῶν μὲν Ἑλληνικῶν, τῶν δὲ βαρβαρικῶν, ὑπερβάλλοντα δὲ τὸ πλῆθος ὑποζύγια καὶ πρὸς κατακοπὴν ἱερεῖα σιτευτά, καὶ πολλοὶ μὲν ἀρτυμάτων

---

4 sqq. Herod. 7. 188, 191   9 Herod. 8. 13   12–p. 52, 5 Theopomp. F 263 FGrHist 115: cf. Athen. 2, p. 67F

1 †ἐπ' εὐθύ†] ἐπ' εὐθὺ ⟨ἄγει⟩ Stephanus: ἐπευθύνει Petra   1–2 locus valde dubius. post ἐκτάδην ego, post ἀπόψυχα interpungunt plerique. sed fortasse praestat ⟨τὰ⟩ ante ἐκτάδην delere   2 παρὰ καιρὸν] παρ' ἄκαιρον Pearce   ἀνακαλούμενα] ἀναχαλώμενα Toup: num ἀνακυκλούμενα?   7 τὸ ὕψος] τοῦ ὕψους Reiske   8–9 ἐκοπίασε... κοπιάσαι] ἐκόπασε... κοπάσαι codd. Herod.   βρασσομένους Man.: δρασσομένους P: ἀρασσομένους Valckenaer   9 ἀχάριστον] ἄχαρι codd. Herod.   ⟨καὶ⟩ add. Rob.   15 τιμίων Man.: τιμῶν P   24 σιτευτά Canter: εἰς ταῦτα P

ΠΕΡΙ ΥΨΟΥΣ

μέδιμνοι, πολλοὶ δὲ [οἱ] θύλακοι καὶ σάκκοι καὶ χύτραι βιβλίων καὶ τῶν ἄλλων ἁπάντων χρησίμων· τοσαῦτα δὲ κρέα τεταριχευμένα παντοδαπῶν ἱερείων ὡς σωροὺς αὐτῶν γενέσθαι τηλικούτους ὥστε τοὺς προσιόντας πόρρωθεν ὑπολαμβάνειν ὄχθους εἶναι καὶ λόφους ἀντωθουμένους." ἐκ τῶν ὑψηλοτέρων εἰς τὰ ταπεινότερα ἀποδιδράσκει, δέον ποιήσασθαι τὴν αὔξησιν ἔμπαλιν· ἀλλὰ τῇ θαυμαστῇ τῆς ὅλης παρασκευῆς ἀγγελίᾳ παραμίξας τοὺς θυλάκους καὶ τὰ ἀρτύματα καὶ τὰ σακκία μαγειρείου τινὰ φαντασίαν ἐποίησεν. ὥσπερ γάρ, εἴ τις ἐπ' αὐτῶν ἐκείνων τῶν προσκοσμημάτων μεταξὺ τῶν χρυσίων καὶ λιθοκολλήτων κρατήρων καὶ ἀργύρου κοίλου σκηνῶν τε ὁλοχρύσων καὶ ἐκπωμάτων φέρων μέσα ἔθηκε θυλάκια καὶ σακκία, ἀπρεπὲς ἂν ἦν τῇ προσόψει τὸ ἔργον, οὕτω καὶ τῆς ἑρμηνείας τὰ τοιαῦτα ὀνόματα αἴσχη καὶ οἱονεὶ στίγματα καθίσταται παρὰ καιρὸν ἐγκατατατττόμενα. παρέκειτο δ' ὡς ὁλοσχερῶς ἐπελθεῖν καὶ οὓς ὄχθους λέγει συμβεβλῆσθαι, καὶ περὶ τῆς ἄλλης παρασκευῆς οὕτως ἀλλάξας εἰπεῖν καμήλους καὶ πλῆθος ὑποζυγίων φορταγωγούντων πάντα τὰ πρὸς τρυφὴν καὶ ἀπόλαυσιν τραπεζῶν χορηγήματα, ἢ σωροὺς ὀνομάσαι παντοίων σπερμάτων καὶ τῶν ἅπερ διαφέρει πρὸς ὀψοποιίας καὶ ἡδυπαθείας, ἢ εἴπερ πάντως ἐβούλετο †αὐτάρκη οὕτως θεῖναι, καὶ ὅσα τραπεζοκόμων εἰπεῖν καὶ ὀψοποιῶν ἡδύσματα. οὐ γὰρ δεῖ καταντᾶν ἐν τοῖς ὕψεσιν ⟨εἰς τὰ ῥυ⟩παρὰ καὶ ἐξυβρισμένα, ἂν μὴ σφόδρα ὑπό τινος ἀνάγκης συνδιωκώμεθα, ἀλλὰ τῶν πραγμάτων πρέποι ἂν καὶ τὰς φωνὰς ἔχειν ἀξίας καὶ μιμεῖσθαι τὴν δημιουργήσασαν φύσιν τὸν ἄνθρωπον, ἥτις ἐν ἡμῖν τὰ μέρη τὰ ἀπόρρητα οὐκ ἔθηκεν ἐν προσώπῳ οὐδὲ τὰ τοῦ παντὸς ὄγκου περιηθήματα, ἀπεκρύψατο δὲ ὡς ἐνῆν καὶ κατὰ τὸν Ξενοφῶντα

---

27 Xen. *Mem.* I. 4. 6

1 [οἱ] om. Athen. καὶ χύτραι Toup : καὶ χάρται P : om. Athen. βιβλίων P, Athen. : βολβῶν Toup   2 τοσαῦτα Rob. : τοιαῦτα P   9 ἐποίησεν] ἐνεποίησεν Rothstein   15 οὓς] ὡς Spengel   16 ἀλλάξας] ἁμάξας Toup   17 ⟨καὶ⟩ καμήλους Toup   19 ἅπερ] ὅσαπερ Richards   20 †αὐτάρκη οὕτως] αὐτὰ ῥητῶς (sive ῥητῶς οὕτως) Richards   22 ⟨εἰς τὰ ῥυ⟩παρὰ Pearce, post Man.   27 περιηθήματα Pearce : περιθήματα P

ΠΕΡΙ ΥΨΟΥΣ

τοὺς τούτων ὅτι πορρωτάτω ὀχετοὺς ἀπέστρεψεν, οὐδαμῇ καταισχύνασα τὸ τοῦ ὅλου ζῴου κάλλος.

Ἀλλὰ γὰρ οὐκ ἐπ᾽ εἴδους ἐπείγει τὰ μικροποιὰ διαριθμεῖν· 6 προϋποδεδειγμένων γὰρ τῶν ὅσα εὐγενεῖς καὶ ὑψηλοὺς ἐργάζεται τοὺς λόγους, δῆλον ὡς τὰ ἐναντία τούτων ταπεινοὺς ποιήσει κατὰ τὸ πλεῖστον καὶ ἀσχήμονας.

Ἐκεῖνο μέντοι λοιπὸν ἕνεκα τῆς σῆς χρηστομαθείας οὐκ 44 ὀκνήσομεν †ἐπιπροσθῆναι, διασαφῆσαι, Τερεντιανὲ φίλτατε, ὅπερ ἐζήτησέ τις τῶν φιλοσόφων πρὸς ⟨ἔμ᾽⟩ ἔναγχος, "θαῦμά μ᾽ ἔχει" λέγων "ὡς ἀμέλει καὶ ἑτέρους πολλούς, πῶς ποτε κατὰ τὸν ἡμέτερον αἰῶνα πιθαναὶ μὲν ἐπ᾽ ἄκρον καὶ πολιτικαί, δριμεῖαί τε καὶ ἐντρεχεῖς καὶ μάλιστα πρὸς ἡδονὰς λόγων εὔφοροι, ὑψηλαὶ δὲ λίαν καὶ ὑπερμεγέθεις, πλὴν εἰ μή τι σπάνιον, οὐκέτι γίνονται φύσεις. τοσαύτη λόγων κοσμική τις ἐπέχει τὸν βίον ἀφορία. ἢ 2 νὴ Δί᾽" ἔφη "πιστευτέον ἐκείνῳ τῷ θρυλουμένῳ, ὡς ἡ δημοκρατία τῶν μεγάλων ἀγαθὴ τιθηνός, ᾗ μόνῃ σχεδὸν καὶ συνήκμασαν οἱ περὶ λόγους δεινοὶ καὶ συναπέθανον; θρέψαι τε γάρ, φησίν, ἱκανὴ τὰ φρονήματα τῶν μεγαλοφρόνων ἡ ἐλευθερία καὶ ἐπελπίσαι, καὶ ἅμα διεγείρειν τὸ πρόθυμον τῆς πρὸς ἀλλήλους ἔριδος καὶ τῆς περὶ τὰ πρωτεῖα φιλοτιμίας. ἔτι γε μὴν διὰ τὰ 3 προκείμενα ἐν ταῖς πολιτείαις ἔπαθλα ἑκάστοτε τὰ ψυχικὰ προτερήματα τῶν ῥητόρων μελετώμενα ἀκονᾶται καὶ οἷον ἐκτρίβεται καὶ τοῖς πράγμασι κατὰ τὸ εἰκὸς ἐλεύθερα συνεκλάμπει. οἱ δὲ νῦν ἐοίκαμεν" ἔφη "παιδομαθεῖς εἶναι δουλείας δικαίας, τοῖς αὐτοῖς ἔθεσι καὶ ἐπιτηδεύμασιν ἐξ ἁπαλῶν ἔτι φρονημάτων μόνον οὐκ ἐνεσπαργανωμένοι καὶ ἄγευστοι καλλίστου καὶ γονιμωτάτου λόγων νάματος, τὴν ἐλευθερίαν" ἔφη "λέγω· διόπερ οὐδὲν ὅτι μὴ κόλακες ἐκβαίνομεν μεγαλοφυεῖς." διὰ τοῦτο τὰς μὲν ἄλλας 4

1 τούτων Man.: τῶν P   3 ἐπ᾽ εἴδους Tollius: ἐπιδοὺς P: cf. 13. 3
8 †ἐπιπροσθῆναι] ἐπιπροσθεῖναι Man., quo accepto praestat vel ⟨καὶ⟩ διασαφῆσαι (Rob., Man.) vel διασαφῆσαί τε (Wilamowitz) scribere. num vero ἐκ προσθήκης?   9 πρὸς ⟨ἔμ᾽⟩ ἔναγχος Cobet: προσέναγχος P: προὔναγχος Valckenaer   13 δὲ Man.: τε P   18 φησίν P: φασίν Toup   19 διεγείρειν Morus: διελθεῖν P: διαίθειν Richards
24 αὑτοῖς P: αὐτῆς p, edd.

ἕξεις καὶ εἰς οἰκέτας πίπτειν ἔφασκε, δοῦλον δὲ μηδένα γίνεσθαι ῥήτορα. "εὐθὺς γὰρ ἀναζεῖ τὸ ἀπαρρησίαστον καὶ οἷον ἔμφρουρον ὑπὸ συνηθείας ἀεὶ κεκονδυλισμένον· "ἥμισυ γάρ τ' ἀρετῆς", κατὰ τὸν Ὅμηρον, "ἀποαίνυται δούλιον ἦμαρ." ὥσπερ οὖν, εἴ γε" φησί "τοῦτο πιστόν ἐστιν ἀκούω, τὰ γλωττόκομα, ἐν οἷς οἱ Πυγμαῖοι καλούμενοι δὲ νᾶνοι τρέφονται, οὐ μόνον κωλύει τῶν ἐγκεκλεισμένων τὰς αὐξήσεις, ἀλλὰ καὶ †συνάροι διὰ τὸν περικείμενον τοῖς σώμασι δεσμόν, οὕτως ἅπασαν δουλείαν, κἂν ᾖ δικαιοτάτη, ψυχῆς γλωττόκομον καὶ κοινὸν ἄν τις ἀποφήναιτο δεσμωτήριον." ἐγὼ μέντοι γε ὑπολαβών, "ῥᾴδιον" ἔφην "ὦ βέλτιστε, καὶ ἴδιον ἀνθρώπου τὸ καταμέμφεσθαι τὰ ἀεὶ παρόντα· ὅρα δὲ μήποτε οὐχ ἡ τῆς οἰκουμένης εἰρήνη διαφθείρει τὰς μεγάλας φύσεις, πολὺ δὲ μᾶλλον ὁ κατέχων ἡμῶν τὰς ἐπιθυμίας ἀπεριόριστος οὑτοσὶ πόλεμος, καὶ νὴ Δία πρὸς τούτῳ τὰ φρουροῦντα τὸν νῦν βίον καὶ κατ' ἄκρας ἄγοντα καὶ φέροντα ταυτὶ πάθη. ἡ γὰρ φιλοχρηματία, πρὸς ἣν ἅπαντες ἀπλήστως ἤδη νοσοῦμεν, καὶ ἡ φιληδονία δουλαγωγοῦσι, μᾶλλον δέ, ὡς ἂν εἴποι τις, καταβυθίζουσιν αὐτάνδρους ἤδη τοὺς βίους, φιλαργυρία μὲν νόσημα μικροποιὸν ⟨ὄν⟩, φιληδονία δ' ἀγεννέστατον. οὐ δὴ ἔχω λογιζόμενος εὑρεῖν ὡς οἷόν τε πλοῦτον ἀόριστον ἐκτιμήσαντας, τὸ δ' ἀληθέστερον εἰπεῖν ἐκθειάσαντας, τὰ συμφυῆ τούτῳ κακὰ εἰς τὰς ψυχὰς ἡμῶν ἐπεισιόντα μὴ παραδέχεσθαι. ἀκολουθεῖ γὰρ τῷ ἀμέτρῳ πλούτῳ καὶ ἀκολάστῳ συνημμένη καὶ ἴσα, φασί, βαίνουσα πολυτέλεια, καὶ ἅμα ἀνοίγοντος ἐκείνου τῶν

3-4 Hom. ρ 322-3:
ἥμισυ γάρ τ' ἀρετῆς ἀποαίνυται εὐρύοπα Ζεύς
ἀνέρος, εὖτ' ἄν μιν κατὰ δούλιον ἦμαρ ἕλῃσιν

---

2 ἀναζεῖ] ἀναζεῖν Weiske : num ἀναζῇ?   5 ἐστιν del. Pearce   ἀκούω Pearce : ἀκούω P   6 δὲ om. Man.   νᾶνοι Man. : νάοι P : γίννοι Immisch   7 †συνάροι] συναρθμοῖ Kaibel : σιναροῖ Meinel : συναραιοῖ Schmid   8 σώμασι Scaliger : στόμασι P   9 ἂν Spengel : δὴ P   ἀποφήναιτο p : ἀποφήνετο P   10 ὑπολαβών Bühler : ὑπολαμβάνω P : ὑπολαμβάνων Tollius   ἔφην Portus : ἔφη P   12 μήποτε οὐχ ἡ Spengel : μή πο****χ η*** P (τῆς add. p)   16 πρὸς]περὶ Wilamowitz   19 μικροποιὸν ⟨ὄν⟩ vel φιλαργυρία μὲν ⟨γὰρ⟩ Spengel   24 ἅμα Pearce ἄλλα P

ΠΕΡΙ ΥΨΟΥΣ

πόλεων καὶ οἴκων τὰς εἰσόδους †εἰς ἃς† ἐμβαίνει καὶ συνοικίζεται. χρονίσαντα δὲ ταῦτα ἐν τοῖς βίοις νεοττοποιεῖται, κατὰ τοὺς σοφούς, καὶ ταχέως γενόμενα περὶ τεκνοποιίαν πλεονεξίαν τε γεννῶσι καὶ τῦφον καὶ τρυφήν, οὐ νόθα ἑαυτῶν γεννήματα ἀλλὰ καὶ πάνυ γνήσια. ἐὰν δὲ καὶ τούτους τις τοῦ πλούτου τοὺς ἐκγόνους εἰς ἡλικίαν ἐλθεῖν ἐάσῃ, ταχέως δεσπότας ταῖς ψυχαῖς ἐντίκτουσιν ἀπαραιτήτους, ὕβριν καὶ παρανομίαν καὶ ἀναισχυντίαν. ταῦτα 8 γὰρ οὕτως ἀνάγκη γίνεσθαι καὶ μηκέτι τοὺς ἀνθρώπους ἀναβλέπειν μηδ' ὑστεροφημίας εἶναί τινα λόγον, ἀλλὰ τοιούτων ἐν κύκλῳ τελεσιουργεῖσθαι κατ' ὀλίγον τὴν τῶν βίων διαφθοράν, φθίνειν δὲ καὶ καταμαραίνεσθαι τὰ ψυχικὰ μεγέθη καὶ ἄζηλα γίνεσθαι, ἡνίκα τὰ θνητὰ ἑαυτῶν μέρη [καπανητα] ἐκθαυμάζοιεν, παρέντες αὔξειν τἀθάνατα. οὐ γὰρ ἐπὶ κρίσει μέν τις δεκασθεὶς 9 οὐκ ἂν ἔτι τῶν δικαίων καὶ καλῶν ἐλεύθερος καὶ ὑγιὴς ἂν κριτὴς γένοιτο (ἀνάγκη γὰρ τῷ δωροδόκῳ τὰ οἰκεῖα μὲν φαίνεσθαι καλὰ καὶ δίκαια ⟨τὰ δ' ἀλλότρια ἄδικα καὶ κακά⟩), ὅπου δὲ ἡμῶν ἑκάστου τοὺς ὅλους ἤδη βίους δεκασμοὶ βραβεύουσι καὶ ἀλλοτρίων θῆραι θανάτων καὶ ἐνέδραι διαθηκῶν, τὸ δ' ἐκ τοῦ παντὸς κερδαίνειν ὠνούμεθα τῆς ψυχῆς ἕκαστος πρὸς τῆς ⟨φιλοχρηματίας⟩ ἠνδραποδισμένοι, ἆρα δὴ ἐν τῇ τοσαύτῃ λοιμικῇ τοῦ βίου διαφθορᾷ δοκοῦμεν ἔτι ἐλεύθερόν τινα κριτὴν τῶν μεγάλων ἢ διηκόντων πρὸς τὸν αἰῶνα κἀδέκαστον ἀπολελεῖφθαι καὶ μὴ καταρχαιρεσιάζεσθαι πρὸς τῆς τοῦ πλεονεκτεῖν ἐπιθυμίας; ἀλλὰ μήποτε 10 τοιούτοις οἷοί πέρ ἐσμεν ἡμεῖς ἄμεινον ἄρχεσθαι ἢ ἐλευθέροις εἶναι· ἐπείτοιγε ἀφεθεῖσαι τὸ σύνολον, ὡς ἐξ εἱρκτῆς ἄφετοι,

3 cf. Pl. *Resp.* 9. 573E

1 †εἰς ἃς† ἐμβαίνει] ἴσα συνεμβαίνει Kaibel: εἰς αὐτὰς ἐμβαίνει Weiske: εὐθὺς ἐμβαίνει Mathews 5 τούτους Tollius: τούτου P 8 ἀναβλέπειν] ἄνω βλέπων Cobet: ⟨πρὸς ἄλλ'⟩ ἀναβλέπειν Wilamowitz 9 ὑστεροφημίας Ruhnken: ἕτερα φήμης P: πέρα φήμης Man. 12 [καπανητα] del. Vahlen: κἀνόνητα Man.: κἀνόητα Toup: κἀπ' ἄκρον Wenkebach 13 τἀθάνατα apogr.: τὰ ἄνατα P δεκασθεὶς Man.: δικασθεὶς P 14 ἔτι Morus: ἐπὶ P 16 ⟨τὰ δ'... κακά⟩ ex. gr. supplevi: lacunam ind. Spengel 19 ⟨φιλοχρηματίας⟩ post Tollium (αὐτοῦ φιλοχρηματίας) supplevi 21 μεγάλων ἢ bis P: corr. Rob. 22 αἰῶνα Portus: ἀγῶνα P κἀδέκαστον apogr.: καθέκαστον P μὴ Man.: μοι P

κατὰ τῶν πλησίον αἱ πλεονεξίαι κἂν ἐπικλύσειαν τοῖς κακοῖς τὴν
11 οἰκουμένην. ὅλως δὲ δάπανον ἔφην εἶναι τῶν νῦν γεννωμένων
φύσεων τὴν ῥᾳθυμίαν, ᾗ πλὴν ὀλίγων πάντες ἐγκαταβιοῦμεν, οὐκ
ἄλλως πονοῦντες ἢ ἀναλαμβάνοντες εἰ μὴ ἐπαίνου καὶ ἡδονῆς
ἕνεκα, ἀλλὰ μὴ τῆς ζήλου καὶ τιμῆς ἀξίας ποτὲ ὠφελείας. 5
12 "κράτιστον εἰκῇ ταῦτ᾽ ἐᾶν," ἐπὶ δὲ τὰ συνεχῆ χωρεῖν· ἦν δὲ
ταῦτα τὰ πάθη, περὶ ὧν ἐν ἰδίῳ προηγουμένως ὑπεσχόμεθα
γράψειν ὑπομνήματι, †ὃ τήν τε τοῦ ἄλλου λόγου καὶ αὐτοῦ τοῦ
ὕψους μοῖραν ἐπεχόντων, ὡς ἡμῖν ⟨εἴρηται, κρατίστην⟩ . . . .

6 Eur. *El.* 379: cf. Nauck², p. 437

1 ἐπικλύσειαν Markland: ἐπικαύσειαν P   2 δάπανον Tollius:
δαπανῶν P: δαπάνην Rothstein: διὰ παντὸς Spengel   3 ᾗ Man.: οἵ P
6 κράτιστον ⟨δ᾽⟩ Man., fortasse recte   7-9 ἐν ἰδίῳ . . . ἡμῖν add. p,
del. Philippson   8 †ὃ] om. apogr.   9 ⟨εἴρηται, κρατίστην⟩
ex. gr. supplevi

COMMENTARY

1-2. *Preface.*

Title. No translation of the title περὶ ὕψους is likely to please everybody. This is largely because of a fundamental and obvious ambiguity in L's thinking. On the one hand he would deny excellence to writing which does not possess ὕψος; on the other, to say that something has ὕψος is not the same thing as to say that it is excellent, for ὕψος possesses definite characteristics—seriousness, tension, dignity of thought and language—which some whole genres of literature cannot achieve. Compare 29. 2, 9. 15. For L there is a particular kind of literature which alone is capable of being the best. It is this consideration which makes such renderings as Grube's *Of Great Writing* or Welsted's *On the Sovereign Perfection of Writing* unsatisfactory. The traditional translation is, of course, *On the Sublime*. This, as Dr. Johnson said (*Dictionary*, s.v.), is 'a Gallicism but now naturalised'. Though used in English as early as 1586 of the *sublime genus dicendi*, 'sublime' became current as a critical, and then as a philosophical, term only with the popularization of L in Boileau's translation (Monk, pp. 18 ff.). Today there adhere to the word connotations which come from the developments of L's ideas by eighteenth-century critics and especially from Burke. It is contrasted with 'the beautiful', terror and darkness are essential to it, it is Hebraic rather than Greek. These accretions perhaps disqualify it as a translation; at any rate we must use it, if at all, in full knowledge of its history and as a kind of technical term. There are, of course, other approaches. Among pre-Boileau renderings, Hall's *Of the Height of Eloquence* (i.e. περὶ ὕψους λόγου, a title which has no authority but that of some of the apographa) is attractive because it is so literal; it would, however, be obscure and affected nowadays. *Of Elevation* remains possible; it is not I think a very serious disadvantage that it suggests something rhetorical and technical, since, however far L widens his theme as he goes on, it is from a specific technical question that he starts. German translators are apparently content with *vom Erhabenen*; the French, in piety to Boileau, consistently use *du Sublime*.

L shows little concern to maintain a consistent terminology in the body of the work; ὕψος and its cognates and μέγεθος and its cognates are often, but not always, used without any discernible difference (Introd. III, xxxi). The translator is therefore fairly free to use 'sublimity,' 'greatness', 'grandeur', 'elevation', 'magnificence', etc., as occasion demands.

On the form of the title in the manuscripts see Introd. II, xxii.

1. 1. τοῦ Καικιλίου: this is almost certainly Caecilius of Calacte or Caleacte in Sicily, a contemporary of Dionysius of Halicarnassus, known to us as an influential writer on figures (below, p. 127) and on other rhetorical subjects. The small residuum of doubt, exploited by some who wish to date L in the third century, is due to the fact that the Suda-article prolongs his life ἕως Ἁδριανοῦ; this indicates a confusion with some other Caecilius but does not seriously affect the identity of L's opponent. Little is known of his life; some said that he was of slave origin, some that he was a Jew by belief. He has sometimes been identified with the Q. Caecilius Niger who was quaestor of Verres in Sicily in 73/72 B.C. and is described by Plutarch as ἔνοχος τῷ ἰουδαΐζειν . . . ἀπελευθερικὸς ἄνθρωπος (*Cic.* 7); but it should be remembered that Plutarch does not make the identification, despite the fact that he has occasion to mention the critic Caecilius in the same pair of Lives (*Dem.* 3). Caecilius was a common name in Sicily, where the Caecilii Metelli were influential; and on other grounds (e.g. Quint. 3. 1. 16, if the names here listed are in chronological order; also the relationship with Dionysius) our Caecilius may well be a generation later.

Dionysius (*ad Pomp.* 3) speaks of agreeing with τῷ φιλτάτῳ Καικιλίῳ—a polite phrase, not necessarily implying intimacy—on the point that Demosthenes imitated Thucydides' thought. Clearly the two critics belong to the same school, though they sometimes disagreed (schol. Dem. *Olynth.* 2 init.), and Caecilius' general position as an opponent of Asianists and so a 'Renaissance writer' in the same sense as Dionysius, is evident from the titles of his books κατὰ Φρυγῶν and τίνι διαφέρει ὁ Ἀττικὸς ζῆλος ('style') τοῦ Ἀσιανοῦ.

Like Dionysius, he was also an historian; he wrote on the slave wars in Sicily. His most important work, περὶ τοῦ χαρακτῆρος τῶν δέκα ῥητόρων (frr. 99–149 Ofenloch), dealt with questions of authenticity in the Attic Orators and had both an historical and a rhetorical side. His περὶ ὕψους is known only from L's refutation. From this we learn (i) that Caecilius tried to describe ὕψος but gave no practical advice on its attainment (1. 1); (ii) that he gave some instances of bad taste in Timaeus, but not those which L gives (4. 2); (iii) that he left out some of what L regards as the sources of ὕψος and said nothing about πάθος (8. 1); (iv) that he found fault with Theopompus' vigorous phrase ἀναγκοφαγῆσαι πράγματα (31. 1); (v) that he talked as though he advocated some restriction on the use of metaphor (32. 2); (vi) that he wrote a book on Lysias in which his dislike of Plato was evident (32. 8). There may also be irony at Caecilius' expense in the comparison of Demosthenes with Cicero, 12. 4; but see note. And, of course, there may be other allusions, though it is dangerous to identify unnamed opponents with Caecilius (e.g. 2. 1, 36. 3), or to suppose him, *qua ἔνοχος τῷ ἰουδαΐζειν*, to be the source of the Genesis quotation of 9. 9. There is no reason to believe that L's arrangement of his material or any large tract of argument comes from him.

See Ofenloch, *Caecilii fragmenta* (1907)—a useful collection of material, but very uncritical in method; Brzoska, P–W, s.v. Caecilius 2; W. Rhys Roberts, *AJP* xvii (1897) 302 ff.; S. F. Bonner, *Dionysius of Halicarnassus* 6 ff.

P has Κεκίλιος, &c., consistently; such spellings are very common in manuscripts and should often be corrected (Cobet, *Variae Lectiones* 121); I have credited L with the more literary spelling (cf. Ὑπερείδης 15. 10, &c.). But note (i) Latin *ae* became a simple vowel both in accented and in unaccented syllables by the first century A.D., so that if L wrote down what he heard, he wrote Κεκίλιος; (ii) Greek αι was pronounced ε in Egypt in Hellenistic times, in Attica by A.D. 150, but standard literary Greek preserved αι as a diphthong (Dion. Hal. *CV* 22. 167; Sturtevant, *The Pronunciation of Greek and Latin* 48).

συγγραμμάτιον: 'essay.' A diminutive with something of a derogatory sense: cf. σχημάτια (17. 1), ποιημάτιον (33. 5), φλογίον (35. 4).

ἀνασκοπουμένοις ἡμῖν . . . ὑποθέσεως: '. . . seemed to us in the course of our joint examination of it, as you know, my dear P. T., inadequate to its general theme . . . .' ὡς οἶσθα does not go exclusively with ἀνασκοπουμένοις κοινῇ but with the whole clause of which ἐφάνη is the verb; compare the (at first sight) misleadingly placed adverbs in ἀριστίνδην ἐκκαθήραντες ἐπισυνέθηκαν (10. 7), ἑτέρως ἐφηδύνας ἐξεφώνησε (15. 6). The contrast between ταπεινός and ὑψηλός gives an additional sting to L's criticism. 'La bassesse de son style répondoit assez mal à la dignité de son sujet', says Boileau; but it is even more lowliness and unworthiness of *thought* that is meant.

Ποστούμιε Τερεντιανέ: Manutius' correction, though not certain, may be defended on the ground that φλω- arose from the following φίλτατε. It is very unlikely that a third name, Φλῶρε or Φλ. = Φλάβιε, was given; the latter suggestion, moreover, involves an abbreviation unlikely in a literary text. T. Vibius Postumius Terentianus, whose name is on a water-pipe probably of the late second century (*CIL* xv. 2. 7373), may be connected with L's friend. Martial (1. 86. 7) knows a Terentianus who *Niliacam regit Syenen*, i.e. commands a cohort or *ala* in Upper Egypt, in A.D. 85/86. T. is a young man (15. 1), but with some experience (1. 4) and no longer an elementary student (1. 3). That he is addressed κράτιστε (39. 1) tells us little, for this style, though appropriate to equestrian officials (κράτιστε Φῆστε Acts xxvi. 25), is also used more generally (κράτιστε Θεόφιλε, Luke i. 3 where *NEB* is surely wrong; cf. Theophr. *char.* 5). See Arndt–Gingrich, s.v.

οὐ πολλήν τε . . . εἴγε . . .: with these readings—P's τε and

Spengel's εἴγε—L makes two points: (i) that C. is inadequate to the subject and misses the vital things; (ii) that he is unpractical. The εἴγε clause enlarges on this second point by saying that he has failed to fulfil the second requirement of any τεχνολογία. Manutius' εἶτα obscures the connexion.

τεχνολογίας: 'technical treatise.' Cf. Philod. *rhet.* i. 128 Sudhaus: ὡς αἱ στοιχειώδεις ('elementary') αὐτοῖς τεχνολογίαι παραγγέλλουσιν. τεχνογραφία is, however, the commoner word in the rhetores.

δευτέρου ... κυριωτέρου: a good instance of L's familiarity with Demosthenes, for the antithesis comes from *Olynth*. 3. 15: τὸ γὰρ πράττειν τοῦ λέγειν καὶ χειροτονεῖν ὕστερον ὂν τῇ τάξει, πρότερον τῇ δυνάμει καὶ κρεῖττόν ἐστιν.

διὰ μυρίων ὅσων: 'at enormous length.' Or possibly 'by means of innumerable examples'.

τὸ δὲ δι' ὅτου τρόπου ... ἰσχύοιμεν: see Analysis, x. Cf. the Stoic critique of Alexandrian scholarship in Philodemus, περὶ ποιημάτων v. 162 Jensen: ἀσθενὲς γὰρ παρατιθέντας ἄλλων ἐπιτυχίας καὶ ἀποτυχίας συμβουλεύειν τὰς μὲν διώκειν τὰς δὲ φεύγειν, πῶς δ' ἂν διώκοι τις ἢ φεύγοι μηδὲν ὑπογράφειν. But note that we also have a reminder that not only the acquisition of a skill but a development in one's own φύσις is needed. Cf. τὰς ψυχὰς ἀνατρέφειν πρὸς τὰ μεγέθη (9. 1).

οὐκ οἶδ' ὅπως: both here and at 31. 1 this phrase has a touch of sarcasm.

1. 2. ὡς αὐτῆς τῆς ἐπινοίας ... ἐπαινεῖν: cf. Proclus, *in Alcib.*, p. 82. 2 Westerink: we admire inventors τῆς ἐπινοίας χάριν καὶ τῶν νοερῶν ἐπιβολῶν.

πάντως: 'without fail', to be taken with ὑπομνηματίσασθαι; see LSJ, s.v. ii. 2, on its use with imperative. Fyfe wrongly takes it with εἰς σὴν χάριν, 'purely for your sake'. It tends to come early in its part of the sentence: cf. 9. 10, 12. 1.

ὑπομνηματίσασθαι: 'set down some notes.' Cf. ἐν ἰδίῳ ... ὑπομνήματι (44. 12). Roughly equivalent to the Latin *commentarius*, at least in some contexts, ὑπόμνημα is often an informal memorandum as opposed to a finished treatise (σύγγραμμα). Cf. Ammonius, *in Categ.* 4 Busse: διενήνοχε τὰ ὑπομνηματικὰ τῶν συνταγματικῶν τάξει τε καὶ ἑρμηνείας κάλλει. Thus an historian prepares ὑπομνήματα as a preliminary to writing history. But the distinction is not hard and fast; περὶ ὕψους, for instance, could be called by either name. There is ironical modesty in the implied comparison with Caecilius' συγγραμμάτιον. See in general G. Avenarius, *Lukian zur Geschichtsschreibung* 85–104.

εἴ τι ... χρήσιμον: 'whether you think any of my observations useful to men in public life.' Judging by the worldly advice of 17, this is the predominant sense of πολιτικός here; L hopes to say something useful to a man who will have to speak in public—in court, on an embassy, before an assembly, &c. But the word has many nuances; in the rhetores it often means simply 'orator' and does not imply any political subject or activity. In Dion. Hal. *CV* 1, ἅπασι τοῖς ἀκούουσι τοὺς πολιτικοὺς λόγους is more general in meaning than I take L's phrase here to be. I take it, in fact, that in L's usage there is an implied contrast between πολιτικός and σοφιστής (cf. 4. 2, 23. 4), not between πολιτικὸς λόγος and the ἀφελὴς λόγος of philosophers and ordinary discourse. See in general K. Brandstätter, *Leipziger Studien* xv. 1 (1894); R. Jeuckens, *Plutarch und die Rhetorik* 41 ff.

αὐτὸς δ' ἡμῖν ... ἀλήθειαν: a polite and roundabout request for friendly criticism, characteristic of literary society in the Roman period. Cf. the requests for *emendatio* which the younger Pliny addresses to his friends (e.g. *ep.* 1. 8. 3, 4. 14) and the services which he performs in return (e.g. 7. 20, to Tacitus: 'librum tuum legi et quam diligentissime adnotavi quae commutanda quae eximenda arbitrarer'). The courteous emphasis on T.'s honesty is perhaps a *locus communis* of prefaces; cf. Dion. Hal. *Thuc.* 2: the addressee is one of those who think nothing to be τιμιώτερον τῆς ἀληθείας.

ὡς πέφυκας καὶ καθήκει: 'as your nature and relation to me require.' καθῆκον is the equivalent of the Latin *officium*; L here means duty as a friend.

συνεπικρινεῖς: future with sense of imperative: see K–G i. 176; Goodwin *GMT*, § 69, p. 19.

εὖ γὰρ ... ἀλήθειαν: *scil.* ἀπεφήνατο. εἴπας is then subordinate to this unexpressed main verb. For the form, Ionic and κοινή, see B–D § 81, Schmid, *Der Atticismus* iv. 603. Of the two variants of the apophthegm, that in Arsenius, who attributes it to Demosthenes, is much closer to L's version.

1. 3. ὡς ἀκρότης ... τὰ ὕψη: 'that sublime passages are some kind of eminence or excellence of discourse.'

ποιητῶν τε ... καὶ συγγράφεων: 'poets and prose-writers.' Cf. 13. 2; Pl. *Phaedr.* 235C, Sex. Emp. *adv. gramm.* 57. Elsewhere συγγραφεύς bears the narrower sense 'historian' and is opposed to ῥήτωρ: e.g. Dion. Hal. *Thuc.* 52, *Lys.* 3. Context must decide.

L commonly regards poets as instructive models for the orator, and in this he follows the general educational tendency of his times (see Helen North, *Traditio* viii (1952) 1 ff.). He therefore quotes freely from the poets and, on the other hand, is prepared to extend the doctrine of inspiration from them to prose-writers. But see also 15. 2, where the distinction drawn between rhetorical and poetical φαντασία suggests fundamental differences which L does not pursue.

ταῖς ἑαυτῶν ... τὸν αἰῶνα: 'clothed their own glorious deeds with eternity.' Writers do for themselves the service—that of immortalization—which it is their pride to do for others. With περιεβάλοντο,

Weiske meant 'won eternal life for their fame'. We could also say 'clothed themselves in eternal life by their fame'. Cf. 40. 1 ὄγκον καὶ διάστημα ... περιεβάλοντο. But this seems to rob ἑαυτῶν of its point.

1. 4. οὐ γὰρ εἰς πειθὼ ... ἀλλ' εἰς ἔκστασιν: a condition of ἔκστασις (see F. Pfister, *Pisciculi ... F. J. Dölger dargeboten* 178 ff.) is one of being out of one's senses or being no longer the same person; it is closely akin to ἐνθουσιασμός or possession. L freely uses these and kindred terms to explain both the effect of great literature and the state of mind of writers. See notes on 13. 2. The idea that speech in general and not only poetical speech produces these effects dates from the claims made by the earliest teachers of rhetoric; note especially *Menexenus* 234A, where Socrates ironically describes the effect on himself of patriotic funeral orations.

πάντῃ δέ γε ... τὸ θαυμάσιον: 'and it is through its power of astonishment that the marvellous always proves superior to the merely persuasive and pleasant.' ἔκπληξις picks up ἔκστασις: see on 15. 2 for this important concept. The sentence πάντῃ ... καθίσταται, as I take it, gives the second part of the proof of the statement that ὕψος is the prime source of literary glory, δέ γε introducing the second premiss: cf. Denniston, p. 154. But text and interpretation are uncertain, and we should perhaps consider reading ⟨τὸ⟩ σὺν ἐκπλήξει ... κρατεῖ [τὸ] θαυμάσιον. Notice that L uses the motif of the three *officia oratoris—docere, delectare, movere*: see Introd. III, xxxvi.

ἐφ' ἡμῖν: 'in our control', in the sense that we can choose whether or not to let a rational argument convince us to act—or vote—in a certain way.

ταῦτα ... καθίσταται: 'but these qualities bring to bear invincible power and might and dominate every hearer.' ταῦτα refers presumably to the complex of τὸ θαυμάσιον and ἔκπληξις.

τὴν μὲν ἐμπειρίαν ... οἰκονομίαν: 'experience in invention, and order and arrangement of material.' These terms correspond to *inventio* and *dispositio*, which together make up the πραγματικὸς τόπος of rhetoric as opposed to the λεκτικὸς τόπος which comprises *elocutio*, with the two appendages of *memoria* and *pronuntiatio* (λέξις, μνήμη, ὑπόκρισις). See *ad Herennium* 1. 3. This important basic scheme can well be seen in the over-all plan of Quintilian's *institutio*: III–VI *inventio*; VII *dispositio*; VIII–X *elocutio*; XI *memoria, actio*. See further on 8. 1.

τά τε πράγματα ... διεφόρησε: 'pulverizes all the facts like a thunderbolt.' For the metaphor see on 12. 4 and Introd., xxxix. For δίκην σκηπτοῦ cf. Plu. *Cato minor* 20: εἰς τὴν πολιτείαν ἐμπεσεῖται δίκην σκηπτοῦ πάντα πράγματα ταράττων. For διεφόρησε cf. Plu *de defectu* 44, 434B: (μαντικὰ πνεύματα) ... εἰκός ἐστι ... κεραυνῶν ἐμπεσόντων διαφορεῖσθαι ('be dissipated').

2. 1]   COMMENTARY   63

2. 1. Ἡμῖν δ' ἐκεῖνο ... τέχνη: Terentianus can himself suggest lines of thought leading to a satisfactory description of ὕψος. L, who has promised practical advice, has to answer the preliminary question whether there can be a τέχνη.

ὕψους ... ἢ βάθους: 'of elevation or profundity.' This is the only way of translating βάθους. It cannot mean *bathos*, despite Pope's *Peri Bathous or on the Art of Sinking*, which apparently created the English word, and the arguments of Leo (*Analecta Plautina* ii. 39 = i. 161 ed. Fraenkel) and of Prickard (in his translation). If ὑψηλός and βαθύς were in fact terms applicable to different positions on the same scale (*high* and *low*), ὕψους ἢ βάθους τέχνη would indeed be, as Leo says, an idiomatic way of conveying L's meaning; but βαθύς is *deep*, not *low*, and the opposite to L's ὑψηλός is ταπεινός. (The antithesis 'depth–height', significant in some other contexts, is not relevant here: we should not quote, for example, Isaiah vii. 11 LXX: εἰς βάθος ἢ εἰς ὕψος. See Arndt–Gingrich, s.v. βάθος). The rendering 'profundity' may be defended by various rough parallels: (i) phrases like βαθεῖα θεωρία (Dion. Hal. *CV* 8. 46), though here the notion of obscurity or secrecy is involved; (ii) moral uses of βαθύς, βαθύτης, βάθος of dignity or *gravitas*: e.g. γενναῖον βάθος of Parmenides, Pl. *Theaet.* 184A; μεγαλοψυχίας ἐστὶ ... ἔχειν ... τι βάθος τῆς ψυχῆς καὶ μέγεθος, [Arist.] *de virtutibus et vitiis* 1250ᵇ34 ff.; τὸ δυσκίνητον ὑπὸ βάθους καὶ μεγαλόψυχον καὶ λεοντῶδες of Fabius Cunctator, Plu. *Fabius* 1. (iii) Hermogenes, *de ideis* 2. 9 (Spengel ii. 395): ἐπεὶ καὶ βίας πολλάκις καὶ βαθύτητος δεῖ καὶ μεγέθους τινός. This last example at any rate is apt enough; the trouble is that, despite L's rich vocabulary for this sort of thing, βάθος does not appear again in the extant parts of the book, and therefore strikes a somewhat alien note. It is very reasonable to think this objection insuperable; those who do, should accept the good easy eighteenth-century conjecture πάθους, attributed by Warton to Upton and by Smith to 'the learned Dr. Tonstal'. So Photiades, Rostagni. Cf. ἐν τοῖς παθητικοῖς καὶ διηρμένοις (2. 2); moreover, it is the connexion between πάθος and ὕψος which especially makes it plausible to deny the possibility of the τέχνη. Diels's μεγέθους is farther from P's reading, and it is an objection to it that this word is often a synonym of ὕψος: cf. 17. 2 τοῖς πάθεσι καὶ μεγέθεσι ... τὰ πάθη καὶ ὕψη: see also **Introd. III**.

ἐπεί τινες ... παραγγέλματα: we do not know to whom L refers; not, presumably, to Caecilius, who (1. 1) 'somehow omitted' the practical side. The argument attacked is in essentials an old commonplace of aristocratic ethics, early and often applied to poetry: cf. Pind. *Ol.* 2. 86: σοφὸς ὁ πολλὰ εἰδὼς φυᾷ· μαθόντες δὲ λάβροι παγγλωσσίᾳ κόρακες ὡς ἄκραντα γαρύετον Διὸς πρὸς ὄρνιχα θεῖον. L's reply, to which he refers later (36. 4, cf. 17. 2, 22. 1), is almost equally venerable: φύσεως καὶ ἀσκήσεως διδασκαλία δεῖται, said Protagoras (B 3). The twin themes of the alliance between art and nature and the part played by ἄσκησις as a supplement to formal teaching had a long history: see, for example, Pl. *Phaedr.* 269D; Isocr. 15. 189 ff.; *ad Herennium* 3. 28 (with Caplan's note); and Hor. *ars poet.* 409–11:

> ego nec studium sine divite vena
> nec rude quid prosit video ingenium; alterius sic
> altera poscit opem res et coniurat amice.

φησί: here and at 29. 1, where P also gives φησί, Manutius proposed the plural φασί. Here the singular comes awkwardly between οἴονται and ὡς οἴονται; in 29. 1 it follows awkwardly on διαχλευάζουσιν. The change is, however, not necessary; parenthetical φησί with no expressed subject is very common and the word becomes in effect a particle: cf. 4. 4, 15. 9, 23. 2, 24. 1, 27. 3, 33. 2, and see E. Kieckers, *Glotta* xi (1917) 184. A close parallel to our passage is Libanius 52. 39: ὃ τοίνυν μέγιστον ἔχειν οἴονται κατὰ τῆς γνώμης, καὶ αὐτός, φησί, τῶν εἰσιόντων ἦσθα.

κατασκελετευόμενα: 'worn down to a skeleton', 'emaciated'. For the metaphorical use of this medical term, cf. Isocr. 15. 268: μὴ περιιδεῖν τὴν φύσιν ... κατασκελετευθεῖσαν ἐπὶ τούτοις [on τέχνη!] μηδ' ἐξοκείλασαν εἰς τοὺς λόγους τοὺς τῶν παλαιῶν σοφιστῶν.

2. 2. ἐγὼ δ' ἐλεγχθήσεσθαι ... εἰ ἐπισκέψαιτό τις ὅτι ...: 'my position, however, is that this will be proved not to be so, if we consider the following points: (i) ....' No fine shade of meaning is to be sought in this irregular conditional, such as one would be justified in seeking in a classical instance (e.g. Thuc. 1. 121). L, like other writers of Hellenistic and Roman times, uses far fewer optatives than classical Attic; at the same time some of these occur where classical rules demand a different mood. Thus here and at 6. 1, 10. 1, 13. 2, 29. 1, an optative in the protasis is combined with an indicative in the apodosis of a conditional sentence; at 7. 1, an indirect question has an optative in primary sequence. These are in fact the commonest irregularities in late writers generally. The usual explanation is that the optative was no longer a living form but tended to be used more or less indiscriminately as an ornament of style; so, for example, Radermacher, *NTGram* 160–5. But the usage is not so haphazard that this can be accepted as a full account of the matter; see Higgins, *Traditio* iii (1947) 1 ff., for the view that 'standard late [Greek'—i.e. the literary language as written by Dionysius of Halicarnassus and his successors—owes something in this matter to the practice of dialects other than Attic.

ἡ φύσις ... οὐκ εἰκαῖόν τι: that nature is purposeful and does nothing at random is a frequent thought in Aristotle: e.g. *de caelo* 290ᵃ31 οὐθὲν γὰρ ὡς ἔτυχε ποιεῖ ἡ φύσις.

2. 2] COMMENTARY 65

ὥσπερ ... οὕτως: concessive in sense, like Latin *ut ... ita*.

καὶ ὅτι αὐτὴ ... ἡ μέθοδος: '(ii) she is herself in every instance a first and primary element of production, but it is method which is competent to provide and contribute quantities and appropriate occasions for everything, as well as perfect correctness in exercise and use.' (i) For παρορίσαι, 'limit, determine', LSJ quote only the three occurrences in L (here and 10. 6, 38. 1). Elsewhere the verb means 'to go (or send) beyond the bounds'. Considerations of sense make the reading doubtful both at 38. 1 (see note) and here; for 'limit and contribute' is surely a curious reversal of natural order. Moreover, παρώρισε in 10. 6 can be taken (as it was by Langbaine) as *exsulare iussit*. It seems to me likely that the word in the sense 'limit' is a ghost, and that we should (with Wilamowitz) adopt πορίσαι from the margin of P, where it is given as a variant. (ii) On the other hand συνενεγκεῖν 'contribute' is probably sufficiently defended by Arist. *SE* 183ᵇ33: πολλοὶ πολλὰ συνενηνόχασι μέρη. (iii) I prefer αὐτὴ to P's αὕτη, because φύσις is the principal agent and μέθοδος her assistant; errors of breathing and accent are common in P.

καὶ ὡς ἐπικινδυνότερα ... λειπόμενα: '(iii) grand effects are particularly dangerous when left on their own, unaccompanied by knowledge, unsteadied and unballasted, abandoned as they are to mere impulse and uninstructed temerity.' The nucleus of the metaphor here is from Pl. *Theaet.* 144A: καὶ ᾄττοντες φέρονται ὥσπερ τὰ ἀνερμάτιστα πλοῖα. Themistius in imitating this (*orat.* 1. 17a) appears to be thinking of a ship at sea, not a ship on a landing-slip. So compare Plu. *animine an corporis* 501D: ἀκυβέρνητος καὶ ἀνερμάτιστος ἐν ταραχῇ καὶ πλάνῃ ... εἴς τι ναυάγιον φοβερὸν ἐξέπεσε. However, ἕρμα may mean either (i) a prop or support such as is put under a ship on a slipway, or (ii) ballast. ἀστήρικτος, 'unsupported', if its literal sense is pressed, suits the slipway picture better; but it is also used quite vaguely and its metaphorical force does not seem to have been strongly felt: cf. 2 Peter ii. 14, iii. 16. 'Suda' and the Plato-scholia use it to explain ἀνερμάτιστος, and the scholiast certainly seems to be thinking of a ship on dry land, for he says (p. 19 Greene): ἕρματα γὰρ τὰ ἐρείσματα ἢ στηρίγματα. But he is probably wrong, both for Plato and for his imitators. See Addenda, p. 193.

Wilamowitz's τὰ μεγαλοφυᾶ for τὰ μεγάλα is unnecessary; L's terminology is seldom precise, and we may compare 33. 2 and 36. 1 for the equivalence of these expressions. Nor is it necessary to complete the comparison by introducing τὰ πλοῖα.

δεῖ ... χαλινοῦ: a metaphor much used by educators. Isocrates is said to have applied it to Ephorus and Theopompus (Cic. *Brutus* 204), Plato to Aristotle and Xenocrates (Diog. Laert. 4. 6), and Aristotle to Callisthenes and Theophrastus (Diog. Laert. 5. 39). Sen. *de vita beata* 25. 6, generalizes: 'quaedam virtutes stimulis, quaedam frenis egent.' Cf. also Proclus *in Alcib.* i, p. 82. 1 ff. Creuzer (p. 36 Westerink).

2. 3. φύσις ... θεωρίαν: this is what is called the 'fragmentum Tollianum', preserved in Par. 985 and Vat. 285 (see Introd. V). Some believe it to be spurious (cf. Schmid, *Gr. Lit.* II. i. 476). The actual contents of the passage perhaps give colour to this, for we might say that it consists of (i) an inevitable completion of the preceding sentence—containing incidentally a similar use of ἐπέχειν to that to be found in another suspect passage, 44. 12, but also in 9. 1; (ii) a very dubious argument, curiously dubbed τὸ κυριώτατον (see below); (iii) a commonplace applicable to Philistines in general rather than to the particular adversaries against whom L is arguing. But loose construction is not alien to L (although admittedly least expected in the climax of the Preface) and these internal arguments do not seem enough to warrant excision. For the tradition of the passage, see Introd. l, n. 1.

τὸ δὲ κυριώτατον ... ἐκμαθεῖν δεῖ: 'the most vital argument is that the very fact that there are some things in literature wholly dependent on nature can itself only be learnt from art.' At first sight this argument seems confused. The rest of the chapter is concerned with the relation of τέχνη and φύσις in composition, whereas the only τέχνη relevant to the point here made is that of criticism. However, L clearly does not make this distinction; so far as his actual argument is concerned, of course, τέχνη is τέχνη whether it directs writers or informs critics, and indeed, were his attention drawn to the ambiguity, he might not think it important; for although he regards criticism as extremely difficult and the fruit of long experience, it has no independent justification for him except as a means to composition (cf. 5–6). A modern American critic, Allen Tate, has attempted to restate the argument of this section ('Longinus and the New Criticism', in *The Man of Letters in the Modern World*, Meridian Books, 1957, 180 ff.). It is, he says, quite proper that L should mean both the art of criticism and that of the poet. 'For our sense of the achievement of the past may issue in a critical acquisition of knowledge which is not to be put away in the attic when the creative moment comes.' He goes on to interpret L's doctrine—going well beyond what L actually says—in terms of the division between style and subject: 'I make Longinus say, we learn from the development of technique that stylistic autonomy is a delusion, because style comes into existence only as it discovers the subject; and conversely the subject exists only as far as it is formed by the style.'

ὁ τοῖς χρηστομαθοῦσιν ἐπιτιμῶν: 'He who finds fault with the students of sound learning'. Cf. χρηστομάθεια 44. 1; Cic. *ad Att.* 1. 6. 2: 'secum habebat hominem χρηστομαθῆ D. Turranium.' Cf. 'bonae artes' (Cic. *de oratore* 1. 158; further material in *Thes. LL*,

3. 1] COMMENTARY 67

s.v. *ars*, p. 661, s.v. *bonus*, p. 2090). In late Greek χρηστομάθεια also means 'summary' or 'anthology'; so also in modern academic usage, e.g. *Chrestomathie néo-hellénique*.

μοι δοκῶ: there is no need to change δοκῶ to δοκεῖ. Cf. *Theages* 121D : δοκῶ γάρ μοι, τῶν ἡλικιωτῶν τινες αὐτοῦ; Athen. 4. 3. 129 a: αὐλητρίδες . . . ἐμοὶ μὲν γυμναὶ δοκῶ; Com. Adesp. *CGF* iii, p. 424 Kock: οἱ δ' ἐπτ' (scil. μέδιμνοι) ἐπὶ Θήβας ἐστράτευσαν, μοι δοκῶ. See Woerpel, *Rh. Mus.* lvii (1902) 311. For the enclitic μοι in this position, cf. also Pl. *Euthyd.* 297C: νεωστί, μοι δοκεῖν, καταπεπλευκότι.

περιττὴν καὶ ἄχρηστον: 'superfluous and useless.' A natural pair of adjectives: cf. (an instance at random) Plu. *de cup. div.* 527 C, D. περιττός—which can mean 'extraordinary' or 'unwanted' as well as 'odd' in the arithmetical sense—is often coupled with a second adjective which determines its meaning.

3. *Faults incident to striving after the sublime:* (i) *turgidity, puerility, false emotion.*

See Introd. I, xi for the connexion of thought.

3. 1. †**καὶ καμίνου . . . μέλος**: '. . . restrain also the furnace's huge glow. For if I see but one beside his hearth, I'll insinuate a tentacle ⟨of flame⟩, quick as a torrent, only one, and fire his roof and reduce it to cinders. So far I've not sung my proper song.' ἑστιοῦχος may perhaps be 'giver of a feast' (cf. Philo, *de ebrietate Noe* 210): πλεκτάνη (cf. πλεκτάνη καπνοῦ, Aristoph. *Birds* 1717) means 'tentacle' as well as 'coil' or 'wreath' and παρείρας makes this the more appropriate rendering here (so van Groningen, *Mnemosyne* iv. 5 (1952) 214 ff.). There is no need to suppose (with LSJ) that a lightning-flash is meant; I take the torrent-like tentacle to be a tongue of flame whipped up by the wind into the roof-timbers; but it may perhaps be the blast of wind itself, getting into the house where the open fire has been left.

The speaker is evidently Boreas, and the passage comes from a play—which should be a tragedy rather than a satyr-play, if παρατράγῳδα is pressed as honest and informed criticism—dealing with the Attic legend of Orithyia the daughter of Erechtheus, whom Boreas carried away as she played beside the Ilissus (see, e.g., Pl. *Phaedr.* 229B; Ov. *Met.* 6. 675 ff.). Boreas is enraged at Erechtheus' refusal to give him his daughter. But is the play by Aeschylus or by Sophocles? An eleventh-century rhetor, John of Sicily (Walz vi. 225, cf. anon., ibid. vii. 963), after commenting on the word στόμφαξ ('bombastic') in Aristophanes (*Clouds* 1367) and its application to Aeschylus, continues: φαίνεται δ' ἡ ἀτοπία τοῦ ποιητοῦ μᾶλλον ἐν τῷ τῆς Ὠρειθυίας δράματι, ὅπου δυσὶ σιαγόσι φυσῶν ὁ Βορέας κυκᾷ τὴν θάλασσαν· οὐ γὰρ φέρω ἐπὶ μνήμης τὰ ἰαμβικὰ ἐπιλαθόμενος. διὸ [? ὃ] καὶ Σοφοκλῆς μιμεῖται. λέγει δὲ περὶ τούτων Λογγῖνος ἀκριβέστερον ἐν τῷ κα' τῶν φιλολόγων. (For the relevance of this to the question of L's identity see Introd. II, xxvi f.) Boreas blowing with both cheeks clearly refers to the same detail which L travesties as Boreas as an αὐλητής—playing the flute being a patently undignified occupation—but the other details in our passage are not in John. There is not enough here to determine the authorship in favour of Aeschylus. Nor do we know that Sophocles could not have written in this style. Indeed, the balance seems in favour of Sophocles: (i) we are told he imitated Aeschylus, and L's οὐ τραγικὰ ἔτι ταῦτα suggests a comparison with some more successful treatment; (ii) Strabo's (7. 295C) way of quoting from Sophocles' play on this theme (οὐδὲ γὰρ εἴ τινα Σοφοκλῆς τραγῳδεῖ... οὐδὲν ἂν εἴη πρὸς τὰ νῦν: fr. 870 N) suggests that the piece was known for a certain extravagance or exuberance; (iii) there is nothing improbable in the supposition that L here compared a passage of Aeschylus with one of Sophocles to the latter's detriment. Cf. Plu. *de prof. in virt.* 79B for a well-known story about the two poets, discussed by Bowra, *Studies in Greek Poetry* 108 ff.

παρατράγῳδα: 'a parody of the tragic.' Cf. [Plu.] *de lib. ed.* 7A: τὸ θεατρικὸν καὶ παρατράγῳδον τῆς λέξεως, opposed to τὴν σμικρολογίαν ... καὶ ταπείνωσιν.

τεθόλωται ... δεδείνωται: 'the result is not so much impressiveness as turbidity of expression and confusion of imagery.' For θολοῦσθαι in this type of context, compare Latin *lutulentus*, e.g. in Hor. *serm.* I. 4. 11.

κἂν ... πρὸς αὐγὰς ἀνασκοπῇς: 'and if you hold them up to the light to examine them....' Cf. Pl. *Phaedr.* 268A; Plu. *quaest. conv.* 623C.

ὑπονοστεῖ: 'sinks to....' Cf. Plu. *de rep. ger.* 811E: καὶ τὸ θαυμαζόμενον... εἰς χλευασμὸν ὑπονοστεῖ καὶ γέλωτα; *SNV* 556D: ὑπονοστούσης τῆς φιλοδοξίας εἰς τὴν φιλαργυρίαν.

ὅπου δέ ... σχολῇ γ' ἄν...: 'but if ... still less....' Cf. 4. 4 for ὅπου (γε) and 44. 9 for a similarly constructed sentence.

πράγματι ὀγκηρῷ φύσει καὶ ἐπιδεχομένῳ στόμφον: 'a genre naturally grand and permitting bombast.' Both ὄγκος and στόμφος—'bulk' and 'stuffing'—and their derivatives belong to what may be called the earliest stratum of Greek critical vocabulary. Thus Aristophanes uses στομφάζειν and στόμφαξ (*Wasps* 721, *Clouds* 1367). ὄγκος is a transfer from the vocabulary of the human body, as are ἰσχνός, ἁδρός, οἰδεῖν, and many other terms (the analogy is made consciously in 3. 4: and cf. *ad Herennium* 4. 15). In the fifth century, too, stylistic criticism largely took the form of a contrast between the swollen style peculiar to tragedy and especially to Aeschylus, and the thin or refined style; so Euripides boasts (*Frogs* 939 ff.):

ἀλλ' ὡς παρέλαβον τὴν τέχνην παρὰ σοῦ [Aesch.] τὸ πρῶτον εὐθὺς

οἰδοῦσαν ὑπὸ κομπασμάτων καὶ ῥημάτων ἐπαχθῶν
ἴσχνανα μὲν πρώτιστον αὐτήν.

See Introd. III, xxxii.

λόγοις ἀληθινοῖς: Grube's 'discourse which deals with facts' is more accurate than Fyfe's 'real speeches' or Rhys Roberts's 'the narration of fact'.

3. 2. ταύτῃ καὶ ... γῦπες ἔμψυχοι τάφοι: both these quotations come from Gorgias' *Epitaphios*, his speech for the Athenian war-dead delivered in 427: we possess one long fragment (6 D–K), one of the most remarkable pieces of early Greek prose.

Ξέρξης ὁ τῶν Περσῶν Ζεύς probably alludes to the story which is also related by Herodotus (7. 56) in which a man from the Hellespont says: ὦ Ζεῦ, τί δὴ ἀνδρὶ εἰδόμενος Πέρσῃ καὶ οὔνομα ἀντὶ Διὸς Ξέρξην θέμενος ἀνάστατον τὴν Ἑλλάδα θέλεις ποιῆσαι; cf. also Isocr. *Paneg.* 151. Persian ruler-cult shocked the Greeks very much in the fifth century.

Γῦπες ἔμψυχοι τάφοι is an early example of one of the most celebrated conceits in European literature. Developed out of such natural if macabre ideas as ἑλώρια τεῦχε κύνεσσιν, οἰωνοῖσί τε δαῖτα (*Il.* 1. 4–5), it first appears in extant literature as a conceit (i.e. with explicit allusion to funeral rites) in Aesch. *Septem* 1020–1:

οὕτω πετηνῶν τόνδ' ὑπ' οἰωνῶν δοκεῖ
ταφέντ' ἀτίμως τοὐπιτίμιον λαβεῖν.

Other fifth-century instances include Soph. *Antigone* 1081 (if καθήγνισαν is read) and *El.* 1487 f. Of many later uses the following are perhaps enough to give an idea of the history: (i) Enn. *Ann.* 141–2: 'crudeli ... sepulchro' of a vulture. (ii) Lucr. 5. 993: 'viva videns vivo sepeliri viscera busto.' (iii) Ovid, *Heroides* 10. 123–4: 'ossa superstabunt volucres inhumata marinae? haec sunt officiis digna sepulcra meis?' (iv) Ignatius, *ad Romanos* 4: μᾶλλον κολακεύσατε τὰ θηρία, ἵνα μοι τάφος γένωνται. (v) Spenser, *Faerie Queene* II. viii. 16: 'To be entombed in the raven or the kight.' (vi) *Macbeth* III. iv. 72: 'Our monuments shall be the maws of kites.' See Norden, *AK* 385; Bonner, *Roman Declamation* 155; E. R. Bevan in *Essays in Honour of Gilbert Murray* 198–9.

Hermogenes (Spengel ii. 292) criticizes the phrase as ψυχρόν on the principle that disproportion between the objects compared is a fault in metaphor. Another rhetor, Athanasius (*rhet. Gr.* xiv. 180 Rabe), has ζῶντες for ἔμψυχοι.

Καλλισθένους: *FGrHist* 124. Of Olynthus, nephew of Aristotle and historian of Alexander; also wrote a general history of Greece. No verbal quotations survive. Other testimonies (e.g. Cic. *de oratore* 2. 58) bear out that of L, that, especially in his work on Alexander, he was a rhetorical and exaggerated stylist.

οὐχ ὑψηλά, ἀλλὰ μετέωρα: 'not lofty so much as right up in the air.' Cf. Latin *praeceps, abruptus* opposed to *sublimis*, Quint. 12. 10. 73, 80. I do not know another case of this pejorative use of μετέωρος. It is perhaps assisted by the classical associations of μετεωρολογία, &c., with nonsense and blasphemy: cf. Pl. *Apol.* 18B, *Rep.* 489C, *Cratylus* 401B, &c. In Dion. Hal. *Isaeus* 19, τὸ μετέωρον καὶ πομπικόν is not pejorative. We learn from Galen (*in Hipp. de victu acut., C. Med. Graec.* v. 9. 1, p. 361. 20) and from Suet. *Claud.* 39 that μετέωρος was a popular word for 'wool-gathering'. L *may* be hinting at this too.

Κλειτάρχου: *FGrHist* 137. Historian, living under Ptolemy II (285–246 B.C), who wrote an account of Alexander. 'Probably a bad historical novel, unfavourable to Alexander and making him an imitative character with a taste for massacres. . . . No critic of antiquity has a good word for him' (Tarn in *OCD*).

φλοιώδης γὰρ ἀνήρ: 'a fellow made up of Puffpaste and Cork' (Hall). φλοιώδης means 'showy': cf. 10. 7 οὐδὲν φλοιῶδες ἢ ἄσεμνον ἢ σχολικόν; Plu. *de prof. in virt.* 81B: ἀρχόμενοι . . . συλλέγειν καρπὸν ἀπὸ τῶν λόγων, τὸ σοβαρὸν καὶ φλοιῶδες ἀποτίθενται. φλοιός is bark or husk; metaphorically φλοιώδης, &c., may therefore indicate either appearance as against reality or simply lack of finish: for the latter cf. Crantor *ap.* Diog. Laert. 4. 27: ἀπελέκητον φωνὴν καὶ φλοιοῦ μεστήν. Cf. Latin *cortex, corticosus*. There is no necessity to change ἀνήρ to ἀνήρ: cf. Pl. *Meno* 99D, *Rep.* 331E (with Adam's note).

κατὰ τὸν Σοφοκλέα: this does not imply that an exact quotation from Sophocles follows, and I take it that L is perverting for his own use the lines quoted by Cicero, *ad Att.* 2. 16. 2:

φυσᾷ γὰρ οὐ σμικροῖσιν αὐλίσκοις ἔτι
ἀλλ' ἀγρίαις φύσαισι φορβειᾶς ἄτερ.

The point is that Clitarchus' instrument is small but he tries to play a resounding tune. The φορβειά is a leather mouth-band which regulates the sound: cf. Aristoph. *Wasps* 582; Plu. *de cohib. ira* 456B. This criticism then accords with that of Demetrius, who (304) accuses Clitarchus of describing some sort of wasp in language grandiose enough for the Erymanthian boar.

It is worth while observing the order in which these writers are criticized. The series runs from Gorgias through the earlier writers about Alexander to the full-blooded Asianists of the school of Hegesias. It indicates a theory of literary history according to which the Ἀσιανὸς ζῆλος was the direct descendant of the worst features in the old sophists. (See Immisch, *Rh. Mus.* xlviii (1893) 512 ff.)

γε μήν: progressive (Denniston, *Greek Particles* 349), not adversative; it adds an item to the list.

Ἀμφικράτους: *FHG* iv. 300. No other literary judgement is preserved about this historian, who fled from Athens to Seleucia in 86 B.C.

Ἡγησίου: *FGrHist* 142. Hegesias of Magnesia was an historian and orator of the third century B.C. A few fragments of his work survive (see Norden, *AK* 134 ff.). He was the *bête noire* of the critics from the age of Cicero, and all the ancient judgements are hostile. His style was affected and jerky and his thought as foolish as his style (*orator* 226). He claimed to imitate Lysias—presumably in syntactical simplicity. In reaction against Isocratean periods and in fear of dullness of any sort, he resorted to a style characterized by broken sentences, eccentric expression, Gorgianic figures, violent hyperbata, and strongly rhythmical short cola, with a special predilection for $-\cup-\cup$ and $-\cup--\cup$ as clausulae. Dion. Hal., a very hostile witness, who conceived his relationship to the Hegesianic school rather as Renaissance Latinists conceived theirs to medieval barbarism, describes Hegesias' σύνθεσις as μικροκομψός, ἀγεννής, and μαλθακή. Fr. 7 is perhaps the most instructive example we have: ὁρῶ τὴν ἀκρόπολιν καὶ τὸ περιττῆς τριαίνης ἐκεῖθι σημεῖον· ὁρῶ τὴν Ἐλευσῖνα καὶ τῶν ἱερῶν γέγονα μύστης. ἐκεῖνο Λεωκόριον, τοῦτο Θησεῖον. οὐ δύναμαι δηλῶσαι καθ' ἓν ἕκαστον. The abuse heaped on Hegesias cannot, however, wholly conceal the fact that these short cola, strong rhythms, and incessant points recur in a good deal of later literature—the declaimers, Seneca, some of Plutarch's rhetorical works for instance—and that we shall never fairly know what the influence of this type of writing was.

Hegesias is the typical representative of 'Asianism'; but we must remember the vagueness of this term, which covers not only such pointed styles but also the full periodic manner exemplified by the great inscription of Antiochus of Commagene (Norden, *AK* 141; Dittenberger, *OGIS* 383). Thus Cicero (*Brutus* 325): 'genera autem Asiaticae dictionis duo sunt: unum sententiosum et argutum, sententiis non tam gravibus et severis quam concinnis et venustis ... aliud ... non tam sententiis frequentatum quam verbis volucre atque incitatum ... nec flumine solum verborum, sed etiam exornato et faceto genere verborum.' On the whole issue, see the summary of the position in Austin's note on Quint. 12. 10. 16.

Μάτριδος: *FGrHist* 39. Of Thebes, another Hellenistic writer, of uncertain date; author of hymns and encomia, and probably to be identified with a person of this name who was an advocate of the simple life and drank only water. See Hobein in P–W, s.v.

πολλαχοῦ γὰρ ... παίζουσιν: 'for they often think themselves inspired when they are not possessed at all but merely playing the fool'. L is very fond of metaphors from this sphere: cf. 8. 1, 15. 1 (ἐνθουσιασμός); 13. 2 (the Pythia); 16. 4, 32. 7 (βακχεία); 3. 5 (παρένθυρσον). For παίζειν of an unreal emotion cf. Dem. π. ἑρμ. 250: κακοτεχνοῦντι ... ἔοικεν ... μᾶλλον δὲ παίζοντι, οὐκ ἀγανακτοῦντι. Perhaps we should also compare Eur. *HF* 952: παίζει πρὸς ἡμᾶς δεσπότης ἢ μαίνεται;

3. 3. ἐν τοῖς μάλιστα δυσφυλακτότατον: cf. 40. 1. The idiom is a classical touch; see K–G i. 28–29. It is a common idea that turgidity is a particular danger of aiming high. Cf. Hor. *ars poet.* 27: 'professus grandia turget'; Plin. *ep.* 9. 26. 5: 'visus es ... annotasse quaedam ut tumida quae ego sublimia ... arbitrabar'; Quint. 10. 2. 16: 'pro grandibus tumidi'; Cic. *Brutus* 202; *ad Herenn.* 4. 15 ff.

φεύγοντες: 'in their endeavour to escape.'

μεγάλων ... ἁμάρτημα: the thought is commonplace, this formulation of it unique. If its source is New Comedy—the second line beginning εὐγενὲς ἁμάρτημ'—the more correct form ἀπολισθάνειν should certainly be adopted. The later form, which P gives here and below (ὀλισθαίνουσι), is generally retained by editors in Hellenistic or later authors. For the general idea cf. Plu. *Crassus* 26: εἰ δεῖ τι καὶ παθεῖν μεγάλων ἐφιεμένους; Ov. *Met.* 2. 328 (of Phaethon): 'currus auriga paterni, quem si non tenuit, magnis tamen excidit ausis.'

3. 4. κακοὶ ... τοὐναντίον: as it stands, this sentence seems to mean: 'Both in the body and in literature, those swellings are bad which are puffy and not genuine and apt to reduce us to the opposite condition.' This, however, is not very good sense, and we should rather expect κακοὶ ... καὶ μήποτε ... to be the predicates. Vaucher's deletion of οἱ χαῦνοι καὶ ἀναλήθεις makes L imply that all ὄγκοι are bad: but cf. 3. 1 πράγματι ὀγκηρῷ φύσει ... παρὰ μέλος οἰδεῖν. We should consider deleting καὶ ('non est vocula quae facilius irrepat', Cobet, *Variae Lectiones* 145; cf. ibid. 191) and translating: 'Puffy and false swellings are bad swellings, for they may well reduce us to ....'

καὶ ... καὶ ... without the second preposition is idiomatic: cf. Aristoph. *Peace* 770: πᾶς γὰρ ἐρεῖ νικῶντος ἐμοῦ κἀπὶ τραπέζῃ καὶ συμποσίοις. But see 7. 1, 17. 2, for some support for Wilamowitz's emendation. As well as meaning physically porous or spongy, χαῦνος has commonly the moral meaning 'vain': see note on next sentence. The point of εἰς τοὐναντίον is that in literature the attempt to achieve great effects may lead to mean and ridiculous results, just as in the body a tumour draws strength and causes emaciation.

οὐδὲν ... ὑδρωπικοῦ: 'for as they say "there's nothing drier than the man with the dropsy".' Dropsy causes thirst; and moralists used it as an analogue of covetousness or insatiable greed: cf. Diog. *ap.* Stob. 3. 10. 45, p. 419 Hense: Διογένης ὡμοίου τοὺς φιλαργύρους τοῖς ὑδρωπικοῖς· ἐκείνους μὲν γὰρ πλήρεις ὄντας ὑγροῦ ἐπιθυμεῖν ποτοῦ; Hor. *Odes* 2. 2. 13. I note an English example in Thomas Flatman (*Poems*, 1686): 'the Golden Flood ... from whence the covetous mind receives no good, but rather swells the dropsy of the soul.' See also *OED*, s.vv. dropsy, hydropic, hydroptic, &c.

In connexion with this section, Rostagni has laid great stress on a passage of Philo (*de plantatione Noe* 156 ff.), which he thinks goes far to prove a close relation between Philo and L. Even if we doubt this (see Introd. xxix f.), it is still important as a striking example of the same sort of use of the same medical metaphors as we have before us. Philo is engaged in a general complaint (cf. L 44) that times are not what they were: σχεδὸν οἱ νῦν ἄνθρωποι τοῖς προτέροις ἔξω μέρους βραχέος οὐδὲν ὁμοιότροπον ζηλοῦν ἀξιοῦσιν, ἀλλὰ καὶ ἐν λόγοις καὶ ἐν ἔργοις τὸ μὴ συνῳδὸν καὶ διαφωνοῦν ἐπιδείκνυνται· τοὺς μὲν γὰρ λόγους ὑγιαίνοντας καὶ ἐρρωμένους εἰς πάθος ἀνήκεστον καὶ φθορὰν περιήγαγον, ἀντὶ σφριγώσης καὶ ἀθλητικῆς ὄντως εὐεξίας οὐδὲν ὅτι μὴ νοσοῦν κατασκευάσαντες καὶ τὸν πλήρη καὶ ναστόν, ὥς ἔφη τις, ὑπ' εὐτονίας ὄγκον εἰς παρὰ φύσιν οἰδούσης καχεξίας [scil. ὄγκον: but it would be simpler to read οἰδοῦσαν καχεξίαν] ἀγαγόντες καὶ κενῷ φυσήματι μόνον ἐπαίροντες, ὃ δι' ἔνδειαν τῆς συνεχούσης δυνάμεως ὅταν μάλιστα περιταθῇ ῥήγνυται. τὰς δὲ πράξεις ἐπαινέσεως καὶ σπουδῆς ἀξίας καὶ αὐτάς, ὡς ἔπος εἰπεῖν, ἄρρενας ἐξεθήλυναν αἰσχρὰς ἀντὶ καλῶν ἐργαζόμενοι, ὡς ὀλίγους εἶναι παντάπασιν ἑκατέροις, ἔργοις τε καὶ λόγοις, ἀρχαιοτρόπου ζηλώσεως ἐρῶντας. I give the sense of this turgid and difficult passage: 'With few exceptions, the present generation feels no call to pursue the ideals of its predecessors; both in literature and in action it displays the difference and contrast. Literature, which once was strong and healthy, has been brought irremediably to ruin. Through the efforts of the moderns, a wholly morbid condition has replaced the old muscular and athletic fitness. The firm, full swelling—to use someone's phrase [? a medical writer; anyway not L, as Rostagni appears to think]—caused by good bodily tone has given way to the swelling that marks the unnatural puffiness of bad condition; they inflate their writing with mere wind and, there being nothing to hold it together, it bursts when fully blown up. In the realm of action too, what is worthy of praise and effort has been itself, as it were, emasculated and disfigured, so that there are few left in either department of life, in actions or in words, who have a passion for the old ways.'

ἀλλὰ τὸ μὲν οἰδοῦν ... ἀγεννέστατον: 'whereas turgidity tries to overreach the sublime, puerility is the direct opposite of grandeur.' The transition to the next κακίας εἶδος, puerility, is managed by means of a scheme based on the Peripatetic doctrine of the mean; ὕψος being regarded as the μεσότης, τὸ οἰδοῦν and τὸ μειρακιῶδες are the extremes, but the latter is the real opposite: cf. Arist. EN 1125ᵃ17–34: τοιοῦτος μὲν οὖν ὁ μεγαλόψυχος, ὁ δ' ἐλλείπων μικρόψυχος, ὁ δ' ὑπερβάλλων χαῦνος ... ἀντιτίθεται δὲ τῇ μεγαλοψυχίᾳ ἡ μικροψυχία μᾶλλον τῆς χαυνότητος· καὶ γὰρ γίνεται μᾶλλον καὶ χεῖρόν ἐστιν. Thus, as well as using this pattern of thought in his literary criticism, L also adopts much of the original terminology. For the general dependence of his ideal of ὕψος on moral ideals such as that of the Aristotelian μεγαλόψυχος, see Introd. xxxviii.

τὸ δὲ μειρακιῶδες: a further fault is puerility or childishness, the effect of pedantic overworked thought, which ends in ψυχρότης. For the derogatory sense of σχολαστικός, cf. the contrast between σχολαστικοί and ἔμπρακτοι ῥήτορες, Philod. *rhet*. ii. 265 Sudhaus. So also Albucius Silus (Suet. *de rhet*. 30) declaimed 'circumcise et sordide' 'ne usquequaque scholasticus existimaretur'. μειρακιώδης is not always an uncomplimentary term (not, for example, in Arist. *Rhet*. iii. 1413ᵃ29: εἰσὶ δὲ ὑπερβολαὶ μειρακιώδεις) but can take its colour from any common characteristic of youth—here L has in mind the enthusiastic but immature and probably ungifted student.

ἢ δῆλον . . . : Wilamowitz (I owe this to Professor Ed. Fraenkel) compared Pl. *Apol*. 26B: ἢ δῆλον δὴ ὅτι . . .; cf. also Julian, *orat*. 1. 2; Aristides 39 (18). 1; Plu. *de adul. et amico* 54E.

εἰς τοῦτο τὸ γένος: i.e. τὸ μειρακιῶδες, not τὸ ψυχρόν, which is here mentioned only in passing. See Introd. xi ff.

Demetrius' terminology (186) clearly cannot be regarded as a guide to L's. He treats ψυχρότης as a fault related to the μεγαλοπρεπὴς χαρακτήρ as κακοζηλία to the γλαφυρὸς χαρακτήρ. Thus he draws a distinction which has no place in L's argument, though he and L coincide in assuming some special association between τὸ κακόζηλον and τὸ ἡδύ.

πεποιημένου: 'artificial.' Cf. 8. 1.

ἐξοκέλλοντες: cf., e.g., Isocr. 15. 268, quoted on 2. 1. Both ἐποκέλλειν and ἐξοκέλλειν mean 'run aground'; but the lexica give no instance of ἐποκέλλειν used metaphorically, and we should probably accept Wilamowitz's suggestion. Cf. also the use of ἐκπίπτειν εἰς, as in 4. 1, 38. 5.

τὸ ῥωπικὸν καὶ κακόζηλον: 'trumpery and affectation.' For ῥωπικός, cf. Plu. *mor*. 495D, Holden on *Demosth*. 9. 5. εὐζηλία has a special association with Atticism and purism: *Anth. Pal*. 11. 144. 2. κακοζηλία itself has a variety of meanings. In Quint. 8. 3. 56 it bears a very wide sense: 'κακόζηλον, id est mala adfectatio, per omne dicendi genus peccat: name et tumida et pusilla et praedulcia et abundantia et arcessita et exsultantia sub idem nomen cadunt.' Demetrius (see above) usurps it for the special fault corresponding to the γλαφυρὸς χαρακτήρ. Cf. also (i) Suet. *Aug*. 86: 'cacozelos [seekers after novelty] et antiquarios [archaizers] ut diverso genere vitiosos pari fastidio sprevit.' (ii) Sen. *controv*. 9. 1 (24). 15: 'foedo genere cacozeliae usus dixit: istud publicum adulterium est, sub Miltiadis tropaeis concumbere [of the adultery of Cimon's wife].' (iii) Donatus, *vita Vergilii* 44: 'M. Vipsanius a Maecenate eum [*scil*. Vergilium] suppositum appellabat novae cacozeliae repertorem, non tumidae nec exilis, sed ex communibus verbis atque ideo latentis.'

3. 5. ἐν τοῖς παθητικοῖς: the two faults just dealt with—τὸ οἰδοῦν and τὸ μειρακιῶδες—are not specially connected with emotion.

ὁ Θεόδωρος: Theodorus of Gadara—the Palestinian home of Menippus and Meleager, and something of a cultural centre (Meleager,

Anth. Pal. 7. 417)—was one of Tiberius' teachers. He and Apollodorus, who taught Augustus, *in se converterunt studia*, and founded rival sects like philosophers. Ancient evidence (Quint. 3. 1. 18; Strabo 13. 4. 3; esp. the rhetorical treatise by the so-called Anonymus Seguerianus, Spengel i. 427 ff.) tells us only of technical, if far-reaching, subjects of controversy. Of these, the most important concerned the parts of a speech. Apollodorus is represented as holding that every speech must consist of prooemium, narrative, argumentation, and peroration, in that order. Theodorus appears to have held that only the argumentation was invariably necessary, and that the choice and arrangement of the other elements depended on the demands of the case. Not unnaturally, Apollodorus' rules were the more restrictive; the elder Seneca (*controv.* 10, *praef.* 15) tells us that Clodius Turrinus 'multum viribus dempserat dum Apollodorum sequitur'.

But it is a question how far this difference between empiricism and rigidity in rhetorical theory is indicative of a real difference of outlook on literature in general. Scholars have made a sort of Romantic out of Theodorus, and attached L to his movement. Schanz (*Hermes* xxv (1890) 36 ff.) speaks of Theodoreanism in rhetoric, anomaly in grammar, and some contemporary legal theories as all 'fragments of one and the same spiritual movement'. See Grube (*AJP* lxxx (1959) 337 ff.) for a good criticism of Schanz and his successors. Schanz's original article, however, remains much the clearest statement of the technical issues.

παρένθυρσον: 'the bogus bacchanalian.' Cf. Eratosthenes' παράβακχος of Demosthenes (Plu. *Dem.* 9). The word (it is neuter, not masculine) seems to be coined on the analogy of ἔνοπλος, 'in arms, armed'. Cf. in general Philostr. *vit. soph.* 1. 19 (of Nicetes of Smyrna, who flourished under the Flavians): ἡ δ' ἰδέα τῶν λόγων τοῦ μὲν ἀρχαίου καὶ πολιτικοῦ ἀποβέβηκεν, ὑπόβακχος δὲ καὶ διθυραμβώδης, τὰς δ' ἐννοίας ἰδίας τε καὶ παραδόξους ἐκδίδωσιν, ὥσπερ οἱ βακχεῖοι θύρσοι τὸ μέλι καὶ τοὺς ἐσμοὺς τοῦ γάλακτος (Eur. *Bacchae* 710–11).

ἐκάλει: the use of the imperfect tells us nothing of the context of the remark—not, for instance, whether it was written or oral. We should beware of arguing from it that L heard Theodorus or belonged to his school.

πολλά: adverbial, equivalent to πολλάκις. Cf. Pl. *Phaedo* 61C: πολλὰ ... ἤδη ἐντετύχηκα τῷ ἀνδρί. K–G i. 315.

ὥσπερ ἐκ μέθης: a natural and quite common comparison. Cf. Sen. *ep.* 19. 9, 114. 4, 22; Aristides, 34 (51). 18: μεθύειν περὶ τοὺς λόγους. In Pl. *Lysis* 222C, ὥσπερ μεθύομεν ὑπὸ τοῦ λόγου has a rather different sense.

εἰς τὰ μηκέτι ... πάθη: 'are carried away into emotions which no longer have anything to do with the subject but are their own private affair, and pedantic too.' Faber's emendation is not certain, but gives reasonably good sense. LSJ are, I think, wrong to take σχολικά as 'long-winded': cf. 10. 7.

εἶτα πρὸς οὐδὲν ... ἐξεστηκότας: 'and then inevitably disgrace themselves before hearers who share none of their feelings and none of their ecstasies.' Cf. Cic. *orator* 99: 'furere apud sanos et quasi inter sobrios bacchari.' Note that the hiatus πάθη, εἶτα (no stronger punctuation is called for, since ὥσπερ ἐκ μέθης applies to the whole sentence) resembles several others justified by pauses: e.g. 9. 5 ἵπποι, οὐκέτι; 9. 6 ταρτάρου, ἀνατροπήν; 9. 12 ἤδη, ἴδιον; 35. 3 ἀρκεῖ, ἀλλά. (See Appendix.)

πλὴν περὶ μὲν ... τόπος: see Introd. xiii.

4. (ii) *Frigidity*.

4. 1. Θατέρου: i.e. the second main fault if the interpretation given in Introd. xii, is right.

τοῦ ψυχροῦ: 'frigidity' was a well-established term in criticism, and, like most terms of abuse, a pretty vague one. In Aristophanes it denotes failure (*Acharn.* 138 ff., *Thesm.* 848): cf. Latin *frigesco*, *refrigesco* (Cic. *ad Q. fr.* 2. 5. 3 [2. 4. 5]). But Aristotle (*Rhet.* 3. 3, 1405ᵇ35 ff.; Cope, *Introduction* 286) uses it in a more positive sense of a particular range of faults of diction—viz. an excessive use of compound words, γλῶσσαι, inappropriate adjectives (λευκὸν γάλα is all right in a poet but ψυχρόν in prose) and absurd, pompous, or obscure metaphors. This is in essentials its use in L, as in Demetrius 114 ff. See La Rue van Hook, *CP* xii (1917) 68 ff.

ὁ Τίμαιος: *FGrHist* 566. Of Tauromenium, historian of Sicily, died 260 B.C. at a great age. L's criticism follows conventional lines. Polybius (xii) made a violent attack on Timaeus' inaccuracy and bad taste. ἀλλοτρίων ἐλεγκτικώτατος ἁμαρτημάτων: cf. Polyb. 12. 23. 1, 24. 5, &c.; Athen. 6. 103, Diod. 5. 1 (Istros called him ἐπιτίμαιος). πολυΐστωρ: cf. Diod. l.c.: τῆς πολυπειρίας πεφροντικώς.

τὰ μὲν ἄλλα ... πλὴν ...: πλήν balances μέν: cf. 9. 7, Luke xxii. 22: ὁ υἱὸς μὲν ἀνθρώπου κατὰ τὸ ὡρισμένον πορεύεται, πλὴν οὐαὶ τῷ ἀνθρώπῳ ἐκείνῳ δι' οὗ παραδίδοται.

ἐπινοητικός: 'ingenious' or perhaps 'original' or 'inventive': cf. 1. 2 τῆς ἐπινοίας.

4. 2. ἐπαινῶν: for the asyndeton, introducing an example, cf. 16. 2.

Isocrates took ten years over the *Panegyricus* (c. 390–380 B.C.), see Dion. Hal. *CV* 25. 208, Quint. 10. 4. 4. T.'s point is elaborated by Plu. *de gloria Atheniensium* 350D–E: (Isocrates) οὐ γὰρ ἀκονῶν ξίφος οὐδὲ λόγχην χαράττων οὐδὲ λαμπρύνων κράνος οὐδὲ στρατευόμενος οὐδ' ἐρέττων, ἀλλ' ἀντίθετα καὶ πάρισα καὶ ὁμοιόπτωτα κολλῶν καὶ συντιθείς ... οἴκοι καθῆστο βιβλίον ἀναπλάττων τοῖς ὀνόμασιν, ὅσῳ χρόνῳ τὰ προπύλαια Περικλῆς ἀνέστησε καὶ τοὺς ἑκατομπέδους.

4. 4] COMMENTARY 77

ἐν ἐλάττοσι⟨ν ἔτεσι⟩ παρέλαβεν: ἔτεσι must be added, and the argument for putting it here rather than after παρέλαβεν is that the error is probably due to the similar ending of ἐλάττοσι.

πρὸς τὸν σοφιστήν: cf. Plutarch's σοφιστικὴ μικροφροσύνη, l.c. L does not use σοφιστής and its derivatives except in a derogatory sense; see 17. 2, 23. 4, and cf. Introd. xxix, n. 1, and A. Boulanger, *Aelius Aristide* 76.

⟨ἐν⟩ τριάκοντα ἔτεσι: all our sources agree that the original conquest of Messene in the eighth century took twenty years. This is based on Tyrtaeus (fr. 4 Diehl). The seventh-century war was also long, and the two add up to more than thirty years. L's words anyway imply one war; we have to choose between supposing that the numeral is corrupt (cf. 26. 2 and, for the facility with which this happened, Polyb. 12. 4a) and saying that L has a unique variant of the tradition. Faber's εἴκοσι is attractive but dangerous. Messenian wars: Bury–Meiggs, *History of Greece* 127.

Cobet's ⟨ἐν⟩ is a desirable and easy change; the preposition is regularly added to express the period within which an event takes place; K–G i. 446, Anm. 6.

4. 3. τοῖς δὲ Ἀθηναίοις ἁλοῦσι περὶ Σικελίαν: the sense required is not 'the Athenians when captured in Sicily', but 'the Athenians captured in Sicily'.

τίνα τρόπον ἐπιφωνεῖ . . .; 'What is his *mot* on . . .?' An ἐπιφώνημα (Dion. Hal. *Thuc.* 48 fin.; Theon, *progymnasmata*, Spengel ii. 91) is especially a comment, summing up details in a single pithy phrase; so here, Timaeus' remark is a kind of *sententia* on the facts related. See Quint. 8. 5 on *sententiae*, especially 8. 5. 11: 'est enim epiphonema rei narratae vel probatae summa acclamatio: tantae molis erat Romanam condere gentem [*Aen.* 1. 33].'

Plutarch (*Nicias* 1) repeats and criticizes Timaeus' conceits: Nicias, whose name comes from νίκη, opposed the expedition; the mutilation of the Hermae threatened destruction from Hermocrates, son of Hermon. 'The etymological thread of connection . . . is strange enough', says Grote; but we should remember that both Greeks and Romans were in the habit of assigning serious importance to names; ill-omened names were avoided and very large numbers of names actually suggest good fortune.

εἰς Διονύσιον: L's point is not valid unless Dionysius really was on some specific occasion irreverent to Zeus and Heracles; no such episode seems to be known.

4. 4. ⟨καὶ⟩ τί δεῖ . . .; I think a connexion *is* needed here. At 36. 1, which Vahlen uses to defend the asyndeton, the connexion of thought is somewhat different. Here we surely expect: '*But* why talk about Timaeus when even Xenophon and Plato . . .?' Of the possible supplements, I am inclined to prefer καί to καίτοι or δέ; it can bear an adversative sense, equivalent to καίτοι (Denniston, p. 292; note especially Pl. *Gorg.* 519D), and καὶ τί δεῖ . . .; is an exceedingly common, indeed stereotyped, formula of transition: see, for example, Dem. 9. 59, 22. 15; Dion. Hal. *Isaeus* 13, *Dem.* 29, *CV* 3. 30 (where ὅπου γε follows as here). Toup *ad loc.* has other instances.

οἱ ἥρωες ἐκεῖνοι: cf. 14. 2, 36. 2; Philod. *rhet.* i, 200 Sudhaus: τῶν ἡρώων καὶ τῶν μετ' αὐτούς of the great orators of olden days as opposed to modern degenerates. On Xenophon's reputation, see on 8. 1.

καίτοιγε . . . ὄντες: καίτοιγε is Hellenistic (e.g. *Axiochus* 364B; see Arndt–Gingrich. s.v.), καίτοι . . . γε being the classical form (Denniston, *Greek Particles* 564); καίτοι with participle meaning 'although' (= καίπερ) is also Hellenistic rather than classical (K–G ii. 85). Cf. 38. 5.

παλαίστρας: 'school.' Cf. Plu. *quaest. conv.* 710B: ἀμυνόμενοι βαθυπώγωνα σοφιστὴν ἀπὸ τῆς Στοᾶς . . . καίτοι παρὼν ἀπὸ τῆς αὐτῆς παλαίστρας Φίλιππος ὁ Προυσιεύς. . . . So γυμνάσιον in Pl. *Gorg.* 493D.

ἐκείνων [μὲν] γοῦν: μέν should certainly be deleted. It is not in Xenophon's manuscripts or in Stobaeus, who excerpts this passage of Xenophon; and μὲν γοῦν (= μέν γε) is a very rare combination (Denniston, *Greek Particles* 459). The intrusion is probably due to the occurrence of μέν γε just above, or of ἧττον μέν just below.

τῶν ἐν τοῖς ὀφθαλμοῖς παρθένων: here L and Stobaeus agree in a reading against the direct tradition of Xenophon, which has θαλάμοις—probably wrongly, for this produces an anticlimax which seems absurd. However, ὀφθαλμοῖς can be attacked as a reading in Xenophon by L's argument that it is ridiculous to believe that everybody's pupils are modest.

κόρη means doll as well as girl, and the pupil (*pupula*) is so called because of the image appearing in it. For exploitations of the ambiguity (besides the passage of Timaeus which L goes on to quote) cf. (i) Diog. Laert. 6. 68 (Diogenes the Cynic to a doctor): μὴ τὸν ὀφθαλμὸν τῆς παρθένου ἰατρεύων τὴν κόρην φθείρῃς; (ii) Prudentius, *hamartigenia* 308–11:

> idcircone, rogo, speculatrix pupula molli
> subdita palpebrae est, ut turpia semivirorum
> membra theatrali spectet vertigine ferri
> incestans miseros foedo oblectamine visus?

παρθένους αἰδήμονας: αἰδήμονας should, I think, be retained; it is not so much the substitution of παρθένος for κόρη which is frigid (Aretaeus, *SD* 17 uses ἡ ἐν τοῖς ὀφθαλμοῖσι παρθένος in a purely medical descriptive context, but it must be admitted that his style is peculiarly affected), but rather the—implied—addition of the anthropomorphic adjective αἰδήμονας.

οἷον δὲ ... πεπεῖσθαι: 'and what an absurdity to believe that everybody's pupils, without exception, are modest!' For ἁπάντων ἑξῆς cf. 33. 5, 34. 2, 3; Introd. xxv n. 1.

It is a common idea that the eyes reveal ἀναίδεια; see, for example, [Arist.] *Physiog*. 807ᵇ28: ἀναιδοῦς σημεῖα ὀμμάτιον ἀνεπτυγμένον καὶ λαμπρόν; 2 Peter ii. 14: ὀφθαλμοὺς ἔχοντες μεστοὺς μοιχαλίδος. Cf. also the related ideas expressed in such passages as Sappho 137 L–P, Aristoph. *Wasps* 447, Eur. *Hec*. 970–2.

ὅπου φασὶν ... φησίν: the abruptness of the quotation (*Il*. 1. 225) is striking and the construction and text of the whole sentence very uncertain. We should note first: (i) that the hiatus οὐδενὶ οὕτως is possible, cf., for example, 10. 4 παντὶ οἶμαι; (ii) that ἐνσημαίνεσθαι may either be active or passive, and the dative with it may be construed either with ἐν or as instrumental (see LSJ, s.v.). It seems, however, most natural in the context to take the words down to ὀφθαλμοῖς as meaning 'shamelessness is revealed in nothing so much as in the eyes' (cf. the previous note). But this means taking ἰταμόν ... φησίν as a separate sentence.

Schol. B on the Homer passage appears relevant: τὸ δ' ἰταμὸν τῶν βασιλέων καὶ δυσπαράκλητον ἀναίδειαν εἶπεν. This note aims at showing how Achilles is able to set a bad interpretation on actions which Agamemnon inevitably performs as king. The scholiast therefore is not using ἰταμός in a bad sense; it is 'bold', not 'shameless'. Both good and bad senses are not uncommon in later Greek; this is no merely poetical or archaic word.

However, if we translate ἰταμόν ... φησίν, 'he calls a bold man "Thou drunkard, with dog's eyes"' (and defend this use of φησίν by φάναι in 4. 7), we get a very abrupt sentence and one that has nothing to do with the scholiast's point that Achilles wilfully misunderstands ἰταμότης as ἀναίδεια.

There are three types of solution: (i) e.g. οὐδὲν οὕτως ... ὡς ⟨τὸ⟩ ἐν τοῖς ὀφθαλμοῖς ἰταμόν. So Immisch; Toup had already suggested ⟨τῷ⟩ ... ἰταμῷ: 'Nothing reveals shamelessness so much as boldness in the eyes.' (With Toup's variation: 'Shamelessness is revealed by nothing so much as by ....') All such attempts, of course, sacrifice what I have referred to as the most natural way of taking the sentence down to ὀφθαλμοῖς. (ii) Delete ἰταμόν (Cumanudes) or ἰταμόν ... φησίν (Kayser). As it is easier to explain how the whole sentence came to be inserted—viz. as a comment by a reader who remembered Homer; cf., for example, Plu. *mor*. 19C, 35B, 678B for the use of this passage—than how this can have happened to the single word, it is better to follow Kayser (iii) Finally—and perhaps best—we may add some supplement to make the reference less abrupt. So

Cobet: for example ὀφθαλμοῖς· ⟨ὁ δ' Ἀχιλλεὺς τῷ Ἀγαμέμνονι ὀνειδίζων τὸ ἐν τοῖς ὀφθαλμοῖς⟩ ἰταμόν.... I have modified this to avoid hiatus.

4. 5. ὡς ... ἐφαπτόμενος: 'laying his hands, as it were, on stolen property.' This is a simple accusation of κλοπή (see on 13. 4), introduced as an incidental aggravation of Timaeus' sins. ὡς probably qualifies the whole phrase, not just φωρίου τινός.

Translators have generally strained at this phrase or felt the need to add something. Rhys Roberts: 'clutches it as though it were hid treasure.' Grube: '. . . as if he had come upon something worth stealing.' Boileau: 'Timée n'a pu voir une si froide pensée . . . sans la revendiquer comme un vol qui avoit esté fait par cet Auteur.' Emendations have been suggested; Rohde's ὡς φώρ ἰοῦ—'like a thief getting hold of poison'—is wonderfully ingenious.

τὰ φώρια, 'stolen property', seems always plural; Lucian (*Hermotimus* 38) even uses the plural of a single cup. However, it is not a very common word, and this fact may be an accident. Singular and plural are both used in the sense 'damning evidence'.

ἐπὶ τοῦ Ἀγαθοκλέους †καὶ τὸ† τὴν ἀνεψίαν . . . ἀπελθεῖν: general sense clear, reading quite uncertain. The only possible defence of καὶ τό is that it introduces a direct quotation τὴν ... ἔχων. I find καί difficult on this hypothesis, and it seems foreign to L's (as to all Greek writers') normal practice to take over a subordinate construction (here acc. and inf.) from his authority without making its syntactical status clear or adapting it to his own sentence. Of proposed emendations, κατὰ τό is to be preferred to καὶ τοῦ; but I think there is probably deeper corruption or a considerable omission.

Agathocles (361–287) was tyrant of Syracuse from 317 and king from 304. For his career see Justin xxii–xxiii (from Timaeus), Diod. xix–xx (from Duris), *CAH* VIII. xix. Despite his bad moral reputation (Polyb. 12. 15 on Timaeus' account) and a history of family feuds, this particular episode does not seem to be mentioned elsewhere.

ἐκ τῶν ἀνακαλυπτηρίων: 'from the unveiling.' This was a ceremony, normally held on the third day after the marriage, at which the bride appeared for the first time unveiled. Presents were given, also sometimes called ἀνακαλυπτήρια. See, for example, Daremberg–Saglio i. 261.

4. 6. ὁ τἆλλα θεῖος Πλάτων: Posidonius spoke of Plato like this; see Galen, *plac. Hipp.* 4. 7: ὁ Ποσειδώνιος . . . θαυμάζων τὸν ἄνδρα καὶ θεῖον ἀποκαλεῖ. Cf. Cic. *de opt. gen. orat.* 17: 'divinus auctor Plato.'

L's quotations, as often, are very free.

4. 7. καὶ τὸ Ἡροδότειον ... ὀφθαλμῶν: this seems a somewhat unfair account of Herodotus' amusing narrative of the entertainment of the Persians in Macedonia. W. Smith's note to his translation (1739) is worth repeating: 'And who but such sots would have given the most delightful objects in nature so rude and uncivil an appellation? I appeal to the ladies for the propriety of this observation.'

καίτοιγε ἔχει τινὰ παραμυθίαν: the suggested defence—that the speakers are barbarians and in drink—is based on the principle of τὸ πρέπον καὶ οἰκεῖον, a hackneyed theme in ancient criticism. See, for example, Arist. *Rhet.* 3. 7, Hor. *ars poet.* 114 ff., and more particularly Plu. *de audiendis poetis* 18D: οὐ γάρ ἐστι ταὐτὸ τὸ καλόν τι μιμεῖσθαι καὶ καλῶς. καλῶς γάρ ἐστι τὸ πρεπόντως καὶ οἰκείως, οἰκεῖα δὲ καὶ πρέποντα τοῖς αἰσχροῖς τὰ αἰσχρά. There is naturally a close relation between aesthetic and ethical theory in regard to the concept of πρέπον.

Plutarch's defence of poets who imitate vice is that they display examples of what to avoid; L, however, will not acquit Herodotus— to make an exhibition of oneself to all eternity is too high a price to pay for realism.

[οἱ] βάρβαροι: Wilamowitz is, I think, right to delete οἱ: this is the predicate and we do not need the article—though we should if the sense required were 'the barbarians in the story'.

5. On the argument here, see de Vries, pp. 55–57. I take the steps to be: (i) the one cause for all these lapses from dignity is the passion for novelty; (ii) the reason why it has this effect is that the general principle that our blessings and banes come from the same causes applies also to the elements of literary style. Immisch took the μία αἰτία to be rather the ambivalence of human ἀγαθά; de Vries thinks that ἀφ' ὧν γάρ, &c., explains not why the cause has the effect it does, but why it is a single cause. Both these views seem unnecessarily complicated. The missing step in L's argument is that τὸ περὶ τὰς νοήσεις καινόσπουδον produces elegances of style as well as faults; it is surely in keeping with L's attitude that it should—must it not be an element in τὸ περὶ τὰς νοήσεις ἁδρεπήβολον (8. 1)?

μάλιστα κορυβαντιῶσιν: 'are most frantic.' Strictly, 'feel like taking part in Corybantic dances'. The Corybantes were priests who danced in the worship of Cybele, and professed to cure mental disorders; see Dodds, *The Greeks and the Irrational* 77 ff., with his references. L uses κορυβαντιασμός of the effects of flute-music (39. 2); in the present passage the sense is farther removed from the original and the metaphor much weaker; cf. Lucian, *de historia conscribenda* 45, 58: ὁ τῆς ποιητικῆς κόρυβας.

μάλιστα may mean *either* 'more than about anything else'—i.e. τὸ καινόσπουδον is the special tune, as it were, to which the lunatics respond, cf. Pl. *Ion* 536C—*or* (better) 'more than at any other time', the fault having existed, though to a less degree, in the days of the great classics (so de Vries; cf. 4. 4). For this complaint against the passion for novelty, cf. especially Sen. *ep.* 114. 10: 'cum assuevit

82   COMMENTARY   [6. 1–

animus fastidire quae ex more sunt, et illi pro sordidis solita sunt, etiam in oratione quod novum est quaerit.'

ἀφ' ὧν ... φιλεῖ: adapted from Democritus, B 172 D–K: ἀφ' ὧν ἡμῖν τἀγαθὰ γίγνεται, ἀπὸ τῶν αὐτῶν τούτων καὶ τὰ κακὰ ἐπαυρισκοίμεθ' ἄν, †τῶν δὲ κακῶν ἐκτὸς εἴημεν†. αὐτίκα ὕδωρ βαθὺ εἰς πολλὰ χρήσιμον καὶ δαῦτε κακόν· κίνδυνος γὰρ ἀποπνιγῆναι. μηχανὴ οὖν εὑρέθη, νήχεσθαι διδάσκειν.

ὅθεν, ἐπεὶ φορόν ... καθίστανται: 'this is why, since beauties of style, elevation, and charm make a contribution to the success of a book, even these excellences are the principle and foundation of failure just as they are of triumph.' Von Arnim's division of ἐπίφορον into ἐπεὶ φορόν should, I think, be accepted—even if at first sight it looks too clever to be true. (i) φορός 'contributing to' is a more usual and in the context a more apt word than ἐπίφορος 'suitable'; cf., for example, Plu. *de comm. not.* 1066C φορὰ καὶ συνεργά, and other examples in LSJ. (ii) The argument too is clearer; the premisses 'goods are ambivalent' and 'beauties of style, &c., are good' lead to the conclusion 'beauties of style, &c., are ambivalent'.

Von Arnim deleted καὶ before αὐτὰ ταῦτα; but it can quite well be taken as 'even'.

For φορόν followed by plurals, cf. the examples given in K–G i. 58 ff. The usage is appropriate to general statements, gnomai, proverbs, &c. Cf., for example, Pl. *Rep.* 364A: καλὸν μὲν ἡ σωφροσύνη τε καὶ δικαιοσύνη.

ἑρμηνεία, 'style' is a synonym of λέξις; see Rhys Roberts, *Demetrius*, index, s.v.

The phrase ἀρχαὶ καὶ ὑποθέσεις comes from Dem. *Olynth.* 2. 10, or from Aristotle (e.g. *EE* 1227ᵃ8, ᵇ30: see Bonitz, Index, 797ᵃ3 ff.).

αἱ μεταβολαί ... ὑπερβολαί ... πληθυντικά: see 23. 1, 38, 23. 2. In 23. 1, however, μεταβολαί are only incidentally mentioned. Wilamowitz thought the reference was more probably to 32, on the danger of metaphors, and therefore suggested μεταφοραί (palaeographically an easy change: note the proximity of ὑπερβ ο λ α ί, which would explain the slip).

τὰς ἀνακεκραμένας κακίας τοῖς ὑψηλοῖς: 'faults involved in sublimity'. For the order of words, cf. 43. 5: τὴν δημιουργήσασαν φύσιν τὸν ἄνθρωπον.

6–7. *Some marks of the sublime.*

6. ἔστι δ' ... εἴ τινα περιποιησαίμεθα: see on 2. 2.

ὦ φίλος: L chooses this form not to avoid hiatus (cf. 44. 1 φίλτατε, ὅπερ), but more probably as an ornament of style; grammarians said that it was Attic (Ap. Dysc. *synt.* p. 301 Uhlig) and it occurs in extant classical literature (e.g. Aesch. *PV* 545). It may be a survival of a time when adjectives had no separate vocative form: cf. the

Homeric φίλος ὦ Μενέλαε and see the discussion by Wackernagel, *Vorlesungen über Syntax* i. 307.

ἡ γὰρ τῶν λόγων κρίσις ... ἐπιγέννημα: 'literary judgement is the ultimate product of great experience.' By ἡ τῶν λόγων κρίσις L means the power to distinguish bad writing from good—e.g. *abrupta* from *sublimia*—whether in one's own work or in others'. It is aesthetic criticism, but its main purpose is practical. So we may compare [Dion. Hal.] *ars*, p. 374 U–R: ὁ μέγιστος κίνδυνός ἐστι καὶ νέῳ καὶ μὴ νέῳ περὶ τὴν τῶν λόγων κρίσιν. ταῖς γὰρ ἡμετέραις δόξαις δίχα ἐπιστήμης (note this phrase; it is also in L 2. 2) εἰκῇ καὶ ἐπαινοῦμεν ἃ ἔτυχεν ἑκάστοτε καὶ ψέγομεν.

Rhetoricians, looking at literary problems unambiguously from the point of view of the composer, regarded κρίσις (*iudicium*) either as a subdivision of οἰκονομία (so Hermagoras, fr. 1 Matthes = Quint. 3. 3. 9; Striller, p. 39) or as a separate division of the πραγματικὸς τόπος (Dion. Hal. *Isocr.* 4); Quintilian (l.c.) sensibly says it is involved in all the parts of the subject.

To grammarians, ποιημάτων κρίσις is the crowning achievement of their art; the scholiast on Dionysius Thrax (p. 15. 26 ff. Hilgard) interprets this in an aesthetic sense.

The practitioner of κρίσις in any sense is the κριτικός; in all literary senses this word is a Hellenistic development, and is especially associated with the Pergamene φιλόλογοι, scholars who made use of Stoic logical and grammatical theories, and, in some opposition to the Alexandrians, attended very much to the subject-matter of the poets. Thus we find it in their leading light, Crates of Mallus, the scholar who introduced grammatical studies into Rome (Suet. *de grammaticis* 2): διαφέρειν τὸν κριτικὸν τοῦ γραμματικοῦ, καὶ τὸν μὲν κριτικὸν πάσης, φησί, δεῖ λογικῆς ἐπιστήμης ἔμπειρον εἶναι, τὸν δὲ γραμματικὸν ἁπλῶς γλωσσῶν ἐξηγητικὸν καὶ προσῳδίας ἀποδοτικὸν καὶ τῶν τούτοις παραπλησίων εἰδήμονα (Sex. Emp. *adv. math.* 1. 79). This is a manifesto claiming a higher professional status. In the Roman period, κριτικοί were often highly specialized γραμματικοί (cf. Philostr. *vit. Soph.* 2. 1. 14; von Arnim, *Dio von Prusa* 160 f.), whose province, which included questions of authenticity and exegesis, was also dealt with by teachers of rhetoric. See in general Gudeman, *Grundriss der Geschichte der klassischen Philologie*² 3 ff., and especially Rutherford, *A Chapter in the History of Greek Annotation* 399 ff.

ὡς εἰπεῖν ἐν παραγγέλματι: 'to speak in textbook fashion.'

αὐτῶν: i.e. τῶν ὑψηλῶν rather than τῶν λόγων; it is easy enough to supply this from τοῖς ὑψηλοῖς above.

7. 1. διότι: 'that.' Cf. 40. 3; the use occurs occasionally in the Attic orators and is common in all later periods. K–G ii. 356. οἷον introduces the clause whose verb is ἂν δόξειεν.

ὅσα ... προστραγῳδούμενον: 'everything else which has a lot of external trappings.' The phrase is echoed below: πολὺ . . . τὸ εἰκῇ προσαναπλαττόμενον. Note also the parallelism between the pendant relative clauses ὧν . . . οὐ μέτριον and ὧν . . . εὐγενέστερον. Cf. 12. 3, 12. 4, 22. 3.

θαυμάζουσι . . . ὑπερορῶντας: a parenthesis, like a modern footnote; γοῦν is a normal particle for introducing such a remark (Denniston, pp. 450 ff.). θαυμάζουσι: 'men generally admire.' For this—quite ordinary—way of expressing the indefinite subject, see K–G i. 36, Wackernagel *Vorlesungen* i. 111.

διὰ μεγαλοψυχίαν: this again (cf. 3. 4) recalls Aristotelian ethics: see *EN* 1124ᵃ13: οὐ μὴν ἀλλὰ καὶ περὶ πλοῦτον καὶ δυναστείαν καὶ πᾶσαν εὐτυχίαν μετρίως ἕξει, ὅπως ἂν γένηται, καὶ οὔτ᾽ εὐτυχῶν περιχαρὴς ἔσται οὔτ᾽ ἀτυχῶν περίλυπος [scil. ὁ μεγαλόψυχος] . . . διὸ ὑπερόπται δοκοῦσιν εἶναι.

τῇδέ που . . . εὐγενέστερον: 'in much the same way we must ask ourselves about elevated writing, poetry or prose, whether particular examples of it in fact possess the sort of show of greatness to which many accidental accretions adhere, and so prove on being opened up mere vanities, which it does a man more honour to despise than to admire.'

τὸ εἰκῇ προσαναπλαττόμενον: cf. Cornutus 34 (p. 71, 17 Lang): ἔξωθεν ἤδη τούτῳ προσπεπλασμένου τοῦ κυνηγετεῖν αὐτὴν (Artemis) τοξότιν οὖσαν.

7. 2. γαῦρόν τι ἀνάστημα λαμβάνουσα: 'acquires an exultant pride.' ἀνάστημα (Ruhnken, anticipated in the Ambrosianus) makes good sense; cf. Diod. 19. 92 (of Seleucus): ἔχων ἤδη βασιλικὸν ἀνάστημα καὶ δόξαν ἀξίαν ἡγεμονίας. Manutius's παράστημα ('exaltation') is also possible, though a little farther from P's reading. Pace Grube, ἀνάθημα is impossible; even in *Hippias minor* 364B the sense of 'votive offering' is unmistakable, and it is quite inappropriate here.

ὡς αὐτὴ γεννήσασα ὅπερ ἤκουσεν: cf. 41. 2 for this sort of attention to the psychology of the audience. Similarly Quintilian (8. 2. 21, on the advantage of setting the audience puzzles): 'gaudent non quasi audierint sed quasi invenerint.'

7. 3. ὅταν οὖν . . . μέχρι μόνης τῆς ἀκοῆς σῳζόμενον: 'when something is heard on a number of occasions by a man of sense and literary experience [cf. 6] and yet fails to dispose his mind to high thoughts or leave his intellect with more to think over than is actually said, but collapses into bathos under repeated inspection, it cannot now be "the true sublime", for it endures only for the moment of hearing.' (i) πολλάκις goes with ἀκουόμενον, not with συνδιατιθῇ, as Immisch takes it. (ii) ἐγκαταλείπῃ may possibly be meant to recall Eupolis' famous lines on Pericles (see Introd. xxxix n. 1), but we should remember that the prefixes in ἐγκαταλείπω lost their special force early and the word means simply 'leave' (see Arndt–Gingrich, s.v.). (iii) For

7. 4] COMMENTARY

τὸ ἀναθεωρούμενον cf. Diod. 13. 35, on the style of the laws of Diocles at Syracuse: ἔστι δὲ καὶ κατὰ τὴν λέξιν σύντομος καὶ πολλὴν τοῖς ἀναγιγνώσκουσιν ἀπολιπὼν ἀναθεώρησιν. L's point suggests an obvious characteristic of sophisticated writing such as we find in much Silver Latin: 'suspiciosae sententiae in quibus plus intelligendum quam audiendum' (Sen. *ep.* 114. 1). (iv) ἂν αὐτὸ συνεχές: so Wakefield. συνεχές is an adverb ('frequently, repeatedly'; cf. Diog. Laert. 2. 32: ὠρχεῖτο συνεχές). L is *not* talking about 'looking at the context'.

(v) ἀπαύξησις is apparently unique in extant literature; LSJ, Rhys Roberts, and others take it to mean 'disesteem'; but it is perhaps rather the opposite of αὔξησις, 'amplification', and should be translated 'bathos'. (vi) To judge by the context, ἀκοή means rather 'moment of hearing' than 'ear'; the point seems to be that the false attempt at ὕψος is not a permanent possession, rather than that it affects the ear and not the mind.

δύσκολος: 'difficult', not 'disagreeable'.

κατεξανάστασις: 'resistance'. Cf. Iambl. *VP* 69: δόξης τε καὶ πλούτου καὶ τῶν ὁμοίων ἀνεπιτήδευτον καταφρόνησίν τε καὶ κατεξανάστασιν. Diod. 37. 20: ἠναγκάζοντο κατεξανίστασθαι τῶν περὶ ψυχὴν παθῶν καὶ περιορᾶν τὰ τέκνα στερισκόμενα τοῦ ζῆν ἐν ὀφθαλμοῖς τῶν γεγεννηκότων.

7. 4. διὰ παντός: 'always.'

ὅταν ... λόγων: ζήλων are 'tastes', whether literary (cf. εὔζηλος, κακόζηλος, ὁ Ἀττικὸς ζῆλος) or more general. ἡλικιῶν are periods of life, youth, age, &c. The meaning of λόγων is uncertain, and the reading has been questioned. In Lucian, *convivium* 6, οἱ ἀπὸ φιλοσοφίας καὶ λόγων means 'the philosophers and literary men'; in, e.g., Arist. *Met.* 1078ᵇ14 Ἡρακλείτειοι λόγοι means 'Heraclitean philosophical arguments'. Phrases like these, however, do not provide convincing parallels for taking οἱ ἀπὸ διαφόρων λόγων as 'people of different literary views' or as 'people of different philosophical outlooks'. Dacier took λόγων as 'languages'; cf. Polyb. 11. 19 of the various races in Hannibal's army: οἷς οὐ νόμος οὐκ ἔθος οὐ λόγος οὐχ ἕτερον οὐδὲν κοινόν—translated by Livy (28. 12): 'quibus non lex, non mos, non lingua communis.' But this does not parallel the plural in L. (It is not, however, an objection to this view that L would not have spoken of a consensus of opinion among people of various tongues; cf. Dio Chrysostom 53. 6 on Homer's reputation not only among ὁμόγλωττοι καὶ ὁμόφωνοι but among many βάρβαροι.)

If λόγων is thought corrupt, Richards's χρόνων—'periods of history' and Professor Dodds's suggestion τρόπων ('character') should be considered.

ἡ ἐξ ἀσυμφώνων ... συγκατάθεσις: 'the judgement and assent, as it were, of discordant witnesses.' For this use of ὡς with a noun (= *quasi*) de Vries (58–59) well compares 13. 4 ὡς ... ἀποτύπωσις and gives other examples. The phrase κρίσις καὶ συγκατάθεσις should not be tampered with; it is a technical philosophical expression (cf., for example, Plu. *adv. Col.* 1123F; Nem. *de natura hominis* 12).

τὴν ... ἀναμφίλεκτον: 'achieves strength and certainty in the conviction it implants regarding the object of admiration'.

8. *The five sources of the Sublime. Plan of the treatise.*

8. 1. πηγαί: a common Platonic metaphor: cf. *Tim.* 85B, *Phileb.* 62D; *Leges* 808D, 891C.

γονιμώταται: 'most productive.' Cf. 31. 1.

ἰδέαις: 'headings.' So καθ' ἑκάστην ἰδέαν below. No technical sense, philosophical or rhetorical, is intended.

τῆς ἐν τῷ λέγειν δυνάμεως: the possession of the ability to speak effectively; without this the natural, or voluntarily developed, qualities of mind and emotion which might issue in ὕψος could not find expression, and the particular kinds of figures, diction, and σύνθεσις which are needed could not be fashioned. In other words, the τέχνη of ὕψος presupposes a capacity already developed by ῥητορική. Cf. Quint. 10. 1. 3.

τὸ περὶ τὰς νοήσεις ἀδρεπήβολον: 'grasp of great thoughts', 'ambitiousness in idea'.

ὡς κἂν τοῖς περὶ Ξενοφῶντος: we learn then that L wrote on Xenophon; so did Aelius Theon, a grammarian of the Flavian period, who thus becomes a possible claimant for the authorship of περὶ ὕψους (so Lana). But Xenophon was much admired (see Münscher, *Philologus*, Suppl. xiii. 2 (1920) for his influence on later literature in general) both for his Attic charm (see, for example, Quint. 10. 1. 82: 'illam iucunditatem inadfectatam ... ut ipsae sermonem finxisse Gratiae videantur') and for his manly and honest temper; he appealed especially to the Stoics (Musonius, Epictetus), and to this school belonged his mimic Arrian, who modelled his own work on Xenophon, not only in style but in content (memoirs of Epictetus, *anabasis* of Alexander). See also Diog. Laert. 2. 57; Cic. *Brutus* 132, 292.

αὐθιγενεῖς συστάσεις: 'natural means of production.' This seems an unusual sense of σύστασις, which is normally either a process of combination or the product of such a process.

αἱ λοιπαὶ δ' ἤδη καὶ διὰ τέχνης: 'the rest involve art.' καί does not mean 'also', since nature does not come into the last three sources. It therefore marks emphasis (see Denniston 319; so de Vries).

The three artificial sources appear to correspond to the means of producing τὸ μέγα καὶ σεμνὸν καὶ περιττὸν ἐν λέξει according to Theophrastus (Dion. Hal. *Isocr.* 3 = p. 6 Mayer): τῆς τ' ἐκλογῆς τῶν ὀνομάτων καὶ τῆς ἐκ τούτων ἁρμονίας καὶ τῶν περιλαμβανόντων αὐτὰ σχημάτων. Indeed, L's whole scheme is based on tradition—essentially on the fundamental division of rhetoric (see, for example, Dion. Hal. *CV* 1. 3) into the πραγματικὸς τόπος (εὕρεσις and οἰκονομία, see on 1. 4) and the λεκτικὸς τόπος (ἐκλογή and σύνθεσις). The principle of this division can be seen at an early date and in a non-technical context in what Thucydides says of Pericles (2. 60. 5): οὐδενὸς ἥσσων γνῶναί τε τὰ δέοντα καὶ ἑρμηνεῦσαι ταῦτα. See also, for example, Dion. Hal. *Dem.* 51; Cic. *part. orat.* 3.

ἥ τε ποιὰ τῶν σχημάτων πλάσις: 'the construction of figures in a particular manner.' L deals with this in 16–29.

τὰ μὲν νοήσεως, θάτερα δὲ λέξεως: this distinction is a standard one in the rhetoricians (e.g. Quint. 9. 1. 17). Roughly speaking, figures of speech are those which do not affect the substance of what is said and are destroyed by mere changes of grammar or word-order; such are anastrophe, asyndeton, homoeoptoton. Figures of thought, on the other hand, depend not on details of expression but on the way in which the thought is cast; rhetorical question, σχῆμα ὁμοτικόν, and aposiopesis are examples of this class. The distinction is not at all a clear one: see Quint. 9. 1. 10 ff.

ἡ τροπικὴ καὶ πεποιημένη λέξις: note that tropes come under λέξις (see 16. 1) not under figures. πεποιημένη probably means 'artificial' (cf. 3. 4, Dion. Hal. *Isaeus* 7; Cic. *de oratore* 3. 184: 'oratio polita et facta quodammodo') rather than 'coined' (cf. Arist. *Poet.* 1457ᵇ2; Demetr. 94, 98, &c.; Hor. *ars poet.* 48 ff.).

ἡ ἐν ἀξιώματι καὶ διάρσει σύνθεσις: 'dignified and elevated composition.' For ἐν with a noun as a periphrasis for an adjective, see K–G i. 466, Arndt–Gingrich, s.v. iii. 2. It is characteristic of Hellenistic Greek to use ἐν in a very wide range of usages. Cf. ἐν ὕψει . . . ἐν χύσει 12. 4.

'Composition' is, of course, to be understood in a technical sense: σύνθεσις, Latin *compositio*, covers word-order and considerations of rhythm and euphony—a particularly important stylistic element in languages in which, as in Greek and Latin, inflexion allows great liberties of word-order without danger of actual ambiguity. See on 39.

By συγκλείουσα τὰ πρὸ αὐτῆς ἅπαντα L means only that it brings up the rear, not that it is most important or all-inclusive.

τῶν πέντε μορίων: Immisch objects that the πηγαί ought not to be called μόρια and would delete πέντε, interpreting the whole sentence as meaning that Caecilius left out some subdivisions of each πηγή and one πηγή (πάθος) altogether. But L is not consistent in his terminology in this matter anyway: cf. 39. 1.

However, it remains a little uncertain whether τῶν πέντε μορίων . . . ἔστιν ἅ means 'some of the five divisions' or 'some points out of the five divisions'. If the former—and more natural—alternative is right, then L appears to say that Caecilius omitted πάθος and at least one other πηγή. But the language of controversy should not be pressed; and in any case it is to be presumed that Caecilius did not divide the subject up in L's way.

88 COMMENTARY [8. 1–

ἀμέλει: cf. 34. 2, 44. 1.

8. 2. εἰ μὲν ὡς ἕν τι ... διαμαρτάνει: a difficult and doubtful passage. (i) Reiske and Vahlen would translate: 'But if he omitted it on the ground that ὕψος and τὸ παθητικόν are one, and thought ....' Vahlen compares Pl. *Gorg.* 495C6: ἄλλο τι οὖν ὡς ἕτερον τὴν ἀνδρείαν τῆς ἐπιστήμης δύο ταῦτα ἔλεγες; Here, however, as in a number of similar passages, it is easy and plausible to add the participle (ὄν after ἕτερον). (ii) A second approach is to take ὡς ἕν τι as 'quasi unum quoddam', and translate: 'But if he thought ὕψος and τὸ παθητικόν, the two together, made as it were a single unit, and always existed together ....' This involves either supplying a verb of thinking in the first clause from ἔδοξεν αὐτῷ in the second, or assuming a hyperbaton by which ἔδοξεν αὐτῷ is displaced, its natural position being after ἀλλήλοις or after συμπεφυκέναι. This seems very forced, if not impossible. (iii) On the whole, I think it best to follow Pearce in omitting καί before ἔδοξεν. Translate: 'But if he thought that the two ... existed and cohered together always as a single entity ....' καί is fairly often inserted erroneously in prose texts to break up syntactical complexities: see note on 3. 4.

οἴκτοι λῦπαι φόβοι: pity, grief, and fear are low. This is in accordance with the established doctrine that the expression of these weaker emotions requires unimpressive language: cf. Arist. *Rhet.* 3. 1408ᵃ18; Hor. *ars poet.* 95 ff. So Marcellinus (56) says of Thucydides: μεγαλοπρεπὴς ὡς μηδὲ ἐν τοῖς οἴκτοις ἀφίστασθαι τοῦ μεγαλοπρεποῦς. All the same, L seems here to have a less catholic view of ὕψος than, say, in 7. Does not this remark exclude the most characteristic effects of tragedy? See Introd. xxxviii. φόβοι, of course, are expressions of timidity; there is no conflict with what is said about τὸ φοβερόν in 10. 4–7.

τὰ περὶ τοὺς Ἀλωάδας: Otus and Ephialtes, the sons of Poseidon and Iphimedeia, were brought up by the giant Aloeus. They grew prodigiously until they were nine fathoms high. They warred against the gods, and were killed—by Zeus, or, according to another version, by a trick of Artemis. Their piling of Pelion on Ossa and of Ossa on Olympus in order to reach heaven made them proverbial for impious presumption. See, for example, Apollodorus 1. 7. 4, with Frazer's notes.

τῷ ποιητῇ: a very well-known and fairly common way of speaking of Homer: cf. Pl. *Gorg.* 485D. So Theon, *progymnasmata*, Spengel ii. 97: Ὅμηρον ... κατ' ἐξοχὴν ... μόνον καλεῖν εἰώθαμεν ποιητήν.

8. 3. τὰ πομπικὰ καὶ ἐπιδεικτικά: 'ceremonial and display themes.' At 32. 5 πομπικῶς means 'impressively', but, despite LSJ, this is not right here. Same spread of meaning in Lat. *pompa*: Lewis–Short s.v. ii B.

ἐγκωμιαστικοί ... ἐπαινετικοί: here synonyms: contrast Arist. *Rhet.* 1367ᵇ27 ff. (Buchheit, pp. 158 ff.).

8. 4. ⟨εἰς⟩ τὰ ὕψη: since συντελεῖν with a direct object means 'to complete', Faber's easy correction is necessary.

ὥσπερ... τοὺς λόγους: 'filled as it were with a frenzy and spirit of possession and inspiring the words with Apollonian power.' Similar metaphors in 13. 2 (see note), 15. 1, 32. 7. Morus's ἐπιπνέον governs λόγους, and perhaps gives a simpler image; but it is not necessary.

For the general thought, cf. Sen. *tranq. an.* 17. 11: 'non potest grande aliquid et supra ceteros loqui nisi mota mens; cum vulgaria et solita contempsit instinctuque sacro surrexit, tum demum cecinit grandius ore mortali.'

9. Μεγαλοφροσύνη and ὕψος.

Gibbon says (*Journal* for 3 Sept. 1762): 'The ninth chapter is one of the finest monuments of antiquity. Till now I was acquainted only with two ways of criticising a beautiful passage: the one, to shew by an exact anatomy of it the distinct beauties of it and whence they sprung; the other, an idle exclamation or a general encomium which leaves nothing behind it. Longinus has shown me that there is a third. He tells me his own feelings upon reading it, and tells them with such energy that he communicates them. I almost doubt which is most sublime, Homer's Battle of the Gods or Longinus' apostrophe to Terentianus upon it.'

9. 1. τῶν ἄλλων: either 'all except πάθος', or (more probably) a pleonastic use of the type exemplified by Hom. *Od.* 5. 105: ἄνδρα... ὀϊζυρώτατον ἄλλων; and Pl. *Charm.* 166E: (ἡ σωφροσύνη) μόνη τῶν ἄλλων ἐπιστημῶν.

L obviously begins with the first source, but there are two features of the language of this first sentence—the choice of the term τὸ μεγαλοφυές and perhaps the allusion to γενναίου παραστήματος—which almost make it look as if he meant to include πάθος with it. See Introd. xiii f.: we can only suppose that the relation between the two αὐθιγενεῖς συστάσεις was further discussed in the missing passage.

τὸ μεγαλοφυές: cf. 2. 1, 9. 14, 15. 3; in all these places, as here, there is emphasis on natural talent. But this does not seem to be so in 36. 1, τῶν ἐν λόγοις μεγαλοφυῶν. See note on 2. 2.

ἐγκύμονας: see on 13. 2, ἐγκύμονα.

παραστήματος: 'feeling' or 'idea'? The word may well cover both, for παρίστασθαι means simply 'to occur to the mind'; the noun παράστημα, however, seems more usually to be used of emotion or excitement rather than simply of thought. A possible exception is M. Aur. 3. 11; but cf. Dion. Hal. *ant.* 8. 39: θείῳ τινὶ παραστήματι κινηθεῖσα; and Diod. 26. 14: εὐγενῆ παραστήματα λαβόντες ἐναπέπνευσαν ταῖς ἀνάγκαις (of steadfast courage).

9. 2. ἀπήχημα: 'echo.' Toup compares Basil, *homilia in martyrem Julittam* (Migne 31. 244D): πεφύκασι γάρ πως αἱ καθ' ὕπνον φαντασίαι... ἀπηχήματα εἶναι τῶν μεθημερινῶν φροντίδων. Other patristic exx. in G. W. H. Lampe, *A Patristic Lexicon*, s.v.

ἡ τοῦ Αἴαντος ἐν νεκυίᾳ σιωπή: cf. schol. λ 536: δῆλον ὅτι καὶ τῶν παρὰ τραγῳδοῖς λόγων βέλτιον αὐτοῦ ἡ σιωπή.

9. 3. πρῶτον . . . ἀγεννές: 'first then we are bound to state to begin with the source of greatness. The thoughts of the true orator must not be humble or mean.'
This section sums up an important part of L's outlook; the expression recalls Dem. *Olynth.* 3. 32: ἔστι δ' οὐδέποτ', οἶμαι, μέγα καὶ νεανικὸν φρόνημα λαβεῖν μικρὰ καὶ φαῦλα πράττοντας· ὁποῖ' ἄττα γὰρ ἂν τἀπιτηδεύματα τῶν ἀνθρώπων ᾖ, τοιοῦτον ἀνάγκη καὶ τὸ φρόνημ' ἔχειν.

9. 4. φρονηματίας: 'men of high thoughts.' This word (see LSJ and especially the example from Xen. *Ages.* 1. 24) seems usually to bear a good sense, 'high-spirited' or the like. Contrast most *-ίας* words, which are commonly deteriorative, e.g. στιγματίας, θηλυδρίας, γυναικίας, καπνίας. Buck (*Reverse Index* 169) thinks that the ending derived its tendency to a bad sense from its use to masculinize feminine nouns.

ὁ γὰρ τῷ Παρμενίωνι . . .: the story in Arrian and Plutarch (*Alex.* 29) is that Parmenio said to Alexander that if he were Alexander he would stop fighting; to which Alexander replied that, if he were Parmenio, he would. It is echoed by Sterne, *Tristram Shandy* xxix: 'If I was you, quoth Yorick, I would drink more water, Eugenius.—And if I were you, Yorick, replied Eugenius, so would I.—Which shows they had both read Longinus.'

9. 4-7. The passage immediately following the lacuna contains a number of Homeric passages; L finds them praiseworthy as showing grandeur and imagination, though some (especially the theomachy) appear objectionable unless explained allegorically. See Introd. xv for the difficulties in the connexion of thought.

9. 4. τὸ ἐπ' οὐρανὸν . . . μέτρον: L refers to Homer's description of Eris (*Δ* 440 ff.) and says that Homer, too, is a colossus stretching from earth to heaven. For an allegorical explanation and defence of Homer's Eris, see Heraclitus, *quaest. Hom.* 29.
For the use of οὐ μᾶλλον . . . ἤ, by a sort of meiosis, where we should say 'not so much . . . as', cf. 34. 3; common in Thuc. (2. 41. 2, 44. 1, 65. 8, etc.), it occurs later also, e.g. Philo, *legatio ad Gaium* 62.

9. 5. εἴγε Ἡσιόδου . . . θετέον: according to the Hypothesis of the *Shield*, Aristophanes of Byzantium suspected it on the ground that the first 56 lines were current ἐν τῷ δ' Καταλόγῳ. Others, including Apollonius of Rhodes and Stesichorus (this must be an inference from a poem), are said to recognize it as genuine.

ὁ δὲ πῶς . . .: see on 10. 5.

τίς οὖν οὐκ . . . τόπον; 'The extraordinary grandeur of this would make anybody say, and with reason, that, if the horses of the gods took two more strides forward, they would find no room in the universe.' Mutschmann (*Hermes* lii. 167) and Grube (*AJP* lxxviii. 365 f.) take the view that τὴν ὑπερβολὴν τοῦ μεγέθους and ὑπερφυᾶ just below imply some blame (cf. ὑπεραίρειν τὰ ὕψη 3. 4). I do not think this is right. There is nothing *in the actual phrase* ὑπερβολὴ μεγέθους to compel us to this (cf. Aristides, εἰς 'Ρώμην 67; Isocr. *Busiris* 14). For ὑπερφυᾶ as a term of praise, cf. 1. 4, 43. 2. The three passages of Homer in 9. 4–6 are in my view all presented for our admiration—two of them by contrast with the piece of Hesiod—but the admiration of the theomachy passage is qualified by an afterthought—namely that, if such things are judged on moral or theological criteria and not just on the effectiveness with which they arouse terror, they must either be condemned or treated as allegories.

9. 6. ἀμφὶ δ' ἐσάλπιγξεν ... θεοί περ: this and the passage quoted in 9. 8 are conflations of lines from various places; they are therefore either memory quotations by L or (more probably, cf. 9. 8 πολλοῖς δὲ πρὸ ἡμῶν ὁ τόπος ἐξείργασται) taken from earlier critics. We possess a number of relevant ancient criticisms. (i) Demetr. 83: ἐσάλπιγξεν needs defence, as it may seem μικροπρεπές. (ii) Schol. B, ad loc.: εἰ γὰρ εἶπεν ἐβρόντησεν, οὐδὲν ἂν εἰσηγήσατο παράδοξον. (iii) Plin. *ep*. 9. 26. 6: ἀμφὶ δ' ἐσάλπιγξεν ... 'opus est examine et libra, incredibilia sint haec et inania, an magnifica et caelestia' (cf. Introd. xli f.). (iv) Plu. *de audiendis poetis* 16D, on the folly of being deceived by the poets into being frightened lest Poseidon burst open the earth and lay Hades bare. (v) Philostr. *Heroicus* 2. 19: both the theomachy and ἀμφὶ δ' ἐσάλπιγξεν are Orphic philosophy; but Homer is to be blamed for mixing up gods and men (cf. 9. 7 below).

ἐπιβλέπεις, ἑταῖρε ...; for the 'apostrophe' cf. 10. 3.

ἀναρρηγνυμένης ... μάχῃ: 'the earth is torn from its foundations, Tartarus is laid bare, the whole universe overthrown and broken asunder, so that all things—Heaven and Hell, things mortal and things immortal—war together and are at risk together in that ancient battle.' For the asyndeta cf. 9. 7, 10. 3; and see L's own remarks (19–20).

9. 7. πλὴν ἄλλως ... λαμβάνοιτο: πλήν answers μέν (cf. 4. 1); ἄλλως is pleonastic, cf. 23. 4 ἐπ' ἄλλων εἰ μή .... The optative λαμβάνοιτο (see on 2. 2) does *not* imply that L thinks allegorical explanations implausible.

εἰ μή ... ἄθεα: cf. Heraclitus, *quaest. Hom.* 1: πάντα γὰρ ἠσέβησεν, εἰ μηδὲν ἠλληγόρησεν. The theomachy is the most obvious subject for allegory of the kind which is directed to explaining away disagreeable features by assuming a hidden meaning. Very probably this was done for it in the sixth century B.C., for we are told that Theagenes of Rhegium (fr. 2 D–K), the earliest allegorist, handled the episode, though it is not clear whether his interpretation was moral (the gods represent wisdom, folly, desire, &c.) or physical (the gods represent fire, water, air, &c.). In later times various allegorizations were given: see [Plu.] *de vita et poesi Homeri* 102; Heracl. *quaest. Hom.* 52–58. See J. Tate in *OCD*, s.v. Allegory, and his references.

πάμφυρτα: 'of all kinds confused together.' Cf. Philo, *de Josepho* 84: ἐκ τῆς πολυμιγοῦς κράσεως ἐν ἀποτελοῦσι πάμφυρτον καὶ παμμίαρον κακόν.

τοὺς μὲν ... ἀνθρώπους: cf. Philostratus, l.c. The same remark serves for the text of the quite differently motivated discussions of modern scholars, whose interest in anthropomorphism is only to describe it and give it an historical placing: cf. the beginning of E. Ehnmark's *The Idea of God in Homer* (Uppsala, 1935): 'To a modern reader the most striking characteristic of the Homeric gods is their humanity.'

λιμὴν κακῶν ὁ θάνατος: a common metaphor: cf. trag. adesp. 369 Nauck: λιμὴν ... Ἀΐδας ἀνιᾶν; Epictetus 4. 10. 27: οὗτος δ' ἐστὶν ὁ λιμὴν πάντων ὁ θάνατος, αὕτη ἡ καταφυγή. L's words fall into iambics; they may, indeed, be a quotation.

οὐ τὴν φύσιν ἀλλὰ τὴν ἀτυχίαν ἐποίησεν αἰώνιον: 'not only immortal natures but immortal sorrows' (Fyfe; Rhys Roberts has the same general view). But although οὐ μόνον ... ἀλλὰ and οὐ ... ἀλλὰ καὶ can do duty for the full οὐ μόνον ... ἀλλὰ καί, οὐ ... ἀλλά cannot. Translate rather (after Grube): 'has made their miseries rather than their divine nature immortal.' The φύσις of the gods includes their main peculiar attribute, τὸ μακάριον. Cf. 20. 3 τὴν φύσιν τῶν ἐπαναφορῶν καὶ ἀσυνδέτων, 'the characteristic nature of epanaphora and asyndeton'.

9. 8. τὰ ὅσα ... παρίστησιν: cf. 16. 1, 43. 3. The idiom by which a relative clause, usually with ὅσα, is treated as a noun and given an article, is not uncommon: Pl. *Protag.* 320D: ἐκ τῶν ὅσα πυρὶ καὶ γῇ κεράννυται.

ἄκρατον: 'unalloyed', *scil.* with weakness or evil. A favourite word with Philo, who applies it to εὐδαιμονία, θεός, δύναμις θεοῦ, &c. No need to emend.

9. 9. ταύτῃ ... ἐγένετο: hardly anything in L has so caught the fancy of readers as this passage (for its influence in the seventeenth and eighteenth centuries see Introd. xlvi). Its authenticity, about which there have been long and violent disputes, was first doubted by Fr. Portus, if indeed he is the author of the notes published under his name in the 1733 reprint of Pearce's edition; he argued that Longinus was not known to be a Christian, and was unlikely to have been versed in Scripture. For later controversies see especially the works of Mutschmann, Norden, and Ziegler listed in the Bibliography.

(i) *Construction and translation.* (*a*) What is the main verb? Is it to be supplied from the context? Is it φησί? Or κἀξέφηνεν (καί meaning 'also') as Immisch suggested? (*b*) How far does the ἐπειδή clause extend, and does it depend on the main verb or on οὐχ ὁ τυχὼν ἀνήρ— 'no ordinary man because . . .'—(so Mutschmann)? These points admit of much doubt. I assume in translating: (1) that φησι is parenthetical (cf. 15. 4, 15. 5) and the main verb to be understood (but elsewhere in L—3. 2, 9. 4, 31. 1—ταύτῃ καί is followed by an expressed verb); (2) that Mutschmann is right about ἐπειδή; (3) that the rhetorical question τί; draws attention to what God said rather than to what Moses says. Translate then: 'A similar effect was achieved by the lawgiver of the Jews—no mean genius, for he both understood and gave expression to the power of the divinity as it deserved —when he wrote at the very beginning of his laws—I quote his words—"God said"—what?—" 'Let there be light.' And there was. 'Let there be earth.' And there was." ¹ Even if one makes the opposite assumptions about the first and third of these points, the resulting translation is not seriously different.

For ἐχώρησε—'was big enough to grasp', and so 'understood'— cf. Philo, *quod deterius* 90: τὸν ἀνθρώπινον νοῦν . . . μέγεθος οὐρανοῦ καὶ κόσμου χωρῆσαι τοσοῦτον. Other examples in Arndt–Gingrich, s.v. Despite Plu. *Cato minor* 64 (Κάτωνες οὐκ εἰσὶν οὐδὲ τὸ Κάτωνος φρόνημα χωροῦσιν) and Plot. 3. 6. 18. 8 Henry–Schwyzer (ἐπειδὴ παρὰ μεγάλου πατρὸς ἔρχεται, οὐ δύναται τὸ ἄλλο χωρῆσαι μέγα) there is some presumption that the usage is most at home in Jewish and Christian literature. This fact has been used, though not with much effect, in attacks on the authenticity of our passage; it does, of course, strengthen the probability of the natural assumption that L's immediate source is a work of Jewish origin.

Similarly, ὁ τῶν Ἰουδαίων θεσμοθέτης recalls ὁ τῶν Ἰουδαίων νομοθέτης in Philo, *de aeternitate mundi* 5 (19), and similar phrases in *quod omnis probus* 7 (43) and Josephus' *Antiquities* (see below). These are all works which seem to be directed at a Gentile audience.

(ii) *Context.* The burden of proof lies with those who think the passage interpolated. The best of their arguments have been derived from a consideration of the connexion of thought. It is said (see Spengel, *Rhet. Gr.* i, praef., p. xvi) that the whole chapter so far has been about Homer, indeed about the *Iliad*, and that a contrast with the *Odyssey* follows (9. 11–15); an intrusive comment about a quite alien writer is therefore out of place. Whether or not this argument would have been put forward had it not been for the natural distrust which many feel at the sight of a Biblical quotation in a pagan writer, the point nevertheless needs answering; I suspect that the answer is that we have here a sort of parenthesis in the discussion, not, as Mutschmann says, its *Schlussglied*; we should compare the reference to Hesiod in 9. 5, which illustrates Homer by contrast as this does by similarity. Neither is essential, both are helpful.

9. 10, so far as I can see, would follow equally well on 9. 9 or on 9. 8: there is no argument here.

(iii) *The significance of the quotation*. After Norden it is unnecessary to labour the point that it is not really unlikely that a pagan writer of the early empire should allude to this passage. (See also R. Harder, *Ocellus Lucanus* 129 ff.; C. H. Dodd, *The Bible and the Greeks* (on Hermetica).) Hecataeus of Abdera had made Jewish things known as early as the third century B.C. In Rome and Alexandria under the Empire there were innumerable chances of cultural contact. Josephus certainly, and probably Philo, wrote for the Gentile world. In the second century Galen made use of this passage to show that Moses did not offer in the Greek sense a philosophical account of the creation (see R. Walzer, *Galen on Jews and Christians* 11). The fact that L gives only the substance of the passage suggests an intermediate source, some popularization of Jewish antiquities; it is also an argument against the theory of a Jewish or Christian interpolator, whom one would expect to quote more accurately. The LXX has: 3 καὶ εἶπεν ὁ θεός, Γενηθήτω φῶς· καὶ ἐγένετο φῶς ... 9 καὶ εἶπεν ὁ θεός, Συναχθήτω τὸ ὕδωρ τὸ ὑποκάτω τοῦ οὐρανοῦ εἰς συναγωγὴν μίαν καὶ ὀφθήτω ἡ ξηρά· καὶ ἐγένετο οὕτως· καὶ ἐκάλεσεν ὁ θεὸς τὴν ξηρὰν γῆν.

A very close parallel to L's language is provided by a passage in Josephus' *Antiquities*, Preface 3: ἤδη τοίνυν τοὺς ἐντευξομένους τοῖς βιβλίοις παρακαλῶ τὴν γνώμην θεῷ προσανέχειν καὶ δοκιμάζειν τὸν ἡμέτερον νομοθέτην, εἰ τήν τε φύσιν αὐτοῦ ἀξίως κατενόησε καὶ τῇ δυνάμει πρεπούσας ἀεὶ τὰς πράξεις ἀνέθηκε, πάσης καθαρὸν τὸν περὶ αὐτοῦ φυλάξας λόγον τῆς παρ' ἄλλοις ἀσχήμονος μυθολογίας. For other possible Jewish connexions of L, see Introd. xxix f., xl f., and notes on 3. 4, 44.

(iv) John of Sicily (vi. 211 Walz) says that Longinus admired this passage: καὶ ὁ Μωϋσῆς· εἶπεν ὁ θεός, Γενηθῇ τόδε· καὶ ἐγένετο τόδε· ὃν οὐ μόνον Χριστιανῶν ἐκθειάζουσιν ἀλλὰ καὶ τῶν Ἑλλήνων οἱ ἄριστοι, Λογγῖνος καὶ ὁ ἐκ Φαληρέως Δημήτριος. For the bearing of this on the authorship question, see Introd. xxvii f.

9. 10. καὶ τῶν ἀνθρωπίνων: i.e. 'idque ex iis quae ad homines pertinent'.

ἐθίζει: 'is accustomed.' For the active used intransitively, cf. M. Aur. 12. 2: ἐὰν ... ἐθίσῃς ποιεῖν.

εἰς τὰ ἡρωικὰ μεγέθη συνεμβαίνειν: 'enter into grandeurs befitting his heroic characters'. For συνεμβαίνειν cf. 13. 4.

ἀχλὺς ἄφνω: note the vivid asyndeton. Schol. BT comments similarly on P 645: θαυμαστὸν τὸ ἦθος (indication of character)· οὐ γὰρ σωτηρίαν αἰτεῖ ἀλλὰ τὸ μὴ ἐμποδίζεσθαι ἀπὸ ἔργων ἀγαθῶν.

αὐτῷ: cf. 15. 4. A good example of this dative (= *apud eum*) is Pl. *Laws* 706D: Ὀδυσσεὺς γὰρ αὐτῷ λοιδορεῖ τὸν Ἀγαμέμνονα; cf. *Rep.* 389E; Arist. *Pol.* 1339^{b}8; Max. Tyr. 32, 1 a (Hobein); Demetrius, π. ἑρμ. 25.

9. 11] COMMENTARY

τὴν τῶν Ἑλλήνων... μάχην: cf. μάχην... Ἀχαιῶν P 261. So 'battle' is sometimes used for 'army' in older English, e.g. *1 Henry IV*, IV. i. 129: 'What may the king's whole battle reach unto?' 'To thirty thousand.'

ἀλλὰ σὺ ῥῦσαι: for ῥῦσαι in a prayer cf. ῥῦσαι ἡμᾶς ἀπὸ τοῦ πονηροῦ Matthew vi. 13; F. R. Chase, *The Lord's Prayer* 71 ff. For this use of ἀλλά to introduce a wish at the end of a speech, see W. Bühler's note on Moschus 2. 27 (*Die Europa des Moschos*, 1960, p. 72).

Αἴαντος: 'of an Ajax.' Cf. Callim. *ep.* 27. 1; de Vries, p. 60.

ἐν ἀπράκτῳ σκότει: 'in the paralysing dark' (Tucker). The neuter form of σκότος, though attested in Attic, is rather the κοινή and Biblical form (see LSJ, s.v.).

ὡς... ἀντιτάττηται: 'hoping at least to find a burial worthy of his valour, even if it is Zeus who opposes him.' ἐντάφιον is literally 'winding-sheet'. Cf. Polyb. 15. 10. 3: ἐὰν δ' ὡς ἄλλως ἐκβῇ τὰ κατὰ τὸν κίνδυνον, οἱ μὲν ἀποθανόντες εὐγενῶς ἐν τῇ μάχῃ κάλλιστον ἐντάφιον ἕξουσι τὸν ὑπὲρ τῆς πατρίδος θάνατον. The metaphor is hardly used without at least some dim recollection of Simonides' Thermopylae dirge (fr. 4 Bergk): ἐντάφιον δὲ τοιοῦτον οὔτ' εὐρὼς οὔθ' ὁ πανδαμάτωρ ἀμαυρώσει χρόνος. Cf. also Isocr. *Archidamus* 45; Plu. *an seni* 783C; Philostr. *VS* 1. 16; Schmid, *Der Atticismus* III 195–6.

9. 11. ἀλλὰ γὰρ... τοῖς ἀγῶσι: 'but here it is the real Homer the gale of whose genius blows high with the excitement of battle.' De Vries (p. 60) rightly defends the order as laying special emphasis on Ὁμήρος.

ἐνθάδε refers specifically to the Ajax example. ἀλλὰ γὰρ marks the dismissal of a topic and the passage to a new and important point (Denniston, p. 103).

μαίνεται... γίγνεται: a slight adaptation of Homer's μαίνετο δ'... γίγνετο. For the didactic habit of using a quotation to describe an author cf. 3. 2, 15. 3, and perhaps 15. 5.

9. 11–15. This comparison between the *Iliad* and the *Odyssey* is admittedly something of a digression, but it is carefully justified (9. 15) as showing how the capacity for ὕψος and πάθος may decline into foolishness and a mere ability to portray characters and scenes of everyday life. It therefore adds something to the discussion in 3–5, where ὕψος is defined by contrast with οὐχ ὑψηλά. L's other major digressions (12. 2 ff., 33–36) are also συγκρίσεις: see on 12. 4.

The *Odyssey* is a sequel, assuming knowledge of the *Iliad*; it is a work of old age and so naturally mythical or fabulous in content; it is concerned with ἤθη rather than πάθη. Schol. BT on Ω 804 and Eustathius on γ 108 represent a similar point of view. The scholiast says: Μενεκράτης φησὶν αἰσθόμενον ἑαυτοῦ ἀσθενείας τὸν ποιητὴν καὶ τοῦ μὴ ὁμοίως δύνασθαι φράζειν, ἐᾶσαι τὰ μεθ' Ἕκτορα· καλῶς δ' ἐταμιεύσατο ἑαυτῷ τὰ λοιπὰ τῶν διηγημάτων εἰς τὴν Ὀδύσσειαν· μικρὰ γὰρ ἦν ἡ ὑπόθεσις περὶ τῆς οἰκίας τοῦ 'Οδυσσέως μόνον· τὰ γὰρ λείψανα ἐκεῖ ἃ μὲν 'Οδυσσεύς, ἃ δὲ Νέστωρ καὶ Μενέλαος, ἃ δὲ Δημόδοκος κιθαρίζων, φησίν, ⟨διηγεῖται⟩, ἄλλως τε πολιορκίαν μακρὰν οὐκ ἄξιον διηγεῖσθαι. The ideas reflected here are therefore those of Menecrates of Nysa (see P–W, s.v. Menekrates 27), a pupil of Aristarchus and himself the founder of a local school of critics (Strabo 14. 1. 48).

Both opinions about the relative priority of the two epics were evidently current in antiquity. In Lucian, *vera historia* 2. 20, Homer, interviewed in Hades, denies the common view that he wrote the *Odyssey* first. This view is implied by the narrative in the Herodotean *vita Homeri* 26; the *Certamen*, on the other hand, makes the *Iliad* the earlier (p. 236 Allen). In Sen. *de brevitate vitae* 13, the question of priority is given as a typical example of the useless προβλήματα of the grammarians.

9. 11. μεγάλης ... τὸ φιλόμυθον: for ὑποφερομένης 'declining', cf. Max. Tyr. 16. 5: σῶμα ... ἐξ ἥβης ὑπονοστοῦν καὶ ὑποφερόμενον. We should take ἤδη with ὑποφερομένης; the hiatus ἤδη, ἴδιον is also more tolerable with a sense-pause. It looks as if ἐν γήρᾳ, too, goes in sense with ὑποφερομένης, despite the complex order; but Hefermehl may be right to delete it as coming from ἴδιον γήρως below.

9. 12. λείψανα: 'left-overs.' This was evidently Menecrates' word; see the scholion quoted above. The point is that Homer is using up what he had left over after finishing the *Iliad*.

τῶν 'Ἰλιακῶν παθημάτων: cf. Pl. *Rep.* 393B: τῶν ἐν 'Ἰλίῳ καὶ ... τῶν ἐν 'Ἰθάκῃ καὶ ὅλῃ 'Οδυσσείᾳ παθημάτων.

[τοῦ Τρωικοῦ πολέμου]: an intrusive gloss on τῶν 'Ἰλιακῶν παθημάτων.

καὶ νὴ Δί' ... προσαποδιδόναι: τοῖς ἥρωσι goes with προσαποδιδόναι. Reiske's easy and attractive προεγνωσμένοις should be adopted; it enables us to take the verb in its normal sense ('already known') and the resulting meaning fits the quotation which follows, which implies previous knowledge of the characters by the audience. Translate: 'not to speak of the fact that he there puts the expressions of lamentation and pity into the mouths of the heroes, as persons already well known.' L seems to have in mind Pl. *Rep.* 387D: καὶ τοὺς ὀδυρμοὺς ἄρα ἐξαιρήσομεν καὶ τοὺς οἴκτους τοὺς τῶν ἐλλογίμων ἀνδρῶν;

οὐ γὰρ ... ἡ 'Οδύσσεια: it seems no improvement, rather the reverse, to transpose this to follow the quotation (Jahn, Lebègue). For οὐ γὰρ ἀλλ' ἤ (conj., not pronoun) cf. LSJ, s.v. ἀλλ' ἤ and, for example, Lysias 19. 28: γῆ γὰρ οὐκ ἦν ἀλλ' ἢ χωρίδιον.

9. 13. ἐν ἀκμῇ πνεύματος: 'at the top of his form' (as an athlete); cf. Plu. *Sertorius* 13: πνεύματος ἀκμαίου γέμοντι.

ὅλον τὸ σωμάτιον: 'the whole body of the poem.' σῶμα and σωμάτιον are used of books or of a corpus of writing (Cic. *ad Att.* 2. 1. 4). LSJ's 'structure' is wrong. In Latin *corpus* is commonly used in this way, *corpusculum* sometimes. Cf. Heraclitus *quaest. Hom.* 1 (δι' ἀμφοτέρων τῶν σωματίων of *Il.* and *Od.*) and Mar. Victorinus *CGL* vi. 68. 13 (*corpusculis* of *Il.* and *Od.*).

οὐ γὰρ ἔτι ... καταπεπυκνωμένον: 'for he no longer sustains the tension as it was in the tale of Troy nor the consistent level of elevation that never admits any falling off; nor is there any such outpouring of passions crowding one on another, nor yet that versatility, realism, and abundance of images taken from the life.' (i) ποιήμασιν is difficult; perhaps 'verses', cf. C. O. Brink, *Horace on Poetry* 62. (ii) ὁμοίαν: *scil.* τῇ Ἰλιάδι, cf. ὁμοίως in schol. Hom. BT, l.c. (iii) τὸ ἀγχίστροφον καὶ πολιτικόν are the qualities of the quick-witted practical speaker with knowledge of the world; cf. 34. 2, 44. 1. L judges Homer here from the standpoint of a teacher of πολιτικοὶ λόγοι. Cf. Hermogenes, περὶ ἰδεῶν 2. 10, περὶ μεθόδου δεινότητος 33; Quint. 10. 1. 46 (with special reference to debates in *I* and *A* and *sententiae* in *B*). (iv) καταπεπυκνωμένον: 'thickly set with . . . .' Cf. πυκνώσει 10. 1; καταπυκνοῦν τοῖς ὑπερβατοῖς Philod. *rhet.* i. 160 Sudhaus. For ταῖς ἐκ τῆς ἀληθείας φαντασίαις cf. 15. 8: τῆς δὲ ῥητορικῆς φαντασίας κάλλιστον ἀεὶ τὸ ἔμπρακτον καὶ ἐνάληθες.

ἀλλ' οἷον ... πλάνος: a very uncertain passage. (i) It is not clear whether the image is taken from North Sea tides or from cataclysmic floods; but it is perhaps worth noting, in favour of the former view, the Latin use of *senescere* and *adolescere* of ocean tides (Gell. 14. 1. 3; Amm. 27. 8. 4). (ii) ἐρημουμένου has not been satisfactorily explained or emended. (iii) τὸ λοιπόν may go either with what precedes it or with what follows.

The older editors and translators insist that the point of comparison must be that, just as at low tide the original bounds of the sea are still seen, so Homer's greatness appears even in the work of his old age. It would follow that we should read πλάνοις (i.e. Odysseus' wanderings). This, however, wrecks the whole argument.

For τὰ ἴδια μέτρα, which there is no reason to suspect, cf. Aelian, *HA* 10. 43 (of the Nile): ὑπονοστεῖ καὶ ἐς τὰ ἑαυτοῦ μέτρα ὑποστρέφει τὰ ἐκ φύσεώς οἱ νενομισμένα.

πλάνος should almost certainly be kept, despite the abrupt abandonment of the ocean metaphor. There is, I think, a conceit: Homer πλανᾶται in his hero's wanderings. For the metaphor in πλάνος, cf. πλάνος καὶ ἄγνοια in *Cebetis Tabula* 5. 3, &c., or (better) πλάνη ποιητική in Athenagoras 22 (Geffcken, *Zwei griech. Apologeten* 139).

†ἐρημουμένου remains an enigma. Probably it conceals some word of the ἠρέμα family; my ἠρέμα κεχυμένου ('quietly flowing') is one possibility. But Toup's ingenious ἠπειρουμένου ('becoming dry land') still deserves serious consideration; cf. Philo, *de aeternitate mundi* 122: μεγάλων πελαγῶν μεγάλους κόλπους ... ἀναξηρανθέντας ἠπειρῶσθαι. It does not, however, satisfactorily explain the difficult—and perhaps

suspect—περί. Translate provisionally: 'What we see, however, is an ebbing of greatness. It is as though the ocean were withdrawing into itself and (? flowing gently) around its limits. In the fabulous and incredible parts of the poem, all is astray.'

9. 14. γήρας διηγοῦμαι, γήρας δ' ὅμως 'Ομήρου: note the anaphora. Since Homer is a god among poets (see below), there is a common element in this thought and that of Virgil's line about Charon (*Aen.* 6. 304): 'iam senior, sed cruda deo viridisque senectus.'

πλὴν ... μυθικόν: 'Yet throughout all these episodes, without exception, fable predominates over real action.'

τὰ περὶ τὸν ἀσκόν ... ἀπίθανα: winds in wine-skin: κ 17; men changed into pigs: κ 237; Zeus supplied with ambrosia by doves: μ 62; shipwreck: μ 447; murder of suitors: χ 79.

ἐν Κίρκης: 'in Circe's palace.' Faber's conjecture, as Dr. W. Bühler has pointed out to me, is confirmed by κ 282, ἐνὶ Κίρκης, and Plu. *de adulatore et amico* 52D: ἐν Κίρκης μεταμορφωθέντας.

συοφορβουμένους: 'kept as swine.' (Valckenaer's attractive συομορφουμένους cannot be said to be necessary, and the tense is *perhaps* against it, since we should expect aorist or perfect). They were given φάρμακα λυγρά to make them forget their homeland and then touched with a wand and driven into the sty. Once turned into pigs, κλαίοντες ἐέρχατο. Does κλαίοντες here mean squealing or weeping? Is Zoilus complaining about the vulgarity of the description or the improbability of pigs shedding tears?

Zoilus was a Cynic of the middle of the fourth century B.C., who taught Anaximenes of Lampsacus. He wrote, or was himself nicknamed, 'Ομηρομάστιξ. Examples of his carping and sophistical criticism are to be found in the Homer scholia: e.g. he complained that it was unworthy to make Apollo attack mules and dogs with the plague (A 50), he objected to Ψ 100 (ψυχὴ δὲ κατὰ χθονὸς ἠΰτε καπνὸς ᾤχετο) on the ground that smoke rises, and he objected that Diomedes (E 7) would have been burnt by the miraculous fire. So far as the evidence goes, therefore, his theme here may have been either implausibility or ταπεινότης or both. Some of his comments (e.g. on Achilles' grief, Σ 22) are moralizing notes and recall Plato's τύποι θεολογίας in *Rep.* ii–iii. See Radermacher, *Artium Scriptores* 198 ff. Z.'s *Encomium of Polyphemus* is a possible source for the details given here.

ὡς νεοσσόν: 'like a chick.' The doves were thought ἄσεμνα, unless interpreted allegorically as the Pleiads (Athen. 11. 490B).

τοῦ Διὸς ἐνύπνια: a difficult phrase; it appears (τῷ ὄντι) to be an allusion to a proverb or familiar quotation. Dio Chrysostom 11. 129 is clearly relevant: ὥστε καὶ τὴν 'Ομήρου ποίησιν ὀρθῶς ἄν τινα εἰπεῖν ἐνύπνιον, καὶ τοῦτο ἄκριτον καὶ ἀσαφές. (Dio—if the passage is his— compares some of the improbabilities in Homer to recorded dreams in which people imagine themselves talking to the gods, flying, &c.) But what about τοῦ Διός? Zeus indeed sends dreams in Homer (καὶ γάρ τ' ὄναρ ἐκ Διός ἐστιν, A 63), but it would be frigid and pointless if this were all that L means. It is probably better to look for the clue in the notion that Homer is the Zeus of poets (cf. Quint. 10. 1. 46); the effect of the phrase 'Zeus' dreams' is then like that of *bonus dormitat Homerus*. (Wilamowitz's deletion of τοῦ is not necessary, given the freedom in the use of the article in all late Greek.)

9. 15. προσιστορήσθω: the perfect is needed, as Weiske saw, since the discussion of the *Odyssey* is now complete. Cf. 39. 2, ἅλις πεφιλολογῆσθαι.

ἡ ἀπακμὴ τοῦ πάθους . . . εἰς ἦθος ἐκλύεται: so Arist. *Poetics* 1459ᵇ14 : ἡ μὲν 'Ιλιὰς ἁπλοῦν καὶ παθητικόν, ἡ δ' 'Οδύσσεια πεπλεγμένον . . . καὶ ἠθική. Aristotle and L mean that the *Odyssey* is more realistic, nearer to everyday life, milder in emotional tone. The antithesis between ἦθος and πάθος, which bears many meanings (see Lockwood, *CQ* xxiii (1929) 180 ff.) and is a tool much used by ancient critics (see, for example, Dion. Hal. *Demosth.* 2, 8, 43, 53), is really a formulation of a common preconception in antiquity—borne out to a great extent by the literature itself—that there is a positive correlation between realism and lack of seriousness and tension. See in general E. Auerbach, *Mimesis* 25–27 (Anchor Books, 1957). Good accounts of the contrast are in Cic. *orator* 128 and Quint. 6. 2. 8–24. Note especially Cic., l.c.: ἠθικὸν . . . 'ad naturas et ad mores et ad omnem vitae consuetudinem accommodatum . . . come, iucundum, ad benevolentiam conciliandam paratum'; Quint., l.c. 9: 'cautiores . . . adfectus igitur πάθος concitatos, ἦθος mites atque compositos esse dixerunt . . . hos imperare, illos persuadere'; ibid. 20: 'illud comoediae, hoc tragoediae magis simile.' So the *Odyssey* stands to the *Iliad* as comedy (i.e. Menandrean comedy) to tragedy. See Grube's note on his translation, p. 16.

We may perhaps think of the change from the great tragedies to *The Tempest* and *The Winter's Tale* as a rough illustration of L's point about Homer's old age.

τοιαῦτα . . . ἠθολογουμένη: 'his realistic description of Odysseus' house, with its depiction of character, is of this kind. It is a sort of comedy of manners.' If we refuse to allow this asyndeton, we must take τοιαῦτα as adverbial and dispense with punctuation after οἰκίαν.

βιολογούμενα implies portrayal of ordinary life, and comedy is *par excellence* the realistic genre. Cf. ὦ Μένανδρε καὶ βίε, πότερος ἄρ' ὑμῶν πότερον ἀπεμιμήσατο; (Aristophanes of Byzantium, *ap.* Syrian. comment. in Hermog. ii. 23 Rabe.)

Similarly, Dion. Hal. (*CV* 3. 13) calls the incidents of the arrival of Telemachus at Eumaeus' hut (π 1–16): πραγμάτι' ἄττα βιωτικά, ἡρμηνευμένα ὑπέρευ.

10. *Proper selection and arrangement of material.*

10. 1. ἔχοιμεν: optative not significant: cf. 2. 2. But we should perhaps read ἔχομεν: cf. 10. 3, where P has θαυμάζοις by error for θαυμάζεις.

ἐπειδὴ ... συνυπάρχοντα: 'since everything has naturally connected with it certain elements inherent in the material.' Cf. Dion. Hal. *CV* 16. 96: τά τε ἤθη καὶ τὰ πάθη καὶ αἱ διαθέσεις καὶ τὰ ἔργα τῶν προσώπων καὶ τὰ συνεδρεύοντα τούτοις.

ὗλαι (plural) is Hellenistic (Polyb., Philo, &c.).

τῶν ἐμφερομένων: 'constituent features.' So 12. 2: πάντων τῶν ἐμφερομένων τοῖς πράγμασι μορίων καὶ τόπων. Cf. Philo, *de migratione Abrahami* 28. 155: ἵν' ὅλον δι' ὅλων τὸ γένος ᾧ πᾶν εἶδος ἐμφέρεται μετέρχηται.

ὃ μὲν γὰρ ... προσάγεται: 'for the one wins over the hearer by the choice of topics, the other by the density in which those selected are set before him.' Notice how the concepts of ἐκλογή and σύνθεσις (cf. 8. 1) are here employed for a new purpose.

λαμβάνει: 'takes up'; cf. λημμάτων, 'points', just above. Sappho 'takes up' the circumstances attendant on passion (συμβαίνοντα = συνυπάρχοντα) by looking at the symptoms as they really are (ἐκ τῆς ἀληθείας αὐτῆς). But it is in her selection of the most important facts and arrangement of those she selects that she shows her excellence.

ποῦ δὲ ...; ὅτι ...: 'in what way ...? In that ....' Wifstrand's conjecture (*Eikota* iii (*Bulletin de la Société Royale des lettres de Lund*, 1934) 11 ff.) is a definite improvement. Cf. for the form of the sentence Lucian, *pro imag.* 19: ἀλλὰ ποῦ τὸ ἴδιον τοῦ ἐπαίνου ἀποτελεῖται; ἢν ὁ κύων τῷ λέοντι ἐοικέναι λέγηται ....

10. 2. For text and interpretation of the poem see especially Page, *Sappho and Alcaeus*, ch. ii, on which the following brief notes are largely based, and Bowra, *Greek Lyric Poetry*² 185–9. This is one of the two poems of Sappho—the other being the Aphrodite hymn in Dion. Hal. *CV* 23—which the indirect tradition has preserved to us at length. It was famous in antiquity: Catullus adapted it (51) and Plutarch alludes to it three times (*de prof.* 81D, *Eroticus* 763A, *Demetr.* 38. 3). In modern times it has been much admired and often translated. Boileau's version, indeed, is tasteless, but his English follower Ambrose Phillips avoids some of the pitfalls and is still worth reading (*Spectator* 229, with a critique by Addison). Two great poets have attempted adaptations—Racine (*Phèdre* I. iii) and Tennyson (*Eleanore* and *Fatima*). Hall's version in his translation of L (1652) seems to be the earliest in English. I reprint it here, as it is difficult of access and of considerable interest:

> He that sits next thee now and hears
> Thy charming voyce, to me appears
> Beauteous as any deity
> That rules the Sky.

COMMENTARY

> How did his pleasing glances dart 5
> Sweet languors to my ravish'd heart!
> At the first sight thou so prevail'd
>   That my voyce fail'd.
> I'm speechlesse, feav'rish, fires assail
> My fainting flesh, my sight doth fail, 10
> Whilest to my restlesse mind my ears
>   Still hum new fears.
> Cold sweats and tremblings so invade
> That like a wither'd flower I fade,
> So that my life being almost lost 15
>   I seem a Ghost.
> Yet since I'm wretched I must dare.

P's text of the poem is written out as prose, like the other poetical quotations. It preserves a number of Aeolic forms, e.g. ἰμέροεν, βρόχε', ὐπαδεδρόμακεν. How should the text be presented in editions of L? Radermacher (*Dionysii Opuscula* ii, praef. xi ff.) discusses the similar (but not identical) problem in *de compositione verborum*. Our papyri of Lesbian lyric are of the Roman period, so that the text they give is a fair guide to the knowledge of early Aeolic which was accessible to L. Whether or not he availed himself of the best direct tradition to be had, we shall never know. I assume he did. See Introd. l.

On the poem in general, see Page, pp. 19 ff.; on the dialect, pp. 327–9.

Lines 1–2. Either 'That man is the gods' equal inasmuch as he ...' *or*, 'That man, whatever is his name, who is sitting opposite you ...' *or again*, 'any man who sits opposite you ...'. 'Equal to the gods', *scil.* in happiness.

Line 5. τό: *either* the girl's voice and laughter, *or* the sight of the man and the girl together. See below.

μ': i.e. μοι.

ἐπτόαισεν: gnomic or referring to a specific occasion? Or just expressing an *instant* reaction (cf. ἤσθην, &c.; Goodwin, *GMT* § 60)?

Lines 7–8. 'For as soon as I look at you for a moment, it is impossible for me to utter a word.'

βρόχε' (=βραχέα) is adverbial: φώναισ' = φώναισαι = Attic infinitive φωνῆσαι. Page inclines to regard εἴκει, like Attic παρείκει, as impersonal ('it is possible'); Bowra (p. 185, n. 1) takes it as ἴκει, 'comes': cf. Hesych. s.v., εἴκει· παρεγένετο.

ὠς ... ὠς: cf. Ξ 294 ὡς δ' ἴδεν, ὥς μιν ἔρως ... ; Theocr. 2. 82 ὡς ἴδον ὡς ἐμάνην; Moschus 2. 74, with Bühler's note. Note that Sappho uses the subjunctive ('whenever' (?)).

Line 9. †ἔαγε is intransitive, 'is smashed'. (κὰμ ... ἔαγε = κατέαγε.)

This is a vigorous expression (what L might call ἰδιωτισμός, cf. 31) but perhaps not out of place. The hiatus γλῶσσα ἔαγε is, however, unexplained. Lobel's ἄκαν means 'in silence'.

Line 13. Very difficult. In *An. Ox.* i. 208 Cramer the passage is quoted as evidence for ἱδρώς as a feminine, of which there is no other example. With Ahrens's conjecture (μ' = μοι) the phrase means 'sweat pours off me'. Page's suggestion, which he renders 'a cold sweat covers me', finds some support in L's ψύχεται (10. 3), unless this alludes simply to τρόμος.

Line 14. Cf. Homeric χλωρὸν δέος, K 376, &c.

Lines 16–17. Page is probably right in supposing that the end of 16 is lost (L may, however, have omitted it: cf. 26. 1, 27. 4 for incomplete metrical quotations) and that ἀλλά begins the new stanza.

For the transition cf. Archilochus fr. 7 Diehl, 5–7:

ἀλλὰ θεοὶ γὰρ ἀνηκέστοισι κακοῖσιν,
ὦ φίλ', ἐπὶ κρατερὴν τλημοσύνην ἔθεσαν
φάρμακον.

General interpretation.

There is no need to imagine that the girl is a bride with her husband, or that Sappho is an emotional schoolmistress talking about a favourite pupil. These are the fictional embellishments of modern scholarship: see Page, p. 27. Nevertheless, the situation is not quite clear. (i) φαίνεται ... ἱμέροεν may refer either to a specific occasion or to a repeated situation (Catullus 51. 4 has *identidem*: it probably follows that he took Sappho to mean that the man had constant opportunities to enjoy the girl's company); (ii) the reference of τό (5) is not certain, nor is the meaning of ἐπτόαισεν (6); (iii) in 7 ff. ὡς ... ἴδω ought to be general ('whenever I see'), and it would follow that all the symptoms are habitual.

Consider these two general summaries, from which the points of legitimate doubt should become clear: (i) 'Any man who enjoys your company is happy! Hearing you talk and laugh excites me: for whenever I see you . . . . Still, one must endure . . . .' (ii) 'How happy that man there is, for he enjoys your laughter and talk! It excites me to see you together; for whenever I see you . . . . Still, one must endure . . . .'

10. 3. οὐ θαυμάζεις; whatever the solution of the puzzle of the last line of the poem, L's comment certainly begins here: cf. 9. 6 ἐπιβλέπεις ...;

ὑπὸ τὸ αὐτό: 'at the same moment.' L's criticism is a little hard to follow: ἀκοάς refers to 8 and 11, γλῶσσαν to 9, ὄψεις to 11, χρόαν to 10 or 14, ψύχεται to 13, and κάεται to 10. The contrast ἀλογιστεῖ φρονεῖ appears to be a general remark on the wonderful incongruity between Sappho's passion and her rational capacity for objectivizing her emotions. φοβεῖται presumably refers to τρόμος δὲ παῖσαν ἄγρει, and so need not be questioned, but ἢ γάρ ... ἤ offends (hiatus, construction). Hermann (*Opuscula* vi. 1. 110) proposed [φρονεῖ] φοβεῖται, παρ' κ.τ.λ. taking γάρ as a development of γρ = γράφεται, the usual note of a marginal variant. But this destroys the ἐναντίωσις of ἀλογιστεῖ φρονεῖ. I am tempted simply to delete ἢ γάρ and ἤ.

οὐ θαυμάζεις ... ἐπιζητεῖ; 'do you not marvel at the way she pursues, all at once, her body and soul, her hearing and tongue, her vision and complexion, all lost to her as though not hers at all?'

ἵνα: here consecutive, not final; the two types of clause became confused in Hellenistic Greek when ἵνα began to extend its empire at the expense of other conjunctions (cf. modern Greek νά). A particularly clear instance of consecutive ἵνα is Epictetus 2. 2. 16: οὕτω μῶρος ἦν ἵνα μὴ ἴδῃ. See Arndt–Gingrich, s.v. ἵνα ii. 2.

10. 4. ὁ ... τὰ Ἀριμάσπεια ποιήσας: traditionally, Aristeas of Proconnesus (fr. 1 Kinkel; on this passage see Bowra *CQ*, N.S. vi (1956) 1–10, and especially J. D. P. Bolton, *Aristeas of Proconnesus* 8–15) whom we know principally from Herod. 4. 13 ff. He disappeared in mysterious circumstances and reappeared in his home town in the seventh year; it was then that he composed this poem, in which he related how he had travelled φοιβόλαμπτος γενόμενος in Siberia, with many strange facts about Issedones, gold-guarding griffins, Hyperboreans, and so on. He was connected with Apollo, whose cult he spread at Metapontum in the south of Italy. Herodotus dates him in the seventh century. Is the passage which L quotes from a poem of such antiquity? Both style and content give rise to doubts, but not overwhelming ones. The style is simple, but of a mannered simplicity, especially the balance of line 4. The subject is uncertain; it is perhaps most likely that it is the surprised comment of innocent continentals on the first ship they have heard of. At any rate, other explanations which have been proposed—dwellers in lake-villages on piles, or amphibious monsters with webbed feet like Lucian's φελλόποδες—do not carry conviction. Is this sort of moralizing likely at such an early date? Bolton (p. 10, 19) clearly thinks not: I do not feel sure, and am inclined to adduce on the other side two famous passages in archaic poetry which, added together, suggest the theme: Hesiod's remarks about the dangers of seafaring, *erga* 618 ff., and the motif in *Od.* 11. 122 ff. of the distant people who know nothing about ships and the sea.

The last line clearly refers to sea-sickness, not to fear or unfavourable extispicy. Ruhnken was right to compare Plu. *de vitando aere alieno* 831C: ἐμοῦντος τοῦ ἑτέρου (a vulture) καὶ λέγοντος τὰ σπλάγχν' ἐκβάλλειν.

The lines do not describe a storm but the permanent discomforts of those who ὕδωρ ναίουσιν ... ἐν πελάγεσσι, so that the comparison with the Homeric passage is not quite fair.

ὄμματ'... ἔχουσιν: 'their eyes are fixed on the stars, their lives depend on the sea.' Cf. Archiloch. fr. 21, quoted on 10. 7 below. A mannered zeugma. The statement would apply to sailors, but not to lake-villagers or web-footed men.

ἄνθος: prettiness, elegance, charm; not what we call floweriness. Cf. Dion. Hal. on Pl. *ad Pomp.* 2: ἱλαρόν τι καὶ τεθηλὸς καὶ μεστὸν ὥρας ἄνθος ἀναδίδωσι.

10. 5. ὁ δὲ Ὅμηρος πῶς; Cf. 9. 5 and Dio Chrysostom 33. 19: ἀλλ' Ἀρχίλοχος μὲν οὕτως εἶπεν, Ὅμηρος δὲ πῶς;

10. 6. Schol. BT on the Homer passage (628) adduce this line of Aratus, which is in turn imitated by Quintus Smyrnaeus 8. 418: τυτθὴ δὲ βίη μέγα πῆμ' ἀπερύκει. [Plu.] *de vita et poesi Homeri* 160 also mentions Aratus' imitation as an instance of the way in which later poets παρέφρασαν Homer's γνῶμαι καὶ παραινέσεις.

Aratus was an exceedingly popular poet in Hellenistic and Roman education, largely because of his instructive content: some knowledge of astronomy was necessary for the formation of the characteristic religious and moral ideas of the period. There are many ancient commentaries and Latin translations. So such comparisons as this are natural; but Posidonius' σύγκρισις Ὁμήρου καὶ Ἀράτου, which was concerned with astronomy, is not a likely source (V. Reinhardt, P-W, s.v. Poseidonios col. 667).

γλαφυρόν: 'smooth, polished.' Cf. 33. 5. This is a term often used in describing types of style (e.g. γλαφυρὸς χαρακτήρ in Demetrius) and it indicates much the same qualities as does ἀνθηρός. See Rhys Roberts, *Demetrius* p. 272.

παρώρισε: see 2. 2, 38. 1. The sense alleged in LSJ ('limit') would suit here, but in view of the lack of confirmatory evidence it is perhaps better to follow Langbaine and say 'banished', 'sent packing'. So below: 'Homer does not get rid of the danger once for all....'

ξύλον ἅϊδ' ἐρύκει: P gives ἀπείργει. There are two ways of dealing with this. (i) Correct to ἐρύκει (Manutius): ' "A mere plank wards off death." Then it prevents it.' This is best; it is highly unlikely that, having quoted Aratus correctly, L should then go on, in repeating his verbal quotation, to make a mistake. On this view, moreover, οὐκοῦν may be taken in its common inferential sense; with P's reading it is progressive: 'well, it does' (Denniston 439). (ii) Correct to ἐρύκει, but also delete οὐκοῦν ἀπείργει as a corruption of ἤγουν ἀπείργει, a gloss explaining the poetical word (Ruhnken). This is an unnecessarily complicated hypothesis.

The conceit did not escape the declaimers: cf. Cestius Pius *ap.* Sen. rhet. *Contr.* 7. 1 (16) 10: 'parva materia seiungit fata.'

ἀλλὰ... εἰκονογραφεῖ: 'but draws a picture of people constantly on the point of death—many times a wave, one might almost say.' Or should we, as Professor Dodds suggests to me, delete πολλάκις as a gloss? As it is, we have a frigid conceit. For the general idea, we may perhaps compare Aristides 47 (23). 2: πόσοις τισὶ τοῖς πᾶσιν ῥοθίοις ἐνέτυχον καὶ ποίας τινὸς τῆς θαλάσσης παρ' ἕκαστον αὐτῶν ἐπειρώμην.

καὶ μὴν ... φέρονται: compound prepositions are rare in prose of all periods. ὑπέκ, like παρέκ, is fairly common in Homer. Wackernagel (*Vorlesungen über Syntax* ii. 231) remarks that ὑπὲκ τῶν γρυπῶν ἁρπάζειν in Herod. 3. 116 may be a poetical quotation—from the *Arimaspea*.

[**ὑπὲκ θανάτοιο**]: we expect to find the quotation at the end of the sentence; cf. 9. 12, 15. 6, &c. The insertion of ὑπὲκ θανάτοιο as a reminder in the middle is very odd: G. S. A. (whose identity I have failed to discover) was, I think, right to delete it: it is probably a marginal note which has intruded into the text.

τῷ μὲν συνεμπίπτοντι ... τὸ ἰδίωμα: 'he has tortured the words to correspond with the emotions of the moment and at the same time magnificently expressed the emotion by the compression of the words, virtually stamping the special character of the danger on the diction.' For βασανίζω in this sense cf. Dion. Hal. *Thuc.* 55: πολὺ τὸ βεβασανισμένον καὶ τὸ σολοικοφανὲς ἐν τοῖς σχηματισμοῖς. It is apparently unusual for ἔπος to mean unambiguously a single word; but τῇ τοῦ ἔπους συνθλίψει certainly refers to the unnatural compounding of ὑπό and ἐκ; *ecthlipsis* is found as a technical term for a sort of synaloephe (Ap. Dysc. *conj.* 230. 10). Note the repeated συν- compounds (cf. 15. 4, 22. 4); like repeated *con-* in Latin (e.g. 'rerum consentiens conspirans continuata cognatio', Cic. *ND* 2. 19), this is a fairly common phenomenon.

10. 7. οὐκ ἄλλως ὁ Ἀρχίλοχος: this perhaps alludes to Archilochus' elegy commemorating the loss at sea of his sister's husband; frr. 10–12 Diehl, with *P. Oxy.* 2356. But there are also iambic fragments on similar subjects; see 21 Diehl (ψυχὰς ἔχοντες κυμάτων ἐν ἀγκάλαις) and 43 (ἴστη κατ' ἠκὴν κύματός τε κἀνέμου).

ἐπὶ τῇ προσαγγελίᾳ ... φησίν: this very well-known passage is Demosthenes' description of the alarm felt at Athens when news came of Philip's occupation of Elatea in 339. The rhetoricians greatly admired it: e.g. Hermogenes (Spengel ii. 349) uses it as an example of γοργότης ('vehemence') and draws attention particularly to the trochaic rhythms. There are many imitations: for two particularly trivial and tasteless ones see Chariton 1. 3. 1, 8. 1. 5.

ἀλλὰ τὰς ἐξοχὰς ... ἐπισυνέθηκαν: 'they polished up and put together the special excellences, taking only the best ....' The metaphor, as in the next sentence, is from building. Editors quote Pl. *Rep.* 361D, where ἐκκαθαίρειν is used of cleaning up statues for exhibition. This is not a very close parallel, but the word may still be right here—blocks of stone need cleaning up before being fitted.

But Ruhnken's ἐπικρίναντες removes the difficulty. For the position of ἀριστίνδην, see on 1. 1, 15. 6.

οὐδὲν ... διὰ μέσου: for φλοιώδες, see on 3. 2. For σχολικόν, see on 3. 5. The metaphor here derives from Homer (Δ 299 f., weaklings in the middle) but is often applied to style: see, for example, *ad Herennium* 3. 10. 18; Quint. 5. 12. 14; Longinus epit. Laur. E 13–20 Prickard[2]: δεῖ ... μιμεῖσθαι τὴν ἐν τοῖς πολέμοις τακτικήν, εἰς μέσον τοὺς χείρους λοχίζουσαν.

λυμαίνεται γὰρ ... συντετειχισμένα: a very difficult sentence. P has αι corrected into ῆ; otherwise the tradition is clear. It is certain, or at least highly probable, (i) that ψύγματα, 'gaps' (Latin *spiramenta*: Vitruv. 4. 7) should not be changed into ψήγματα ('dust', 'chippings') or anything else: cf. Dion. Hal. *CV* 20. 141: τὸ μεταξὺ τῶν ὀνομάτων ψῦγμα; (ii) that ἀραιώματα, 'crevices', is also correct. Almost everything else is in doubt. (i) Dem. *de corona* 303: πάντα ταῦτ' ἐλυμαίνετο τοῖς ὅλοις suggests that τὸ ὅλον is the object of λυμαίνεται (the dative is not essential) but we cannot rule out the possibility that it is adverbial. (ii) There is uncertainty about συνοικονομούμενα, but this does not much affect the total interpretation; Manutius' συνοικοδομούμενα fits in well with the building metaphor and is supported by 39. 3 τῇ τῶν λέξεων ἐποικοδομήσει τὰ μεγέθη συναρμόζουσαν, a passage with obvious resemblances to this. (iii) The construction of ἐμποιοῦντα is doubtful: I take it, however, that ψύγματα ἢ ἀραιώματα is its object, whether its subject be μεγέθη or ταῦτα. (iv) There is no clear evidence that μεγέθη can mean 'large blocks of stone', though some translators take it like this; it often, on the other hand, means 'examples of literary μέγεθος', as in 39. 3. (v) The most intractable difficulty of all lies in συντετειχισμένα; we have no proof that this could mean anything but 'enclosed within the same circuit of walls'; but if the word is right here, it apparently means 'put together to make a wall'. Its tense, too, is to be noted: it can hardly be co-ordinate with the present participle συνοικοδομούμενα.

I offer two tentative translations. The first assumes that συνοικοδομούμενα ... σχέσει is subordinate to συντετειχισμένα. 'For they utterly spoil, by producing as it were gaps or crevices, grand expressions which have been (? built into one structure) by being fitted together in virtue of their relation to one another.' The second is based on admitting the possibility of an elaborate interlacing of subject and object, ταῦτα ... συνοικοδομούμενα going together as subject and μεγέθη ... συντετειχισμένα as object. Cf. (on a small scale) Pl. *Laws* 798D: τὰ μὲν οὖν ἄλλα ἐλάττω μεταβαλλόμενα κακὰ διεξεργάζοιτ' ἄν, 'changes in the others would produce lesser evils'. 'For the building of these things into the structure, by producing as it were gaps or crevices, utterly ruins grand expressions which have been

(? built into one construction) in virtue of their relation to one another.'

But it is, of course, not impossible that there is some corruption or considerable omission. I give below three recent English translations; two of them assume changes. I hope the natural points of controversy may appear from the comparison. (i) Grube retains the reading of P. 'Such things spoil a whole work, as massive stones that are being fitted into a wall spoil a whole edifice when they leave chinks and fissures as they are fitted together.' συνοικονομούμενα is subordinate to ἐμποιοῦντα. Again the meaning and tense of συντετειχισμένα cause difficulty; so does the meaning of μεγέθη. (ii) ⟨τὰ⟩ μεγέθη . . . τῇ ⟨τε⟩ πρός . . . Fyfe (adopting Toll's τε). 'For all such irrelevancies are like the introduction of gaps or open tracery in architecture; they utterly [τὸ ὅλον] spoil the effect of sublime ideas, well ordered and built into one coherent structure.' Here 'open tracery' surely gives quite a wrong impression. (iii) Rhys Roberts reads ἐμποιοῦντα ⟨ἐς⟩ and translates: 'For these faults mar the effect of the whole, just as though they introduced chinks or fissures into stately and co-ordinated edifices whose walls are compacted by their reciprocal adjustment.' μεγέθη is here wrongly interpreted; but this is not inherent in Rhys Roberts's suggestion for the text, which has much to commend it. Ruhnken was a brave man to preface his own radical but implausible solution with the words: 'Locus vehementer vexatus, verumtamen posthac non amplius vexandus.'

11–12. 2. *Amplification.*

L distinguishes αὔξησις both from ὕψος and from the synthesis of details described in 10. He criticizes the rhetoricians' definition as being too wide and attempts one of his own. Observe that in 12 (i) ὕψος is clearly distinguished from πάθος and both are thought of as means to ποιόν τι μέγεθος, (ii) as in 1. 4 it is a special characteristic of ὕψος that it can be seen in single *sententiae*.

In all this L seems to be following a line of his own. The theory of αὔξησις was developed in the early days of rhetoric and had special reference to epideictic oratory, and also to the exciting of emotions (see Buchheit, pp. 15 ff. and his index; Caplan's note on *ad Herennium* 2. 30. 47; Aristotle's discussion is mostly in *Rhet.* A 9 and 14). In the most general terms αὔξησις includes all means of making things seem bigger (or, for example, more terrible) than they are.

Quintilian's account of *amplificatio* (8. 4) gives the best idea of the types of technical device discussed under this head in L's time. He lists the following species: (i) *in ipso rei nomine*, e.g. calling an honest man *latro*: (ii) *per incrementum*, e.g. 'ut de vomitu in Antonium Cicero' (*Phil.* 2. 25. 63): 'in coetu vero populi Romani, negotium publicum gerens, magister equitum': (iii) *per comparationem*, e.g. 'if my slaves feared me as your fellow citizens fear you, I should think it wise to leave home' (*in Cat.* 1. 17): (iv) *per ratiocinationem*, when we are led to infer the greatness or horror of the subject from some allied details; e.g. 'in his slaves' chambers were purple coverlets which had been Pompey's' (*Phil.* 2. 27. 67) lets us infer *a fortiori* what luxury there must be in the master's house: (v) *per congeriem*—the multiplication of phrases of the same meaning.

11. 1. ταῖς προεκκειμέναις: if we lay weight on the plural, this must refer to the qualities described in 9 and 10; but the examples in the extant parts of 9 do not bear any obvious kinship to αὔξησις. A slightly careless connecting formula?

ὅταν ... κατ' ἐπίτασιν: 'when the facts of the case and the issues involved admit many starts and pauses, section by section, and impressive phrases are brought into position one after another and introduced so as to intensify the whole.'

(i) κατὰ περιόδους can hardly refer to periods in the technical sense (though L does, *pace* Grube, so use the word in 40. 1); Weiske was probably right in suggesting *Abschnitt*, 'section'. Grube renders 'from time to time', comparing ὁ ἐκ περιόδου πυρετός, 'intermittent fever' (Lucian, *Philopseudes* 9). (ii) ἀρχαί, 'fresh starts', is at any rate possible. Rothstein's ἀργίαι—places where the argument idles and does not advance—is suggested by Anon. *de figuris*, Spengel iii. 176: ἐπιμονὴ (= Latin *commoratio*) δὲ ἡ ἐπὶ τοῦ αὐτοῦ καὶ ἑνὸς πράγματος ἀργία καὶ ἀναστροφὴ χάριν αὐξήσεως. (iii) The building metaphor is still maintained in ἐπεισκυκλούμενα ... ἐπεισάγηται. (iv) Wilamowitz's κατ' ἐπίτασιν, 'by way of intensification', is preferable to P's κατ' ἐπίβασιν—'by way of climax' (?)—and is a very slight change. The word occurs in a similar context but in a much more restricted sense in Phoebammon, *de figuris*, Spengel iii. 47: ἐπίτασις δέ ἐστιν ἐπιμονῆς μὲν εἶδος, οὐκ ἐπίσης δὲ δηλοῦν τὸ πρᾶγμα, ἀλλ' ἐξαλλαγὴν ἔχον ἐπὶ τὸ μεῖζον.

11. 2. τοῦτο δὲ ... γίνοιτο: 'whether this is achieved by the use of commonplaces or by exaggeration or insistence on circumstances or arguments, or by the building up of actions or emotions.' (i) τοπηγορία 'use of commonplaces' (cf. 12. 5, 32. 5) subserves αὔξησις by providing material to expand the basic idea. Cf. also *ad Herennium* 2. 30, 47: 'amplificatio est res quae per locum communem instigationis auditorum causa adsumitur.' (ii) δείνωσις in Quintilian (6. 2. 24) is 'rebus indignis asperis invidiosis addens vim oratio'. (iii) Portus's deletion of ἤ makes a neater sentence, but is not imposed upon us. (iv) For ἐπίρρωσις cf. Anon. Seg., Spengel i. 430. (v) For the emendation of ἐποικονομίαν—which is not found elsewhere and would be inappropriate in meaning—cf. 10. 7, 39. 3, and *Rhet. ad Alex.* 1426ᵇ3 ἐποικοδομοῦντα τὸ ἕτερον ὡς ἐπὶ τὸ ἕτερον αὔξειν.

πλὴν εἰ μὴ ... ἐν εὐτελισμοῖς: for this use of ἄρα, indicating that the hypothesis is one the possibility of which has only just been realized, cf., e.g., Aristoph. *Birds* 601: οὐδεὶς οἶδεν τὸν θησαυρὸν τὸν

12. 2–13. 1] COMMENTARY 109

ἐμόν, πλὴν εἴ τις ἄρ' ὄρνις: see Denniston, p. 38; Dion. Hal. *Dem.* 23 (p. 180. 5 U–R): πλὴν εἴ τις ἄρα; Demetrius π. ἑρμ. 83: πλὴν εἰ μή τις ἄρα .... But νὴ Δία would be much more apt in the second clause (cf. 33. 5, 39. 4, 44. 1 for ἦ νὴ Δία) and I think we should not hesitate to make this small transposition.

εὐτελισμοῖς: 'disparagement'—Latin *elevatio*—is from one point of view the opposite of αὔξησις, since it diminishes the worth of things; but so far as rhetorical technique is concerned it is just another form of exaggeration. 'To make great things small and small things great' is a traditional function of rhetoric (Pl. *Phaedr.* 267A; Isocr. *Paneg.* 8). On pity, see 8. 2.

εὐθὺς ... συνεπιρρωνύμενον: 'their practical element loses all vigour and fullness when deprived of the support of elevation.' I see no reason to question κενοῦται: cf. Theophr. *HP* 9. 14. 3 (quoted by LSJ) ῥιζῶν ... μανουμένων καὶ κενουμένων. The context here (σώματος ... ἀτονεῖ ... συνεπιρρωνύμενον) suggests that the metaphors are medical.

11. 3. τοῦ ἀρτίως εἰρημένου: 10. 1.

12. 1. ὁ μὲν οὖν τῶν τεχνογράφων ... τοῖς ὑποκειμένοις: cf. Anon. Seg. (Spengel i. 457): λόγος μεῖζον ποιῶν φαίνεσθαι τὸ πρᾶγμα. Arist. *Rhet.* 1. 9. 1368ᵃ27: ἡ μὲν αὔξησις ἐπιτηδειοτάτη τοῖς ἐπιδεικτικοῖς· τὰς γὰρ πράξεις ὁμολογουμένας λαμβάνουσιν, ὥστε λοιπὸν μέγεθος περιθεῖναι καὶ κάλλος.

καὶ ἐν πλήθει: αὔξησις does not always involve δίαρμα, so καὶ should not be translated 'also'. See Denniston, p. 305 for some similar examples.

κοινὸς οὗτος ὅρος: οὗτος is probably the subject and κοινὸς ὅρος the predicate; Manutius's ὁ is then not needed.

12. 2. συμπλήρωσις ἀπὸ ... τὸ κατεσκευασμένον: 'an aggregation of all the details and topics which constitute the situation, strengthening the argument by dwelling on it ....' For ἐμφερομένων cf. 10. 1. For ἀπὸ or ἐκ added to genitives where classical usage would have no preposition, see Blass–Debrunner, §§ 169, 172. 180. An obvious example is John xii. 3: ἡ οἰκία ἐπληρώθη ἐκ τῆς ὀσμῆς.

τῇ ἐπιμονῇ: cf. Anon. *de fig.* quoted on 11. 1; also *ad Herenn.* 4. 45. 58; Cic. *de oratore* 3. 53. 202.

ταύτῃ ... ἀποδεί⟨κνυσιν⟩: some part of ἀποδεικνύναι is clearly needed. The general sense is that πίστις demonstrates, whereas αὔξησις impresses by iteration or development of the original idea.

12. 2–13. 1. Where P resumes, the same general subject is still being discussed, with the help of a *contrast between the abundance of Plato and the vehemence of Demosthenes*. This leads (12. 4–5) to a short *comparison of Demosthenes and Cicero*, which is incidental to the main plan. L returns to Plato at 13. 1; in him at least fullness is compatible with μέγεθος (οὐδὲν ἧττον μεγεθύνεται 13. 1; this is presumably not μέγεθος in its widest sense—ποιόν τι μέγεθος of 12. 1—but simply ὕψος).

L often shows his enthusiasm for Plato; see 12. 3, 13. 1, 13. 3, 32. 5–7, 35. 1. Caecilius had clearly disparaged him, perhaps in the same way as his friend Dionysius in *Demosth.* 5 ff. (same passage repeated in *ad Pomp.* 2; more moderate opinions in *CV* 18. 117 and *de imitatione* 6. 4, p. 210 U–R). When writing simply, says Dionysius, Plato is charming and his work possesses a delightful archaic patina (πίνος, cf. εὐπίνεια, L 30. 1), but in his more elaborate moments he becomes obscure and long-winded and does not even write good Greek. He affects long periphrases and poetical and archaic words. His use of figures and tropes is unhappy, καὶ μάλιστα τοῖς Γοργιείοις ἀκαίρως καὶ μειρακιωδῶς ἐναβρύνεται (i.e. parisosis and the like), καὶ πολὺς ὁ τελέτης ἐν τοιούτοις παρ' αὐτῷ ('the witch doctor is strong in him') ὡς καὶ Δημήτριος ὁ Φαληρεὺς εἴρηκέ που. Such criticism was widespread; even Plutarch, a devoted Platonist, admitted that Gorgianism ἥψατο ... καὶ τοῦ θαυμαστοῦ Πλάτωνος (fr. 138 Bern.). It found its justification in the *Laws* and the *Phaedrus* myth, much of which was not unfairly labelled διθυραμβῶδες. Further, rhetoricians sometimes took the *Menexenus* seriously as a model λόγος ἐπιτάφιος (cf. Hermogenes, Spengel ii. 446; Synesius, *Dion*, p. 237, 13 Terzaghi) and very naturally found it wanting. (Cf. Cic. *orator* 151; Dion. Hal. *Demosth.* 23 ff.).

See in general the material collected by F. Walsdorff, *Die antiken Urteile über Platons Stil*, Bonn, 1927.

πλουσιώτατα ... μέγεθος: the subject is clearly Plato.

12. 3. ὅθεν ... ἐπέστραπται: 'accordingly, Demosthenes, with his stronger passions, abounds, as is natural, in fieriness and the heat of anger, while Plato, consistently magniloquent, solemn, and grand, is altogether less intense—though far indeed from frigidity.' Bentley's brilliant ἀπαστράπτει (cf. σκηπτῷ ... ἢ κεραυνῷ below) is unnecessary: cf. Philostr. *VS* 1. 17: σεμνότης δ' ἡ μὲν Δημοσθένους ἐπεστραμμένη μᾶλλον, ἡ δ' Ἰσοκράτους ἁβροτέρα τε καὶ ἡδίων. Plato's ὄγκος gives rise to a danger of ψυχρότης, which, however, he avoids, though at the cost of intensity.

12. 4. ὡς Ἕλλησιν: as Hellenized Jews could regard themselves as Greek (cf. Philo, *de confusione linguarum* 129; de Vries 61 f.) this passage cannot be used to disprove theories that L was a Jew.

We know from Plutarch (*Dem.* 3) that Caecilius infelicitously attempted to compare Cicero and Demosthenes. I doubt if this was in περὶ ὕψους (and Plutarch's reference perhaps implies a separate work), as it seems not to be in L's mind, at any rate in the extant part of this argument; he would hardly have contented himself with so oblique a reference, to judge by the controversial tone of 1. 1 and 8. 2–4.

On συγκρίσεις see the excellent article of Fr. Focke, *Hermes* lviii

12. 4] COMMENTARY 111

(1923) 327 ff. Note especially (i) that all the three great digressions in L are of this form; cf. 9. 11-15, 33-36; (ii) that comparisons between Greeks and Romans are not a novelty in Plutarch; see Cic. *Brutus* 43. The σύγκρισις became a regular rhetorical exercise (just as it is today a regular form of examination question) and rules for it are to be found in the rhetores: see, for example, Theon, *progymnasmata*, Spengel ii. 112; Nicolaus, *progymnasmata* 59 ff. Felten (= Spengel 485). Examples of its use in literary criticism are very numerous; see, for example, Quint. 10. 1. 93, 98, 101, 105; A. Gell. 2. 23. 9 ff.; Plu. *comparatio Aristophanis et Menandri*.

οὐ κατ' ἄλλα δὲ ... ἀνατρεφόμενον: 'This and no other seems to me ... to be the difference between Cicero and Demosthenes in their grand passages. Demosthenes uses generally an abrupt sublimity; Cicero spreads himself. Demosthenes, with the violence, rapidity, force, and vehemence with which he always burns and ravages, may be compared to lightning or the thunderbolt; Cicero, like some spreading conflagration, ranges everywhere, as it were, and rolls along, having within him a fire which is huge, persistent, renewed in various forms as time goes on, and repeatedly refuelled.' This is to take ἐν αὐτῷ with ἔχων and construe πολὺ ... καὶ ἐπίμονον ... καὶ διακληρονομούμενον ... καὶ κατὰ κ.τ.λ. together. Wilamowitz, by deleting καὶ after καῖον, a very easy change, gave the ensuing participles a subordinate relationship to ἔχων. This is attractive, but I think unnecessary.

The sense of διακληρονομούμενον is uncertain. LSJ, without authority, give 'dispersed'; perhaps 'distributed' is better, or, as I have suggested in translating, 'succeeded by a series of fresh fires', δια- having the same force as in διαδέχεσθαι: compare κληρονομεῖσθαι, 'to be succeeded by an heir', κληρονομεῖν, 'to succeed'.

As in 11-12. 2, ὕψος is here a means to μέγεθος, and is contrasted with a quality connected with αὔξησις (πλῆθος or χύσις). This metaphor of χύσις (*flumen*, &c.) is extremely common in both Greek and Latin criticism; see, for example, Cic. *de oratore* 2. 62, 64, *Brutus* 274, 325.

ἀποτόμῳ: cf. 39. 4.

τάχους ῥώμης δεινότητος: note the apt asyndeton. For δεινότης—which L uses again of Demosthenes, 34. 4—see Rhys Roberts, *Demetrius*, Glossary, s.v. δεινός, and especially Dion. Hal. *Thuc.* 23.

σκηπτῷ ... ἢ κεραυνῷ: cf. 1. 4 and note. So Cic. *orator* 234: '(Demosthenis) non tam vibrarent fulmina illa nisi numeris contorta ferrentur.' So also Milton, *Paradise Regained* 4. 267 ff.:

The famous orators . . .
    . . . whose resistless eloquence
Shook th' arsenal and fulmin'd over Greece
To Macedon and Artaxerxes' throne.

12. 5. ὑμεῖς: i.e. you Romans.

ἔν τε ταῖς δεινώσεσι: see on 11. 2.

καὶ ἔνθα δεῖ ... ἐκπλῆξαι: 'and in short where it is necessary to astonish the hearer.'

τῆς δὲ χύσεως ... ἁρμόδιος: types of context where χύσις is especially valuable. For τοπηγορίαι, see on 11. 2. παρέκβασις, not παράβασις, is the normal word for digression (Spengel ii. 34, iii. 203, 224 for example) and should probably be restored here: see, however, Strabo 1. 2. 2: παράβασίν τινα ... ἀπὸ τῶν ἄλλων τῶν ἐγκυκλίων ('diversion' from regular studies). τοῖς φραστικοῖς: descriptive passages, cf. 32. 6. ἱστορίαις τε καὶ φυσιολογίαις: is this to be taken as explaining the preceding words, or as a new item? ἱστορίαι include all sorts of historical and mythological excursuses, not only what we call history. φυσιολογίαι are scientific excursuses of any kind. Good examples are the digressions on Sicily and on the rape of Proserpina in the Verrines (ii. 2. 2 ff., ii. 4. 106 ff.).

καταντλῆσαι: 'deluge.' Cf. Pl. *Rep.* 1. 344D, of Thrasymachus' shower-bath of words.

13. 1. ἀψοφητὶ ῥέων: 'softly flowing.' From Pl. *Theaet.* 144B.

There is humour in using a Platonic phrase of Plato himself. Cf. also Dion. Hal. *Dem.* 20 on Isocrates 8. 48: ὑγρὰ καὶ ὁμαλὴ καὶ ὥσπερ ἔλαιον ἀψοφητὶ διὰ τῆς ἀκοῆς ῥέουσα. With less taste, Olympiodorus, *in Phaedonem*, p. 14. 28 Norvin: ἀψοφητὶ τῆς μεταβάσεως γενομένης δίκην ἐλαίου ῥέοντος· οὐ γὰρ λογογραφικὸν τὸ διαιρεῖν εἰς αʹ καὶ βʹ κεφάλαιον.

τὸν τύπον: 'the style' or possibly 'the kind of thing'. In either case there is a slight confusion of construction; οὐκ ἀγνοεῖς governs both the ὅτι-clause and the accusative.

13. 2-14. *Imitation*.

Mimesis in the special sense of imitation of earlier writers plays a large part in ancient criticism and rhetoric from the fourth century B.C. onwards; see especially the remains of Dion. Hal. *de imitatione* and the first two chapters of Quintilian X. Good modern discussions by Kroll (P-W suppl. vii. 1113-17), R. McKeon (*MP* xxxiv (1936) 1 ff.), P. Bompaire (*Lucien écrivain* 13-154). Much material also in E. Stemplinger, *Das Plagiat*.

In this, as in other matters, L is free from the more pedantic elements of the rhetorical teaching. He does not attempt any systematic treatment of the subject; it is just another road to τὰ ὑψηλά. He does not stop to examine the stock theoretical question of its relation to φύσις, τέχνη, and ἄσκησις (see Quint., l.c.). Nor does he interpret imitation as a matter of copying traits from the older authors or avoiding non-Attic locutions; the kind of imitation he has in mind in fact is obviously a matter not of teachable tricks but of being steeped in an author and reproducing his spirit. He would agree with the writer of the *ars* attributed to Dionysius (10. 19) that μιμεῖται τὸν Δημοσθένην οὐχ ὁ τὸ ⟨Δημοσθένους λέγων ἀλλ' ὁ⟩ Δημοσθενικῶς.

L finds the justification of mimesis in the practice of the ancients; with 13. 3 compare Dion. Hal. *Dem.* 33 (on Demosthenes' eclecticism) and the Dionysian *ars* 8. 8 (on Demosthenes and Plato). In practising it therefore we do not disparage ourselves as ἐπίγονοι but give ourselves a place in the sacred tradition. But we must not forget the special importance of mimesis in a narrower sense in L's age, when the literary speech of the classical writers was becoming increasingly remote from ordinary language, and could only be written by deliberate effort and persistent vigilance. Even to an Aristides, τὸ Δημοσθενικῶς λέγειν would not come quite naturally.

A similar notion of the importance of imitation prevailed in Renaissance literature and education, and indeed still prevails in classical education, though in no other form of literary teaching, to the present day. See Bolgar, *The Classical Tradition*, especially pp. 265–75 on Petrarch and his successors; for 'imitation' in present-day Greek and Latin composition, see T. F. Higham, *Some Oxford Compositions*, pp. xix ff.

13. 2. οὗτος ἀνήρ: P's reading may be retained: cf., for example, Pl. *Gorg.* 467B1; K–G i. 629.

μίμησίς τε καὶ ζήλωσις: cf. κατὰ ζῆλον 14. 1. There is sometimes a difference between μίμησις and ζῆλος: Dion. Hal. *de imitatione*, fr. 28 (p. 200 U–R): μίμησίς ἐστιν ἐνέργεια διὰ τῶν θεωρημάτων ἐκματτομένη τὸ παράδειγμα· ζῆλος δέ ἐστιν ἐνέργεια ψυχῆς πρὸς θαῦμα τοῦ δοκοῦντος εἶναι καλοῦ κινουμένη. This distinction, however, should not be read into passages where it is not expressed, and it is certainly not relevant to L's point here. It is clear from the tenor of all this section that he places no value on mere pastiche, and is not talking about the mechanical reproduction of a model by rule.

καί γε: 'and.' Not a classical combination, but not rare in later Greek (Galen, Lucian, Libanius, LXX). See Denniston, p. 157.

ἀπρὶξ ἐχώμεθα: 'let us hold fast to . . . .' Cf. Soph. fr. 328 Nauck: τοῦ γε κερδαίνειν ὅμως ἀπρὶξ ἔχονται.

πολλοὶ γὰρ . . . κατ' ἐπίπνοιαν: 'for many are possessed by a spirit not their own, just as, according to the story, the Pythian priestess, as she sits on her tripod where there is a cleft in the ground exhaling —or so they say—a divine vapour, is thereby impregnated by the supernatural power and forthwith prophesies under inspiration.'

Manutius' ἀναπνέον, 'exhaling', gives this verb a normal sense, and makes the construction clear; no connective—⟨καὶ⟩ αὐτόθεν or αὐτόθεν ⟨δ'⟩—is then needed.

(a) The theory that the Pythia was inspired by vapour from the chasm was widely held in Hellenistic and Roman times. The geology of Delphi, with its caverns in the limestone, gives it no support, and no ῥῆγμα or στόμιον has been discovered. See A. P. Oppé, *JHS* xxiv (1914) 214–20; P. Amandry, *La Mantique apollinienne à Delphes* 52, 216, 248.

There are a number of statements of the theory in literature. Note especially: (i) Strabo 9. 3. 5: φασὶ δ' εἶναι τὸ μαντεῖον ἄντρον κοῖλον κατὰ βάθους οὐ μάλα εὐρύστομον, ἀναφέρεσθαι δ' ἐξ αὐτοῦ πνεῦμα ἐνθουσιαστικόν, ὑπερκεῖσθαι δὲ τοῦ στομίου τρίποδα ὑψηλόν. (ii) [Arist.] *de mundo* 395ᵇ28: ὁμοίως δὲ καὶ πνευμάτων πολλὰ πολλαχοῦ γῆς στόμια ἀνέῳκται· ὧν τὰ μὲν ἐνθουσιᾶν ποιεῖ τοὺς ἐμπελάζοντας, τὰ δ' ἀτροφεῖν, τὰ δὲ χρησμῳδεῖν, ὥσπερ τὰ ἐν Δελφοῖς καὶ Λεβαδείᾳ (i.e. the oracle of Trophonius). (iii) Justin 24. 6. 9: 'profundum terrae foramen, quod in oracula patet; ex quo frigidus spiritus vi quadam velut vento in sublime expulsus mentes vatum in vecordiam vertit impletasque deo responsa consulentibus dare cogit.' (iv) The narrative in Diodorus (16. 26) of how the oracle was discovered by a goatherd.

Amandry's conclusion, that the whole story is a philosophical hypothesis, is surely right. The στόμιον, as he suggests, may be simply the gorge of Castalia. Plutarch, the one writer of this age who knew Delphi intimately, does not subscribe to the 'mephitic vapour' theory.

(*b*) Poets and prophets having much in common, the language in which divine inspiration and possession are described is often applied to literary activity. See in general Dodds, *The Greeks and the Irrational* 80 ff., Kroll, *Studien* 24 ff. Thus we have here a modification of a set of ideas which has a long history. So far as I know, however, it is not exploited by other writers as it is by L in connexion with imitation and the influence of the great models on their successors. This adaptation may, however, owe something to the magnetic chain metaphor of Plato's *Ion* 533D (Homer—rhapsode—audience).

As L uses this range of ideas a good deal (see 1. 4, 3. 2, 3. 5, 8. 1, 8. 4, 15. 1, 38. 5), I give here a few broad indications about their history and development in ancient times. (i) So far as Hellenistic and Roman writers are concerned, the chief sources of the doctrine are Plato (*Phaedr.* 245A, &c., *Ion* 533C ff., *Meno* 99C–D) and Democritus (B 17–18, especially ποιητὴς δὲ ἅσσα μὲν ἂν γράφῃ μετ' ἐνθουσιασμοῦ καὶ ἱεροῦ πνεύματος καλὰ κάρτα ἐστίν). Cf. Cic. *de oratore* 2. 194. (ii) These ideas are often repeated in Roman literature; Cic. *pro Archia* 18 is a good instance: 'poetam natura ipsa valere et mentis viribus excitari et quasi divino quodam spiritu inflari.' Sometimes the native—or Gallic?—word *vates* seemed apter than the Greek *poeta* to express this side of poetry (cf. Enn. *Ann.* 222; Virg. *Ecl.* 9. 34; Hor. *epist.* 2. 1. 26; Tac. *dial.* 9 with Gudeman's note). (iii) Not only poetry but the higher forms of prose came to be regarded as inspired; cf. Cic. *Tusc.* 1. 64; Sen. *tranq. an.* 17. 10. This is a consequence of the blurring of the distinction between poetry and prose, on which see notes on 1. 3, 15. 1. (iv) We should beware of taking the metaphors too seriously. No one suspects Dionysius of Halicarnassus of a tendency to mysticism, but observe how he describes his feelings on reading Demosthenes (*Dem.* 22): ἐνθουσιῶ τε καὶ δεῦρο κἀκεῖσε ἄγομαι, πάθος ἕτερον ἐξ ἑτέρου μεταλαμβάνων . . . διαφέρειν τε οὐδὲν ἐμαυτῷ δοκῶ τῶν τὰ μητρῷα καὶ τὰ κορυβαντικὰ καὶ ὅσα τούτοις παραπλήσιά ἐστι τελουμένων.

ἐγκύμονα: cf. 9. 1, Pl. *Symp.* 209B: ἐγκύμων τὴν ψυχήν; Max. Tyr. 8. 1 b: ἡ πρόμαντις καθίζουσα ἐπὶ τρίποδος ἐμπιμπλαμένη δαιμονίου πνεύματος χρησμῳδεῖ. Any kind of contact with a god may make a prophet; in particular sexual union with him inspires women, e.g. the Sibyl. W. R. Halliday, *Greek Divination* 82; Norden on *Aen.* 6. 77–80. Christian polemists vulgarize this; e.g. Origen, *contra Celsum* 3. 25 (221–2 Koetschau): διὰ τοῦ Πυθίου στομίου περικαθεζομένῃ τῇ καλουμένῃ προφήτιδι πνεῦμα διὰ τῶν γυναικείων ὑπεισέρχεται τὸ μαντικόν.

δαιμονίου: apparently feminine, the adjective being treated as of two terminations; cf. Lys. 6. 32: ὑπὸ δαιμονίου τινὸς ἀγόμενος ἀνάγκης (δαιμονίου can hardly be a substantive here); Philostr. *imag.* 2. 34: δαιμονίου τέχνης; Plu. *Demosth.* 19. 1: τύχη . . . δαιμόνιος.

καὶ οἱ μὴ λίαν φοιβαστικοί: 'even those who are not particularly promising subjects.' Cf. κἂν ἄμουσος ᾖ τὸ πρίν, 39. 2.

13. 3. μόνος ... ἐγένετο; an abrupt question followed by a curt answer. Text probably sound. It is not quite certain to what features L refers. There are many Homeric words and phrases in Herodotus (see, for example, 1. 84 ἐφράσθη καὶ ἐς θυμὸν ἐβάλετο, 3. 14 ἐπὶ γήραος οὐδῷ, 6. 11 ἐπὶ ξυροῦ ἀκμῆς, 7. 217 ἠώς τε δὴ διέφαινε) but the judgement may just as well be based, say, on Herodotus' battle scenes and heroic temper, his methods of narrative and digression, his frequent use of direct speech, his dialect (cf. Hermogenes, *de ideis* 2 = Spengel ii. 362), or his rhythms. Dionysius (*ad Pomp.* 3) says that Herodotus ποικίλην ἐβουλήθη ποιῆσαι τὴν γραφὴν Ὁμήρου ζηλωτὴς γενόμενος. See in general Jacoby in P-W suppl. ii. 502, where other criticisms in rhetores are quoted.

Στησίχορος ... ὅ τε Ἀρχίλοχος: cf. Dio Chrysostom 55. 6: οὕτως μὲν οὐδ' Ἀρχίλοχον εἴποις ἂν Ὁμήρου ζηλωτήν, ὅτι μὴ τῷ αὐτῷ μέτρῳ κέχρηται εἰς ὅλην τὴν ποίησιν, ἀλλ' ἑτέροις τὸ πλέον, οὐδὲ Στησίχορον, ὅτι ἐκεῖνος μὲν ἔπη ἐποίει, Στησίχορος δὲ μελοποιὸς ἦν. Stesichorus' claim to be Homeric rests on his treatment of epic themes, dactylic metres, and use of epic vocabulary. Archilochus' claim may be on the score of vocabulary (A. M. Hauvette, *Archiloque* 235 ff.) or on that of the imitation or adaptation of Homeric themes; thus Theon (*progymnasmata*, Spengel ii. 62) compares σ 136–7:

τοῖος γὰρ νόος ἐστὶν ἐπιχθονίων ἀνθρώπων
οἷον ἐπ' ἦμαρ ἄγῃσι πατὴρ ἀνδρῶν τε θεῶν τε

with Archilochus' paraphrase, fr. 68 Diehl:

τοῖος ἀνθρώποισι θυμός, Γλαῦκε Λεπτίνεω πάϊ,
γίνεται θνητοῖς ὁκοίην Ζεὺς ἐφ' ἡμέρην ἄγει.

Heraclides Ponticus wrote περὶ Ἀρχιλόχου καὶ Ὁμήρου (fr. 178 Wehrli), and this work, which probably had a rhetorical side, may be the source of some of the later comparisons.

ὁ Πλάτων ... ἀποχετευσάμενος: 'diverting to himself countless rills from the Homeric spring.' (i) Plato and Homer. (a) Longinus epit. Laur. F 15 Prickard[2]: ὁ πρῶτος ἄριστα πρὸς τὴν πεζὴν λέξιν τὸν Ὁμηρικὸν ὄγκον μετενεγκὼν Πλάτων ἐστίν. (b) Quint. 10. 1. 81 speaks of Plato's 'eloquendi facultas divina ... et Homerica'; this is just a vague expression of praise. (c) Proclus, in remp. i. 163. 19 Diehl compares Plato's power of delineation of character with Homer's; people weep in sympathy with Apollodorus' outburst (Phaedo 117D) as they do with Achilles'. (d) Heraclitus (quaest. Hom. 18) tracing the psychology of the Phaedrus and Timaeus from the allegorical understanding of Homer (A 194 ff.) says: ταῦτα ὥσπερ ἐκ πηγῆς τῶν Ὁμηρικῶν ἐπῶν εἰς τοὺς ἰδίους διαλόγους ὁ Πλάτων μετήρδευσεν. (e) Dion. Hal. ad Pomp. 1. 13: Plato was jealous of Homer and this is why he threw him out of the ideal state. (f) Hermogenes, de ideis 2. 10 (= Spengel ii. 405): both Plato and Demosthenes owe a great debt to Homer, the greatest orator of all. (g) Max. Tyr. 32 (Hobein) 8 b: Homer gave Plato grandeur. These diverse comparisons naturally reflect the different educational attitudes of philosophers, rhetores, and grammatici through the ages. Nearest to L's view is (a); nearest to his expression is (d).

(ii) The metaphor. Besides (d) above, compare the following: (a) Pl. Rep. 485D: ὥσπερ ῥεῦμα ἀπωχετευμένον, clearly the source of L's ἀποχετευσάμενος. (b) Dion. Hal. de imitatione, fr. 6 (ii. 203 U–R): οὕτω καὶ λόγων μιμήσεσιν ὁμοιότης τίκτεται, ἐπὰν ζηλώσῃ τις τὸ παρ' ἑκάστῳ τῶν παλαιῶν βέλτιον εἶναι δοκοῦν καὶ καθάπερ ἐκ πολλῶν ναμάτων ἕν τι συγκομίσας ῥεῦμα τοῦτ' εἰς τὴν ψυχὴν μετοχετεύσῃ. (c) Dion. Hal. CV 24. 187: κορυφὴ μὲν οὖν ἁπάντων καὶ σκοπός

ἐξ οὗ περ πάντες ποταμοὶ καὶ πᾶσα θάλασσα
καὶ πᾶσαι κρῆναι

δικαίως ἂν Ὅμηρος λέγοιτο.

(d) Manilius 2. 8–10:

(Homeri) ex ore profusos
omnis posteritas latices in carmina duxit
amnemque in tenues ausa est diducere rivos.

(e) Mr. M. L. West adds Page, Greek Lit. Pap., p. 414: (Homer) πόντος τις ὅπως ἔπτυσας ἄλλοις ... φωσίν.

τὰ ἐπ' εἴδους: 'particular examples.'

13. 4]   COMMENTARY   117

οἱ περὶ Ἀμμώνιον: i.e. 'Ammonius'. Cf. Philo, *de vita contemplativa* 15, where οἱ περὶ Δημόκριτον is a periphrasis for Democritus. Examples of this idiom are numerous in Hellenistic texts—according to K–G i. 270 it occurs first in grammarians, which is interesting in view of its context here—but it is by its very nature difficult to recognize. The ambiguity may sometimes be meant to avoid the μικροπρέπεια of blunt accuracy, but no doubt very often it simply covers ignorance. So we might naturally say 'people like Ammonius'. There is a similar usage with ἀμφί. See Arndt–Gingrich, s.v. περί 2 δ.

This Ammonius was the successor of Aristarchus and wrote a Homeric commentary (see *P. Oxy.* ii. 221). Schol. A on *I.* 540 alludes to his work περὶ τῶν ὑπὸ Πλάτωνος μετενηνεγμένων ἐξ Ὁμήρου.

13. 4. ἔστι δ' οὐ κλοπὴ τὸ πρᾶγμα: if it were, it would be highly reprehensible. κλοπή (*furtum*, plagiarism) was one of the stock themes of ancient criticism and formed one of its least intelligent departments. Since Caecilius is among the writers περὶ κλοπῆς listed by Porphyry (*ap.* Euseb. *PE* 10. 3. 12), it is possible that L has him in mind here. κλοπή is a very large subject: see Kroll, *Studien* vii (Latin); E. Stemplinger, *Das Plagiat*; K. Ziegler in P–W, s.v. Plagiat. It is important to consider ancient opinions on this topic because it focuses attention on some of the ways in which Graeco-Latin literature differs from ours—its traditionalism, its fixed genres, its allusiveness, the slow and uncertain growth of the idea of individual property in literary work. Confessed borrowings were not κλοπή: see Cic. *Brutus* 76 'a Naevio ... sumpsisti multa, si fateris, vel, si negas, subripuisti'; Sen. *suas*. 3. 7 (of Ovid's borrowing from Virgil) 'non subripiendi causa sed palam mutuandi, hoc animo ut vellet agnosci'. L naturally is here looking at the question not only as a critic but as a teacher; he wishes to defend the school practice of *mimesis* from the brusque accusation to which its duller exponents laid it open. See also 4. 5, 10. 5, 15. 6, 16. 3.

ἀλλ' ὡς ... ἀποτύπωσις: this defence of Plato's *mimesis* of Homer remains obscure. Does L mean to compare it (*a*) with the imitation of good *mores* in works of art, or (*b*) with the formation of the mind by the imitation of good *mores* or works of art? If (*a*), we should probably read the first ἤ as ἡ, since πλασμάτων ἤ δημιουργημάτων is a natural couple of nearly synonymous words (cf. Lucian, *de morte Peregrini* 8: τὸ τῆς φύσεως τοῦτο πλάσμα καὶ δημιούργημα, ὁ τοῦ Πολυκλείτου κανών). This is best. If (*b*), we have a list of disparates, and the temptation to emend ἠθῶν is stronger, even if none of the suggestions made carries conviction.

For ἀποτύπωσις, cf. Theon, *progymnasmata*, Spengel ii. 61: ἡ δ' ἀνάγνωσις ... τροφὴ λέξεώς ἐστι· τυπούμενοι γὰρ τὴν ψυχὴν ἀπὸ καλῶν παραδειγμάτων κάλλιστα καὶ μιμησόμεθα. Theon's argument, however, has no particular relevance to our passage.

ἐπακμάσαι: 'flourish upon ....' The verb is intransitive, and, if the text is right, its subject must be τηλικαῦτά τινα and the construction must be broken, for the subject of συνεμβῆναι can only be Plato. De Vries (p. 64) compares Pl. *Rep.* 414D : ὥσπερ ὀνείρατα ἐδόκουν ταῦτα πάντα πάσχειν τε καὶ γίγνεσθαι περὶ αὐτούς and ibid. 492C. Even apart from this, however, the expression is strange and perhaps we should adopt some transitive verb, like Morus's ἐπιπάσαι, 'sprinkle upon' (cf. Lucian, *Piscator* 22 ἐπίπαττε οὖν καὶ τῆς εἰρωνείας), though this does not seem dignified enough.

φιλονικότερον: cf. Cobet, *Nov. Lect.* 691 and LSJ, s.v. φιλόνικος. νεῖκος would form *φιλονεικής. The late spelling ει for ι confuses matters, but we should be clear that the word we have here derives from νίκη. 'The sense *contentious* arises from *fond of victory*' (LSJ).

διαδορατιζόμενος: 'breaking a lance.'

ἀξιονικότατος: 'worth winning.' LSJ give no parallel for this passive use of the word, which normally means 'deserving to win'.

εὐκλείας ... στέφανος: a poetical reminiscence; cf. Soph. *Ajax* 465 στέφανον εὐκλείας and similar phrases in Eur. (*Suppl.* 315, fr. 853).

14. *When we write, we must consider how our great predecessors would have met our problems, how they would have judged our work, and what posterity will think of it.*

14. 1. ἡνίκ' ἂν ... δεόμενον: 'when we are working on something which needs lofty speech and grandeur of conception.'

πῶς ἂν ... Θουκυδίδης: the thought that one should ask 'How would X have done this?' is natural in any exhortation: πρόβαλε σαυτῷ, τί ἂν ἐποίησεν ἐν τούτῳ Σωκράτης ἢ Ζήνων; (Epictetus, *encheiridion* 33. 12; cf. *diatrib.* 2. 13. 14 ff.)

εἰ τύχοι: 'perchance.' A fixed formula, no matter what the tense-sequence. See B–D, § 385. 2.

ὕψωσαν: for the plural, cf. Dem. 27. 12 : ἃ μὲν οὖν Δημοφῶν ἢ (καὶ F) Θηριππίδης ἔχουσι; other examples in K–G i. 81. Though corruption would be easy (note that ἢ and καί are readily confused: Wyse on Isaeus 5. 5), it is rash to emend what seems a perfectly natural irregularity.

Θουκυδίδης: Thucydides is perhaps mentioned as the typically ὑψηλός historian, though L would certainly not deny ὕψος to Herodotus, whom he often quotes. The more pedantic critical tradition (e.g. Marcellinus, *vita Thucydidis* 40) contrasted Thucydides as the typical exponent of the ὑψηλὸς χαρακτήρ with Herodotus (μέσος) and Xenophon (ἰσχνός).

προσπίπτοντα: Manutius' correction should be accepted; cf. 21. 1, 23. 2, 39. 4.

οἷον διαπρέποντα: 'as it were standing out conspicuously'. διαπρέπειν cannot be transitive; see Pl. *Gorg.* 485E and Dodds's note.

14. 3] COMMENTARY 119

πρὸς τὰ ἀνειδωλοποιούμενα μέτρα: 'towards the standards it imagines.' Cf. [Plu.] *placita* 904 F (= Diels, *Dox. Gr.* 416ᵃ16): ἀνειδωλοποιουμένης τῆς ψυχῆς τὸ συμφέρον αὐτῇ καὶ τὸ πάντως ἐσόμενον. But μέτρα is difficult, and we should certainly consider emendation; μεγάλα and μεγέθη are both possible.

14. 2. ἔτι δὲ μᾶλλον ... διετέθησαν: 'all the more will they do so if we further [προσ-, if this is right] imagine to ourselves how Homer or Demosthenes, if present, would have reacted to such-and-such an expression which we use, and what their attitude to it would have been.'

Sir Joshua Reynolds imitates this (Discourse II, 1769): 'Instead of treading in their footsteps, endeavour only to keep the same road.... Consider with yourself how a Michael Angelo or a Raffaelle would have treated this subject; and work yourself into a belief that your picture is to be seen and criticized by them when completed.'

θέατρον: 'audience.' Cf. Pl. *Symp.* 194A (humorously for a small group?); Plu. *de genio Socratis* 575F.

ἐν τηλικούτοις ἥρωσιν: cf. 4. 4, 36. 2.

πεπλάσθαι: πεπαῖχθαι should probably be regarded as a conjecture: there is no reason to suppose that it can mean 'pretend that', as the sense requires. It is also difficult to account for it as an interpolation (Wilamowitz thought it was a comment—'a joke'—but there *is* no joke). Reiske's πεπεῖσθαι (cf. 4. 4) is plausible; better, I think, is πεπλάσθαι (middle) from πλάσσομαι 'imagine' (cf. Aeschin. *epist.* 2, init.).

14. 3. εἰ δέ τις ... ὑπερήμερον: 'but anyone who is frightened just by the thought of giving utterance to something which will overstay his own life and time ....' ὑπερήμερος is a legal term meaning 'that which has gone over the date', hence 'too late for ...'. It is difficult to say whether L conceives the μικρόψυχος in literature as feeling himself unworthy to create lasting works, or simply as afraid that he will not reap his reward in his lifetime. The second idea is probably dominant. Cf. Lucian, *Hermotimus* 67: the study of philosophy takes so many years ὡς ὑπερήμερον γίγνεσθαι τἀληθὲς τοῦ ἑκάστου βίου.

ἀνάγκη ... χρόνον: 'incomplete and abortive, his mind's conceptions must needs miscarry and never be brought to birth whole and perfect for the day of posthumous fame.'

The metaphor of conception and birth is maintained throughout the sentence; cf. the vocabulary of Cornutus, p. 73. 15 f. Lang: φανερῶς δ' ἡ σελήνη τελεσφορεῖσθαι τὰ συλλαμβανόμενα ποιεῖ. So τυφλά, 'abortive'; cf. Themistius, *or.* 32. 356: τυφλάς τε εὐθὺς καὶ ἀγόνους τὰς ὠδῖνας λαχὼν βαρύνεται. For the general thought cf. Lucian, *de conscribenda historia* 39. 61: πρὸς τοὺς ἔπειτα μᾶλλον σύγγραφε καὶ παρ' ἐκείνων ἀπαίτει τὸν μισθὸν τῆς γραφῆς.

15. Φαντασία. ('Visualization', though an ugly word, is preferable as a translation to 'fantasy', 'vision', or 'imagination'—all of which have too many other associations.)

15. 1. Ὄγκου ... ἀγῶνος: 'weight, grandeur, and the sense of contest.' All these are closely associated with ὕψος; this introductory sentence is parallel to εἴ τι καὶ ἕτερον ἔχοιμεν ὑψηλοὺς ποιεῖν τοὺς λόγους δυνάμενον (10. 1) and ὁδὸς ἐπὶ τὰ ὑψηλά (13. 2).

For ἀγών see 9. 13, 15. 9, 18. 2, 26. 3; the notion of the urgency and excitement of a real case is always present. Cf. Arist. *Rhet.* 1413ᵇ9; Cic. *ad Att.* 1. 16. 8 ('illo studio contentionis, quem ἀγῶνα vos appellatis'). See also Introd. xxxiii.

οὕτω γοῦν ... παριστάμενον: 'this is the name I give them; some call them εἰδωλοποιίαι. The term φαντασία is used generally for anything which in any way suggests a thought productive of speech.' οὕτω γοῦν refers immediately back; we expect then a defence of the usage L proposes to follow. The defence turns out to be that it is an accepted specialization. What then is the point made? It must be either that ἔνιοι are authorities for L's terminology or else that he is using the term φαντασίαι for what they call εἰδωλοποιίαι. With the former alternative, we need ⟨τὰς⟩ before εἰδωλοποιίας and αὐτάς is difficult. So Fyfe: 'That at least is what some people call the actual mental picture.' With the latter alternative, which gives the more natural sense, we must follow Martens in assuming a lacuna after γοῦν—the suggestion in the text is simply a more economical variant of his—so that the meaning is: 'That at least is what I call them; some call them εἰδωλοποιίαι.'

Striller (*de Stoicorum studiis rhetoricis* 56 ff.) and most translators take παριστάμενον intransitively. But the middle can be transitive and the word-order does not decide the matter. Rostagni takes it transitively, and this is better; cf. Antiochus' definition of φαντασία (S.E. *adv. math.* 7. 201 = fr. 65 Luck): φαντασίαν ῥητέον εἶναι πάθος τι περὶ τὸ ζῷον ἑαυτοῦ τε καὶ τοῦ ἑτέρου παραστατικόν ('capable of bringing to mind itself and the other object'). This Stoic definition, of course, includes those φαντασίαι which produce physical changes or bodily movements as well as those which produce λόγος; what L is talking about is naturally λογικὴ φαντασία. For this see the Stoic account in Diog. Laert. 7. 49: προηγεῖται γὰρ ἡ φαντασία, εἶθ' ἡ διάνοια ἐκλαλητικὴ ὑπάρχουσα, ὃ πάσχει ὑπὸ τῆς φαντασίας, τοῦτο ἐκφέρει λόγῳ.

εἰδωλοποιίας: 'production of images.' In the rhetoricians this word has a specialized significance as a kind of prosopopoeia in which the dead are made to speak, as in the much admired appearance of Appius Claudius in Cic. *pro Caelio* 33 ff. (cf. Spengel iii. 108, 241). It is also a philosophers' word for a mental image. As an equivalent for φαντασία, it occurs only here; but note εἰδωλοποιήσας, Plu. *de gloria Ath.* 347A.

15. 2] COMMENTARY 121

ἤδη ... κεκράτηκε τοὔνομα: cf. Herod. 4. 149: καί κως τὸ οὔνομα τοῦτο ἐπεκράτησε. Philo, *in Flaccum* 20: τοῦτο γὰρ κεκράτηκέ πως τοὔνομα (of the vogue word ταραξιπόλιδες).

ὅταν ... τοῖς ἀκούουσιν: 'when inspiration and emotion make you appear actually to see what you describe and bring it before your hearers' eyes.'

For this concept see especially Quint. 6. 2. 29: 'quas φαντασίας Graeci vocant, nos sane visiones appellemus, per quas imagines rerum absentium ita repraesentantur animo ut eas cernere oculis ac praesentes habere videamur.' There can be no doubt that this chapter of Quintilian—which, be it noted, is περὶ παθῶν—uses much the same material as L here. Quintilian begins by saying that the most important thing about stirring emotions is to be moved oneself; this is not, one would think, in our power, but in fact a practical suggestion towards attaining it can be made. We need to be εὐφαντασίωτοι; and this can be practised by exploiting our natural vice of daydreaming ('otia animorum et spes inanes et velut somnia quaedam vigilantium') and visualizing the situation with which we are concerned in all possible detail; ἐνάργεια will follow. Thus in Quintilian, as in L, φαντασία is a means to ἐνάργεια; only he does not, as L does, limit ἐνάργεια to oratory, but uses the term freely also of poetical effects. With *somnia vigilantium* we should compare Plu. *Amat.* 759B: ὥς τις εἶπεν, αἱ ποιητικαὶ φαντασίαι διὰ τὴν ἐνάργειαν ἐγρηγορότων ἐνύπνιά εἰσιν.

By the rhetoricians, ἐνάργεια is commonly defined as λόγος ὑπ' ὄψιν ἄγων τὸ δηλούμενον (Anon. Seg., Spengel i. 439) or the like. The notion was perhaps developed as a label of praise to be attached to descriptive passages in Homer, especially similes (Kroll, P-W, suppl. viii. 1111). The term has various synonyms, ὑποτύπωσις, διατύπωσις, &c. In Latin we find *evidentia*, *repraesentatio*, *sub oculos subiectio*, *demonstratio* (see *ad Herennium* 4. 68 and Caplan's note). The concept is particularly important in the criticism of the historians; e.g. (i) Polyb. 2. 56. 8 on Phylarchus: πειρώμενος ἑκάστοις ἀεὶ πρὸ ὀφθαλμῶν τιθέναι τὰ δεινά (see F. W. Walbank's notes on the whole passage): (ii) Plu. *de gloria Atheniensium* 347A on Thucydides: ἀεὶ τῷ λόγῳ πρὸς ταύτην ἁμιλλᾶται τὴν ἐνάργειαν, οἷον θεατὴν ποιῆσαι τὸν ἀκροατὴν καὶ τὰ γιγνόμενα περὶ τοὺς ὁρῶντας ἐκπληκτικὰ καὶ ταρακτικὰ πάθη τοῖς ἀναγιγνώσκουσιν ἐνεργάσασθαι λιχνευόμενος.

15. 2. ὡς δ' ἕτερόν τι ... ἐνάργεια: L develops this distinction in 15. 8–11, from which it is clear that what is said here is not to be pressed; the real difference is that rhetoric deals more with reality, not that it does not admit ἔκπληξις; see 15. 11 and what is said on ὕψος, 1. 4. All the same, the introduction of the contrast here shows L to be aware of differences between poetry and rhetoric which affect the usefulness to practical speakers of imitation of the poets (cf. 15. 8), and in this he is more far-sighted than many of his contemporaries and successors.

ἔκπληξις is surprise or fear which 'knocks you out'; less often (e.g. Pl. *Protag.* 355C) it is used of other violent feelings. From an early date it is associated with the effect of the startling and fantastic; *Frogs* 962: οὐδ' ἐξέπληττον αὐτούς, Κύκνους ποιῶν καὶ Μέμνονας κωδωνοφαλαροπώλους.

Aristotle uses the term of poetry, both of the effect of a fantastic situation (*Poet.* 1460ᵇ25) and of that of a striking ἀναγνώρισις (1454ᵃ4). Hellenistic theory laid considerable stress on it as an aim of poetry; and we see the effects of this, for example, in the Latin epic, where both choice of subject and treatment often reveal a desire to astonish or frighten (see Heinze, *Vergils epische Technik*, II. v, Die Ziele, and especially p. 466 n. 1). It was well understood that fear and pleasure are compatible (cf. Plu. *de aud. poet.* 25D: τὸ γὰρ ἐμπαθὲς καὶ παράλογον, ᾧ πλείστη μὲν ἔκπληξις ἕπεται, πλείστη δὲ χάρις). But if a poet aims at either or both of these, he does not seek to teach, as the Stoics thought he should and as they thought, for instance, Homer did. See especially the important Stoic discussion in Strabo 1. 2 against Eratosthenes, who held ποιητὴν πάντα στοχάζεσθαι ψυχαγωγίας, οὐ διδασκαλίας.

τό τε ⟨παθητικόν⟩: cf. 29. 2. There can be no doubt of the sense which has to be supplied, though naturally the precise word cannot be certain.

ὦ μῆτερ ... μου: the mad scene of the *Orestes* seems to have been very popular. Plutarch alone refers to it six times (Helmbold and O'Neil, *Plutarch's Quotations* 31). It is worth noting that Quintilian (12. 10. 6) tells us that Theon of Samos, a painter who excelled 'concipiendis visionibus quas φαντασίας vocant', painted 'Orestis insaniam'. It is, as Austin (ad loc.) says, only a coincidence that L uses this illustration of φαντασία. But the same quotation turns up in philosophical discussions of illusion (*Dox. Graec.* 401 ff. Diels, Sex. Emp. *adv. math.* 7. 242 ff.) and was clearly used by the early Stoics to illustrate the διάκενος ἑλκυσμός ... ἀπ' οὐδενὸς φανταστοῦ γινόμενος. L may well have found it in the Stoic or Stoicizing text to which he owes the general definition of φαντασία in 15. 1, and have used it for his own purposes.

οἴμοι, κτενεῖ με: the manuscripts of Euripides do not offer the epic future κτανεῖ here, though they do have this form in some other places (e.g. *Ion* 1210, *Iph. Aul.* 873, 880, 1131, *Or.* 1578).

15. 3. The remarks on Euripides' skill in delineating love and madness and his lack of native grandeur are in the main critical tradition. Compare, besides 40. 2–3, (i) Quint. 10. 1. 68 for πάθη and οἶκτος, (ii) Dion. Hal. *de imitatione*, fr. 6 (ii. 206 U–R) for realism, failure to achieve τὸ πρέπον καὶ κόσμιον, and success only with ἄσεμνα καὶ

15. 4] COMMENTARY 123

ἄνανδρα καὶ ταπεινά in character and emotion. Note also the scholiast's comment on the dramatic ironies in Oedipus' speech in Soph. *OT* 264: αἱ τοιαῦται ἔννοιαι οὐκ ἔχονται μὲν τοῦ σεμνοῦ, κινητικαὶ δ' εἰσὶ τοῦ θεάτρου· αἷς καὶ πλεονάζει Εὐριπίδης.

μανίας: especially Orestes, Heracles, Agaue, and the Bacchae.
ἔρωτας: especially Medea, Phaedra.
ἐκτραγῳδῆσαι: 'make fit subjects for tragedy', not much more than 'dramatize'. The normal metaphorical extension of τραγῳδία and its cognates is (as here) in the direction of gorgeousness or exaggeration, rather than in that of sadness and (in the modern sense) pathos. Aristotle's τραγικώτατος τῶν ποιητῶν of Euripides (*Poetics* 1453ᵃ30) acquires a special meaning from its context. Examples of the modern sense of 'tragic' (e.g. Himerius 8 (23) 2 ὦ τῆς τραγικῆς καὶ ἀπηνοῦς ἡμέρας, of his son's death) are rather rare and mostly late (see H. Zilliacus, *Arctos* ii (1958) 217–20).

κἂν ... ἐπιτυχέστατος: 'successful as in nothing else.' This adds little, and Stanley's εἴ τις ἕτερος is tempting; cf. 34. 2 = p. 42, 26.

τὴν αὐτὸς αὐτοῦ φύσιν: Wilamowitz on *Heracles* 961 collects instances of this word-order. Rare in classical prose (an example—unique according to Wilamowitz but note Arist. *EE* 1245ᵇ18—is Aeschin. 3. 233: καταλέλυκεν τὴν αὐτὸς αὐτοῦ δυναστείαν), it is a favourite with the more mannered later writers. Cf., for example, Dion. Hal. *Dem.* 7: ἐπιλαμβάνεται τῆς ἀκαιρίας τῆς αὐτὸς αὐτοῦ; Synes. *orat.* 1. 6 (p. 13. 16 Terzaghi): τὰς αὐτὸς αὐτοῦ πάσας ὀρέξεις.

οὐρῇ [δὲ]: δέ spoils the construction; I suggest it has been added by a scribe out of Homer and in the interests of metre; by no means all L's quotations are metrically complete.

15. 4. On Euripides' *Phaethon* see Wilamowitz, *Hermes* xviii 396 ff.; von Arnim, *Suppl. Eur.* 67 ff.; A. W. Pickard-Cambridge, in *New Chapters in Greek Literature*, Series III, 143 ff. This charming and exotic play is a great loss; considerable fragments, especially the light and beautiful lyrics of the parodos, survive to tantalize us. The scene is laid in the remote Orient. Phaethon, who believes himself to be the son of Clymene and King Merops, is about to marry a goddess—we do not know whether it is Aphrodite or a daughter of Aphrodite. His mother reveals to him that his true father is Helios; he therefore goes to Helios and begs to be allowed to drive the sun's chariot.

Helios does not appear on the stage to give the instructions from which L quotes. Both these passages come from a messenger's speech relating Phaethon's ride and death.

ἔλα ... διήσει: 'drive without entering either the Libyan air—it has no moisture in it and will let your wheel fall ....' καίων, revived by Richards, is ingenious but unnecessary: he compared Aesch. *Persae* 504–5, where διῆκε perhaps means 'went through, melted': but see Broadhead ad loc.

ἴει: imperative. Helios' advice ends here. The messenger continues. There is no need to mark a lacuna, as is often done, nor to assume, with Jahn, that L has left some lines out.

Σειρίου: this seems a good piece of fantasy (in the modern sense), given the association of Sirius with scorching heat. Rutgers objected that it would be painful to Helios' *nates* to ride 'tam ferventi sideri velut eculeo'. Hall translates Rutgers's σειραίου, which surely gives an inappropriate picture:

Whilest that his father as Postilion rode
Instructing him which way and how to drive.

συνεπιβαίνει ... συγκινδυνεύουσα ... συνεπτέρωται: for repeated συν-compounds cf. 10. 6, 22. 4; similarly ἐν-compounds, 15. 8–9.

'Would not any man say the soul of Euripides hath here taken coach with Phaeton?' (Hall).

ὅμοια ... Τρῶες: a very compressed note. The quotation is perhaps from the *Alexandros*. The point is not clear, and cannot be clear without the rest of the passage. Cf. 10. 7 for an illustrative quotation reduced to a few words. We should assume that Terentianus is expected to remember what Cassandra said rather than that L's tradition is at fault—though this is, of course, not impossible.

αὐτῷ: for the dative cf. 9. 10.

15. 5. ⟨οἱ⟩ Ἑπτὰ ἐπὶ Θήβας: *Septem* 42 ff. δίχα οἴκτου below is from the same context (51). Most editors treat the quotation as an example of Aeschylus' heroic visualizations. The lines come near the beginning of the speech in which the messenger gives an eyewitness report of the vivid scene where the heroes pledge themselves to conquer or die. This is just the sort of martial and heroic subject congenial to Aeschylus and difficult to Euripides. And it is fair to take the whole speech into account, not only the lines quoted.

Nevertheless, I think it better (as apparently do Hickie and Lebègue) to take the lines as a description of Aeschylus himself; cf. 3. 2, 15. 3, for this didactic trick. This gives a point to καί after ὥσπερ and a less impeded train of thought. The whole passage 15. 3–6 is about Euripides; Aeschylus is introduced only incidentally to illustrate Euripides' attitude towards him. We do not want an instance of Aeschylean φαντασία independent of any Euripidean imitation.

ποκοειδεῖς ... ἀμαλάκτους: 'crude ... unsoftened.' The metaphor is from preparing wool.

15. 6. θεοφορεῖται: 'is possessed.'

ἐνθουσιᾷ ... στέγη: probably from Ἠδωνοί, the first play of the trilogy Ἠδωνοί, Βασσάραι, Νεανίσκοι, Λυκοῦργος, which told the story of the Thracian king Lycurgus. In Homer (Z 130 ff.), Lycurgus drives away the infant Dionysus. In Aeschylus, he refused passage to

Dionysus on his march to India, the Bacchae whom he imprisoned were miraculously released, and he himself was driven mad and killed his son Dryas under the delusion that he was a vine-stock. His land brought forth no crops and he was ultimately, in obedience to an oracle, torn to pieces by four horses on Mt. Pangaeus. See E. R. Dodds, ed. of *Bacchae*, Introd., pp. xxv ff.

ἐφηδύνας: L's point is presumably that Euripides' line is ἥδιον and less παράδοξον than Aeschylus' because of the addition of συν-, which I take him to understand (rightly, see Dodds on *Bacchae* 726) as meaning 'with the Bacchae.'

ἑτέρως goes with the whole phrase ἐφηδύνας ἐξεφώνησε, not solely with ἐφηδύνας. For the order, see note on ὡς οἶσθα 1. 1.

15. 7. ἄκρως ... πεφάνταοται: 'Sophocles too has achieved a brilliant visualization in the scene of Oedipus dying and giving himself burial amid divine portents.' The closing scene of *Oed. Col.*

ἐπὶ τἀχιλλέως: presumably, as Ruhnken suggested, in the *Polyxena* (frr. 479 ff. Nauck). The ghost appeared over the tomb and spoke to the Greek leaders, certainly to Agamemnon. Various versions of the stories are known; see Euripides' *Troades* and *Hecuba*, and Quint. Smyrn. xiv. Of the lyric poets, Ibycus (fr. 26 Page) as well as Simonides handled it.

15. 8. οὐ μὴν ἀλλὰ ... ὑπεραίρουσαν: 'but the exaggeration in poetical passages is, as I said, of a more fabulous kind and altogether beyond credibility.' ὡς ἔφην: in 15. 2. For ὑπερέκπτωσις cf. Andronicus Rhodius, p. 572 Mullach: δεισιδαιμονία ... ὑπερέκπτωσις τῆς πρὸς θεοὺς τιμῆς. ὑπεραίρειν occurs also in 3. 4. The terminology of the present passage, too, may perhaps not unfairly be said to be Peripatetic.

παραβάσεις: 'deviations, excesses' rather than 'digressions'. Cf. 12. 5. I take it that again we have a word that suggests that the right thing is a mean or norm and the error an 'overstepping'.

τοῦ λόγου ... τὸ πλάσμα: 'the content of the passage.' πλάσμα is here 'story', not 'style', though it sometimes means this too. Cf. note on πλάσις, 40. 3.

προεκπῖπτον: Morus's easy correction is right: cf. 38. 1. προσ- would mean 'in addition to . . .', and we do not need this.

[τὸ] ἀδύνατον: Mr. West's suggestion that ἀ- should *replace* the unwelcome τό seems the best solution.

οἱ καθ' ἡμᾶς δεινοὶ ῥήτορες: declaimers or sophists. Cf. 5, 41. Such criticisms are commonplace over a very long period.

ὁ λέγων Ὀρέστης: for the order, cf. Dem. 3. 22: οἱ διερωτῶντες ... ῥήτορες, Τί βούλεσθε; [Plu.] *de ed. lib.* 2 (= *mor.* 1C): ὁ λέγων ποιητής φησι . . . .

15. 10. Ὑπερείδης: for the form of the name see Blass, *Att. Beredsamkeit* iii. 2.

Hyperides was accused of an unconstitutional act for his proposal to enfranchise aliens and free slaves after Chaeronea (cf. Lycurg. *c. Leocr.* 41), and was acquitted. His reply is given in a more elaborate form by Rutilius Lupus, p. 119 Halm, probably from Gorgias, the first-century-B.C. authority on figures: 'Leges igitur quae prohibebant haec nonne neglegebas? non poteram aliter, propterea quod litteris earum arma Macedonum opposita obficiebant.'

The bold personification quoted by L is something very different from the φαντασία or ἐνάργεια illustrated just above from Demosthenes. By ἅμα τῷ πραγματικῶς ἐπιχειρεῖν . . . πεφάντασται, L presumably means that the picture (the battle drafting the decree) is at the same time an argument from fact. For a somewhat similar use of the term φαντασία cf. Sen. *suas.* 2. 14: 'Cestius . . . adiecit: "per sepulcra nostra iurabitur." Nicetes longe disertius hanc phantasiam movit.'

15. 10–11. ἅμα . . . περιλαμπόμενον: 'for the orator has employed a visualization in the moment of making his factual argument, with the result that his thought has taken him beyond the limits of mere persuasiveness. Now our natural instinct is, in all such cases, always to attend to the stronger influence, so that we are distracted away from the demonstration to the amazing effect of the visualization, which by its very brilliance conceals the factual aspect.' Cf. 1. 4 for the contrast between persuasion and astonishment.

15. 11. δυεῖν . . . περισπᾷ: 'for of two things joined together the stronger always attracts to itself the force of the weaker.'

15. 12. Τοσαῦτα . . . ἀρκέσει: 'this will suffice for an account of the elevated in thought, produced by greatness of mind or imitation or visualization.' This summary is puzzling. On the omission of πάθη see Introd. xiv. The contents of 9 (μεγαλοφροσύνη), 13–14, and 15 are mentioned; but nothing is said of the quality described in 10 or of amplification. This may be mere casualness or it may be that the two are not thought worth separate mention because they are more closely linked with μεγαλοφροσύνη than are μίμησις and φαντασία. According to normal usage in lists ἤ is needed before μιμήσεως. The suggested introduction of διά complicates the thought without gain. καί is explanatory: it connects phrases in apposition.

16–29. *Figures.*

See Introd. xviii f. for the place of this section in the treatise.

General Note.

By σχήματα L means 'figures'. He distinguishes them from tropes (τρόποι), which fall under φράσις (30–38). He also (8. 1) knows of a distinction into 'figures of thought' and 'figures of speech', but he does not make use of this division in these chapters, which are deliberately selective.

A σχῆμα in L's sense is some abnormal arrangement of words or expression of thought, which has a pleasant or elevated effect; by τρόπος he means a deviation—such as occurs in metaphor, synecdoche, or metonymy for example—from the natural use or meaning of a word. He would presumably accept Caecilius' definition of σχῆμα: τροπὴ εἰς τὸ μὴ κατὰ φύσιν (cf. ἡ κατὰ φύσιν χρῆσις 16. 2) [τὸ] τῆς διανοίας καὶ λέξεως (fr. 50 Ofenloch = Phoebammon, Spengel iii. 44). An attempt at a τρόπος which failed would produce a barbarism; an unsuccessful attempt at a σχῆμα, on the other hand, ends in solecism (Alexander, Spengel iii. 9–10).

Σχῆμα and τρόπος are commonly used in these or similar technical senses from about the time of Cicero. In Aristotle, however, as in the *Rhetorica ad Alexandrum* and in the Alexandrian critics whose work filtered through to the Homer-scholia (see Schrader, *Hermes* xxxix (1904) 563 ff.), both words as applied to speech bear a variety of other senses. Thus Aristotle (*Poet*. 1456ᵇ9) means by σχήματα τῆς λέξεως command, wish, question, and the like, while Zoilus (Phoebammon, l.c.) defined σχῆμα as ἕτερον μὲν προσποιεῖσθαι, ἕτερον δὲ λέγειν. Such usages have clearly little or nothing to do with the later classification, which was a Hellenistic development, to which both Stoics and Peripatetics contributed; the systematizations of the subject which proved definitive were the work of two writers of the first century B.C., Gorgias and Caecilius. (In Latin, too, the terminology long fluctuated: e.g. in *ad Herennium*, *figura* is used for χαρακτήρ, while σχῆμα is rendered by *exornatio*.) Even after the period of systematization, however, the subject remained confused; the difficulties in the basic distinctions and the continual process of refinement in the definition of individual figures soon produced the jungle of absurdities with which opponents of rhetoric have always been able to make merry.

Indeed, the only distinction between figure and trope which is reasonably plausible is the one mentioned above, which was also held by the Stoics, according to which tropes are confined to deviating uses of single words; Quintilian in opposing this (8. 6. 3) shows very plainly what a tangle the subject had got into by his time. One basic assumption of the whole theory must be emphasized— namely, that there really is a κατὰ φύσιν χρῆσις, deviations from which can be recognized. This was L's assumption; in reading him—and indeed all the writers on figures—we must remember that they think of this φύσις as something immutable and that they are quite without the historical sense of modern scholarship, which recognizes from the start that 'natural expression' varies from age to age, place to place, and genre to genre—if indeed there is such a thing at all.

Thus few good insights into the problems of language and style are to be expected from the ancient discussions of tropes and figures. Nevertheless, for all their complexity and triviality, they possess great historical interest—not only because a good deal of later Greek and Roman literature was written by people who had themselves studied them, but because the same is true of some branches of modern literature also—Elizabethan poetry for example. The most important Latin texts are *ad Herennium* iv, *de oratore* 3. 148–71, and Quint. viii–ix. Cousin's *Études sur Quintilien* contains much useful comment. The Greek treatises are in Spengel iii; those of Tryphon and Phoebammon are the most interesting and preserve early material—as does the Latin treatise of Rutilius Lupus (in Halm's *Rhetores Latini Minores*), which is largely based on Gorgias. The best modern summary is Volkmann's, *Rhetorik* 415–505. H. Lausberg, in the relevant section of his recent *Handbuch der literarischen Rhetorik* (1961), also gives many facts and examples; but his method makes it almost impossible to use the material for historical or interpretative purposes. See also D'Alton 105 ff.; Kroll in P–W, s.v. Rhetorik; W. Barczat, *de figurarum disciplina et auctoribus* (1904); and K. Barwick, *Probleme der stoischen Sprachlehre und Rhetorik* (1957). There are some stimulating things in English: W. G. Rutherford, *A Chapter in the History of Annotation* 183 ff.; J. P. Postgate in *Proc. Brit. Acad.* 1908 ('Some Flaws in Classical Research'); and R. J. Getty's Introduction to his edition of Lucan i, pp. xliv–lxvi. The Elizabethan *Arte of English Poesie* by George Puttenham (1588) contains much of interest; it has been conveniently edited by Willcock and Walter, 1936.

16. *An example of the value of figures.* See Introd. xlviii.

16. 1. ὡς ἔφην: in 8. 1.

οὐ μὴν ἀλλ'... ἀπεριόριστον: cf. the preface of Alexander, *de figuris*, Spengel iii. 9: καὶ γὰρ αὐτὰ τῷ πλήθει δυσπεριόριστά (Dindorf, for δυσπόριστά) ἐστι, τῶν μὲν καὶ ἄπειρα φασκόντων εἶναι τὰ σχήματα, τῶν δὲ οὐκ ἄπειρα μέν, πολλὰ δὲ καὶ ἀπερίληπτα.

The latter view is also L's. Cf. Dion. Hal. *CV* 8. 46; Quint. 9. 1. 10.

πολὺ ἔργον ἐν τῷ παρόντι: Dr. W. Bühler has pointed out to me that πολὺ ἔργον, not πολυέργον is required. Among many examples, cf. Dion. Hal. *CV* 16. 100: πολὺ ἂν ἔργον. For πολύ... μᾶλλον δ' ἀπεριόριστον, cf. Plu. *aqua an ignis* 956B πολλῶν γὰρ ὄντων μᾶλλον δ' ἀπείρων, and *de sera numinis vindicta* 559A πολλὰς... μᾶλλον δ' ἀπείρους. In Philo *de somniis* 2. 48 πολύεργος means 'elaborate'; this is not a valid parallel for the sense required here, 'involving much work'.

τῶν ὅσα μεγαληγορίας ἀποτελεστικά: cf. 9. 8, 43. 4 note.

καὶ δὴ διέξιμεν: 'I will now explain.' For this usage of καὶ δή and the late position in the sentence, cf. Dem. 4. 13: τὸν δὲ τρόπον τῆς παρασκευῆς... καὶ δὴ πειράσομαι λέγειν (Denniston, p. 252); [Plu.] *de lib. ed.* 10B: ἃ τοίνυν... ἐπιτηδευτέα τοῖς νέοις, καὶ δὴ λεκτέον.

16. 2. ἀπόδειξιν... αὐτῆς; 'Demosthenes advances a demonstration on behalf of his policy. What was the natural way of putting it?'

This passage of Demosthenes was immensely admired throughout antiquity. See Quint. 9. 2. 62, 11. 3. 168, 12. 10. 24; Plu. *de gloria Atheniensium* 350C; Hermogenes, Spengel ii. 306, 404; Tiberius, Spengel iii. 69. The thought naturally became banal; cf. Sen. *suas.* 2. 14 for a development by the declaimers.

Demosthenes' originality here was a subject of discussion. Clement of Alexandria (*strom.* 6. 20. 1, writing περὶ κλοπῆς) well compares the phrase with Thuc. 1. 73. 4 φαμὲν γὰρ Μαραθῶνί τε μόνοι προκινδυνεῦσαι. ... Quint. (12. 10. 24) thinks that Demosthenes here shows himself Plato's pupil, and Hermogenes (Spengel ii. 442) connects it with Pl. *Gorg.* 489E: οὐ μὰ τὸν Ζῆθον, ὦ Καλλίκλεις (!).

παραδείγματα: L inserts the missing step. Cf. Tiberius, l.c.: τὸ μὲν οὖν πρᾶγμα παράδειγμα ἐποίησεν, ἀντὶ δὲ τοῦ εὐθέως εἰπεῖν ἐσχημάτισεν. Similarly also Hermogenes, Spengel ii. 306.

ἀλλ' ἐπειδὴ ... φρονεῖν: this long sentence (see Appendix for an analysis) needs a lot of breaking up in translation. 'But instead of this, as though under inspiration and possession, he suddenly gives voice to the oath by the heroes of Greece—"By those who risked their lives at Marathon, you have not done wrong!" Observe what he effects by this single figure of conjuration—here I call it apostrophe. He deifies his audience's ancestors, suggesting that one should swear by men who fell so bravely just as though they were gods. He inspires the judges with the temper of those who risked themselves. He transforms his demonstration into an extraordinary passage of elevation and passion, and into the convincing appeal of this strange, amazing oath. At the same time he injects into his hearers' minds a healing specific, so as to relieve them by these paeans of praise and make them as proud of the battle with Philip as of the triumphs of Marathon and Salamis.'

ἐν Μαραθῶνι: L gives the preposition here and in his verbatim quotation, but not in 16. 4. Demosthenes has the locative; this is also found in some late writers (Aristides, Lucian). Both locutions are good classical Attic; both are used freely by the orators. See J. H. T. Main, *Locative Expressions in the Attic Orators*, Baltimore 1894, p. 37.

ἐμπνευσθεὶς ... φοιβόληπτος: inspiration metaphor again; cf. 13. 2. For φοιβόληπτος cf. Plot. 5. 8. 10: ὑπὸ θεοῦ κατασχεθεὶς φοιβόληπτος ἢ ὑπό τινος Μούσης; J. D. P. Bolton, *Aristeas of Proconnesus* 134 ff.

τὸν ⟨κατὰ⟩ τῶν ἀριστέων ... ὅρκον: the plain genitive can hardly be justified by β 377 θεῶν μέγαν ὅρκον and other poetical passages. The early conjecture ⟨κατὰ⟩ should be accepted; so Toup.

ἀποστροφὴν: not the usual sense of this term, for which see Quintilian's (9. 2. 38) example from *pro Milone*: 'Vos enim iam Albani tumuli atque luci ...' (85).

COMMENTARY   [16. 2-

ἀποθεώσας: cf. Plu. l.c.: καὶ τούτους ἀπεθέωσε τοῖς ὅρκοις ὁ ῥήτωρ ὀμνύων.

μεθεστακώς: transitive: cf. παρέστακεν 27. 3.

ἀξιοπιστίαν: cf. Tiberius, l.c.: πρός τε τὸ λαμπρὸν ἅμα καὶ τὸ ἀξιόπιστον εἰς ὅρκου φαντασίαν μεταβάλλων.

τῇ μάχῃ: for omitted preposition, see K–G i. 548 (poetical examples). But it is perhaps best to supply ἐπί.

16. 3. παρὰ τῷ Εὐπόλιδι: see *New Chapters in Greek Literature* iii. 161 ff.; Page, *Greek Literary Papyri* 202 ff. In the *Demoi*, produced in 412, Eupolis brought great men of old *ab inferis* to comment on the current situation: Miltiades, Aristides, Pericles, Solon, and Myronides. These lines were spoken by Miltiades. They are a parody of Eur. *Medea* 395 ff.: οὐ γὰρ μὰ τὴν δέσποιναν, ἣν ἐγὼ σέβω ... χαίρων τις αὐτῶν τοὐμὸν ἀλγυνεῖ κέαρ.

τὸ δὲ ποῦ καὶ πῶς καὶ ἐφ' ὧν καιρῶν: for such a combination of relative with interrogative forms, cf. [Isocr.] 1. 5: μέλλομέν σοι συμβουλεύειν ὧν χρὴ ... ὀρέγεσθαι καὶ τίνων ἔργων ἀπέχεσθαι ... καὶ πῶς τὸν ἑαυτῶν βίον οἰκονομεῖν. See K–G ii. 439.

πρὸς εὐτυχοῦντας ἔτι: L is unaware—or rather thinks it insignificant—that the play was produced after the disaster in Sicily. By contrast with the situation after Chaeronea, the whole history of independent Athens is εὐτυχία: certainly anything before 404 could be so described.

[ὅρκων] πίστις: we need simply a list of the oratorical functions successfully performed by the *figura iurisiurandi*. Kayser, Wilamowitz, and Dr. Bühler are surely right to delete ὅρκων.

16. 4. κἀπειδήπερ ... ῥήτορι: 'and, when the orator was faced with the possible objection ....'

Faber's τις is unnecessary; and we may follow LSJ and take λέγεις κ.τ.λ. as in effect the subject of ὑπήντα.

λέγεις ... ὀμνύεις: 'you are speaking after producing a defeat by your policy—and then you swear by victories!' But Jahn's ⟨τί⟩ λέγεις is attractive.

κανονίζει ... ἄγει: 'regulates and makes safe (?)'. I mark καί as corrupt; but Photiades is perhaps on the right lines in positing a lacuna.

κἂν βακχεύμασι νήφειν: the phrase recalls Eur. *Bacchae* 317: καὶ γὰρ ἐν βακχεύμασιν οὖσ' ἥ γε σώφρων οὐ διαφθαρήσεται. H. Lewy, *Sobria Ebrietas* 28 ff., draws parallels between L's oxymoron and Philo's νηφάλιος μέθη (e.g. *quod omnis probus* 13). He regards L's expression as a transposition from the religious to the aesthetic plane. So, of course, it is. But L's immediate antecedents here are much more likely to be purely literary and rhetorical, and it would be wrong to attach too much importance on this occasion to his use of this familiar range of imagery (see on 13. 2).

17. 1] COMMENTARY 131

πάντη ... ὄνομα: 'has throughout withheld the word for the final event with intent to deceive.'

17. *Dangers in the use of figures; the best camouflage is a brilliant context.*

17. 1. ἕν τι τῶν ἡμῖν τεθεωρημένων: cf. 1. 2 τεθεωρηκέναι.

The observation that important people sometimes take offence at what they regard as deceitful cleverness was naturally nothing new. Cf., for example, Arist. *Rhet*. 3. 1404ᵇ18 ff.: διὸ δεῖ λανθάνειν ποιοῦντας καὶ μὴ δοκεῖν λέγειν πεπλασμένως ἀλλὰ πεφυκότως· τοῦτο γὰρ πιθανόν, ἐκεῖνο δὲ τοὐναντίον· ὡς γὰρ πρὸς ἐπιβουλεύοντα διαβάλλονται, καθάπερ πρὸς τοὺς οἴνους τοὺς μεμιγμένους. Disclaimers of δεινότης are, of course, common in Attic oratory (Antiphon 5. 1; Pl. *Apology* 17B), while incompetence is sometimes a positive recommendation (αὐτῷ τῷ βατταρισμῷ πείθοντες τοὺς δικαστάς Philod. *rhet*. ii. 136 Sudhaus). For the specific point that figures should be used with caution, see Quint. 9. 2. 72, Demetrius 67. So it is not this which L claims as original, but the proposition that ὕψος defends figures as figures assist ὕψος.

I follow a suggestion of Tucker and regard καὶ ταῦθ' as corrupt. If it is right, we must say either that it is used in the strange and unnatural sense of 'in particular', or else that there is a contrast between the judge and the other great personages: 'playing tricks with figures is of its nature suspicious ... even when one is addressing a judge with full powers, but it is particularly so with tyrants ....' Neither of these explanations is convincing. Since the sentence has another awkward feature—we expect μάλιστα δ' ὅταν πρὸς κ.τ.λ.—the corruption may possibly be more extensive. It is perhaps worth while suggesting that something has fallen out: e.g. καὶ ⟨φυλακτέα⟩ ταῦθ'....

ἐνέδρας ἐπιβουλῆς παραλογισμοῦ ... ἡγεμόνας: note the asyndeta. ἡγεμόνας may refer primarily to provincial governors (see Arndt–Gingrich, s.v. 2), βασιλέας could refer to the *principes* or to client kings; τυράννους must I think apply to holders of usurped or unjust power. This last point shows that in fact the situations are described in general terms and we should be cautious in finding precise reference to contemporary institutions.

Some words have again to be supplied before ἐν ὑπεροχαῖς, but the asyndeton probably continues. The plural ὑπεροχαῖς is perhaps used simply to avoid hiatus. For the phraseology cf. 1 Timothy ii. 2: ὑπὲρ βασιλέων καὶ πάντων τῶν ἐν ὑπεροχῇ ὄντων.

ἀγανακτεῖ ... εἰ ...: observe the return to the singular, as though μάλιστα ... ὑπεροχαῖς were in parenthesis.

For ἀγανακτεῖ εἰ, 'is angry that', a colloquial usage, cf. Pl. *Laches* 194A: ἀγανακτῶ εἰ ... μὴ οἷός τ' εἰμὶ εἰπεῖν; Aristoph. *Frogs* 1007. See K–G ii. 369.

σχηματίοις: the diminutive has a depreciatory sense. See on 1. 1.

εἰς καταφρόνησιν . . . τὸν παραλογισμόν: 'taking the trickery for contempt of himself.' Cf. Philostr. *imag.* 2. 32. 3: εἰ δ' εἰς κόρην λαμβάνοιτο, ἔφηβος δόξει, 'if it (a picture of Palaestra) is taken for a girl, it will seem a boy'.

ἀποθηριοῦται: 'goes wild.' Cf. Polyb. 1. 67. 6: οὐ γὰρ οἷον ἀνθρωπίνῃ χρῆσθαι κακίᾳ συμβαίνει τὰς τοιαύτας δυνάμεις, ὅταν ἅπαξ εἰς ὀργὴν καὶ διαβολὴν ἐμπέσωσι πρός τινας, ἀλλ' ἀποθηριοῦσθαι τὸ τελευταῖον καὶ παραστατικὴν λαμβάνειν διάθεσιν.

διόπερ . . . ἐστι: cf. 38. 3. 'Art concealing art' is a commonplace topic. Cf. Quint. 12. 9. 5; Dion. Hal. *Isaeus* 16; and Caplan's note on *ad Herennium* 4. 7. 10.

17. 2. περιλαμφθεῖσ' ἡ: Bury's conjecture—'surrounded by the brilliance of'—is supported by περιαυγούμενα below and περιλαμπόμενα 15. 11.

δέδυκε . . . ἐκπέφευγεν: gnomic perfects. See *GMT*, §§ 154–5; B–D, § 344.

κάλλεσι: Toll's πάθεσι would accord with ὕψος καὶ πάθος above and τὰ πάθη καὶ ὕψη below. All the same, L's terminology is not so consistent and predictable that we should feel confident about the change. Prickard by an oversight attributes πάθεσι to P.

σχεδὸν γὰρ . . . τὸ μέγεθος: for the application of this commonplace image to literature, cf. Quint. 8. 5. 29: 'ne apparent quidem (*sc.* sententiae) ubi tota lucet oratio, ut in sole sidera ipsa desinunt cerni.'

ἐπὶ τῆς ζωγραφίας: analogies from painting are often used in ancient literary criticism: see H. Nettleship, *Lectures and Essays* 54 ff.; Sandys, *Orator* pp. lxxi ff. Interesting examples include: Dion. Hal. *CV* 21. 146, *Isocr.* 2, *Isaeus* 4; Cic. *orator* 36, 75, 228, 261, 298; Quint. 12. 10. 3 and 10 (see Austin's notes). The comparison between the two arts from the point of view of scope and method is of great importance in the history of aesthetics; see especially R. W. Lee, 'Ut Pictura Poesis', *Art Bulletin* xxii (1940). An important ancient text is Plu. *de gloria Atheniensium* 3. 346F–347C.

ἐπὶ γὰρ τοῦ αὐτοῦ . . . φαίνεται: 'when shadow and light lie side by side in colours on the same plane, the light nevertheless seems more prominent to the eye, and not only stands out but actually appears much nearer.' In the application of the simile, light corresponds to ὕψος and shade to σχήματα and their artifice. It is therefore used differently and less aptly than in Plin. *ep.* 3. 13. 4: 'nec vero adfectanda sunt semper elata et excelsa. nam ut in pictura lumen non alia res magis quam umbra commendat, ita orationem tam submittere quam attollere decet.' L's modest language (οὐ πόρρω δ' ἴσως . . . -ι συμβαίνει) is perhaps not just conventional but an admission that his simile is inexact.

18. 2] COMMENTARY 133

κἀ⟨π⟩ὶ τῶν λόγων: the change is very slight, and seems desirable: cf. κἀπὶ τῶν διηρμένων 7. 1.

διά τε φυσικήν τινα συγγένειαν: an important point introduced incidentally. Cf. 35. 4 for man's natural kinship with τὰ ὑψηλά.

διά τε . . . λαμπρότητα should be taken with ἐγγυτέρω κείμενα.

ἐπισκιάζει: 'casts shadow over . . .', 'puts in the shade . . .'. The ἐπι-compound is preferable, as Reiske saw. Cf. Lucian *conscr. hist.* 11: οὐδ' ἐπισκιάζουσι τὴν θωπείαν.

18. *Rhetorical questions.*

Cf. Demetrius 279: the effect of the rhetorical question is to shake the reader and make him feel he does not know the answer. All the writers on figures handle this topic; see Spengel iii. 24–25, 64–65, 163, 179–80; Quint. 9. 2. 7 ff.; Volkmann 491 f.; Rehdantz, s.v. Frage.

The technical writers distinguish between πύσμα and ἐρώτημα. ἐρωτήματα can be answered yes or no, while πύσματα need longer explanations; this seems originally to have been a distinction of Stoic logic, cf. Diog. Laert. 7. 66. L treats the terms as synonymous.

Note that the chapter begins with two rhetorical questions. This is no doubt deliberate, and there are other certain or possible instances of this sort of teaching by example in 19, 20. 1, 22. 1, 22. 3–4, 26. 3, 42.

18. 1. ταῖς τῶν σχημάτων εἰδοποιίαις: 'by means of the specific characters of the figures.' LSJ translate 'descriptive qualities', Roberts 'visualizing qualities' as though the word were equivalent to εἰδωλοποιία: but cf. rather Aristotle's εἰδοποιὸς διαφορά (*Topica* 143^{b}7: cf. *EN* 1174^{b}5), or Plutarch's εἰδοποιεῖν τὸν ἑκάστου βίον, 'to characterize the life of each' (*Alexander* 1).

τὸ ἔνθουν καὶ ὀξύρροπον: 'the impassioned rapidity.' Some doubt attaches to ἔνθουν, since at 13. 2 we have ἔνθεον; but the contracted form occurs not infrequently in the manuscripts of late authors (e.g. App. *Hisp.* 18, &c.; Lucian, *Dem. enc.* 25) and it is better retained.

18. 2. ἡ δ' ἐρώτησις . . . ἐπίκαιρον: 'and it is just this momentary quality of emotion that is represented by the self-directed question and its answer.'

σχεδὸν γὰρ . . . ἀνθυπαντῶσιν: 'just as those who are unexpectedly asked questions by others are annoyed and reply to the point with vigour and exact truth . . . .' Note the involved order.

τὸν ἀκροατὴν . . . παραλογίζεται: 'as well as carrying away the hearer, actually cheats him into believing . . . .'

τὸ Ἡροδότειον: εἰ οὕτως is presumably part of L's comment (e.g. 'if X had said . . . it would not have been so striking . . .'). It is, of course, impossible to identify the passage with certainty; but Schmid's suggestion (*Gr. Lit.* i. 2. 653, n. 2) that it is 7. 21 (the passage imitated by Theopompus in the description quoted by L in 43) satisfies the requirements: τί γὰρ οὐκ ἤγαγε ἐκ τῆς Ἀσίης ἔθνος ἐπὶ τὴν Ἑλλάδα Ξέρξης; κοῖον δὲ πινόμενον ὕδωρ οὐκ ἐπέλιπε, πλὴν τῶν μεγάλων ποταμῶν; 5. 106. 3 (Histiaeus and the king) is perhaps another possibility.

19. *The conclusion of a discussion of asyndeton, with two disparate examples.*

For other ancient treatments, see Arist. *Rhet.* 3. 1413ᵇ19; Demetrius 194; Hermogenes, Spengel ii. 435; *ad Herennium* 4. 30. 41; Quint. 9. 3. 50. For modern treatments, see (besides Volkmann 473) Denniston, *Greek Particles*, p. xlv, *Greek Prose Style*, ch. vi.

⟨ἀσύμ⟩πλοκα: 'unconnected.' This word (Philo) or ἀνεπίπλοκα (Apoll. Dysc.) is preferable to the simple ἄπλοκα (Oppian).

καὶ συμβαλόντες ... ἀπέθνησκον: this type of thing is a mannerism with Xenophon: see *Hell.* 2. 4. 33, *Anab.* 3. 4. 25, *Cyr.* 7. 1. 38.

ἤλθομεν ... καλά: Homer has ᾔομεν and εὕρομεν. Eustathius (1657. 34) praises the effect: καλὸν ἐν τούτοις ἡ ἀσύνδετος εἰσβολή. So Stanford: 'The absence of a connecting particle shows the speaker's agitation.' Rather, it stresses the immediate sequence of the events; cf. *E* 169, *Λ* 197, *O* 239—all with εὑρίσκω.

τὰ γὰρ ... συνδιωκούσης: 'for phrases both disconnected and at the same time hurried convey an impression of an agitation which both halts the reader and drives him on.'

τοιαῦθ': 'formal' asyndeton (Denniston), with no special rhetorical point, the sentence being introduced by a backward-looking pronoun. All the same, L probably means it to be noticed.

20. *Combinations of figures. Asyndeton in conjunction with anaphora and diatyposis.*

20. 1. ἡ ἐπὶ ταὐτὸ σύνοδος: 'the conjunction in one phrase.' Rhys Roberts's 'for tne same purpose' is wrong. Cf. Philo, *quod deterius* 8: τὴν τῶν στοιχείων εἰς ταὐτὸ σύνοδόν τε καὶ κρᾶσιν.

κινεῖν: *scil.* τὰ πάθη.

οἷον κατὰ συμμορίαν: 'joining their resources, as it were.' This metaphor—from a party to which all present contribute—is continued in ἐρανίζῃ.

τὴν ἰσχὺν τὴν πειθὼ τὸ κάλλος: certainly a deliberate asyndeton; the illustration to be discussed next contains an exact parallel.

ὁποῖα ... τὰ ἀσύνδετα: P's reading gives a harsh, if not impossible, sentence. I have adopted a modification of Rothstein's suggestion. If we follow Weiske, we must take τὰ εἰς τὸν Μειδίαν ... ἀσύνδετα together, and this seems a little odd.

ταῖς ἀναφοραῖς: Puttenham englishes anaphora as 'figure of report'. L uses the terms 'anaphora' and 'epanaphora' apparently without distinction; strictly, anaphora is the generic term and epanaphora should be confined to the repetition of a word at the beginnings of cola, repetition at the ends being called antistrophe. Naturally

20. 3] COMMENTARY 135

these terms cover a great range of phenomena, from the very natural and ordinary (πολλὰ μέν ... πολλὰ δέ..., &c.) to the highly mannered and artificial (e.g. the type illustrated by τοῦ δ' ἐγὼ ἀντίος εἶμι, καὶ εἰ πυρὶ χεῖρας ἔοικεν, εἰ πυρὶ χεῖρας ἔοικε, μένος δ' αἴθωνι σιδήρῳ, Υ 371–2, cf. Herodian, Spengel iii. 97). The best ancient discussions are Arist. *Rhet.* 1414ᵃ1; *ad Herenn.* 4. 13. 19; Demetrius 61, 141; see also Alexander, Phoebammon, and Herodian in Spengel iii (20, 46, 96). Modern works: Volkmann 467 ff.; Denniston, *Greek Prose Style* 84 ff.; Rehdantz, s.v. Anaphora.

τῇ διατυπώσει: 'vivid description.' A vague term; see Spengel iii. 25, 51, 79. Phoebammon calls it ἔκθεσις ἑνὸς πράγματος διὰ πλειόνων, i.e. the building up of a picture by adding detail. Caecilius reckoned it among figures of thought.

πολλὰ γὰρ ἄν ...: the quotation is a favourite; Tiberius uses it once to exemplify anaphora (72. 27) and once to exemplify asyndeton κατὰ κόμμα producing ἐνάργεια (78. 1). Anon. Seg. uses it to illustrate ἐνάργεια (§ 111 = Spengel i. 440).

συγκίνησις: 'motion.' Cf. συγκεκινημένον 15. 2, συγκεκινημένους λόγους 29. 2. συν- here merely emphasizes the completeness or thoroughness of the disturbance: LSJ speak of 'sympathetic emotion' in connexion with 15. 2 and 29. 2, but this is, I think, wrong.

It is a commonplace to think of πάθος as a movement. Latin, indeed, has no word for 'emotion' except *animi motus* and the like.

20. 2. ὅταν ἐπὶ κόρρης: Demosthenes has ὅταν ἐπὶ κόρρης (cf. Pl. *Gorg.* 486c for this) which L duly repeats just below. P's ὅταν ὡς δοῦλον may therefore (i) have displaced this phrase here as an intrusive gloss upon it, or (ii) have been added by L or a scribe as an explanation of ὅταν κονδύλοις, or (iii) have arisen by dittography from the preceding ὅταν κονδύλοις (Radermacher; but it seems perverse to advance a palaeographical hypothesis when the sense provides a clue to what has happened.) It is a possible assumption that ὅταν alone is to be deleted as an accidental repetition, but it does not seem likely that L would have thought an explanation necessary. We should choose between simply deleting the whole phrase and replacing it by ὅταν ἐπὶ κόρρης: so Manutius, and this seems better.

ἐργάζεται· ... πλήττει: a common form of asyndeton with πάσχειν, δρᾶν, and their synonyms. The 'blank cheque' verb forecasts the nature of the coming statement. Denniston, *Greek Prose Style* 110.

αἱ καταιγίδες: 'squalls.' Used of storms that 'rush down'. Also metaphorically of the passions—apparently in particular in the Epicureans, see LSJ, s.v., and Usener, *Epicurea*, fr. 413 (καταιγισμοί).

20. 3. οὐκοῦν ... μεταβολῇ: 'thus he consistently preserves the natural effect of the epanaphorae and asyndeta through frequent variation.' μέν is not answered and φύσιν seems a little strange; hence Vaucher's μεγαλοφυΐαν and Photiades' much more plausible ἔμφασιν (cf. 19. 2).

But the text is probably sound: (i) cf. τὴν τῆς ἀποδείξεως φύσιν 16. 2, ταῖς τῶν σχημάτων εἰδοποιίαις 18. 1; (ii) the idea contrasted with φύσιν is contained in τῇ συνεχεῖ μεταβολῇ and μέν needs no formal answer. The point is a paradoxical one: variation actually maintains the pattern of the asyndeton and anaphora, violence and emotion being of their essence.

μεταβολῇ: not in a specific technical sense; cf. 5, 23. 1. The phenomenon meant is the variation produced by the new asyndeton and anaphora in ταῦτα κινεῖ, ταῦτα ἐξίστησιν, and the new asyndeton in οὐδεὶς ἂν ταῦτα κ.τ.λ.

οὕτως ... τάξιν: 'thus his order becomes disorderly and his disorder in turn embraces a certain order.' For this oxymoron we may perhaps compare not only Plu. *QC* 8. 9. 731C (ἔχει δέ τινα τάξιν τὸ ἄτακτον αὐτῆς [*scil.* -ῆς ψυχῆς]) but also the play made by Latin poets with *concordia discors* (Hor. *ep.* 1. 12. 19; Ov. *Met.* 1. 433; Lucan 1. 98) and *discordia concors* (Manil. 1. 142).

21. *Polysyndeton.*

L's doctrine about the contrast between asyndeton and the addition of conjunctions is essentially the same as that of Demetrius 194, 269, and Plu. *quaestiones Platonicae* 1010E ff. Thus Demetrius 194: ὅτι δὲ ὑποκριτικόν (dramatic) ἡ λύσις, cf. Arist. *Rhet.* 1413ᵇ17 ff.) παράδειγμα ἐγκείσθω τόδε· "ἐδεξάμην ἔτικτον ἐκτρέφω, φίλε." οὕτως γὰρ λελυμένον ἀναγκάσει καὶ τὸν μὴ θέλοντα ὑποκρίνεσθαι διὰ τὴν λύσιν· εἰ δὲ συνδήσας εἴποις "ἐδεξάμην καὶ ἔτικτον καὶ ἐκτρέφω," πολλὴν ἀπάθειαν τοῖς συνδέσμοις συνεμβαλεῖς, πανὺ δὲ τὸ ἀπαθὲς ἀνυπόκριτον. And the general point is no doubt valid; see, for instance, how Demosthenes (4. 36) uses polysyndeton to depict the leisurely care of the Athenians in their festival preparations and asyndeton when he comes to the chaos of the military situation: ἐκεῖνα μὲν πάντα νόμῳ τέτακται, καὶ πρόοιδεν ἕκαστος ὑμῶν ἐκ πολλοῦ τίς χορηγὸς ἢ γυμνασίαρχος τῆς φυλῆς, πότε καὶ παρὰ τοῦ καὶ τί λαβόντα τί δεῖ ποιεῖν, οὐδὲν ἀνεξέταστον οὐδ' ἀόριστον ἐν τούτοις ἠμέληται· ἐν δὲ τοῖς περὶ τοῦ πολέμου καὶ τῇ τούτου παρασκευῇ, ἄτακτα ἀδιόρθωτα ἀόρισθ' ἅπαντα. But polysyndeton, too, can have on occasion the effect of repeated blows; see, for instance, Romans viii. 38–39. An interesting passage for the combined effect of polysyndeton and its opposite is Plu. *de fortuna Alexandri* 3. 335E ff.—an exceptionally rich piece of epideictic prose, the technique of which repays careful study.

L's rewriting of the *Midias* passage (cf. 22. 2, 39. 4 for this didactic trick) involves adding conjunctions which explicitly serialize the items enumerated (πρῶτον μέν ... εἶτα δέ ... εἶτά γε μήν): note that he adds δέ to εἶτα though it is idiomatic to omit it.

κατὰ τὸ ἑξῆς οὕτως παραγράφων: 'as you proceed with these insertions.'

τὸ συνδεδιωγμένον καὶ ἀποτραχυνόμενον: 'the urgency and asperity.'

ἐὰν ... ἐξομαλίσῃς εἰς λειότητα, ἄκεντρόν τε προσπίπτει: 'if you ... level it out to smoothness, [it] falls ineffectually on the ear.' So Rothstein; cf. 23. 2 for this use of προσπίπτω. The alternative is to punctuate after ἐξομαλίσῃς, but this is very unsatisfactory: προσπίπτειν εἰς ... is unnatural, and τε is now awkwardly postponed.

21. 2. ἐμποδιζόμενον ἀγανακτεῖ: 'frets at being impeded.' For the use with a participle, cf. Pl. *Phaedo* 62E ἀγανακτεῖν ἀποθνῄσκοντας, but the personification is bold, and we expect rather some word meaning 'flags'. Haupt's ἀπακταίνει is based on Hesychius: ἀπακταίνων· ὁ κινεῖσθαι μὴ δυνάμενος.

τὴν γὰρ ἐλευθερίαν ... ἀφίεσθαι: 'for it loses the free abandon of its movement and the sense of being as it were catapulted out.'

Finckh's simple correction (ἀπολλύει is a later form for ἀπόλλυσι, 'loses': cf. F's ἀπολύει and the ἀπολλύει of the other manuscripts in Pl. *Gorg.* 496B2: I owe this reference to Professor Dodds) should be adopted: τὸ πάθος is the subject. ἡ ἐλευθερία τοῦ δρόμου is a much more positive concept than the English 'freedom of movement', which implies only the absence of impediment.

22. *Hyperbaton.*

The adjective ὑπερβατός is first applied to transposed words by Plato in his discussion of Simonides' ἄνδρ' ἀγαθὸν μὲν ἀλαθέως γενέσθαι, where he wishes to take ἀλαθέως with γενέσθαι and not with ἀγαθόν (*Protag.* 343E): ἀλλ' ὑπερβατὸν δεῖ θεῖναι ἐν τῷ ᾄσματι τὸ ἀλαθέως. It is therefore a term current in the period of the sophists.

Hyperbaton is treated by the rhetores sometimes as a figure, sometimes as a trope: see Quint. 9. 1. 3, Caecilius fr. 66 Of. Tryphon's definition λέξις μετακεκινημένη ἀπὸ τῆς ἰδίας τάξεως (Spengel iii. 197) is typical. The Latin is *transgressio* (*ad Herennium* 4. 32. 44; Quint. 8. 6. 62). Modern discussions in Volkmann 436, in the works of Postgate and Getty quoted in the general note at the beginning of 16–29, and in Denniston, *Greek Prose Style* 47 ff. For the rhetores see T. Schwab, *Alexander Numeniu, Rhet. Stud.* 5, especially 87–97.

22. 1. Τῆς δ' αὐτῆς ἰδέας: i.e. the class of figures productive of grandeur (16. 1).

καὶ οἱονεὶ * * * χαρακτήρ: Wilamowitz was probably right to suggest a lacuna. χαρακτήρ hardly needs an apology and the transition is very abrupt. As to the content of the lacuna, it is perhaps (i) a bold or metaphorically used adjective agreeing with τάξις (e.g. συντεταραγμένη) and (ii) a new beginning (e.g. καὶ λέγοιτ' ἄν ...). (I owe to Professor Fraenkel the information that Wilamowitz at one time suggested σύγχυσις for (i), and compared 'Quintilian', perhaps thinking of 8. 6. 67 'hyperbatis . . . confusis').

πολλὰ γὰρ . . . δύναιτο: 'for there are many, indeed innumerable, emotions, and one could not possibly say how many.' Wilamowitz's ⟨τὰ⟩ πάθη would make this the subject, which it need not be. Cf. Aristides 26 (14) (εἰς 'Ρώμην) 82: οὐ δέκα παρασάγγαι . . . οὐδ' εἴκοσιν οὐδ' ὀλίγῳ πλείους, οὐδ' εἴποις ἂν εὐθὺς ὁπόσον.

παραπίπτοντες: 'going astray.' See LSJ, s.v. iv.

ἄλλα προθέμενοι . . . τάξιν: 'often put forward one thing and then rush off on to another, irrationally inserting some remark, and then hark back to their first point and are all the time dragged rapidly about, this way and that, by their excitement, as by a constantly veering wind, and vary expression, thought, and the order of the natural sequence in innumerable ways.' L displays asyndeton once again, and a remarkable hyperbaton (τὴν . . . τάξιν). The present παρεμβάλλοντες is to be preferred to the aorist: it is subordinate to μεταπηδῶσι but distinct in time from προθέμενοι.

ἀνακυκλοῦντες is probably intransitive: see LSJ.

ἡ μίμησις . . . τὴν τέχνην: the mimesis here meant is the imitation of things, not that of literary models. For what is said here about 'art' and 'nature', cf. 17. 1, 38. 3.

ἐπὶ ξυροῦ . . . τοὺς πολεμίους: L—or the tradition—has roughly atticized Herodotus' words. Such interjected γάρ-clauses—which are a natural idiom, and particularly common in Herodotus, e.g. 1. 8, 1. 97, 9. 109; and see K–G ii. 334—are often discussed by the rhetores. Cf. Hermogenes (Spengel ii. 438): καὶ οὕτως γίνεται σαφηνείας ὄργανον τὸ ὑπερβατόν, οἷον (κ 191)

ὦ φίλοι, οὐ γάρ τ' ἴδμεν ὅπῃ ζόφος οὐδ' ὅπῃ ἠώς,
οὐδ' ὅπῃ ἠέλιος φαεσίμβροτος εἶσ' ὑπὸ γαῖαν
οὐδ' ὅπῃ ἀννεῖται· ἀλλὰ φραζώμεθα θᾶσσον·

εἰ γὰρ εἰρήκει, ῏Ω φίλοι, φραζώμεθα θᾶσσον, ἐτάραξεν ἂν αὐτούς, καὶ ἐποίησεν ἐρωτῆσαι τί γέγονεν. διὰ τοῦτο διὰ μέσου τὰς αἰτίας τοῦ φράζεσθαι θᾶσσον ἔταξε. Similarly, L shows here (i) how the natural place for ἄνδρες Ἴωνες is first, but the speaker is so eager to come to the point that he delays it; (ii) how the order of the thought is disturbed by the insertion of the reason before the exhortation. So τὸ μὲν Ἄνδρες Ἴωνες is balanced by ἔπειτα δέ.

22. 2. προεισέβαλε γάρ: we do not need οὖν; one of the two corrections proposed should be adopted, and there is not much to choose. I take it, however, that P's οὖν is a misguided emendation, and accordingly adopt the conjecture nearer palaeographically to ἄν. For προεισέβαλεν ἀπό . . ., 'began from', cf. LSJ, s.v. εἰσβάλλω, ii. 4.

ὡς . . . προσαγορεῦσαι: 'not even having the time to address them by name in face of the pressing alarm.'

23. 1] COMMENTARY 139

ἐφεστώς: cf. παρεστώς 39. 3. See K–B ii. 236 for this neuter form.
αὐτούς: emphatic, therefore placed before δεῖ πονεῖν.
22. 3. ἔτι δὲ μᾶλλον ... δεινότατος: 'even more does Thucydides excel in separating by hyperbata even expressions which are wholly unified and indivisible.' Cf. Dion. Hal. *Thuc.* 52 on τὰς ὑπερβάτους καὶ πολυπλόκους καὶ ἐξ ἀποκοπῆς πολλὰ σημαίνειν πράγματα βουλομένας καὶ διὰ μακροῦ τὰς ἀποδόσεις λαμβανούσας νοήσεις (an example as well as a description!). A classic instance in Thuc. is 1. 132. 3 : τὸ μὲν οὖν ἐλεγεῖον οἱ Λακεδαιμόνιοι ἐξεκόλαψαν εὐθὺς τότε ἀπὸ τοῦ τρίποδος τοῦτο ....

22. 3–4. ὁ δὲ Δημοσθένης ... ἐκπλήττει: a very long and involved sentence, in which L describes the psychological effect of hyperbata—the impression of impromptu speech and the anxiety felt by the hearer as a result of the suspension of meaning. The sentence itself, with its participial phrases and short final colon, is probably meant as an illustration of the point.

'Demosthenes is indeed less wilful than Thucydides, yet no one is so insatiate as he for this kind of effect; he produces by his transpositions not only a great sense of urgency but the appearance of extemporization, and drags his hearers with him into the hazards of his long hyperbata. For he often holds up the meaning which he sets out to declare and, introducing one extraneous item after another in an alien and unusual place before getting to the main point, throws the hearer into a panic lest the sentence collapse altogether, and forces him in his excitement to share the speaker's peril, before, at long last and beyond all expectation, appositely paying off at the end the long-due conclusion; the very audacity and hazardousness of the hyperbata add to the astounding effect.'

Wilamowitz's μεταξύ πως should probably be accepted not so much as avoiding a hiatus as because τάξις needs no apology.

The vocabulary of this passage recalls 10. 7–11. 1 (τάξις ~ ἐγκατατάττοντες, ἐπεισκυκλῶν ~ ἐπεισκυκλούμενα). For the order τὸν κίνδυνον τῶν μακρῶν ὑπερβατῶν see on 28. 4.

22. 4. παραβόλῳ: cf. Plin. *Ep.* 9. 26. 3: 'sunt enim maxime mirabilia quae maxime inexspectata, maxime periculosa, utque Graeci magis exprimunt παράβολα.'

23. *Polyptoton: changes of tense, person, number, and gender.*

23. 1. τά γε μὴν πολύπτωτα. Polyptoton in the rhetores is the effect produced by the occurrence of the same word in various inflexions. Some expressions so describable are, of course, normal idioms (ἕτερος ἕτερον, ἄλλος ἄλλο and the like): on these see Wackernagel, *Vorlesungen* ii. 97. But the same principle can be developed rhetorically to great heights of elaboration: see, for example, Plu. *de fortuna Alexandri* 339A: πρόσγραψον εἰ βούλει τῇ Τύχῃ τὰ Ἄρβηλα καὶ τὴν Κιλικίαν καὶ τἆλλα, ἃ γέγονε βίας ἔργα καὶ πολέμου· Τύχη τὴν Τύρον ἔσεισεν αὐτῷ καὶ Τύχη τὴν Αἴγυπτον ἀνέῳξε· διὰ Τύχην Ἁλικαρνασσὸς ἔπεσε.... See also Volkmann 470. In the strict sense, ἀθροισμοί and μεταβολαί and κλίμακες, though related figures, cannot be said to be species of the genus polyptoton. Hence Martens's κάθροισμοί: but it is safer to assume that L's terminology is different, and that he uses the term polyptoton in a rather loose sense.

ἀθροισμοί: this is probably what is more usually called συναθροισμός; cf. Alexander's instance (Spengel iii. 17) from Dem. 18. 71: τὴν Εὔβοιαν ... σφετεριζόμενος καὶ κατασκευάζων ἐπιτείχισμ' ἐπὶ τὴν Ἀττικήν, καὶ Μεγάροις ἐπιχειρῶν καὶ καταλαμβάνων Ὠρεὸν καὶ κατασκάπτων Πορθμόν.... Quintilian (8. 4. 26–27) calls it 'plurium rerum congeries' and distinguishes it from 'congeries verborum ac sententiarum idem significantium'. His example is not a polyptoton; his example of the other *congeries* does in fact involve one, but the definition makes it clear that this is not an essential feature. The distinction which Quintilian is making is one of content not of verbal form.

μεταβολαί: Tiberius (Spengel iii. 76) clearly distinguishes this figure from polyptoton: μεταβολὴ δ' ἐστὶν ὅταν μὴ τὰς πτώσεις μόνον ἀλλὰ καὶ τὰ ῥήματα μεταβάλλῃ, οἷον· τίς γὰρ συμμαχία σοῦ πράξαντος γέγονε τῇ πόλει; ποῖαι τριήρεις; ποῖοι νεώσοικοι; τίς ἐπισκευὴ τειχῶν; ποῖον ἱππικόν; (Dem. 18. 311). Same doctrine and example in Alexander, ibid. 35. Quintilian, in a difficult and probably corrupt passage (9. 3. 38), attributes to Caecilius (fr. 69 Ofenloch) the use of μεταβολή for 'rerum coniuncta diversitas' and gives as an example *pro Cluentio* 41: 'illum tabulas publicas ... corrupisse decuriones universi iudicaverunt, cum illo nemo rationem, nemo rem ullam contrahebat, nemo illum ... tutorem umquam liberis suis scripsit.' Here there is, indeed, polyptoton as well as anaphora.

ἀντιμεταβολαί, which Manutius or another sixteenth-century scholar conjectured here, are a variety of polyptoton: 'I do not live to eat but eat to live' is a traditional example (see Caplan on *ad Herennium* 4. 28. 39).

κλίμακες: the stock instance (e.g. in Demetrius 270) is Dem. 18. 179: οὐκ εἶπον μὲν ταῦτα, οὐκ ἔγραψα δέ· οὐδ' ἔγραψα, οὐκ ἔπεισα δὲ Θηβαίους. 'The figure is called a ladder, because on a ladder we start again from the step on which we stop.' It inevitably involves some repetitions, but is not necessarily polyptoton. St. Paul is a virtuoso at climax; see Romans v. 3, viii. 29–30. See also *ad Herennium* 4. 25. 34; Volkmann 474. The use of the term 'climax' for any series of statements in ascending importance and also its use for the last term in such a series seem to be modern; the latter perhaps does not appear before the eighteenth century.

τί δὲ ... εὑρίσκεται: 'but what of changes of case, tense, person, number, and gender? How do they diversify and enliven the style?'

23. 2] COMMENTARY 141

I hold indeed that, if we consider phenomena affecting number, it is not only the singular forms found on reflexion to be plural in sense which have an agreeable effect....' This is not without difficulty. (i) I assume that πῶς ποτε is little more emphatic that πῶς; but at 44. 1 L uses it with some intensive force, as in normal classical Greek (LSJ, s.v. iii. 3). (ii) I accept the old conjecture δή for P's δέ, which is clearly unsatisfactory. L answers an imagined objection by giving his own opinion.

For γενῶν 'genders', cf., for example, Arist. *Rhet.* 1407ᵇ7 = Protagoras A27 D-K.

What is here called ἐνάλλαξις is more commonly called ἀλλοίωσις, and this was apparently the term which Caecilius used (Tiberius, Spengel iii. 80; see Schwab, pp. 8 ff.).

τὰ ἑρμηνευτικά: a mannered use of the neuter plural for the abstract noun (τὴν ἑρμηνείαν), perhaps suggested by the subject of the chapter.

τοῖς τύποις ἑνικά: 'singular in form.' Cf., for example, Herodian (Spengel iii. 87): τὸν μὲν τύπον ἑνικόν ... τὴν δὲ σημασίαν πληθυντικήν. See K-G i. 52 ff. for this type of *constructio ad sensum*.

23. 2. αὐτίκα ... κελάδησαν: 'straightway the innumerable multitude cried "Tunny!" as they scattered over the shore.' Presumably they scatter to pull in the nets when the watchman (θυννοσκόπος) has signalled that the tunny have entered the trap. Pizzimenti and Wyttenbach made the attractive suggestion that this is about tunny-fishing. For θύννον as the actual cry, see Fraenkel on Aesch. *Ag.* 47 μέγαν ... κλάζοντες Ἄρη. The tunny fisheries were—rightly—thought spectacular; see the elaborate descriptions in Oppian, *hal.* 3. 631 ff. and Aelian, *NH* 15. 5. Ancient and modern material in D'Arcy Thompson, *A Glossary of Greek Fishes*, s.v. θύννος. The source of the quotation is unknown. Rhetores (e.g. Herodian, l.c.) illustrate the same point by means of quotations from Homer and Demosthenes. A good instance in a late writer is Lucian, *Scytha* 11: ἥ γέ τοι πόλις ἅπασα κεχηνότες αὐτοῦ ἀκούουσιν. See also W. Schmid, *Der Atticismus* iii. 93. See Addenda, p. 193.

προσπίπτει ... μεγαλορρημονέστερα: cf. 21. 1 ἄκεντρόν τε προσπίπτει.

αὐτῷ δοξοκοποῦντα τῷ ὄχλῳ τοῦ ἀριθμοῦ: 'courting success by the mere multitude of the number.' An odd phrase; δοξοκοπεῖν usually has a bad sense—'to curry favour with the mob'—and ὄχλος ἀριθμοῦ is both strange in itself and, taken with the verb, appears to suggest a very frigid conceit. Wilamowitz not very plausibly proposed ὄγκῳ, comparing Pl. *Laws* 737C: τὸν ... ὄγκον τοῦ ἀριθμοῦ, 'the numerical amount' (England).

For the point cf. Arist. *Rhet.* 1407ᵇ26: εἰς ὄγκον δὲ τῆς λέξεως συμβάλλεται ... καὶ τὸ ἓν πολλὰ ποιεῖν, ὅπερ οἱ ποιηταὶ ποιοῦσιν· ... δέλτου μὲν αἵδε πολύθυροι διαπτυχαί (Eur. *Iph. Taur.* 727).

23. 3. ταὐτό: but Jebb (ad loc.) is probably right in conjecturing ταὐτοῦ in Sophocles, whose manuscripts have ταὐτόν: the sense is 'in turn you released seed of the same man' (*scil.* to whom you gave birth).

ἐπὶ ... Ἰοκάστῃ: despite the two hiatuses, this phrase must be retained as being a necessary explanation of νύμφας γυναῖκας μητέρας τε.

χυθεὶς ... ἀτυχίας: 'the expansion of the number to the plural forms pluralizes the misfortunes too.'

ἐξῆλθον ... Σαρπηδόνες: a different type of example from the preceding: this must mean 'from Troy came forth men like Hector and Sarpedon'. This turn, in which the plural enhances either the good or the bad qualities of a person or thing, is rarer in Greek than in Latin; but cf. Aesch. *Ag.* 1439: Χρυσηΐδων μείλιγμα τῶν ὑπ' Ἰλίῳ; Eur. *HF* 454–5: ὦ τέκν', ἀγόμεθα ζεῦγος οὐ καλὸν νεκρῶν, ὁμοῦ γέροντες καὶ νέοι καὶ μητέρες—a line which, as Wilamowitz (ad loc.) says, L might have quoted here.

ἑτέρωθι: not necessarily in περὶ ὕψους, though it may well have been in the lost comparison of Plato and Demosthenes, 12. 2.

23. 4. καὶ τὰ ἑξῆς: but the context in *Menexenus* 245D contains no further example of what L wants to illustrate.

φύσει ... κομπωδέστερα: 'for the facts naturally acquire a grander sound ....' If this is right, ἐξακούω is just a synonym of ἀκούω, but ἐξακούεται ... κομπωδέστερα seems neither very apt nor very natural. ἐξογκοῦται ('puffed out') would be more to the point (cf. 3. 1, 28. 2, &c., for L's fondness for ὄγκος and its cognates) and it is fairly close palaeographically.

ἀγεληδὸν ... ἐπισυντιθεμένων: 'with such a piling up of the names in crowds.' Unless L has forgotten what he is about, we must suppose that ἀγεληδόν refers not to the fact that there is a list but to the pluralizing, the production of 'crowds' of Cadmuses, &c. So Weiske.

ἐπ' ἄλλων: cf. 9. 7.

[τὰ] πλείονα: the article—'most of them'—is out of place. See LSJ, s.v. πλείων i. 2.

τὸ πανταχοῦ κώδωνας ἐξῆφθαι: from [Dem.] 25. 90: καὶ ἃ τῶν ἄλλων τῶν ἠτυχηκότων ἕκαστος ἀψοφητὶ ποιεῖ, ταῦθ' οὗτος μόνον οὐ κώδωνας ἐξαψάμενος διαπράττεται. According to LSJ the metaphor is from a crier's bell, but this does not fit ἐξάπτομαι; we should think of war-horses or (less probably) other animals with bells; cf. Aesch. *Septem* 386, 399; [Eur.] *Rhesus* 308; Aristoph. *Frogs* 963 (Μέμνονας κωδωνοφαλαροπώλους); [Lucian] *asinus* 48.

24. *Collective nouns with singular.*

24. 1. ἔπειθ' ἡ ... διειστήκει: same quotation in Alexander, Spengel iii. 33.

εἰς δάκρυα ⟨ἔπεσε ... ἀντὶ τοῦ⟩ ἔπεσον: without some correction or supplement, L fails to make his point. Vahlen's supplement is,

I think, fairly satisfactory, despite the asyndeton with which the following sentence begins. Wilamowitz is more ingenious: 'for to concentrate the number out of diversity into unity gives a more solid effect than "the spectators fell".' The order of the phrases, however, seems to me much against this.

24. 2. ὅπου τε γὰρ ... ἐν τῷ παραλόγῳ: a crabbed sentence, in L's more hurried manner. Given the correction ἐμπαθοῦς or ἐκπαθοῦς, it is at any rate not impossible to translate. 'Where the nouns are singular, to pluralize them is a mark of unexpected emotion; where they are plural, to unite the plurality of them under one well-sounding word is again surprising because of the opposite metamorphosis of the facts.' The common αἴτιον is surprise; so παρὰ δόξαν goes with ἐμπαθοῦς rather than with πολλὰ ποιεῖν: see R. Ellis, *Hermathena* ix (1896) 386. For ἐν τῷ παραλόγῳ cf. Theophr. *CP* i. 3. 2 (in LSJ): εἴ τι σπάνιον καὶ ὡς ἐν παραλόγῳ.

25. *Past events represented by present tense.*

Past events are related in the present tense in Greek from the sixth century onwards, and notably in Herodotus. The use is conspicuously absent from Homer. The effect in classical writers is not so much to annihilate distance in time as to mark out a specially important event, to fix an occurrence as a lasting picture, or to set down a headline. Some verbs (those of seeing, hearing, going, attacking, dying, speaking, for instance) are particularly prone to this usage. The use is rare in subordinate sentences and very rare indeed with negatived verbs. By Plato's time it is banal.

Latin usage is different; the historic present is common at all periods and in all styles and conveys vividness, immediacy, and rapidity of action. English is again different; there is clearly a colloquial use, a naïve use as in ballads, and the various mannered uses of modern literature.

L and Aristides (Spengel ii. 552) are the only Greek rhetoricians to discuss the phenomenon. L simply repeats Aristotle's distinction of διήγησις and ἀγών (*Rhet.* 1413^{b}14), thereby making it clear that for him at least the historic present *does* annihilate time. Aristides says that the usage produces ἀφέλεια (see on 34. 2) and has a certain novelty.

Since papyri and NT have it, the usage did not die out in Hellenistic times; nevertheless, its occurrence in later writers is patchy and must be largely a matter of conscious effort; Josephus and Arrian (Xenophon's mimic) use it; Dio Cassius does not.

See Wackernagel, *Vorlesungen* i. 162 ff.; K. von Fritz, 'The So-called Historical Present in Early Greek', *Word* v (1949) 186–201; K. Eriksson, *Das Präsens Historicum in der nachklassischen griechischen Historiographie*, Lund, 1943. Also Schwyzer ii. 271; K–G i. 132 ff.

ὁ δὲ πίπτει: not in Xenophon.

Θουκυδίδης: see, for example, the narrative in 1. 136 ff. In fact, Thucydides has far fewer instances than Xenophon.

26. *The imaginary second person.*

Again, L is concerned with the deliberate use of a phenomenon which also occurs unstudied. The imaginary second person (i.e. 'you' = French *on*, German *man*, Greek τις) is much less common in Greek than in Latin (where all styles welcome it) or in English (where it has a strongly colloquial flavour) but it is not exactly rare. It seems to be confined to potentials (past or present) and futures. Futures occur especially in travel narratives, as in the Herodotus passage here quoted.

See Wackernagel, *Vorlesungen* i. 109 ff.; Schwyzer ii. 244; K–G i. 172 n. 1, 557 n. 3.

26. 1. [καὶ] πολλάκις: καί spoils the sentence, and may have been introduced either accidentally from the καί above or as an apparent simplification of the syntax: see note on 3. 4.

φαίης ... ἐμάχοντο: for omissions in the middle of metrical quotations, cf. 27. 4 and Demetrius 129. But naturally it is possible that ἀλλήλοισιν is an accidental omission in P or an ancestor.

κείνῳ ἐνὶ μηνὶ: in midwinter. Note that this is the same part of Aratus' poem as L quotes in 10. 6.

26. 2. The passage of Herodotus is atticized and considerably abridged. Herodotus has: (2) ἀπὸ Ἐλεφαντίνης πόλιος ἄνω ἰόντι ἄναντές ἐστι χωρίον . . . . (3) καὶ ἔπειτα ἀπίξεαι ἐς πεδίον λεῖον . . . . (6) διεξελθὼν δὲ ἐν τῇσι τεσσεράκοντα ἡμέρῃσι τοῦτο τὸ χωρίον, αὖτις ἐς ἕτερον πλοῖον ἐσβὰς (*v.l.* ἐμβὰς) δυώδεκα ἡμέρας πλεύσεαι καὶ ἔπειτα ἥξεις ἐς πόλιν μεγάλην τῇ οὔνομά ἐστι Μερόη.

δύ' ἡμέρας: a period of twelve days, not two, fits the facts and is given by the unanimous reading of the tradition of Herodotus; see How and Wells on Her. 2. 29. 4. But for all we know, L's text of Herodotus may have been in error here. See Introd. l.

τὴν ἀκοὴν ὄψιν ποιῶν: cf. 15. 1 on ἐνάργεια. Behind all this theory lies the common thought ὀφθαλμοὶ τῶν ὤτων ἀκριβέστεροι μάρτυρες— 'seeing's believing'. See Heraclitus B 101 a; Herod. 1. 8, &c.

πάντα ... ἐνεργουμένων: 'all such things, when directed to the actual persons, bring the hearer right into the presence of events.'

26. 3. καὶ ὅταν ... λαλῇς: 'and when you speak not as you would to all and sundry . . . .' For order, cf. Thuc. 1. 78. 1: βουλεύεσθε οὖν βραδέως ὡς οὐ περὶ βραχέων; A. C. Moorhouse, *Studies in the Greek Negatives* 39 n. 1.—λαλεῖν here implies private conversation as opposed to λέγειν, public speaking. Cf. 34. 1, note.

λαλῇς ... ἀποτελέσεις: L uses the trick himself. The example seems in no way different from *O* 697 above.

27. *Changes of persons. The switch from* oratio obliqua *to* oratio recta. *Apostrophe.*

27. 1. ὁ συγγραφεύς: here this includes poets; contrast 1. 3.

εἰς ... πρόσωπον: 'to the person of the character concerned.'

ἐκβολή τις πάθους: 'an outburst of passion.' Cf. 33. 5.

Ἕκτωρ ... μητίσομαι: in the lines from Homer, L clearly takes 347 as depending on ἐκέκλετο, since it is the 'sudden threat' (ὃν δ' ἂν ἐγών κ.τ.λ.) that he thinks is appropriately put into direct speech. Inverted commas should therefore precede ὃν δ' ἂν ἐγών (Prickard is wrong here). L's judgement apart, there is no reason why ἐπισσεύεσθαι and ἐᾶν should not be regarded as imperatival in sense (Monro, *Homeric Grammar*, § 241).

οὐκοῦν ... περιέθηκαν: 'the poet has given himself the narrative as being appropriate to him, and then suddenly and without warning put the abrupt threat in the mouth of the angry prince.'

The point is perhaps that the first two lines, containing no 'outburst of temper', are 'appropriate' to the poet, as objective narrator.

ἐψύχετο: for the omission of ἄν see *GMT* § 431; K–G i. 215–16.

ἔφθακεν ... μετάβασις: 'the change in construction has in a flash got ahead of the writer who makes it'; cf. Dion. Hal. *CV* 19. 142: ἔφθακε τὴν τοῦ λίθου φορὰν τὸ τῆς ἀπαγγελίας τάχος.

27. 2. ἡ πρόσχρησις: 'use', or 'application'. (i) πρόχρησις, the reading of P, elsewhere means 'loan'; (ii) against taking it here as 'preferable use' is also the fact that προ- in compounds seldom (perhaps never) means 'in preference', unless some clear idea of choice or value is present in the simple verb—as, for example, in προαιρεῖσθαι, προτιμᾶν. Corruption should be assumed; the minimal change is Manutius' πρόσχρησις, and, since προσχράομαι may be used without the notion of *additional* use being present (see LSJ), we may assume the same of the noun, even though in the few recorded occurrences it does mean 'additional use', and this sense is certainly inappropriate here.

ἡνίκ' ἄν: for ἡνίκ' ἄν see 14. 1, 15. 8, 22. 1; for ἡνίκα with the subjunctive without ἄν see 32. 5. Since P has the α, it is probably better to accept Jahn's correction here.

ὀξὺς ... καιρός: cf. Plu. *praec. ger. reip.* 8. 804A: ὀξεῖς γὰρ οἱ καιροὶ καὶ πολλὰ φέροντες ἐν ταῖς πολιτείαις αἰφνίδια; Hippocr. *aphor.* 1. 1: ὁ καιρὸς ὀξύς.

παρὰ τῷ Ἑκαταίῳ: the story was that after the death of Heracles the Heraclidae fled to Trachis; but the king Ceyx, a nephew of Amphitryon, was forced by Eurystheus to refuse them hospitality.

τοὺς [Ἡρακλείδας] ἐπιγόνους: I take Ἡρακλείδας to be a gloss on Hecataeus' confusing use of ἐπιγόνους. It cannot form part of the sentence, as von Scheliha saw. Hecataeus must mean either (i) *Ceyx'* young relations, not his actual descendants, or (ii) the descendants of Heracles. (i) seems very difficult; (ii) would involve a specialized use of a word which became specialized in quite another sense—namely, for the descendants of the original Seven against Thebes. This would be natural enough for Hecataeus, if made clear earlier in the narrative, but in an isolated quotation certainly needs an explanation. I assume this was added in the margin in the course of the transmission of L.

Licymnius, whom Morus's emendation introduces, was Alcmena's half-brother and also fled to Trachis.

τρώσητε: 'do an injury.' Cf. Eur. *Hipp.* 703.

ἀποίχεσθε: von Scheliha and Lebègue retain ἀποίχεσθαι, treating it as imperatival in sense.

27. 3. ὁ μὲν γὰρ Δημοσθένης: L evidently has no doubts about the authenticity of the speech (*contra Aristogitonem* i), though Dionysius rejected it (*Dem.* 57), as do most modern critics (Blass, *Att. Ber.* III. i. 408 ff.).

ἐμπαθὲς ... παρέστακεν: καὶ ἀγχίστροφον may go as predicate with ἐμπαθές or be part of the subject with τὸ πολυπρόσωπον; the former gives the better sense: 'has made his change of person produce the effect of strong emotion and quick reactions.' For ἀγχίστροφον, cf. 9. 13; for παρέστακεν transitive, cf. μεθεστακώς 16. 2.

καὶ οὐδεὶς ... παρανοίξειεν ἄν τις: it is worth noting that Alexander (Spengel iii. 33), quoting this passage to illustrate μεταβολὴ προσώπων, agrees with L against the tradition of Demosthenes (*a*) in εὑρεθήσεται for φανήσεται, (*b*) in adding οὗτος after βδελυρός, (*c*) in omitting ἄνθρωπος after ἀναιδής and τοὺς νόμους after βιάζεται.

This passage and the following one have only a formal resemblance to the passages discussed above; their ethos is, of course, quite different (so L says κατ' ἄλλον τινὰ τρόπον). They are in fact instances of apostrophe.

εἶτα πρὸς τὸν Ἀριστογείτονα ⟨τὸν⟩ λόγον ἀποστρέψας: I follow Toll and Weiske and suppose that τὸν has been displaced.

ἐπέστρεψεν: 'has intensified.' Cf. ἐπέστραπται 12. 3. There is no contrast in sense with ἀποστρέψας, and if the jingle is deliberate (as it seems to be) it is frigid. See Addenda, p. 193.

27. 4. κῆρυξ ... οἷος Ὀδυσσεὺς ἔσκε: Penelope meets the herald at the door; he gives her no message but she assumes that the suitors have sent him and asks why. There is no doubt that ἢ εἰπέμεναι must stand in Homer. But L may have forgotten the context and think of 681–3 as all one sentence: 'why have they sent you to tell . . .?' We should either insert ἢ or (better) do without a question-mark at ἀγανοί.

Cf. 26. 1 for a similarly incomplete quotation: see also Introd. l.

28–29. 1 *Periphrasis*.

Quintilian (8. 6. 59) states the essentials about this device, which L (like Caecilius, Quint. 9. 3. 98) treats among the figures: 'Pluribus enim verbis cum id quod uno aut paucioribus certe dici potest, explicatur, περίφρασιν vocant, circuitum quendam eloquendi, qui nonnumquam necessitatem habet, quoties dictu deformia operit, ut Sallustius "ad requisita naturae", interim ornatum petit solum, qui est apud poetas frequentissimus . . . et apud oratores non rarus, semper tamen adstrictior.'

Thus the two essential uses are *ornandae rei* and *celandae turpitudinis*. For the employment of the concept of periphrasis in scholia, &c., see, for example, Servius on *Aen.* 4. 6 and the Index to Schwartz's *Scholia in Euripidem*.

28. 1. ὡς οὐχ ὑψηλοποιόν, οὐδεὶς ἂν διστάσειεν: 'no one would doubt that periphrasis is a means of achieving elevation'. For the 'redundant' negative, see K–G ii. 209.

διὰ τῶν παραφώνων καλουμένων: 'viderint *μουσικῶν παῖδες*', said Toup. The passage has been discussed not only by eighteenth-century musical theorists but more recently by C. A. Moberg, *Zeitschr. f. Musikwissenschaft* xii (1930) 220–5, and J. Handschin, *Philol.* lxxxvi (1931) 52 ff. (i) παράφωνοι are sounds blended simultaneously with the melody or κύριος φθόγγος; the technical writers differ over the interval between the παράφωνοι and the κύριος φθόγγος, but the latter is the lower note (cf. Plu. *conj. praec.* 139c: ἂν φθόγγοι δύο σύμφωνοι ληφθῶσι, τοῦ βαρυτέρου γίνεται τὸ μέλος); see especially Gaudentius, pp. 337–8 Jan. (ii) So far as the interpretation of our passage is concerned, the principal difficulty is that the analogy does not seem to be exact. Periphrasis, unlike paraphonia, is essentially a *replacement* of the κύριον. However—as Mr. E. K. Borthwick, who kindly advised me on the passage, suggests—we should not make too much of this; it may be that L has been attracted by an illustration which he does not use with precision—musical analogies are not uncommon in Plutarch and περὶ κόσμου for instance, and these are writers of the same school in a sense as L—or the analogy may be between an instrumental accompaniment to a voice melody and an occasional periphrasis diversifying a passage mostly composed of κύρια ὀνόματα. 'Accompaniment' is a sufficiently close translation.

καὶ μάλιστ' ἂν μὴ . . . κεκραμένον: either (i) 'especially if it has nothing bombastic or tasteless about it, but only what is pleasantly blended' (*scil.* ἔχῃ τι) or (ii) '. . . but is pleasantly blended', understanding ᾖ, as in Demetrius 303: καὶ ἐπὰν τὰ κῶλα μηδεμίαν ἔχῃ πρὸς ἄλληλα σύνδεσιν ἀλλ' ὅμοια διερρηγμένοις. See Radermacher, *Demetrius* 86. Wilamowitz's ⟨ᾖ⟩ is needless and introduces a bad hiatus.

28. 2. κατὰ τὴν εἰσβολὴν τοῦ Ἐπιταφίου: for the use of the *Menexenus* as a serious model, see above, p. 110. ἆρα... εὐμέλειαν; 'Is it in small degree that he has thus magnified the thought? Or has he rather turned the bare expression into lyric song, pouring as it were the melodiousness of his periphrasis around it as a harmony?' Reiske's punctuation seems preferable—question mark, at νόησιν—and ἤ is *an potius?* Or should we read καί for ἤ, allowing μετρίως to go with ἐμελοποίηε also?

28. 3. νομίζετε ... συγκεκόμισθε ... χαίρετε: the verbs are indicatives, not imperatives. ἡγεμών is not uncommonly used to personify abstracts; cf. *Cyr.* 1. 2. 7; Pl. *Meno* 97B, *Laws* 688B, 963A.

νομίζετε ... ποιεῖσθε: a curious inconsistency.

μεγάλην ... προσπεριωρίσατο: 'has included in his encomium a magnificent sentiment'.

καὶ τὸ ἀμίμητον ἐκεῖνο τοῦ Ἡροδότου: for the order cf. τὸν κίνδυνον τῶν μακρῶν ὑπερβατῶν 22. 3; K–G i. 618. A complete sentence may be produced by transposing τό to follow ἐκεῖνο, but this is not necessary.

The Scythians who plundered the temple at Ascalon while raiding Palestine were struck down by Aphrodite Ourania with this mysterious complaint, which they transmitted to their descendants. Hippocrates (περὶ ἀέρων 22) speaks of effeminacy and impotence among them; he presumably means the condition to which Herodotus alludes, though he gives various rationalizing explanations (e.g. swellings due to riding and their cure; or even wearing trousers).

29. 1. Ἐπίκηρον μέντοι [τὸ] πρᾶγμα: I think Weiske probably right to omit the article. 'Periphrasis is a thing fraught with danger.' For the idiom, cf. Dem. 19. 136: ὁ δῆμός ἐστιν ἀσταθμητότατον πρᾶγμα.

εἰ μὴ ... λαμβάνοιτο: 'if it is not employed with a degree of moderation.' With συμμέτρως, we must take τινί as dative of the agent. Morus's easy correction is convincing, and is rightly accepted by Lebègue and Rostagni.

ἀβλεμές: a very rare and poetical word; LSJ connect it with βλεμεαίνω and take ἀβλεμέως πίνων (Panyasis) as 'drinking heavily'; but see Gow *CQ* N.S. i (1951) 97 for the meaning 'ineffective' in Nic. *Alex.* 32.

παχύτητος: I follow Toup and Weiske in adopting Manutius's suggestion.

τὸν Πλάτωνα: cf. Dion. Hal. *Dem.* 5: ἐκχεῖται ... εἰς ἀπειροκάλους περιφράσεις and (ibid.) ἄκαιρος ἐν ταῖς μετωνυμίαις. In view of this, and of the general sense, we should probably adopt Manutius's ⟨τὸ⟩ σχῆμα, though against this may be cited Dion. Hal. *Dem.* 32: τὸ τροπικόν, περὶ ὃ μάλιστα δεινὸς ὁ Πλάτων εἶναι δοκεῖ.

ἀκαίρως: sc. δεινός, but note Schurzfleisch's ἄκαιρος.

προβάτειον ... καὶ βόειον πλοῦτον: 'ovine and bovine wealth.'

29. 2. *Conclusion of the section on figures.*

πάθος ... ἡδονῆς: 'emotion is as important an ingredient in elevation as characterization is in charm.' For the πάθος–ἦθος contrast and its various forms, see on 9. 15. The contrast between ἡδονή and ὕψος is related (i) to that between the middle and high styles in the theory of χαρακτῆρες, (ii) to that between the *officium commovendi* and the *officium delectandi*. See in general Introd. III.

30. *Beginning of the discussion of diction.* (*The fourth 'source' of* 8. 1.) *Choice of words.*

30. 1. δι' ἑκατέρου διέπτυκται: 'are completely entangled with one another.'

[ἂν] ... λοιπὰ ἔτι: I assume εἴ τινα λοιπὰ ἔτι to be sound; it is convincingly idiomatic. ἄν and δή are easily confused in uncial writing (see, for example, 44. 5; Pl. *Parm.* 141C1, *Gorg.* 452C3; Wyse, *Isaeus*, p. xlvi; Bywater, *JPhil.* 32 (1913) 225), and I suggest we have here two readings of the same word.

Spengel's ᾖ is, however, an easy change, and produces sense if not elegance. On any view, there is a difficulty about the general meaning. L seems to be making the admission that some topics which might be considered as falling under the head of diction—e.g. periphrasis—have already been dealt with.

μέγεθος ... παρασκευάζουσα: 'making as it does grandeur, beauty, charm, weight, force, strength, and a certain lustre bloom upon our words as upon beautiful statues.'

πίνος is patina on metal or bloom on fruit. Cf. schol. Dion. Hal. *Dem.* 5: ὁ ῥύπος, ἤτοι ὁ ἐπικείμενος χνοῦς ὡς ἐπὶ μήλων καὶ ἀπίων καὶ δαμασκηνῶν. πίνος and εὐπίνεια in literary criticism are attractive qualities of earlier literature—a sort of archaic charm (ὁ τῆς ἀρχαιότητος πίνος, Dion. Hal., l.c.; see above p. 110).

πρὸς εἰδότας: like ἐν εἰδόσι (e.g. Thuc. 6. 77. 1), a fixed phrase. In using it, L neglects the fact that he is formally addressing a single individual. There is no need to emend. Cf. Dion. Hal. *CV* 22. 165, *Lys.* 10 (p. 17. 14 U–R), *Dem.* 42 (p. 223. 10 U–R), &c.

φῶς γὰρ ... τὰ καλὰ ὀνόματα: this famous sentence resembles one in Cassius Longinus' *ars*, p. 558 Walz: φῶς γὰρ ὥσπερ τῶν ἐννοημάτων τε καὶ ἐπιχειρημάτων ὁ τοιοῦτος λόγος, ἀποσαφῶν τοῖς δικασταῖς τὴν πιθανότητα τῆς πίστεως. It means 'beautiful words are indeed thought's own illumination'—i.e. they set a lustre on thought. For καλὰ ὀνόματα see Demetrius 173–5. Theophrastus defined these as words pleasant to ear or eye (i.e. names of things pleasant to see) or τῇ διανοίᾳ ἔντιμα (e.g. ἀρχαῖοι for παλαιοί). Cf. also Arist. *Rhet.* 3. 1405^{b}13 ff.

τῷ ὄντι implies an allusion of some sort; it may be to the speculation that φωνή derives from φῶς νοῦ (schol. Dion. Thrac., p. 181. 33 Hilgard).

The νοῦς is the speaker's, not the hearer's. This sort of language may be used (i) of the fact that words, as it were, bring thoughts to light: cf. Philo, *quod deterius* 128: τὰ ἐνθυμήματα ἐν ἀοράτῳ χωρίῳ, διανοίᾳ, ταμιεύεται, μέχρις ἂν οἷα φῶς ἐναυγάσασα ἡ φωνὴ πάντ' ἐκκαλύψῃ; (ii) of the special effect of καλὰ ὀνόματα, cf. Cic. *de oratore* 3. 24: 'neque esse ullam sententiam inlustrem nisi luce verborum.'

There is no direct connexion with any philosophical doctrine of mental 'illumination'.

30. 2. ὡς εἴ τις . . . νηπίῳ: 'as if one were to fit a huge tragic mask on a small child.' A fairly common image: cf. (i) Philod. *rhet.* i. 199 Sudhaus, quoting Hieronymus of Rhodes (fr. 52a Wehrli) on the unsuitability of Isocratean 'study oratory' to the rough-and-tumble of δημηγορίαι: ὅμοιον γοῦν εἶναι τῷ δασὺ καὶ μέγα περιθέμενον πρόσωπον παιδίου φωνὴν ἀφιέναι καὶ τὸ τοῖς Ἕλλησιν συμβουλεύοντα καὶ πλάσμα καὶ τὴν ἄλλην κατασκευὴν δημηγόρου περιβαλλόμενον ἐπ' ἀναγνώστου παιδὸς φωνὴν ἀποδεδρακέναι, μήτε τόνον μήτε πάθος μήθ' ὑπόκρισιν δυναμένου φέρειν. Cf. Dion. Hal. *Isocr.* 13 (Hier. fr. 52b); (ii) Quint. 6. 1. 36: 'nam in parvis quidem litibus has tragoedias movere tale est quasi si personam Herculis et cothurnos aptare infantibus velis'; (iii) Lucian, *de conscr. hist.* 23. 31: ἐοικέναι παιδίῳ, εἴ που Ἔρωτα εἶδες παίζοντα, προσωπεῖον Ἡρακλέους πάμμεγα ἢ Τιτᾶνος περικείμενον.

καὶ ἱ⟨στορίᾳ⟩: presumably L now proceeds to a contrast between poetry and history, on the one hand, and oratory on the other. 'Historia . . . proxima poetis' (Quint. 10. 1. 31). Dionysius too (*Thuc.* 51) expects some poetical graces in history and an avoidance of τὸ ἰδιωτικόν. Hellenistic and Roman historians, of course, practised this doctrine, and some of the most striking characteristics of their work are due to it.

31. *Where the text resumes, L is discussing* τροπικὴ λέξις—*the second division of the* φραστικὸν μέρος—*with special reference to the vigorous effect of colloquial idioms.*

. . . †πτικώτατον . . . ⟨πώλου⟩ ἐπιστρέφομαι: I mark the word with which the extant text begins as doubtful, and also †τὸ δ' . . . οὐκέτι†, on the ground that both reading and punctuation are unsure.

Bergk (Anacreon, fr. 96) read οὐκέτι Θρηικίης ⟨πώλου⟩ ἐπιστρέφομαι. Cf. πῶλε Θρηκίη, fr. 75 Bergk (= 72 Page). This makes L refer to Anacreon's calling a girl a filly, and both Bergk and L's editors and translators assume that his comment on the expression is favourable. This involves emending τὸ δ' Ἀνακρέοντος, perhaps to τὸ τἀνακρέοντος, for Petra's τόδ' clearly will not do. But all this is uncertain, since it is also possible, even if less likely, that the stop should come after, not before, οὐκέτι; i.e. '*X* is impressive, but Anacreon's phrase, by contrast, is not'.

ταύτῃ καὶ . . . καταμέμφεται: much debated (see apparatus), but

32. 1] COMMENTARY 151

I think Hammer was on the right lines. Translate: 'Similarly, Theopompus' much admired phrase seems to me to be particularly expressive because of the aptness of the analogy; yet Caecilius somehow manages to find fault with it.' I take the antecedent of ὅπερ to be τὸ ... ἐπαινετόν.

ἀναγκοφαγῆσαι: 'stomach, eat under compulsion.' A medical term; cf. Philostr. *VS* 2. 17 of an athlete's regimen: ἀναγκοφαγῶν καὶ διαπονῶν.

ἰδιωτισμός: 'common expression.' Cf. the Stoic definition of κατασκευή as λέξις ἐκπεφευγυῖα τὸν ἰδιωτισμόν (*SVF* iii. 214); Sen. *contr.* 7 *praef.* 5: 'idiotismus est inter oratorias virtutes res quae raro procedit; magno enim temperamento opus est et occasione quadam.'

ἤδη πιστότερον: i.e. just by virtue of being familiar. ἤδη is logical, not temporal: see LSJ, s.v. 4. I think this is somewhat more pointed than taking ἤδη with σύνηθες, though ἤδη tends to the end of its phrase (9. 11), and there is a prima-facie case for taking it so here.

31. 2. ἐγγὺς παραξύει τὸν ἰδιώτην: 'come near the common man.' Cf., for example, Dion. Hal. *Lys.* 13: ἡ τῆς συνθέσεως τῶν ὀνομάτων ἡδονὴ μιμουμένης τὸν ἰδιώτην. For the verb, see LSJ, s.v. παραξέω ii.

ἀλλ' οὐκ ἰδιωτεύει τῷ σημαντικῶς: 'but is not commonplace because it is expressed in a significant way.' The ellipse of, for example, λέγεσθαι, is in L's more hurried manner.

32. *Multiplication of metaphors.*

32. 1. περὶ δὲ πλήθους [καὶ] μεταφορῶν: the uncertainty about this passage partly depends on the fact that we cannot be sure whether the type of thing described in the preceding paragraph falls under metaphor or not. We may (i) retain καί, translating either 'number of metaphors *too*' (as though what had preceded was a discussion of *number* of idiotismi) or simply 'number of *metaphors*' (cf. the examples of καί in Denniston, p. 320); (ii) supply a second noun: the sense of the context precludes, for example, Toll's τόλμης, but Lebègue's συνεχείας gives a less exceptionable meaning; (iii) delete καί: this gives quite satisfactory sense, and we may compare 34. 2 for a not dissimilar intrusion of καί between two words (there adverbs, here genitives).

δύο ... τρεῖς: cf. 1 Cor. xiv. 27: δύο ἢ τὸ πλεῖστον τρεῖς.

ὁ γὰρ ... συνεφέλκεται: 'with this sort of thing too, Demosthenes is the standard, and the proper occasion for use is when there is a rushing torrent of emotion which drags along the multiplicity of the metaphors as a necessary concomitant.' With P's reading, μέν is unanswered and the connexion ὁ γὰρ Δημοσθένης follows from a missing step: we must mentally supply some such response to ὁ μὲν Καικίλιος as 'but wrongly, for ...'. Schück and Wilamowitz read ὁ δὲ ... χρείας γάρ, making the argument easy and assuming a quite likely corruption (for the confusion of δέ and γάρ, see Wyse, *Isaeus* xlvii: 'a mental rather than a visual error').

For ὅρος, cf. Dion. Hal. *CV* 18. 119: ὅρος γὰρ δή τίς ἐστιν ἐκλογῆς τε ὀνομάτων καὶ κάλλους συνθέσεως ὁ Δημοσθένης; *Dem.* 1, 23, *Lys.* 18, *Thuc.* 2, Plin. *ep.* 9. 25. 8: 'Demosthenes ipse, illa norma oratoris et regula' (cf. Introd. xli).

ὁ τῆς χρείας δὲ καιρός: Lebègue, following Vahlen, translates 'Mais c'est l'occasion convenable qui décide de l'emploi', and puts a colon after καιρός. This is most implausible. For the phrase cf. Plu. *de cohibenda ira* 454A: ὅταν ὁ τῆς χρείας ἀφίκηται καιρός . . . .

32. 2. ἐνταῦθα . . . θυμός: 'here the orator's anger against traitors hides the multiplicity of his metaphorical expressions.' ἐπιπροσθεῖν is used of heavenly bodies obscuring or eclipsing others; for a metaphorical use cf. Plu. *de audiendo* 41C: ὁ μὲν γὰρ Μελάνθιος . . . περὶ τῆς Διογένους τραγῳδίας ἐρωτηθεὶς οὐκ ἔφη κατιδεῖν αὐτὴν ὑπὸ τῶν ὀνομάτων ἐπιπροσθουμένην ('because the words got in the way').

32. 3. ὁ μὲν . . . Θεόφραστος: there is no other evidence that Aristotle and Theophrastus said precisely this, but the doctrine is certainly Peripatetic. Cf. Arist. *Rhet.* 1408ᵇ2: ἄκος δ' ἐπὶ πάσῃ ὑπερβολῇ τὸ θρυλούμενον· δεῖ γὰρ αὐτὸν αὑτῷ προσεπιπλήσσειν (προ- Quint. 8. 3. 37)· δοκεῖ γὰρ ἀληθὲς εἶναι, ἐπεὶ οὐ λανθάνει γε ὃ ποιεῖ τὸν λέγοντα. Demetrius 80: ἐπὰν μέντοι κινδυνώδης ἡ μεταφορὰ δοκῇ, μεταλαμβανέσθω εἰς εἰκασίαν (*scil.* by adding ὥσπερ, which turns it into a simile).

32. 4. ὅμως δὲ . . . λέγοντι: 'nevertheless—and I said the same about figures—strong and appropriate emotion and genuine elevation are, in my opinion, a very particular palliative for multiplied or daring metaphors, because their nature is to sweep and hurl along all these other things by the surging tide of their movement, or rather positively to demand audacity as an essential, and never let the hearer have leisure to make a count of the metaphors, because he too shares the speaker's enthusiasm.'

For τῷ ῥοθίῳ -ῆς φορᾶς cf. Plu. *praec. ger. reip.* 819F: τὸ παρὰ τῶν ὄχλων ῥόθιον πολλάκις συνεξαῖρον αὐτήν (*scil.* τὴν φιλοτιμίαν).

32. 5. ἔν γε ταῖς τοπηγορίαις καὶ διαγραφαῖς: 'in commonplaces and descriptions.'

δι' ὧν . . . παρὰ τῷ Πλάτωνι: 'this is the method by which Xenophon achieves his elaborate—and Plato his yet more divine—description of man's bodily tabernacle.' Note the involved order, by which ἔτι μᾶλλον is separated from θείως. Professor Fraenkel (see *Horace* 84 ff.) compares the examples given by Vahlen, Arist. *Poetics*³ 284 (e.g. *Meteorol.* 1. 13. 350ᵇ8 περὶ ὧν λίαν εἰσὶν οἱ λεγόμενοι λόγοι μυθώδεις), and a variety of Latin passages with *magis* (Hor. *serm.* 1. 2. 80 sq.), *maxime, minus, nimis*.

παρὰ Ξενοφῶντι: Xenophon's teleological account of human anatomy, perhaps derived from Diogenes of Apollonia, was very

32. 5] COMMENTARY 153

influential in Hellenistic and Roman times; see Festugière, *Le Dieu cosmique* (= *La Révélation d'Hermès Trismégiste II*) 75 ff., and Nock and Festugière's notes on *Corpus Hermeticum* 5. 6.

σκήνους: the word is not in Xenophon, but it has a long history in both pagan and Christian writings in the sense of the body as the 'tabernacle' of the soul: cf., for example, Democritus B 37, 187, 223; *Axiochus* 366A; *Timaeus Locrus* 100A, 101 C, E; 2 Cor. v. 1. The references to the *Timaeus* are best set out in the form of a table.

L	Plato
ἀκρόπολιν	70A6: ἐκ τῆς ἀκροπόλεως.
ἰσθμόν ... τὸν αὐχένα	69E1: ἰσθμὸν καὶ ὅρον διοικοδομήσαντες τῆς τε κεφαλῆς καὶ τοῦ στήθους, αὐχένα μεταξὺ τιθέντες, ἵν' εἴη χωρίς.
σφονδύλους ... στρόφιγγας	74A1: καὶ περὶ τὸν διαυχένιον ἅμα καὶ νωτιαῖον μυελὸν ἐξ αὐτοῦ σφονδύλους πλάσας ὑπέτεινεν οἷον στρόφιγγας.
ἡδονὴν ... κακοῦ δέλεαρ (Note 1)	69D1: ἡδονὴν μέγιστον κακοῦ δέλεαρ.
γλῶσσαν ... γεύσεως δοκίμιον	65C7: οἱόνπερ δοκίμια τῆς γλώττης τεταμένα ἐπὶ τὴν καρδίαν.
ἄναμμα τῶν φλεβῶν τὴν καρδίαν (Note 2)	70A7: τὴν δὲ δὴ καρδίαν ἅμμα τῶν φλεβῶν.
καὶ πηγὴν τοῦ περιφερομένου σφοδρῶς αἵματος, εἰς τὴν δορυφορικὴν οἴκησιν κατατεταγμένην	70B1: καὶ πηγὴν τοῦ περιφερομένου κατὰ πάντα τὰ μέλη σφοδρῶς αἵματος εἰς τὴν δορυφορικὴν οἴκησιν κατέστησαν.
στενωπούς	70B5: διὰ πάντων τῶν στενωπῶν.
τῇ δὲ ... λυμαίνηται (Note 3)	70C1: τῇ δὲ δὴ πηδήσει τῆς καρδίας ἐν τῇ τῶν δεινῶν προσδοκίᾳ καὶ τῇ τοῦ θυμοῦ ἐγέρσει, προγιγνώσκοντες ὅτι διὰ πυρὸς ἡ τοιαύτη πᾶσα ἔμελλεν οἴδησις γίγνεσθαι τῶν θυμουμένων, ἐπικουρίαν αὐτῇ μηχανώμενοι τὴν τοῦ πλεύμονος ἰδέαν ἐνεφύτευσαν, πρῶτον μὲν μαλακὴν καὶ ἄναιμον, εἶτα σήραγγας ἐντὸς ἔχουσαν οἷον σπόγγου κατατετρημένας, ἵνα τό τε πνεῦμα καὶ τὸ πῶμα δεχομένη, ψύχουσα, ἀναπνοὴν καὶ ῥᾳστώνην ἐν τῷ καύματι παρέχοι· διὸ δὴ τῆς ἀρτηρίας ὀχετοὺς ἐπὶ τὸν πλεύμονα

L	Plato
	ἕτερον καὶ περὶ τὴν καρδίαν αὐτὸν περιέστησαν οἷον μάλαγμα, ἵν' ὁ θυμὸς ἡνίκ' ἐν αὐτῇ ἀκμάζοι, πηδῶσα εἰς ὑπεῖκον καὶ ἀναψυχομένη, πονοῦσα ἧττον, μᾶλλον τῷ λόγῳ μετὰ θυμοῦ δύναιτο ὑπηρετεῖν.
καὶ τὴν μὲν ... ἀνδρωνῖτιν	69E6: διοικοδομοῦσι τοῦ θώρακος αὖ τὸ κύτος, διορίζοντες οἷον γυναικῶν, τὴν δ' ἀνδρῶν χωρὶς οἴκησιν, τὰς φρένας διάφραγμα εἰς τὸ μέσον αὐτῶν τιθέντες.
τόν γε μὴν σπλῆνα τῶν ἐντὸς μαγεῖον	72C6: πάντα ἡ σπληνὸς καθαίρουσα αὐτὰ δέχεται μανότης, ἅτε κοίλου καὶ ἀναίμου ὑφανθέντος· ὅθεν πληρούμενος τῶν ἀποκαθαιρομένων μέγας καὶ ὕπουλος αὐξάνεται.
μετὰ δὲ ταῦτα ... προθέμενοι	74B7: τὴν δὲ σάρκα προβολὴν μὲν καυμάτων, πρόβλημα δὲ χειμώνων, ἔτι δὲ πτωμάτων οἷον τὰ πιλητὰ ἔσεσθαι κτήματα.
	74D7: μετὰ ταῦτα σαρξὶν πάντα αὐτὰ κατεσκίασεν ἄνωθεν.
νομὴν δὲ σαρκῶν ἔφη τὸ αἷμα	80E6: ὃ καλοῦμεν αἷμα, νομὴν σαρκῶν καὶ σύμπαντος τοῦ σώματος.
τῆς δὲ τροφῆς ... νάματα	77C6: ταῦτα δὴ τὰ γένη πάντα φυτεύσαντες οἱ κρείττους τοῖς ἥττοσιν ἡμῖν τροφήν, τὸ σῶμα αὐτὸ ἡμῶν διωχέτευσαν τέμνοντες οἷον ἐν κήποις ὀχετούς, ἵνα ὥσπερ ἐκ νάματος ἐπιόντος ἄρδοιτο.
	79A2: οἷον ἐκ κρήνης ἐπ' ὀχετοὺς ἐπὶ τὰς φλέβας ἀντλοῦν αὐτά, ῥεῖν ὥσπερ αὐλῶνος διὰ τοῦ σώματος τὰ τῶν φλεβῶν ποιεῖ ῥεύματα.
ἡνίκα ... ἐλευθέραν	85E6: ἔλυσεν τὰ τῆς ψυχῆς αὐτόθεν οἷον νεὼς πείσματα μεθῆκέν τε ἐλευθέραν.

Notes

(1) P has κακόν, so that Burnet is wrong to report 'κακῶν Longinus'. Cicero's *escam malorum*, on the other hand, *is* evidence for κακῶν.

(2) The better Plato manuscripts have ἅμμα, F and Galen ἅμα (see

Taylor's note): L's ἄναμμα probably arises by a dittography from the neighbouring καρδίαν.

(3) L's μάλαγμα ('cushion'), confirmed by Albinus, *isagoge* 23, is clearly right; Plato's manuscripts and Galen have ἅλμα μαλακόν, or the like.

Thus these quotations, except so far as the actual metaphors under discussion are concerned, are quite unreliable in detail and wording. They are not even given in the order of the original. The accuracy of those which profess to be direct quotations is no higher than that of admitted paraphrases. And yet in one place a right reading—μάλαγμα—is given against the consensus of the direct tradition of Plato. Such passages are a good control for 'fragments'. What sort of idea of this part of the *Timaeus* should we have had if we depended on L?

Since the whole passage is rather difficult, I translate the greater part of 32. 5:

'The head he calls its "citadel"; the neck is an "isthmus" constructed between the head and the chest; the vertebrae, he says, are fixed underneath "like pivots". Pleasure is a "lure of evil" for mankind; the tongue is a "taste-meter". The heart is a "knot of veins" and "fountain of the blood that moves impetuously round", allocated to the "guard-room". The word he uses for the various passages of the canals is "alleys". "Against the throbbing of the heart", he continues, "in the expectation of danger and in the excitation of anger, when it gets hot, they contrived a means of succour, implanting in us the lungs, soft, bloodless and with cavities, a sort of cushion, so that, when anger boils up in the heart, the latter's throbbing is against a yielding obstacle, so that it comes to no harm." Again: he calls the seat of the desires "the women's quarters", and the seat of anger "the men's quarters". The spleen is for him "a napkin for the inner parts, which therefore grows big and festering through being filled with secretions". "And thereafter", he says again, "they buried the whole under a canopy of flesh", putting the flesh on "as a protection against dangers from without, like felting". Blood he called "fodder of the flesh". For the purpose of nutrition, he says too, "they irrigated the body, cutting channels as in gardens, so that the streams of the veins might flow as it were from an incoming stream, the body being a narrow aqueduct". Finally: when the end is near, the soul's "ship's cables" are, in Plato's words, "loosed", and she herself is "set free".'

For a complete translation of the passages of Plato, with comment, see especially F. M. Cornford's *Plato's Cosmology* 266 ff.

μεταξὺ τοῦ στήθους: i.e. between the head and the chest. For μεταξύ with one of the two extreme terms unexpressed, see LSJ, s.v. ii a.

156   COMMENTARY   [32. 6–

32. 6. ἀπόχρη * * * δεδηλωμένα: the supplement ⟨δὲ τὰ⟩ in a later hand in P is an unsatisfactory makeshift. There can be little doubt about the general sense: 'these examples are sufficient, out of many possible ones in the context, to prove that ....' Professor Dodds suggests to me ἀπόχρη δὲ δηλῶ⟨σαι τὰ δεδειγ⟩μένα. There is, however, some illogicality in ταῦτα ... ἑξῆς : we should consider the possibility that L wrote something like ταῦτα ... παραπλήσια (μυρί' ... ⟨δὲ τὰ⟩ δεδηλωμένα) ⟨δείκνυσιν⟩ ὡς ....

τροπικαί: scil. λέξεις, presumably. If this seems unsatisfactory, we should consider reading φύσεις (cf. 33. 2); Arist. Poet. 1459ᵃ6 τὸ μεταφορικόν ... εὐφυΐας σημεῖον.

φραστικοί: 'descriptive.' Cf. 12. 5.

32. 7. ἀπηνεῖς: 'harsh', 'forbidding'. Cf. Dion. Hal. CV 22. 166: ἀπηνῆ καὶ αὐστηρὰν ... ἁρμονίαν.

32. 8. τοῖς τοιούτοις ... ἀποφήνασθαι: 'attacking faults of this kind, Caecilius (? nevertheless) in his book on Lysias (? actually) has the hardihood to declare Lysias in every respect superior to Plato ....'
(i) αὐτό is somewhat doubtful Greek: the best we can do is to compare (with Vahlen) Aristoph. Knights 339: ἀλλ' αὐτὸ περὶ τοῦ πρότερος εἰπεῖν πρῶτα διαμαχοῦμαι; Dio Chrys. 12. 43; αὐτό γε ὥς φασιν ἀπλύτοις ποσὶ διεξίασι. (ii) There is no such antithesis in the thought as ὅμως suggests, unless we look forward to what follows on C.'s inconsistency. There may well be a serious corruption or omission; compare the doubts expressed on ἀκρίτοις below.

ἐν τοῖς ὑπὲρ Λυσίου συγγράμμασιν: probably a separate work from Caecilius' comprehensive περὶ τοῦ χαρακτῆρος τῶν δέκα ῥητόρων: see Brzoska, P–W, s.v. Caecilius, 1183–4. According to Photius (Bibl. 489ᵇ13 Bekker), Caecilius judged Lysias' οἰκονομία not up to the standard of his εὕρεσις. Cf. Pl. Phaedr. 264B.

ἀκρίτοις: translators hedge here. 'Confused', 'blind', 'uncritical', 'non sereni'? We should perhaps have suspicions about the text, though neither ἀσυγκρίτοις ('irreconcilable') nor ἀκράτοις appears an obvious improvement. ἀκρίτως 'without discrimination', taken with χρησάμενος, is possible: Plu. de aud. poet. 36D : οὐδ' ἀκρίτως ἀνάπλεως ὦν ἤκουε τῆς μητρός.

[τῷ παντί]: wrongly repeated from two lines above; meaningless here.

πλὴν ... ᾠήθη: 'but Caecilius, for his part, spoke out of desire to score a point, nor are his assumptions admitted, as he thought.'

τὰ θέματα: 'his assumptions', namely that Lysias is faultless—not that faultlessness is to be preferred to real greatness. See 35. 1. This interpretation is required by L's argument. That what is said is, to judge from Photius, l.c., unfair to Caecilius is simply to be observed as a mark of L's polemical methods.

πολλαχῇ: with διημαρτημένου.

33. 3] COMMENTARY 157

33–36. *Digression on the contrast between genius and mere faultlessness.*
Wilamowitz edited these chapters, with commentary, in his *Griechisches Lesebuch*, under the title *Regel und Genie* (a phrase with echoes of Goethe and the Romantics generally, cf., for example, *Dichtung und Wahrheit* xix).
Cf., in general, Sen. *ep.* 114. 12: 'nullum sine venia placuit ingenium.'

33. 1. τῷ ὄντι: i.e. not a false claimant to faultlessness, like Lysias.

περὶ αὐτοῦ τούτου: 'about this very point.' Neuter, not masculine.

μέγεθος ἐν ἐνίοις διημαρτημένον: 'grandeur in some respects faultily executed.' Cf. διημαρτημένου above and 36. 3 ὁ Κολοσσὸς ὁ ἡμαρτημένος. With P's διημαρτημένοις, translate: 'with some failures.' The correction is much neater and nearer in idiom to the other passages. The error in P may well be due to the proximity of ἐνίοις.

τὸ σύμμετρον ... ἀδιάπτωτον: 'a modest degree of success, though wholly sound and free from fault.'

αἱ πλείους ἀρεταί: for ἀρεταί cf. 34. 1, 2. L alludes to the rhetoricians' technique of criticizing by the enumeration of good qualities. It was fatally easy for any would-be critic to count the numbers of virtues instead of assessing their quality and appeal (Bonner, *Dionysius* 15 ff.). Dionysius' ἀρεταί—the list goes back in part to Theophrastus—are ἑλληνισμός (purity of language), σαφήνεια (clarity), συντομία (brevity), ἐνάργεια (vividness), the imitation of ἤθη and πάθη, ἰσχύς (strength), πειθώ (persuasion) or ἡδονή (charm), τὸ μέγα καὶ θαυμαστόν, and τὸ πρέπον (propriety). See, for instance, *ad Pomp.* 3, where a comparison between Herodotus and Thucydides is conducted on this principle.

33. 2. τὸ γὰρ ... μικρότητος: a notion rooted in Greek notions of social propriety; it is degrading to count the cost. Cf. Arist. *EN* 1122^{b}8: ἡ ἀκριβολογία μικροπρεπές.

εἶναι ... παρολιγωρούμενον: cf. Hor. *ep.* 1. 6. 45: 'exilis domus est ubi non et multa supersunt et dominum fallunt et prosunt furibus.'

μήποτε ... μέγεθος: cf. Pl. *Rep.* 6. 497D: τὰ γὰρ δὴ μεγάλα πάντα ἐπισφαλῆ καὶ τὸ λεγόμενον τὰ καλὰ τῷ ὄντι χαλεπά. For the application of the theme to literature, see the discussion in Dion. Hal. *ad Pomp.* 2, where the language recalls the present passage: Pompeius had written: ἐν δὲ τοῦτο διϊσχυρίζομαι, ὅτι οὐκ ἔστι μεγάλων ἐπιτυχεῖν ἐν οὐδενὶ τρόπῳ, μὴ τοιαῦτα τολμῶντα καὶ παραβαλλόμενον ἐν οἷς καὶ σφάλλεσθαί ἐστιν ἀναγκαῖον. Dionysius replies: ἐγώ τέ φημι τῆς ὑψηλῆς καὶ μεγαλοπρεποῦς καὶ παρακεκινδυνευμένης φράσεως ἐφιέμενον Πλάτωνα μὴ περὶ πάντα τὰ μέρη κατορθοῦν, πολλοστὴν μέντοι μοῖραν ἔχειν τῶν κατορθουμένων τὰ διαμαρτανόμενα ὑπ' αὐτοῦ (cf. 35. 2 below).

33. 3. ὅτι ... ἀπορρεῖ: another commonplace; cf. Cic. *de oratore* 1. 129: 'nihil est enim tam insigne nec tam ad diuturnitatem memoriae stabile quam id in quo aliquid offenderis.'

33. 4. καὶ αὐτός: i.e. even I, with my belief that genius should be pardoned its faults. The reference may be to 9. 7 or to a lost passage, perhaps in the discussion of turgidity in 3.

ὅμως δὲ ... παρενηνεγμένα: 'deeming them nevertheless not so much voluntary mistakes as accidental slips let fall at random through inattention and with the negligence of genius.'
For οὐ μᾶλλον ... ἤ cf. 9. 4.

ἀρετάς: Petra's correction is essential.

κἂν εἰ μηδενὸς: this change seems necessary, since διά with the genitive can hardly mean 'because of'.

Ἀπολλώνιος: cf. Quint. 10. 1. 54: 'non contemnendum reddidit opus aequali quadam mediocritate.'

κἂν τοῖς βουκολικοῖς ... ἐπιτυχέστατος: τοῖς βουκολικοῖς may be masculine or neuter. If the latter, L excludes Theocritus' non-pastoral poems. τῶν ἔξωθεν is also difficult. Neither Morus's suggestion—'locus, occasio, initia colloquii, descriptiones donorum et praemiorum'—nor that of Wilamowitz—'learned details not in harmony with the realistic setting'—is at all convincing. Grace B. Ruckh (*CP* xxix (1942) 256) approaches the question by examining the criticisms made in the scholia: e.g. 1. 72 b, no lions in Sicily; 5. 141/43 b, φριμάσσεο is used properly of horses not goats; 15. 139, Hecuba had nineteen children not twenty. It seems very plausible that L should allude to some such fault-finding by grammatici.

ἆρ' οὖν Ὅμηρος ... γενέσθαι: 'would you rather be Homer or Apollonius?' ἤ should be translated 'or', not 'than'. The genitives of comparison in the next sentence depend on μείζων.

33. 5. ἐν τῇ Ἠριγόνῃ: in this learned elegiac poem (fragments in J. U. Powell, *Collectanea Alexandrina* 64 ff.; the main source for the story is Hyginus fab. 130) the astronomer-poet Eratosthenes told the story of Erigone, the daughter of the Attic countryman Icarius, whom Dionysus once visited. In return for a hospitable welcome, the god gave Icarius a skin of wine, at that time a novelty. Icarius shared this with some shepherds, some of whom thought he had poisoned them and proceeded to beat him to death. The barking of his dog Maira revealed to Erigone the whereabouts of her father's body. She hanged herself for grief. Dionysus then caused an epidemic of madness among the Athenian girls, driving them also to suicide by hanging. Apollo, consulted on the problem, replied that the deaths of Icarius and Erigone had not been avenged. The murderers were punished (but versions vary here) and in memory of Erigone a ritual of swinging from trees (αἰώρα, *oscillatio*) was instituted: on this see L. Deubner, *Attische Feste* 118. The principal characters in the story were all translated to the stars. The poem probably contained other αἴτια in explanation of various Attic Dionysiac festivals: L's description ἀμώμητον ποιημάτιον does not mean that it was very short (it could be 400–500 lines) but it does mean that we should not attribute to it the exuberances of Nonnus' version (*Dion.* 47. 34–264), which is far from ἀμώμητον. L.'s judgement coincides apparently with Plutarch's: cf. τὸν κομψὸν Ἐρατοσθένην, *quaest. conv.* 7. 1. 699A.

Ἐρατοσθένης . . . ποιητής; 'Is Eratosthenes . . . a greater poet than Archilochus with his abundant, uncontrolled flood and that bursting forth of the divine spirit, so hard to bring under the rule of law?' The comparisons go by genres, and for this purpose elegy and iambic count as one. The hendiadys Ἀρχιλόχου . . . κἀκείνης τῆς ἐκβολῆς is admittedly hard; ὑπ' ἐκείνης seems a simple remedy, but gives an unconvincing word-order. It is wrong to put a question-mark after δύσκολον; ἆρα is postponed to the vital point in the sentence, cf. Pl. *Gorg.* 467E : τὰ δὲ μήτ' ἀγαθὰ μήτε κακὰ ἆρα τοιάδε λέγεις; (See Denniston, p. 49; Riddell, *Digest of Platonic Idioms* 246.)

Βακχυλίδης: L's implication that Bacchylides is a good second-rate poet is borne out by the judgement of most modern critics since the discovery of the papyri. For knowledge of Bacchylides in Roman times see Snell, *Bacchylidis carmina,* *14.

Ἴων ὁ Χῖος: another writer of the second class. Von Blumenthal (*Ion von Chios* 3–4) concludes that about a dozen plays of Ion were known to the Alexandrians, and many poems. His prose works (ἐπιδημίαι, ὑπομνήματα) were perhaps better known; Plutarch read them and we have some interesting fragments, notably the account of the visit of Sophocles as a strategos to Chios in the Samian war (Athen. 13. 603E ff.). Ion has a special importance in the history of scholarship because of Bentley's pioneering work in collecting and discussing his fragments in *Epistola ad Millium* (1691).

ἐν τῷ γλαφυρῷ πάντῃ κεκαλλιγραφημένοι: 'examples of uniformly beautiful writing in the smooth manner.' γλαφυρός (see 10. 6) is associated with the middle style and with ἀνθηρός, &c. Introd. xxxiv ff.

ἤ: so Radermacher: 'ipse sibi respondet auctor.' If ἤ is retained, the sentence is a question (*an potius* . . . ?).

τοῦ Οἰδίποδος: L echoes the Aristotelian view that *Oedipus Tyrannus* is *the* classic tragedy.

⟨πάντ'⟩ ἀντιτιμήσαιτο ἑξῆς: πάντα has surely fallen out: for πάνθ' ἑξῆς see Introd. xxv n. 1.

34–35. 1. *Hyperides and Demosthenes.*

34. 1. τῷ ἀληθεῖ: if this can mean 'by their real value', with the implication that mere counting gives a false account, the text should stand. I do not, however, know a parallel. Vahlen, Wilamowitz, and Rostagni adopt Pearce's μεγέθει; cf. 35. 1.

Ὑπερείδης: ancient critics generally characterize Hyperides particularly by his *acumen*; see, for example, Quint. 10. 1. 77; Cic.

orator 110. Dion. Hal. *de imitatione* 5, p. 213 U–R, says that he exceeds Lysias in τῇ τῆς φράσεως κατασκευῇ and all men in ingenuity of invention; is relevant, sensible, and graceful; and combines δεινότης with apparent simplicity. L's critique of him, though more detailed, does not conflict with the common opinion. A rather different appreciation is given by Dion. Hal., *Dinarchus* 7.

πολυφωνότερος: 'more versatile', cf. Dion. Hal. *CV* 16. 97: πολυφωνότατος ... Ὅμηρος (with a more specific reference to sound-effects than in our passage).

ὕπακρος: 'second best.' Cf. [Pl.] *Erastae* 136c, 138E, where as here the word is associated with πένταθλος (competitor in the five contests of jumping, running, discus, javelin, and wrestling: hence 'all-rounder').

Sir Joshua Reynolds (Discourse V) uses this chapter as the basis of a comparison between Michelangelo and Raphael. 'If (the first rank) is to be given to him who possessed a greater combination of the higher qualities of the art than other men, there is no doubt that Raffaelle is the first. But if, as Longinus thinks, the sublime abundantly compensates the absence of every other beauty—then Michael Angelo demands the preference.'

34. 2. ὁ μέν γε ... χάριτας: 'Hyperides, besides imitating all the good features of Demosthenes, apart from his composition, has also acquired the virtues and graces of Lysias to an extraordinary degree.' χάρις—grace, charm—is something different from, and less definable than, the other ἀρεταί. Cf. Dion. Hal. *Lysias* 10: ἡ πᾶσιν ἐπανθοῦσα τοῖς ὀνόμασι κἀπ' ἴσης χάρις, πρᾶγμα παντὸς κρεῖττον λόγου καὶ θαυμασιώτερον. ῥᾷστον μὲν γάρ ἐστιν ὀφθῆναι ... χαλεπώτατον δὲ λόγῳ δηλωθῆναι.

μετὰ ἀφελείας: 'with simplicity.' ἀφέλεια is a word of various meanings. It is often applied to such writers as Lysias (Dion. Hal. *Dem.* 2), but it also serves to distinguish the philosophical style as opposed to the forensic generally. In later times it applies particularly to the arch naïveté and nursery syntax of Aelian, Philostratus, and their like.

πάντα ἐξῆς [καὶ] μονοτόνως: ἐξῆς simply emphasizes πάντα (see on 33. 5) and καί is, I believe, intrusive (see on 3. 4, 8. 2).

λέγει: 'delivers himself.' Note the contrast between λαλεῖ and λέγει. Cf. 26. 3, and Eupolis, fr. 95: λαλεῖν ἄριστος, ἀδυνατώτατος λέγειν. As Wilamowitz points out, this contrast was intelligible in L's time only to the highly cultured. For λαλεῖν as the general late word for 'speak', see, for example, Arndt–Gingrich, s.v.

P's λέγεται is impossible: there can be no point in mentioning an *alleged* fault of Demosthenes.

τό τε ἠθικὸν ... ἐφηδυνόμενον: Weiske was right, I think, to delete ἡδύ. The pleonasm ἡδὺ ... ἐφηδυνόμενον is intolerable. ἡδύ may be due to the scribe's eye glancing at ἐφηδυνόμενον or be a trace of a variant ἡδύτητος for γλυκύτητος. 'He has good sense of character, with a certain sweetness, dressed with a simple sauce.' For ἐφηδύνεσθαι, cf. 15. 6. Emendations like Lebègue's ἢ δριμύτητος which touch λιτῶς destroy another characteristic word of praise: cf. Dion. Hal. *Dem.* 2, *de imitatione*, 6, p. 206 U–R, &c. From λιτός comes λιτότης, the typical Attic feature of understatement.

περὶ αὐτόν: 'in him.' Cf. Philostr. *vit. soph. praef.*: τὰς περὶ αὐτὸν ἀρετὰς καὶ κακίας.

ἀστεϊσμοί: 'urbanities.' ἀστεῖος (= *urbanus*) has a wide range of derived meanings, from 'morally good' to 'smart and clever'. Aristotle (*Rhet.* 3. 10) has a long and valuable discussion of literary ἀστειότης—'good style'. In the rhetores, ἀστεϊσμός is a sort of εἰρωνεία which they try to distinguish from various related forms of humour and sarcasm. See Quint. 8. 6. 57 ff., and A. M. Finoli in *Rend. Ist. Lomb.* (*classe di lettere, &c.*) xcii (1958) 569 ff.

μυκτὴρ πολιτικώτατος: 'highly sophisticated sarcasm.' Cf. Plu. *de mal. Herod.* 860E: εὔρυθμός γε καὶ πολιτικὸς ὁ μυκτὴρ τοῦ συγγραφέως, εἰς Κᾶρας ὥσπερ εἰς κόρακας ἀποδιοπομπουμένου τὸν Ἰσαγόραν. Lucian, *Prometheus es* 1: ὅρα μή τις εἰρωνείαν φῇ καὶ μυκτῆρα οἷον τὸν Ἀττικὸν προσεῖναι τῷ ἐπαίνῳ. Eunapius, *vit. phil.*, p. 524 Wright (p. 84, 2 Giangrande): μυκτῆρα καὶ ἀστεϊσμόν (*si vera lectio*).

Cf. also Quint. 8. 6. 59: 'μυκτηρισμός dissimulatus quidam sed non latens derisus.' Puttenham translates 'the fleering Frumpe', i.e. mocking jeer. So in Latin *nasus*, *nasutus*; Sen. *suas.* 1. 6: 'belle illis cesserat, si nasus Atticus ibi substitisset.' Plin. *NH, praef.* 7: '(Lucilius) primus condidit stili nasum.' Distinguish from these phrases ἀπομύττειν, *emunctae naris*, &c., which imply neatness, cleanness, and smartness, but not scorn.

εὐγένεια: 'high breeding.' Cf. Quint. 10. 1. 113 on Messalla (see on 34. 3 below): 'nitidus et candidus et quodammodo prae se ferens in dicendo nobilitatem suam.' Since Messalla was literally *nobilis*, the criticism has an additional point when applied to him.

τὸ . . . εὐπάλαιστρον: 'proficiency.' For the metaphor, cf. Quint. 9. 4. 56: 'quos palaestritas esse nolumus, tamen esse nolumus eos qui dicuntur ἀπάλαιστροι.'

οὐκ ἄμουσα οὐδ' ἀνάγωγα: 'not tasteless or rude.' Cf. Philo, *de ebrietate* 33: ψυχῶν ὅσαι μὴ ἀνάγωγοι καὶ ἄμουσοι; Dion. Hal. *de ant. orat.* 1 (of Asianist style): ἀφόρητος ἀναιδείᾳ θεατρικῇ καὶ ἀνάγωγος.

κατὰ τοὺς Ἀττικοὺς ἐκείνους ἅλας ἐπικείμενα: a very doubtful passage. (i) If κατὰ τοὺς Ἀττικοὺς ἐκείνους goes closely with what precedes, it implies a criticism of the vulgarity of the classics. This is in itself not impossible, though it does not seem relevant or consistent with L's general attitude: we should have to compare the remarks on Old Comedy in Plutarch's *comparatio Aristophanis et Menandri*, or those on the invectives in Demosthenes and Aeschines in *praecepta gerendae reipublicae* 810D): καίτοι γε καὶ Δημοσθένης ἐν τῷ δικανικῷ τὸ λοίδορον ἔχει μόνον, οἱ δὲ Φιλιππικοὶ καθαρεύουσι καὶ σκώμματος καὶ βωμολοχίας. (ii) If κατὰ ... ἐκείνους is an independent phrase, parallel to οὐκ ἄμουσα οὐδ' ἀνάγωγα, or if it goes with what follows, then ἀλλά, if not also ἐπικείμενα, is to be emended. Now there is no evidence that ἐπικείμενα can mean 'relevant' or 'pointed', as LSJ say, and as most translators assume. Everything points to its meaning 'wearing, covered with'. It therefore needs an object. Hence the attraction of Richards's χάριν and more especially of Tucker's very ingenious ἅλας for ἀλλ'. The latter gives good sense, 'seasoned with salt as the old Attic writers were' (or 'as the Attic writers say', or again, if we are prepared to treat κατά as corrupt, 'with Attic salt'). But though *sales*, 'wit', is familiar in Latin, the evidence for the Greek ἅλες in this sense is not strong. Cf., however, Plu. *comp. Ar. et Men.* 854C: αἱ Μενάνδρου κωμῳδίαι ἀφθόνων ἁλῶν καὶ ἱερῶν μετέχουσι ... οἱ δὲ Ἀριστοφάνους ἅλες, πικροὶ καὶ τραχεῖς ὄντες.... I follow Tucker, though with some hesitation.

διασυρμός τε ἐπιδέξιος: 'a smart way of running things down ....' Cf. Finoli, l.c., for διασυρμός in rhetoric.

καὶ πολὺ τὸ κωμικὸν ⟨ἔχων⟩ ... κέντρον: Selb's addition—he compares 12. 3 πολὺ τὸ διάπυρον ἔχει καὶ θυμικῶς ἐκφλεγόμενον—is, I think, a marked improvement. No other phrase in this list is introduced by καί: the main divisions are marked by τε, the subordinate are in asyndeton. Further, with P's text, κωμικόν seems to be an adjective of κέντρον, and this seems less suitable than taking it substantivally. The whole phrase qualifies διασυρμός. So translate: '... and one in which the comic element is strong and which possesses a sting as well as apt humour.'

εὐστόχου: 'apt.' Cf. Dion. Hal. *de imitatione*, p. 213 U-R: ὁ δ' Ὑπερείδης εὐστοχος μέν, σπάνιον δ' αὐξητικός.

εἰπεῖν: 'sehr kühn für ὡς εἰπεῖν', says Wilamowitz. It is surely impossible in this sense. We should either insert ὡς (or, for example, τὸ σύνολον) or (better) assume that ἀμίμητον εἰπεῖν can mean 'impossible to represent'. This seems a reasonable extension of meaning.

ἐπαφρόδιτον: Latin *venustum*. So ἀφροδίτη is *venustas*, Dion. Hal. *Lys.* 11, &c.

οἰκτίσασθαί τε ... ἄκρως: 'with great natural talent for exciting pity, he is also remarkably facile in narrating myths in a copious style and pursuing a topic with fluency.'

A difficult and uncertain sentence. (i) In support of Blass's κεχυμένως, note P's ἄκρος for ἄκρως below. (ii) For διεξοδεῦσαι see the examples of διέξοδος in LSJ, s.v. II (narrative, description, continued argument), which seem to give the sense of the derived verb here. (iii) Hyperides is praised first for his οἶκτοι, and then for his epideictic qualities as evinced in mythology and in the handling of τόποι in the *epitaphios*. The second ἔτι is not needed and indeed spoils the sense; despite the resulting harsh hiatus, it seems best on balance to omit it as an accidental duplication of the first. Buecheler's τι deserves serious consideration.

τὰ ... περὶ τὴν Λητώ: in the lost *Deliacus* (frr. 67-75 Kenyon), which dealt with Athenian claims at the sanctuary of Delos. Hyperides was sent to plead before the Amphictyones about 343 B.C., when the Delians had asked Philip to support their claims to the temple of Apollo on Delos, which they had not controlled since 422. Rhetoricians quote several passages from this speech as a model for treatment of mythology (Hermog. *de ideis* 1. 6, ii 288 Spengel).

ποιητικώτερα: if the text is right (and Wilamowitz's correction is extremely easy), the predicatively used adjective alternates with the adverb ἐπιδεικτικῶς. The sense does not require us to give the comparative an elative sense (cf. B-D §§ 60, 244), though this is possible.

τὸν δ' Ἐπιτάφιον: Hyperides' *epitaphios*, delivered in 322 as a funeral oration over those who fell in the Lamian war, was first published from a British Museum papyrus in 1858.

34. 3. ἀνηθοποίητος: 'without sense of character.' Cf. Marcellinus, *Thuc.* 57: τὸ ἄπλαστον καὶ ἀνηθοποίητον in the speeches of Thucydides conforms to the heroic character of his speakers; Dion. Hal. *Lysias* 8: πρόσωπον ... ἀνηθοποίητον. ἤθη are *par excellence* the milder and more human facets of character; hence in some contexts ἀνηθοποίητος comes to mean 'unattractive': cf. Cic. *ad Att.* 10. 10. 6 ('difficult' of a person).

μᾶλλον ἤ: see on 9. 4.

περὶ Φρύνης: the famous hetaira Phryne was accused of ἀσέβεια some time in the 340's by one Euthias; the charge was that she ἐκώμασεν ἐν Λυκείῳ and had introduced some θίασοι. The case was naturally very celebrated. Hyperides produced Phryne in court, intending her beauty to persuade if his eloquence failed. Fragments of his speech in Kenyon, frr. 171-80. M. Valerius Messalla Corvinus, the friend of Tibullus and other Augustan poets, translated the speech into Latin (see H. Malcovati, *Oratorum Romanorum Fragmenta* 533). See A. Raubitschek P-W s.v.; Kowalski *Eos* xlii (1948) 50 ff.

ἢ Ἀθηνογένους: a large part of this speech was published from a Paris papyrus in 1892. It dates from the 320's, and is a lively private action about a contract for the purchase of slaves; it is, indeed, full of ἠθοποιία, but the legal complexities make the story very difficult to unravel.

ἔτι μᾶλλον ἂν Ὑπερείδην συνέστησεν: 'would have been an even better advertisement for Hyperides.' συνιστάναι is common for 'recommend, introduce': cf. συστατικαὶ ἐπιστολαί, 'letters of recommendation', 2 Cor. iii. 1.

34. 4. ἀμεγέθη: 'without dignity.' Cf. 40. 2.

"καρδίῃ νήφοντος ἀργά": 'inert in the heart of a sober man.' The Ionic form and the trochaic rhythm both suggest that this is a quotation (? Anacreon). Note the proverb to the effect that τὸ ἐν τῇ καρδίᾳ τοῦ νήφοντος ἐπὶ τῆς γλώττης ἐστὶ τοῦ μεθύοντος; Plu. *de garr.* 503F, *paroem. Graec.* i. 313, &c.

ὁ δ' ἔνθεν ἑλὼν ... καὶ δύναμιν: a difficult sentence, though the general sense is clear and the choice of words recalls Dion. Hal. *Thuc.* 23, where the style of the early historians is judged by the standard of Demosthenic oratory: τὰς δ' ἐπιθέτους (*scil.* ἀρετάς) ἐξ ὧν μάλιστα διάδηλος ἡ τοῦ ῥήτορος γίνεται δύναμις οὔτε ἀπάσας (*scil.* ἔχει ἡ λέξις αὐτῶν) οὔτε εἰς ἄκρον ἠκούσας, ἀλλ' ὀλίγας καὶ ἐπὶ βραχύ, ὕψος λέγω καὶ καλλιρρημοσύνην καὶ σεμνολογίαν καὶ μεγαλοπρέπειαν· οὐδὲ δὴ τόνον οὐδὲ βάρος οὐδὲ πάθος διεγεῖρον τὸν νοῦν οὐδὲ τὸ ἐρρωμένον καὶ ἐναγώνιον πνεῦμα, ἐξ ὧν ἡ καλουμένη γίνεται δεινότης. (Herodotus makes an honourable exception.) Wilamowitz took τοῦ μεγαλοφυεστάτου as explanatory of ἔνθεν ἑλών ('he starts from supreme natural grandeur . . .') and also read ἀρετῆς συντετελεσμένης. This latter change is extremely unlikely, since we need the plural ἀρετάς because of the coming enumeration (and cf. Dion. Hal. l.c.). The phrase ἔνθεν ἑλών comes out of Homer θ 499 ff. φαῖνε δ' ἀοιδὴν ἔνθεν ἑλὼν ὡς οἱ μὲν ... ἀπέπλειον ... ('taking it up from the point where ...') and had a certain vogue in late Greek in the sense of 'thereupon' with verbs of saying; e.g. Diog. Laert. 1. 102: ἔνθεν ὁ Ἀνάχαρσις ἑλὼν ἔφη; Chariton 1. 7. 6: ὁ δὲ Θήρων ἔνθεν ἑλών, 'Εωράκατε, ἔφη .... But, of course, in all such cases ἔνθεν has a point of reference in the preceding words. So it has in Dio Chrysostom 33. 4: ὅτι δ' ἂν ἀξιώσητε ὑμεῖς ... ἔνθεν ἑλὼν ἄθρουν καὶ πολὺν ἀφήσει λόγον. Wilamowitz attempts here to refer it to the genitive; this seems very difficult. I think rather that L imagines Demosthenes as coming forward to speak after Hyperides and taking his cue from him. I take τοῦ μεγαλοφυεστάτου as depending on ἐπ' ἄκρον and the whole phrase as qualifying συντετελεσμένας. The view which Toup suggests and Havell and Tucker adopt, that L is speaking of Demosthenes' debts to *Thucydides* (cf. Dion. Hal. *Thuc.* 53, a passage with several points of contact with L) would lead to much rewriting. The construction completely breaks down at δύναμιν, and ἐπειδή repeats ἐπειδήπερ above (*pace* de Vries, p. 66).

Translate: '... but he, when he takes over, gathers all at once to himself excellences finished to the highest perfection of his sublime genius—the intensity of lofty speech, living emotions, abundance, versatility, rapidity where it most matters, all his unapproachable vehemence and power ....'

τινα: so Manutius for δεινά; but as this may well be due to δεινότητα above it may be thought sounder method to delete, with Jahn.

καὶ ὑπὲρ ὧν οὐκ ἔχει: obscure. *Either* 'even in relation to the quali-

35. 2–36] COMMENTARY 165

ties which he does not possess', *or* 'so as to compensate even for his defects'. Wilamowitz improbably assumes a poetical tmesis: 'vel quibus re vera superior non est' (i.e. καὶ ὧν οὐχ ὑπερέχει).

τοὺς ἀπ' αἰῶνος ῥήτορας: 'the orators of all time.'

35. 1. ἐπὶ μέντοι ... λείπεται: I adopt Manutius' ὁ Λυσίας for ἀπουσίας, despite Grube's ingenious arguments for P's reading. The phrase τῷ πλήθει ἀπουσίας, 'the frequency of their absence', is surely quite impossible. ὡς ἔφην refers to 32. 8 (so Vahlen) and to the allegation, which L does not argue, that Lysias is not without faults. L is playing with two συγκρίσεις: as Hyperides is to Demosthenes, so is Lysias to Plato, except that (i) even on the assumption that we should *count* ἀρεταί Lysias would lose, whereas Hyperides would win; (ii) inferior both in the value and in the number of his ἀρεταί, Lysias is still (ὅμως) guilty of more faults than Plato. οὐ ... ἀλλὰ καί is for οὐ μόνον ... ἀλλὰ καί (Denniston, p. 3).

35. 2–36. *A philosophical justification of the attitude of the great writers who neglect trivialities. Man's natural instinct to admire the sublime.*

The themes of this passage are for the most part philosophical commonplaces, some Stoic in origin, some Platonic or even Pythagorean. L is a typical, though unoriginal, witness to a type of piety and moral reflection which formed the common spiritual fare of the educated in the first two centuries or so of the Empire. His evidence is discussed briefly by M. Pohlenz, *Die Stoa* ii. 121, and by E. Norden, *Agnostos Theos* 104 ff. We may distinguish four themes, which I shall briefly illustrate by one or two other examples.

(i) The nobility of man. This is basically Platonic: φυτὸν οὐκ ἔγγειον ἀλλ' οὐράνιον, *Timaeus* 90A. In οὐ ταπεινὸν ζῷον, L may also have in mind the teleological explanation of man's upright stature; cf., for example, Cic. *ND* 2. 140: 'qui [i.e. deus] primus eos humo excitatos celsos et erectos constituit, ut deorum cognitionem caelum intuentes capere possent.'

(ii) Man is in the cosmos as a spectator and contestant in a marvellous panegyris. See Cic. l.c.: 'sunt enim ex terra homines non ut incolae atque habitatores sed quasi spectatores superarum rerum atque caelestium, quarum spectaculum ad nullum aliud genus animantium pertinet.' Cf. also Epictetus 1. 6. 19, and Cic. *ND* 2. 38, with Pease's long note and his many parallels. Traditionally (Heraclides Ponticus, fr. 88 Wehrli) this image was a Pythagorean recommendation to the contemplative life. It was, however, later adapted to recommend moral effort as well. So Posidonius (who was a very eloquent and influential preacher of these attitudes, whether or not he contributed much that was original to their development) *ap*. Clem. *strom*. 2. 21. 129: τὸ ζῆν θεωροῦντα τὴν τῶν ὅλων ἀλήθειαν καὶ τάξιν καὶ συγκατασκευάζοντα αὐτὴν κατὰ τὸ δυνατόν (a definition of man's τέλος); our actions should be guided by the consideration that we too contribute to the order and harmony of the universe. (Sylburg's conjecture αὐτὸν for αὐτὴν is rejected, I think rightly, by Pohlenz and Reinhardt.)

(iii) The human mind is capable of passing in thought everywhere, even beyond the bounds of the cosmos. This is naturally a protreptic commonplace, equally attractive to philosophers of all schools. Thus the Epicurean Lucretius 1. 72: 'ergo vivida vis animi pervicit et extra processit longe flammantia moenia mundi atque omne immensum peragravit mente animoque.' And the pseudo-Aristotelian *de mundo* 1: ἐπειδὴ γὰρ οὐχ οἷόν τε ἦν τῷ σώματι εἰς τὸν οὐράνιον ἀφικέσθαι τόπον καὶ τὴν γῆν ἐκλιπόντα τὸν οὐράνιον ἐκεῖνον χῶρον κατοπτεῦσαι, καθάπερ οἱ ἀνόητοί ποτε ἐπενόουν Ἀλωάδαι, ἡ γοῦν ψυχὴ διὰ φιλοσοφίας, λαβοῦσα ἡγεμόνα τὸν νοῦν, ἐπεραιώθη καὶ ἐξεδήμησεν, ἀκοπίατόν τινα ὁδὸν εὑροῦσα . . . ῥᾳδίως οἶμαι τὰ συγγενῆ γνωρίσασα καὶ θείῳ ψυχῆς ὄμματι τὰ θεῖα καταλαβοῦσα. And the Stoic Seneca (*de otio* 5. 6): 'cogitatio nostra caeli munimenta perrupit nec contenta est quod ostenditur scire. Illud, inquit, scrutor quod ultra mundum iacet, utrumne profunda vastitas sit an et hoc ipsum terminis suis cludatur.'

(iv) For what purpose were we born? For this type of question cf., for example, Epictetus 1. 6. 25 (ἐπὶ τί γεγόναμεν;), 2. 4. 19 (ἐπὶ τί γέγονεν;), M. Aur. 8. 52: ὁ μὲν μὴ εἰδὼς ὅτι ἐστὶ κόσμος οὐκ οἶδεν ὅπου ἐστίν. ὁ δὲ μὴ εἰδὼς πρὸς ὅτι πέφυκεν οὐκ οἶδεν ὅστις ἐστὶν οὐδὲ τί ἐστι κόσμος. ὁ δ' ἕν τι τούτων ἀπολιπὼν οὐδ' ἂν πρὸς ὅτι αὐτὸς πέφυκεν εἴποι.

35. 2. τῶν μεγίστων . . . τῆς συγγραφῆς: 'the great prizes in literature.'

οὐ ταπεινὸν . . . οὐδ' ἀγεννές: for this (common?) combination of adjectives, cf., for example, Plu. *de adul. et amico* 66D; Epictetus 1. 3. 1 ff., 1. 9. 10.

†ἐ..κρινε: the only compounds of κρίνω which are possible are ἐξέκρινε (Selb), 'selected' (cf., for example, Thuc. 6. 96. 3, of élite troops), and (less probable) ἐνέκρινε in the sense 'selected for inclusion': the word is used of admitting athletes to a competition after a qualifying test. But the parallel from Clement (see next note) makes it possible that we should have here a word meaning 'created', e.g. ἔκτισε, ἐποίησε, or ἔπλασε.

τὸν ἄνθρωπον: Wilamowitz wished to delete τὸν ἄνθρωπον, perhaps rightly. There is a similar case in Clem. *protrepticus* i. 71. 22 Stählin: μόνος ὁ τῶν ὅλων δημιουργὸς . . . τοιοῦτον ἄγαλμα ἔμψυχον ἡμᾶς τὸν ἄνθρωπον ἔπλασεν. Cf. ibid. i. 46. 7. It is possible, however, that the mannered apposition ἡμᾶς . . . τὸν ἄνθρωπον, both in L and in Clement, is the product of art, not of blundering scribes incorporating obvious glosses. If this is so, it comes from a common source and has some emotive power as part of the accepted language of piety.

35. 5]   COMMENTARY   167

αὐτῆς: i.e. τῆς πανηγύρεως. Reiske's τῶν ἄθλων (a slight change) fits in well with the metaphor, which is to be pursued in ἀγωνιστάς: τῶν ὅλων is unintelligible.

35. 3. τῇ θεωρίας καὶ διανοίας τῆς ἀνθρωπίνης ἐπιβολῇ: despite the hiatus it produces (ἐπιβολῇ οὐδ'), Ruhnken's correction should probably be accepted. διανοίας ἐπιβολή, *iniectus animi*, is familiar enough as a technical term of the Epicureans (e.g. Diog. Laert. 10. 31; *Kuriai Doxai* 24), to be readily borrowed for a non-technical context. P's reading, which Wilamowitz calls *Kühnheit* (cf. note on εἰπεῖν 34. 2), is hardly to be translated. There remains, of course, the possibility of some omission.

35. 4. This section was very popular in the eighteenth century. See especially the imitation by Akenside, *Pleasures of the Imagination* i, where the whole context is based on L and on Addison:

> Who but rather turns
> To Heaven's broad fire his unconstrained view,
> Than to the glittering of a waxen flame?
> Who that from Alpine heights his laboring eye
> Shoots round the wide horizon, to survey
> Nilus or Ganges rolling his bright wave
> Through mountains, plains, through empires black with shade
> And continents of sand, will turn his gaze
> To mark the windings of a scanty rill
> That murmurs at his feet?

οὐδέ γε ... πυρός: 'nor are we so much amazed at this little flame that we kindle ourselves, because it keeps its light clear, as at the fires of heaven, though often obscured; nor do we think it more wonderful than the craters of Etna, whose emissions bring up rocks and whole hills out of the depths, and sometimes pour forth rivers of the earth-born, spontaneous fire.'

Cf. Heraclitus, *quaest. Hom.* 26 (p. 42. 4 Oel.): ἐνταῦθα γὰρ ἀνίενται γηγενοῦς πυρὸς αὐτόματοι φλόγες. Hence Markland rightly restored γηγενοῦς and Haupt αὐτομάτου in L.

There is naturally a reminiscence of the famous literary descriptions of Etna, Pind. *Pyth.* 1. 21 ff. ποταμοὶ δ' ἁμέραισιν μὲν προχέοντι ῥόον καπνοῦ αἴθωνα, and Aesch. *PV* 367 ff.: ἐκραγήσονταί ποτε ποταμοὶ πυρὸς κ.τ.λ.

In contrasting the fires of heaven with the little flames we kindle, L also alludes, though briefly, to the Stoic distinction between the destructive fire which men use (χρειῶδες πῦρ, e.g. in Philo *de Abr.* 157) and the creative and maintaining fire of the ether (see, for example, Diels, *Dox. Graec.* 467; Cic. *ND* 2. 41, 57 with Pease's note).

35. 5. ὡς ... παράδοξον: 'the useful and necessary are easily available to man; the unusual always excites our wonder.' Commonplace, but with a decided Epicurean flavour: cf. Usener, *Epicurea* 469: χάρις τῇ μακαρίᾳ φύσει, ὅτι τὰ ἀναγκαῖα ἐποίησεν εὐπόριστα, τὰ δὲ δυσπόριστα οὐκ ἀναγκαῖα; *Kuriai Doxai* 15, 21; *ep. ad Menoec.* 130. Cf. also Demetrius 60: πᾶν δὲ τὸ σύνηθες μικροπρεπές, διὸ καὶ ἀθαύμαστον.

36. 1. οὐκοῦν . . . ἐπάνω τοῦ θνητοῦ: 'when we come then to great geniuses in literature—where by contrast grandeur is not independent of service and utility—we have to conclude from this that, though such men are far from being faultless, they are far above all mortal stature.'

I adopt Pearce's παντός (cf. for the order 1. 4 παντὸς ἐπάνω τοῦ ἀκροωμένου) and take τῶν μεγαλοφυῶν as masculine, since this seems to fit what follows better. The antecedent of ἐφ' ὧν is, I think, λόγοις.

τοὺς χρωμένους ἀνθρώπους ἐλέγχει: 'proves their users to be but men . . . .'

τὸ μέγα δὲ καὶ θαυμάζεται: not 'as well . . .', as if it were worth while to tell us that greatness is exempt from censure; καί is emphatic. So de Vries; and this is quite right if we consider the logic of the passage. See, however, the other version of the saying, [Plu.] *de lib. educ.* 7A: τὸ μὲν γὰρ ἀσφαλὲς ἐπαινεῖται μόνον, τὸ δ' ἐπικίνδυνον καὶ θαυμάζεται. Here καί certainly means 'also'. Should we not then suppose that the form of the remark which both writers remember, in other words their common source, contained the words καὶ θαυμάζεται, and that L retains this without really considering the point of the καί?

36. 2. ὕψει καὶ κατορθώματι: a clear case of hendiadys: 'successful attempt at sublimity.'

τῶν ἄλλων: Lebègue's ⟨τὰ⟩ is not necessary. For the omission of the article in items of a list, cf. (a random example) Philo, *quod deterius* 7: τὰ τρία γένη τῶν ἀγαθῶν, τά τε ἐκτὸς καὶ περὶ σῶμα καὶ ψυχήν.

ὁ πᾶς . . . αἰὼν καὶ βίος: 'all posterity and human experience.' Cf. 7. 4. These judges cannot be held mentally incapacitated by any envious detractors. Cf. Aesch. *c. Ctes.* 251: ὁ δῆμος . . . ὥσπερ παραγεγηρακὼς ἢ παρανοίας ἑαλωκώς.

αὐτοῖς: i.e. τοῖς ἥρωσι.

φέρων ἀπέδωκε: 'man sieht den Kranz in der Hand des *Αἰών*, der einen Homer etwa kränzen will' (Wilamowitz). For the expression cf. 43. 3; the model is Homeric, *I* 331: καὶ πάντα φέρων Ἀγαμέμνονι δόσκον. See Addenda, p. 193.

καὶ ἄχρι νῦν . . . τηρήσειν: 'and maintain it irrevocably and will continue in all likelihood to keep it so . . . .' τὰ νικητήρια are a sort of challenge cup, which the judge is never likely to award to any but the present holders.

ἔστ' ἂν . . . τεθήλῃ: the 'Homeric' epigram on the tomb of Midas is quoted by Plato (*Phaedr.* 264C) and by various later writers. It is sometimes attributed to Cleobulus of Lindos. In *Anth. Pal.* 7. 153 it runs:

χαλκῆ παρθένος εἰμί, Μίδα δ' ἐπὶ σήματι κεῖμαι.
ὄφρ' ἂν ὕδωρ τε νάῃ καὶ δένδρεα μακρὰ τεθήλῃ,
αὐτοῦ τῇδε μένουσα πολυκλαύτου ἐπὶ τύμβου
ἀγγελέω παριοῦσι, Μίδας ὅτι τῇδε τέθαπται.

ἔστ' ἄν is commoner in the quotations than ὄφρ' ἄν; νάῃ and ῥέῃ are both found. The Herodotean *Vita Homeri* 11 has the same selection of variants as L. The origin of the epigram is unknown; the 'maiden' is a sphinx or siren; each verse is self-contained and they can be arranged in various orders (as though round the sides of a monument?). See H. Stadtmüller's or H. Beckby's note on *Anth. Pal.* l.c.

36. 3. ὁ Κολοσσὸς ὁ ἡμαρτημένος: the reference has been much discussed. (i) The Colossus of Rhodes, the huge statue set up at the beginning of the third century B.C. and damaged by an earthquake sixty years later. ἡμαρτημένος is difficult on this view; Wolters suggested ὁ Χάρητος, the sculptor's name. (ii) A colossal statue of Nero by Zenodorus (Plin. *NH* 34. 46), the failure of which *indicavit interisse fundendi aeris scientiam* (Buchenau). (iii) Wilamowitz thought of Phidias' Zeus at Olympia, which Strabo (8. 3. 30) criticizes as too big; on this view ἡμαρτημένος would mean 'faulty in proportions'. (iv) No particular colossus, but any large statue imperfectly made (Jahn, Kaibel). κολοσσός and *colossus* at this period are common nouns for very large statues; and cf. Strabo 1. 1. 23: ἐν τοῖς κολοσσικοῖς ἔργοις οὐ τὸ καθ' ἕκαστον ἀκριβὲς ζητοῦμεν ἀλλὰ τοῖς καθόλου προσέχομεν μᾶλλον εἰ καλῶς τὸ ὅλον. There are certain things to be said for Wilamowitz's guess: we expect a named statue to be contrasted with the Doryphorus; the Doryphorus was famous for its perfect proportions; Strabo's remark on Phidias' Zeus is that if he stood up he would take off the roof of the temple—i.e. the lower parts were too big. But it is really a very obscure way of talking about this famous work, and it is safer to confess our ignorance of L's meaning.

It rather looks as if τὸν γράφοντα must be immediately recognizable to Terentianus. L may mean Caecilius.

ὁ τοῦ Πολυκλείτου Δορυφόρος: for this famous statue—of which a number of Roman copies survive—see, for example, G. M. A. Richter, *The Sculpture and Sculptors of the Greeks*, 245–7; *Handbook of Greek Art*, Phaidon, 1959, p. 110 and fig. 153.

παράκειται . . . τὰ ἀνθρώπινα: L denies that sculpture provides a valid analogy. He argues (i) that ἀκρίβεια ('accurate craftsmanship') is the admired quality of art, μέγεθος (cf. 35. 4) of the works of nature, and, since man is φύσει λογικὸν ζῷον, human λόγοι can be judged by the criterion applicable to works of nature; (ii) that sculpture should be realistic, literature should aim above τὰ ἀνθρώπινα. In the last resort these curious attitudes rest on the ambiguities in the notion of λόγος—'speech' and 'reason'—and chime perfectly with L's depreciation of realism in literature (9) and his assertion of the superiority of literature to music (39). It is the general tendency of ancient art theory to treat the visual arts as purely representational. See in general the article by R. W. Lee, quoted on 17. 2.

36. 4. ἐπὶ τὴν ἀρχὴν τοῦ ὑπομνήματος: i.e. in 2.

τὸ δ' ἐν ὑπεροχῇ πλὴν οὐχ ὁμότονον: 'erratic excellence.' For πλήν, cf. 9. 7.

χαιρέτω . . . οἷς ἥδεται: 'but let everyone enjoy what he finds pleasant', i.e. there is no disputing about tastes. Cf. Dion. Hal. *ant. Rom.* 7. 66. 5: κρινέτω δ' ἕκαστος ὡς βούλεται.

37. *Similes.*

The argument is resumed from the end of 32. L seems to be making the well-known point (Arist. *Rhet.* 3. 4; Quint. 8. 6. 8–9) that similes are extended metaphors and metaphors compressed similes.

38. *Hyperbole.*

This trope (like metaphor and simile) falls under γενναία φράσις; it is discussed by many ancient writers, notably Arist. *Rhet.* 3. 11; *ad Herenn.* 4. 33. 44; Cic. *top.* 10. 45; Quint. 8. 6. 67–76. Quintilian's account is the most detailed and illuminating. See especially 73 ff.: 'sed huius quoque rei servetur mensura quaedam. quamvis enim est omnis hyperbola ultra fidem, non tamen esse debet ultra modum, nec alia via magis in cacozelian itur ... monere satis est mentiri hyperbolen, nec ita ut mendacio fallere velit. quo magis intuendum est quousque deceat extollere quod nobis non creditur.' He comments on its occurrence *apud rusticos*, as does Aristotle on its being natural to youth. He also, like L, relates it to the comic.

Puttenham calls it 'the Overreacher, otherwise the Loud Lyer'.

38. 1. εἰ μὴ . . . φορεῖτε: 'unless you carry your brains in your heels and walk on them.' This passage was used in antiquity to prove *On Halonnesus* spurious; see the *Hypothesis*: ὁ μὲν γὰρ Δημοσθένης εἴωθε παρρησίᾳ χρῆσθαι, τοῦτο δ' ὕβρις ἐστὶ καὶ λοιδορία μέτρον οὐκ ἔχουσα, εὐτέλειά τ' αὐτῷ δεινὴ πρόσεστι κατὰ τὴν ἑρμηνείαν. πρὸς δὲ τούτοις καὶ εὔηθες τὸ νομίζειν ἐν τοῖς κροτάφοις ἔχειν τοὺς ἀνθρώπους τὸν ἐγκέφαλον.

τὸ . . . ἕκαστον: a very doubtful passage. See note on 2. 2. (i) If the text is entirely right here, we should translate: 'to what point each should be pushed over the boundary.' (ii) If we retain παροριστέον, we should consider ἑκάστοτε: 'to what point we should encroach on each occasion'. (iii) But Seager's προοιστέον ('is to be pushed . . .') and possibly προσοιστέον ('is to be applied . . .') d ;erve serious attention. (iv) For μέχρι ποῦ, cf. Plu. *mul. vir.* 259D; Dion. Hal.

38. 4] COMMENTARY 171

AR 4. 13. 4 (I owe these references to Dr. Bühler). But note the apparently common combination of μέχρι πόσου with the verbal in -τέον: Plu. *SNV* 550A: μέχρι πόσου κολαστέον ἕκαστον; Epicurus περὶ φύσεως κη', p. 303 Arrighetti: μέχρι πόσου φροντιστέον αὐτῶν; Epictetus 1. 25. 14: μέχρι πόσου ... ὑπακουστέον; I think μέχρι πόσου should certainly be considered here in place of the more colloquial μέχρι ποῦ, though I do not venture to promote it to the text.

τὸ γὰρ ἐνίοτε ... ἀντιπεριίσταται: 'for going too far sometimes destroys the hyperbole; too great intensity in such things causes relaxation, and sometimes produces the contrary result.' Note the hyperbaton with ἐνίοτε.

38. 2. οὐκ οἶδ' ὅπως: cf. 1. 1, 31. 1.

παιδὸς πρᾶγμα ἔπαθε: 'has fallen into childishness.' There is something odd about the combination of πάσχειν with a noun meaning 'action': compare the more normal πρᾶγμα ἐχθροῦ ποιῶν, Dion. Hal. *Dem.* 35; but a partial parallel is provided by Lucian, *Hermotimus* 75 παίδων πράγματ' ἔχοντες, 'behaving like children'. The general sense is clear; cf. 3. 4 on τὸ μειρακιῶδες.

ἔπειθ' ... διελθεῖν: a free quotation from Isocr. *Panegyricus* 8. This *locus communis* on the power of oratory (cf. Aristoph. *Frogs* 1105 ff.; Pl. *Phaedr.* 267A; Radermacher, *Artium Scriptores* 167) is essentially the teaching of Gorgias. We may admit that Isocrates' love of antitheses has here led him to stultify his argument, but where precisely is the hyperbole?

σχεδὸν ... ἐξέθηκε: 'for in his eulogy of oratory, he has, we may say, published to his hearers a preamble warning them to distrust him' (after Rhys Roberts).

μήποτ': 'perhaps.' See Arndt–Gingrich, s.v. 4.

38. 3. ὡς ... προείπομεν: in 17. 1.

γίνεται δὲ ... περιστάσεως: 'this sort of thing happens when hyperboles are uttered in some great crisis under stress of violent emotion.'

For περίστασις in this sense cf. Epict. 2. 6. 16: κλάοντες καὶ στένοντες πάσχομεν ἃ πάσχομεν καὶ περιστάσεις αὐτὰ καλοῦντες. There is, of course, no reason to think that Thucydides is at all exaggerating, though it is interesting to note that L assumes he is, or at any rate directs his criticism at the literary effect without asking whether or not the fact is historically true. Cf. 38. 3 below.

ἡ ... περίστασις: 'the extraordinary emotion and the crisis.'

ἔτι goes with περιμάχητα.

38. 4. ἐν τούτῳ ... οἱ βάρβαροι ⟨βάλλοντες⟩: the passage is partly atticized. βάλλοντες should be added; otherwise βέλεσι below is unintelligible. Once again, there is no need to think of this as an exaggeration. Tucker observes that he has seen 'a crude picture of a fight in the Greco-Bulgarian war showing a Greek with his teeth fixed in the cheek of an enemy and drawing streams of blood'.

172 COMMENTARY [38. 5–

38. 5. ὡς οὐ διαλείπω λέγων: see 17. 2, 32. 4.

ἀγρὸν ... ⟨Λακωνικῆς⟩: cf. Strabo 1. 2. 30: καὶ καθάπερ εἰσί τινες ὑπερβολαὶ ἐφ' ὑπερβολαῖς, ὡς τὸ κουφότερον εἶναι φελλοῦ σκιᾶς, δειλότερον δὲ λαγὼ Φρυγός, ἐλάττω δ' ἔχειν γῆν τὸν ἀγρὸν ἐπιστολῆς Λακωνικῆς . . . . Source unknown (though probably New Comedy), and we do not know how accurately L quotes. P's text is not satisfactory. 'Smaller than a letter', despite Strabo, is not really a self-sufficient hyperbole like 'lighter than cork' or 'more cowardly than a hare'. It is not even like the English equivalent 'smaller than a postage stamp', since a postage-stamp is a particularly small piece of paper, whereas a letter is not a particularly small piece of papyrus. Apart from this, we expect the boldest possible comic effect for the sake of L's point. We must surely restore the doubly hyperbolical phrase as given in Strabo, with Λακωνικῆς. If the quotation is continuous, the line-ending is at ἀγρόν.

καὶ γὰρ ... ἡδονῇ: ancient theory naturally associated laughter with pleasure (Arist. *Rhet.* 1371^{b}35) and it is normally dealt with in rhetoric under the general head of emotion (Cic. *de oratore* 2. 236; Quint. 6. 3). For the value of hyperbole in comedy see also Demetrius 126 and 161: ἐκ δὲ ὑπερβολῶν χάριτες μάλιστα αἱ ἐν ταῖς κωμῳδίαις.

38. 6. αἱ δ' ὑπερβολαὶ ... αὔξησις: 'hyperboles may be found which diminish an impression as well as those which magnify; intensification is the common factor. Vilification is in a sense an amplification of lowness.'

39–42. Σύνθεσις. *The fifth source* (cf. 8).

Σύνθεσις is 'composition' in the technical sense: word-order and its determinants, among which rhythm and euphony play a much larger part in Greek and Latin *Kunstprosa* than in English. See on 8. 1. Dionysius in *CV* deals largely with euphony and, for all his bookishness and pedantry, is our best evidence for the feelings of sensitive ancient readers. Rhythm, which is to a certain extent readily reduced to rule, is dealt with by most theorists from Aristotle onwards. See A. C. Clark, *Fontes prosae numerosae*, for a selection of typical texts. General sketch and some bibliography by W. H. Shewring in *OCD*, s.v. Prose-rhythm: see below, Appendix on L's style and language.

39. 1. ἐν ἀρχῇ: in 8.

κράτιστε: see on 1. 1.

ἦν δὲ τῶν λόγων αὕτη ποιὰ σύνθεσις: 'and this was word-order of a certain kind.' I print ἦν δέ (cf. 44. 12 ἦν δὲ ταῦτα τὰ πάθη), though with hesitation; but P's διά is impossible, and even if we delete this and adopt Spengel's αὐτή, translating 'the particular type of word-order itself', αὐτή is in an awkward place and the whole phrase strange.

39. 2-3]   COMMENTARY   173

ἐν δυσίν: 'in two books.' So L is not Dionysius of Halicarnassus, whose *CV* is a single book. Not that we need proof of this: see Introd. II, xxiv.

ἀποδεδωκότες: 'having given an account.' Cf. Arist. *EN* 1095ᵃ20: περὶ τῆς εὐδαιμονίας ... οὐχ ὁμοίως οἱ πολλοὶ τοῖς σοφοῖς ἀποδιδόασιν.

ὅσα ... ἐφικτά: 'so much of the subject as was within my reach.' For this use of θεωρία cf. Dion. Hal. *CV* 1. 4: περὶ ἀμφοτέρας τὰς θεωρίας, 'about both subjects'.

ἀλλὰ καὶ μεγαληγορίας: some word like Toll's μεγαληγορίας is needed. For the general sense cf. Quint. 9. 4. 9: 'eam [*scil.* compositionem] .... valere non ad delectationem modo sed ad motum quoque animorum.'

ὄργανον goes with both clauses.

39. 2-3. οὐ γὰρ αὐλὸς μὲν ... οἰόμεθα δ' ἄρα ... ἐπικρατοῦσαν; in this vast sentence, οὐ negatives the contrast expressed by μὲν ... δέ and we should expect 'it cannot be that, while music is effective, σύνθεσις is not'. Cf., for example, Dion. Hal. *AR* 3. 9. 6: οὐ γὰρ δὴ Σαβίνοις μὲν καὶ Τυρρηνοῖς καλῶς εἶχεν ... ὑμῖν δ' ἄρα ... οὐχ ἕξει καλῶς. Either (*a*) the second half is a deliberative question (for the indicative see K–G i. 203); *or* (*b*) the structure goes: 'It cannot be that, while the aulos ..., we are not to think ....' There is a rather similar structure in 44. 9. Wenkebach's ὅπου is not necessary.

In translating, the complex must, of course, be broken up: 'The aulos fills the audience with certain emotions and makes them in a manner of speaking beside themselves and possessed; it sets a rhythm, it makes the hearer walk to the rhythm and assimilate himself to the tune, all untouched by the Muses though he be. The notes of the lyre, too, though they have no signification, yet often, as you know, cast a wonderful spell of harmony with their varied sounds and blended and mingled notes. Yet these are but sham images and imitations of persuasion, not the genuine activities proper to human nature of which I spoke. Composition, on the other hand, is a harmony of words, man's natural instrument, for they penetrate not only the ears but the very soul. It arouses all kinds of conceptions of words and thoughts and objects, beauty and melody—all things native and natural to mankind. The mingling and variety of its sounds convey the speaker's emotions to the minds of those around him and make the hearers partake of them. It fits his great thoughts into a coherent structure by the way in which it builds up patterns of words. Shall we not then believe that by all these methods it bewitches us and elevates to grandeur, dignity, and sublimity both every thought which comes within its compass and ourselves as well, holding as it does complete sway over our minds?'

Quintilian's chapter on *compositio* (9. 4) also makes use of the analogy with music.

39. 2. αὐλός: the music of the aulos ('clarinet' would be more exact than 'flute') was regarded as particularly emotional. Cf. Pl. *Rep.* 398C ff.; Arist. *Pol.* 1341ᵃ21 (οὐκ ἔστιν ὁ αὐλὸς ἠθικὸν ἀλλὰ μᾶλλον ὀργιαστικόν); Dio Chrys. 32. 57 ff. Auloi and kettledrums are the typical instruments of maenadism and orgiastic cults. See in general P. Boyancé, *Le Culte des Muses* I. vi, and E. R. Dodds, *The Greeks and the Irrational*, p. 97 n. 95.

κορυβαντιασμοῦ: see on 5. 1.

βάσιν ... ἐν ῥυθμῷ: cf. Xen. *anab.* 6. 1. 11 : ᾖσάν τε ἐν ῥυθμῷ πρὸς τὸν ἐνόπλιον ῥυθμὸν αὐλούμενοι. In L βάσιν needs ῥυθμοῦ for clarity, and βαίνειν ἐν ῥυθμῷ is a set phrase (see, for example, Lucian, *Harmonides* 1, *Prometheus es* 6). It is a curious coincidence that both L and Xenophon repeat the word ῥυθμός like this.

κἂν ἄμουσος ᾖ: in full, ποιητὴν δ' ἄρα Ἔρως διδάσκει, κἂν ἄμουσος ᾖ τὸ πρίν. These lines, from Euripides' *Stheneboea*, are a very hackneyed quotation indeed: see, for example, Aristoph. *Wasps* 1074; Pl. *symp.* 196E; Plut. *mor.* 405F, 622C; Stemplinger, *Das Plagiat* 249.

τῇ πρὸς ἀλλήλους κράσει: with P's reading, we have 'striking *against* one another and blending'. I think Toup was right to adopt the Renaissance conjecture κράσει. For the close association of the two words and their familiarity in philosophical writing see, for example, Arist. *de gen. et corr.* 328ᵃ8; Sex. Emp. *Pyrrh. hyp.* 3. 56; Philo, *de confusione linguarum* 184. Strictly, μεῖξις is the more general word, κρᾶσις occurs only in liquids; but all that matters for us here is that they are often associated.

39. 3. καὶ πᾶν ... περιλαμβάνει: translators say 'and all the qualities it holds within itself' (Grube), or the like. But κηλεῖν (charm) and πρὸς ὄγκον ... συνδιατιθέναι (i.e. elevate) are specifically distinct in a way which makes it impossible for 'all the qualities of σύνθεσις' to be included under the second head. I prefer therefore to take καί ... καί as 'both ... and', and interpret the passage as meaning that σύνθεσις gives elevation and dignity both to the subject of the composition and to the hearer.

ἀλλ' εἰ καὶ μανία: cf. Dem. 19. 95: μανία γὰρ τοῦτό γε; also 21. 69, 25. 95, 27. 55, *al.*

39. 4. τῷ ψηφίσματι: i.e. the decree, passed in the alarm following Philip's advance to Elatea, making provision for preparation for war and for alliance with Thebes. The text in Dem. 18. 181 ff., however, is spurious (see Goodwin *ad loc.*).

ἀλλ' αὐτῆς ... πεφώνηται: 'but the thought has found expression as much through the arrangement as through the meaning.' For the genitive of comparison following a dative see K-G ii. 308. πεφώνηται is, I think, possible; it implies *successful* expression: cf. φωνήεντα γίγνεται 40. 1 and perhaps Philo, *quod deterius* 79: πάνυ δὲ πεφώνηται καὶ πρὸς κάλλος ἑρμηνείας καὶ πρὸς νοημάτων εὕρεσιν τὰ ἐπιλεγόμενα ταῦτα.

39. 4. ὅλον τε γάρ ... τὸ ἀπότομον: on the interpretation of this very difficult passage see G. Amsel, *de vi atque indole rhythmorum quid veteres iudicaverint* 88 ff. The marked rhythm is certainly cretic rather than dactylic, but the two are closely related (cf. the existence from an early period of dactylo-epitrite verse), and L is not a metrician. Similarly, Aristides Quintilianus (1. 15) knows of various loose uses of the term dactylic.

The best clue to what L means is, I think, provided by the rearrangements he offers (for this method of criticizing metrical effects, cf. Dion. Hal. *CV* 7. 43 ff.; Cic. *orator* 214, 232; Bonner, *Dionysius* 68, 76). They produce respectively the clausulae $-\cup--$, $-\cup\cup----\cup-$, and $-\cup-\cup-\cup-$. Of these, the first—a dichoreus—was used to excess by 'Asianists' (Norden, *AK* 135; Cic. *orator* 212) and the last is avoided by rhythmically conscious authors. The second rearrangement both destroys the double cretic ($-\cup--\cup-$) at the end and replaces one earlier on by $\cup\underset{\smile}{\cup}-\cup\cup--$, thereby perhaps giving the impression of a hexameter ending. But all interpretation of aesthetic judgements of this kind must inevitably be guessing in the dark.

εὐγενέστατοι ... συνιστᾶσι: 'and these are extremely noble and productive of sublimity; which is why they go to make the heroic metre, the most beautiful we know.' A generally held doctrine from Aristotle onwards: see *Rhet.* 1408ᵇ32, *Poet.* 1459ᵇ32; Dion. Hal. *CV* 17. 108.

τό τε * * *: several words missing; the clause balanced ὅλον τε γάρ .... Pearce was probably right in thinking the general sense to have been 'and the closing words are particularly fine'.

ἐπὶ μακροῦ ... χρόνοις: 'stands upon its long first foot, which measures four shorts.' So Toll. The spondee ὥσπερ occupies four χρόνοι, in the sense of *morae*. With P's καταμετρούμενον, χρόνοι are 'syllables', as below; but what then is the sense of τοῦ πρώτου?

ἀκρωτηριάζει: presumably middle, not active.

προσπίπτει: cf. 21. 1, 23. 2, 29. 1.

ὅτι ... τὸ ἀπότομον: two quite different interpretations are possible. (i) As the length of the closing syllables is broken up, so the sublimity is destroyed. If we adopt this, we should (*pace* de Vries, p. 69) take συν- as meaning 'with', and indeed assume it with the second verb διαχαλᾶται also. (ii) The sublimity is lost because the closing syllables (i.e. the closing phrase, I suppose) are lengthened (so Rhys Roberts, for example). I think the first explanation to be preferred.

τὸ ὕψος τὸ ἀπότομον: cf. 12. 4: ἐν ὕψει ... ἀποτόμῳ. Toup preferred to read τοῦ ὕψους: cf. 18. 2 τοῦ πάθους τὸ ἐπίκαιρον; Demetrius 8: οὕτως ἐκτεινόμενον ἐκλύεται τοῦ λόγου τὸ θυμικόν. Emendation, however, does not seem necessary.

40. 1. Ἐν δὲ τοῖς μάλιστα ... φωνήεντα γίνεται: if we punctuate with a colon after σύστημα and take ἡ ... ἐπισύνθεσις as the subject, the syntax becomes straightforward. But we must then take τῶν μελῶν metaphorically, and οὕτως does not answer καθάπερ. This is an impossible situation. It is better to suppose that the construction breaks down. The expected subject of μεγεθοποιεῖ is replaced by a sentence with the finite verbs συνδιαφορεῖ and γίνεται. There is no expressed verb of which ἡ ἐπισύνθεσις is the subject.

Translate: 'I now come to a principle of particular importance for making what is said impressive. Just as the beauty of bodies depends on the way in which the limbs are joined together, each one when severed from the others having nothing remarkable about it but the whole together forming a perfect unity, so great conceptions which are not held together dissipate both themselves and the total sublime effect, whereas if they co-operate to form a single whole and are furthermore linked by the bonds of "harmony", then they come to life and speak in virtue of the actual periodic form of the passage.'

καὶ σχεδὸν ... τὰ μεγέθη: 'it is in fact generally true that in periodic sentences elevation results from the total contribution of many elements.' For πλῆθος cf. 12. 1 ἐν διάρματι ... ἐν πλήθει. For ἔρανος cf. ἐρανίζῃ, 20. 1. Grube takes the sentence more literally: 'A great work is like a feast to the courses of which many people contribute.' This seems implausible; and all the words have a quite appropriate metaphorical sense in the vocabulary of literary criticism. Cf. especially Dion. Hal. *CV* 9. 48 (on *Menex.* 236): τὴν ... περίοδον ... τίς οὐκ ἂν φαίη παραπληρώματι λέξεως οὐκ ἀναγκαίῳ προσηρανίσθαι;

40. 2. οὐκ ὄντες ... ἀμεγέθεις: 'who are not by nature sublime and may indeed have an incapacity for greatness.' Cf. 15. 3 on Euripides. For the general sense cf. Dion. Hal. *CV* 3. 11: πολλοὶ γοῦν καὶ ποιηταὶ καὶ συγγραφεῖς ['historians', contrast our passage and L 1. 3] φιλόσοφοί τε καὶ ῥήτορες λέξεις πάνυ καλὰς καὶ πρέπουσας τοῖς ὑποκειμένοις ἐκλέξαντες ἐπιμελῶς, ἁρμονίαν δ' αὐταῖς ἀποδόντες εἰκαίαν τινὰ καὶ ἄμουσον οὐδὲν χρηστὸν ἀπέλαυσαν ἐκείνου τοῦ πόνου, ἕτεροι δ' εὐκαταφρόνητα καὶ ταπεινὰ λαβόντες ὀνόματα, συνθέντες δ' αὐτὰ ἡδέως καὶ περιττῶς, πολλὴν τὴν ἀφροδίτην τῷ λόγῳ περιέθηκαν.

ταῦτα †δ' ὅμως†: this second ὅμως would be careless writing. Immisch's ingenious δολίως is, as de Vries says, ruled out by the consideration that δόλιος has always a bad sense. Perhaps we should read ἀμεγέθεις ὅλως above and omit δ' here.

διάστημα: it seems natural that a word meaning 'difference' (including 'difference of rank': see Clem. Al. *strom.* 2. 3. 3) should also on occasion mean 'distinction'. As Toup observes, ὄγκος καὶ διάστημα is equivalent to ὄγκος καὶ δίαρμα in Plu. *comp. Aristoph. et Men.* 853C.

Φίλιστος: a fourth-century historian from Syracuse, whom Cicero (*ad Quintum fratrem* 2. 12. 4) called 'paene pusillus Thucydides'. He wrote a history of Sicily from the earliest times down to his own day, and closely imitated Thucydides. L's view is evidently more favourable than that of Dionysius, who thought him inferior, confused, and dull (*ad Pomp.* 5, *de imitatione*, p. 208 U–R).

It is interesting that a comic writer can qualify to be called ὑψηλός: so also Platonius on Eupolis (Kaibel, *CGF* p. 6, 86 f.).

ἱκανῶς ἡμῖν δεδήλωται: probably in the two books περὶ συνθέσεως (so Morus).

γέ τοι: L's use of this rather unusual collocation is quite in accord with Attic idiom. 'A livelier equivalent of the much commoner γοῦν' (Denniston, p. 550).

40. 3. γέμω ... τεθῇ: 'I'm full of evils, there's no place for more' (Hall). Manuscripts of Euripides have ὅπῃ, Plutarch (*mor.* 1048A, 1063D) has L's ὅπου and the unmetrical οὐκ for οὐκέτι.

τῇ πλάσει ἀναλογοῦν: the usual rendering is 'in accordance with the structure', though it is not clear precisely what this means. πλάσις in rhetoric normally means 'invention, invented situation'. So it is perhaps better to say 'in keeping with the situation in the play'. In other words, the situation demands τὸ ὑψηλόν, and this is provided not by the words, which are ordinary, but by the σύνθεσις.

διότι: 'that.' Cf. 7. 1.

τῆς συνθέσεως ... τοῦ νοῦ: 'it is the arrangement rather than the sense of which Euripides is the poet'; i.e. it is the σύνθεσις which shows the great poet. It is, I think, misleading to translate 'Euripides is a poet of arrangement rather than of ideas'. These would be strange genitives; and the judgement is specific, not general. L is, indeed, thinking of the view expressed in Arist. *Rhet.* 1404ᵇ24: κλέπτεται δ' εὖ [i.e. artifice is well concealed] ἐάν τις ἐκ τῆς εἰωθυίας διαλέκτου ἐκλέγων συντιθῇ· ὅπερ Εὐριπίδης ποιεῖ καὶ ὑπέδειξε πρῶτος. But he means by σύνθεσις something more than Aristotle there intends: not only 'putting the words together', but 'putting them together in an effective and euphonious order'. When he invites us ἄλλως συναρμόσαι, he means a rearrangement of the present words, not the use of others: cf. the Demosthenes example, 39. 4–5. L. P. Wilkinson (*CQ*, N.S. ix (1959) 182) follows Immisch in thinking the example inappropriate, as though it really illustrated the value of plain words in grand contexts, and not the value of right order. But I think this is unjust to L; we *could* arrange the words in various involved and cacophonous ways (it does not matter here that the metre would not be preserved); and see above on τῇ πλάσει ἀναλογοῦν.

ἐπὶ δὲ ... μεταλλάσσων ἀεί: from *Antiope* (see Pickard-Cambridge in *New Chapters in Greek Literature* iii. 105–13, and von Arnim, *Supplementum Euripideum* 19 ff.). Antiope, the daughter of Nycteus, had twin sons by Zeus—Amphion and Zethus. Lycus, Nycteus' brother and successor, carried off Antiope and handed her over to his wife Dirce to be tortured. She escaped and joined her sons (now shepherds), but they failed to recognize her. In the play, Dirce is a bacchanal; she arrives raving and tries to drag off Antiope. The sons learn of their mother's identity and rescue her. They then bind Dirce to a bull which tears her apart, and try to kill Lycus. Hermes intervenes and bids Lycus abdicate in favour of Amphion. There are considerable fragments of this very famous play. The closing scenes are known from a papyrus (Page, *Greek Literary Papyri* 60 ff.) and the *agon* between Zethus and Amphion (active *versus* contemplative life) was used by Plato in a striking passage of the *Gorgias* (484c–486d).

εἰ δέ που ... ἀεί: we must insert πάνθ' or some other stop-gap, or else suppose that L has deliberately omitted ταῦρος after ἑλίξας (Valckenaer), having already mentioned the bull. See Introd. l for metrically incomplete quotations. Presumably the bull drags along everything with which it becomes entangled in its mad course, and as it were juggles with Dirce, the rock, and the oak, tossing them about one after the other.

τὸ λῆμμα: 'the subject', P's λῆμα being impossible.

ἁδρότερον: 'greater.' Cf. ἁδρεπήβολον, 8. 1; and, for ἁδρός as a term describing style, Introd. xxx f.

ἐν ἀποκυλίσματι: 'on rollers.' Cf. Dion. Hal. *CV* 20. 142 συγκυλίεται ... ἡ τῶν ὀνομάτων σύνθεσις, of Homer's expressiveness in describing the rock rolling down: λ 596–7.

ἀλλὰ ... μέγεθος: 'but the words are supported one against another and rest on the intervals between them, being set wide apart, so as to give the impression of solid greatness.'

All this refers to such effects as πέριξ ἑλίξας and πέτραν δρῦν, where the collocation of consonants slows down the reader. This is the same sort of criticism as is practised by Dionysius in his analysis of the sound-effects used in *Odyssey* λ 593 ff. to depict the laboured efforts of Sisyphus with his stone (*CV* 20). Note especially διαβεβήκασιν αἱ τῶν ὀνομάτων ἁρμονίαι διαβάσεις εὐμεγέθεις καὶ διεστήκασι πάνυ αἰσθητῶς [double consonants, vowels in hiatus] ... αἱ μὲν μονοσύλλαβοί τε καὶ δισύλλαβοι λέξεις πολλοὺς τοὺς μεταξὺ χρόνους (so χρόνων in L?) ἀλλήλων ἀπολείπουσαι τὸ χρόνιον ἐμιμήσαντο τοῦ ἔργου, αἱ δὲ μακραὶ συλλαβαὶ στηριγμούς τινας ἔχουσαι καὶ ἐγκαθίσματα τὴν ἀντιτυπίαν καὶ τὸ βαρὺ καὶ τὸ μόλις.

41. *Effeminate rhythm.*

This concludes the account of σύνθεσις and forms a transition to 42 and 43, which deal with features in vocabulary and sentence-structure which tend to diminish ὕψος. But these sections are little more than isolated notes, and L seems to be in a hurry to complete his task. See Introd. xxi–xxii.

This type of criticism of rhythm is common. See Sen. *suas.* 2. 10, *contr.* 2. 1. 26; Sen. *ep.* 114. 15; Tac. *dial.* 26; Quint. 11. 3. 57 ff.; Plin. *ep.* 2. 14. 12 ff.; Norden, *AK* 294–5. Note the moral tone of it all, the prevalence of the notion of effeminacy, &c.

41. 1. μικροποιόν: Photiades' conjecture is supported by 28. 1 and 44. 6, and also by ὑψηλοποιὸν αἱ μεταφοραί in 32. 6. It is a very easy change.

κεκλασμένος: Latin *effractus*, 'effeminate, emasculated'.

σεσοβημένος: 'agitated.'

πυρρίχιοι: i.e. ∪ ∪.

τροχαῖοι: probably ∪ ∪ ∪ rather than – ∪ (cf. Cic. *orator* 212, 217; Quint. 9. 4. 82). The point is that runs of short syllables should be avoided.

διχόρειοι: – ∪ – ∪. See 39. 4, note.

τέλεον ... συνεκπίπτοντες: 'which absolutely end up in dance rhythm.' For the association of trochaics with the dance, cf. Arist. *Poet.* 1449ᵃ23, 1459ᵇ37.

τὰ κατάρρυθμα ... ἐπιπολάζοντα: 'all the rhythmical parts immediately appear artificial and tawdry, being constantly repeated without the slightest emotional effect in their monotony.' (i) ἐπιπολάζω, to judge from LSJ, means 'be frequent' rather than 'be apparent' or 'conspicuous', though there is no obvious reason why it should not also bear this latter meaning, as does ἐπιπόλαιος. The dictionary sense, however, will surely do here. (ii) I venture to remove καί before ἀπαθέστατα, and take the latter as an adverb. φαίνεται ... κομψὰ καὶ μικροχαρῆ go well together; what follows does not, I think, depend on φαίνεται. Moreover, if we take ἀπαθέστατα as a superlative adjective, it goes badly in a list with the two positives. (iii) By κατάρρυθμα L means the clausulae and beginnings; he does not think of rhythm as running through the whole texture of prose. So de Vries. I take κατάρρυθμα (a word of doubtful meaning) as 'that which is reduced to rhythmical form' rather than 'that which is excessively rhythmical'.

41. 2. τὰ κατερρυθμισμένα τῶν λεγομένων: 'the rhythmical parts of discourse.' Here LSJ say 'over-rhythmical'; but again I think it better to take the force of κατα- as giving '*reduced to* rhythmical form'.

ὡς ... τὴν βάσιν: 'so that they foresee the endings which are due and sometimes themselves beat time for the speaker and anticipate him in giving the step—just as in a dance.'

For this taunt (similar things are often said about declaimers and sophists) compare (i) Demetrius 15: οἵ τε ἀκούοντες ναυτιῶσι διὰ τὸ ἀπίθανον, τοτὲ δὲ καὶ ἐκφωνοῦσι τὰ τέλη τῶν περιόδων προειδότες καὶ προαναβοῶσι. (ii) Aristides 34 (50) (= κατὰ τῶν ἐξορχουμένων) 47: οὐκ ἀνταποδιδόντες ὥσπερ ἠχὼ τὴν φωνήν, ἀλλὰ καὶ προλαμβάνοντες. (iii) Dio Chrysostom 32. 68: πάντες δὴ ᾄδουσι καὶ ῥήτορες καὶ σοφισταί, καὶ πάντα περαίνεται δι' ᾠδῆς· ὥστ' εἴ τις παρίοι δικαστήριον, οὐκ ἂν γνοίη ῥᾳδίως πότερον ἔνδον πίνουσιν ἢ δικάζονται. See Norden, *AK* 372–9.

41. 3. Ὁμοίως δὲ ... ἐπισυνδεδεμένα: 'devoid of greatness also are phrases too closely fitted together, and those which are cut up into short elements of short syllables, fastened together as it were by a succession of bolts at rough intersections.'

This is all very uncertain. (i) The obvious clue to the meaning of λίαν συγκείμενα is Demetrius 13, in an extended building metaphor: ἔοικε ... τὰ τῆς διαλελυμένης ἑρμηνείας διερριμμένοις πλησίον λίθοις μόνον καὶ οὐ συγκειμένοις. (ii) But if we follow this clue and suppose that λίαν συγκείμενα means 'too well fitted together', i.e. too smooth in σύνθεσις, we cannot apply it to the same sentences as those described by εἰς μικρὰ ... συγκεκομμένα. (iii) The only way to avoid this, it seems to me, is to look elsewhere for the metaphor in συγκείμενα; this word (see LSJ) sometimes means 'collapsed, emaciated' in medical contexts, and so could presumably be applied to writing from which all the padding had been removed. But the general metaphor of the passage is, as so often, from building, and to import something quite foreign to this sphere would be to spoil it. (For the metaphor in κατ' ἐγκοπὰς καὶ σκληρότητας cf. Sen. *ep.* 114. 15: 'nolunt sine salebra esse iuncturam.') (iv) For the bad effect of short phrases cf. Demetrius 4 on short κόμματα: ὁ βίος βραχύς, ἡ τέχνη μακρά, ὁ καιρὸς ὀξύς· κατακεκομμένη ἔοικεν ἡ σύνθεσις καὶ κεκερματισμένη καὶ εὐκαταφρόνητος διὰ τὸ μικρὰ σύμπαντα ἔχειν. I give 41. 3 as a separate paragraph. Note the connexions: μικροποιόν 41. 1, ὁμοίως δὲ ἀμεγέθη 41. 3, ἔτι γε μὴν ὕψους μειωτικόν 42. 1. We are still on σύνθεσις, but have finished with rhythm.

42. *Cramped expression.*

A separate point, expressed with (deliberate?) brevity.

τὰ [οὐ] δεόντως: I think it certain that Manutius was right. The following sentence explains the distinction made in this. The usual translation of P's reading—'things which are simply not properly compressed'—introduces an extraordinary complexity.

συντομία: the opposition συγκοπή—συντομία seems not to occur elsewhere. For συντομία as a virtue see, for example, Demetrius 137: πρώτη ἐστὶ χάρις ἡ ἐκ συντομίας, ὅταν τὸ αὐτὸ μηκυνόμενον ἄχαρι γένηται, ὑπὸ δὲ τάχους χάριεν. For its ambivalence, ibid. 103: ἡ συντομία ... πῇ μὲν μεγαλοπρεπής ... πῇ δὲ μικροπρεπής.

†ἐπ' εὐθύ: 'guides' or 'concentrates' would be satisfactory sense. For ἐπ' εὐθὺ ἄγει (hiatus! but see Appendix), cf. Lucian *hist. conscr.* 6. See Addenda, p. 193.

δῆλον ... ἀνακαλούμενα: another difficult passage. (i) Does ἐκτάδην mean 'laid out flat' (cf. Lucian, *dial. mort.* 12 (14) 5: τὸν νεκρὸν τοῦ θεοῦ ἐκτάδην κείμενον) or 'extended at length' (cf. Philostr. *vit. soph.* 1. 481 (p. 202 Kayser): ἡ ἀρχαία σοφιστική ... διῄει αὐτὰ ἀποτάδην καὶ ἐς μῆκος)? (ii) ἀπόψυχα is not attested elsewhere and in such a doubtful context must itself attract suspicion. If it is right, it probably means 'lifeless', and this suggests that the first meaning proposed for ἐκτάδην is more likely (and note ἀποψύχοντα 'fainting' in Lucian, l.c.). (iii) παρ' ἄκαιρον and παρὰ καιρόν are both possible readings of the tradition. (iv) ἀνακαλούμενα 'calling in to their aid' is very difficult; Toup's ἀναχαλώμενα ('relaxed'—a medical term) is possible, as is ἀνακυκλούμενα, 'repeated' (cf. Plu. *Demosth.* 29).

We are free to punctuate in various ways. Retaining P's text, I think it best to put a colon after ἐκτάδην and translate: 'It is obvious that the converse holds with fully extended expressions: what invokes the aid of length out of season is dead.' This assumes that L means that, as with brevity, so also with fullness of expression, there is both desirable moderation and deplorable excess. This interpretation, however, involves the less probable way of taking ἐκτάδην.

For a solution admitting some change, I suggest the following, *exempli gratia* and as a means of bringing the problems to light: ἔμπαλιν [τὰ] ἐκτάδην ἀπόψυχα τὰ παρ' ἄκαιρον μῆκος ἀνακυκλούμενα. Translate: 'Conversely, what is repeated at unseasonable length is stone dead and laid flat.'

Other suggestions in Jahn–Vahlen. Certainty seems far off.

43. *On lowness of diction.*

This topic is connected with what is discussed in 31. The principle that some words are low and to be avoided in formal writing is of the greatest importance in ancient, as also in Renaissance, literature. It is the negative side of the doctrine that the use of certain words actually imparts dignity and distinction. Both notions rest on the concept of propriety; writing and speaking are social activities possessing a certain degree of formality and must be conducted according to the requirements of good manners. The qualities which blackball words from 'good' literature are (i) obscenity, (ii) association with the common material things of life, (iii) technicality. It is a source of wonderment to modern tastes to see how the ancients appear to confuse and conflate these criteria. Genre is, of course, always an important consideration: thus, for instance, words excluded from history may be quite permissible in a dialogue. And, of course, there is much caprice. Both Greek and Roman writers show great sensitivity about this aspect of style; the Romans seem, however, somehow the more anxious.

There are many ancient discussions of *vilitas*, ταπεινότης, *sordida verba*, εὐτελῆ ὀνόματα. (i) For the principle that the proper names for things are low, see Arist. *Poet.* 1458ᵃ18 ff.: λέξεως δὲ ἀρετὴ σαφῆ καὶ μὴ ταπεινὴν εἶναι. σαφεστάτη μὲν ... ἡ ἐκ κυρίων ὀνομάτων, ἀλλὰ ταπεινή. (ii) For the way in which a poet was expected to avoid *vilitas*, see

Servius on *Aen.* 1. 177 (Cerealiaque arma): 'fugiens vilitaligeneralitatem transiit propter carminis dignitatem et rem vilem auxit honestate sermonis' (see Norden, *Aen. VI*³ 115 n. 1). (iii) The two sides—positive and negative—of the matter are clearly brought out in Petronius 118: 'refugiendum est ab omni ut ita dicam vilitate et sumendae voces a plebe submotae.' (iv) For a rational moderate view, see Quint. 10. 1. 9 or Dion. Hal. *CV* 12. 69–70: οὐδὲν γὰρ οὕτω ταπεινὸν ἢ ῥυπαρὸν ἢ ἄλλην τινὰ δυσχέρειαν ἔχον ἔσεσθαί φημι λόγου μόριον, ᾧ σημαίνεταί τι σῶμα ἢ πρᾶγμα ὃ μηδεμίαν ἕξει χώραν ἐπιτηδείαν ἐν λόγοις. (But he excludes the obscene.) Finally, two examples, both Roman: (i) Velleius (2. 41) has to bring himself to say that Caesar when captured by the pirates never *took his shoes off* or *undressed*; he steels himself for his task with the words: 'cur enim quod vel maximum est, si narrari verbis speciosis non potest, omittatur?' (ii) Albucius (Sen. *contr.* 7, *praef.* 3) apparently put Dionysius' more catholic view into practice: 'splendidissimus erat; idem res dicebat omnium sordidissimas, acetum et puleium et lanternas et psilothrotum et spongias; nihil putabat esse quod dici in declamatione non posset. erat autem illa causa: timebat ne scolasticus videretur.'

For the eighteenth century, Boileau's *Réflexion* ix is important. Typical is the point that *âne* is a word *de la dernière bassesse*, and that *génisse* would do well in an eclogue, whereas *vache* would be intolerable anywhere.

See also G. Tillotson, 'Eighteenth-Century Poetic Diction', in *Essays and Studies* xxv (1939) 59–80.

43. 1. κατὰ μὲν τὰ λήμματα: 'so far as the conception goes.'

τινὰ ... καὶ τοῦτο μὲν ἴσως ... ἀλλ' ...: 'some things ... one might instance .... But he does worse than this: ....' Fyfe well reproduces the effect of the rather tortuous structure of this sentence.

The objection to ζεσάσης is not only homeliness but cacophony. Greek and Latin writers were highly conscious of the effect of sibilants. Cf. Dion. Hal. *CV* 14. 80: ἄχαρι δὲ καὶ ἀηδές τὸ σ, καὶ πλεονάσαν σφόδρα λυπεῖ. θηριώδους γὰρ καὶ ἀλόγου μᾶλλον ἢ λογικῆς ἐφάπτεσθαι δοκεῖ φωνῆς ὁ συριγμός.

βρασσομένους: cf. Hdt. 7. 188, 190 (ἐκ-); *Anth. Pal.* 6. 222, 7. 294. P's δρασσομένους περὶ ... is hardly intelligible.

ἐκοπίασε: 'flagged.' ἐκόπασε is the form found in Herodotus and in most later writers: κοπιάω 'feel tired', does not seem to be used, as κοπάζω often is, of things. Cf. also Matthew xiv. 32 ἐκόπασεν ὁ ἄνεμος. But all this does not compel emendation.

⟨καὶ⟩ ἰδιωτικόν: ἰδιωτικόν can hardly be a substantive; so this or Wilamowitz's ἰδιωτικὸν ⟨ὄν⟩ is necessary.

ἀχάριστον: ἄχαρι in Herodotus, whom L paraphrases freely. It is a little odd that he should disapprove of this litotes. One might have expected more appreciation of this kind of heroic if macabre understatement, natural to many courageous races and generations. For this particular example, see Homer, ν 392:

> δόρπου δ' οὐκ ἄν πως ἀχαρίστερον ἄλλο γένοιτο
> οἷον δὴ τάχ' ἔμελλε θεὰ καὶ καρτερὸς ἀνήρ
> θησέμεναι.

43. 2. This passage of Theopompus describes the preparations for the expedition of Artaxerxes Ochus against Egypt in the middle of the fourth century: Diod. 16. 44 ff. Athenaeus preserves other similar passages, too, mostly about τρυφή and clearly second-hand (see G. Kaibel, *Stil und Text der Πολιτεία Ἀθηναίων* 106 f.). L's quotation is very probably also at second hand. Gilbert Murray (*History of Greek Literature* 390, *Greek Studies* 164) oddly thought that the passage read like intentional satire and that L's criticism is therefore beside the point and unappreciative.

πρὸς κατακοπὴν ἱερεῖα σιτευτά: 'victims fattened for the knife.'

πολλοὶ δὲ [οἱ] θύλακοι ... χρησίμων: quoted by Athen. 2. p. 67 F but with some variations: πολλοὶ μὲν ἀρτυμάτων μέδιμνοι, πολλοὶ δὲ σάκκοι καὶ θύλακοι βιβλίων καὶ τῶν ἄλλων ἁπάντων τῶν χρησίμων πρὸς τὸν βίον.

L's text should not be brought into line. But οἱ is stylistically impossible and should be deleted. Again, καὶ χάρται ... χρησίμων is surely nonsense: χάρται cannot contain ἄλλα χρήσιμα, and it is odd, even if possible, that they should *contain* books. I cannot think that L thought Theopompus wrote this. Theopompus, indeed, very probably wrote Toup's χύτραι βολβῶν, 'jars of onions'. Should we accept this in L? Athenaeus has βιβλίων: it is therefore reasonable to think that this reading was found in a source common to him and L—the excerptor of Theopompus whom they use. Athenaeus does *not* have either χάρται or χύτραι: he has avoided the difficulty. Now χάρται is (*a*) close in form to χύτραι, (*b*) close in sense to βιβλίων. It may therefore be either (*a*), as Professor Dodds suggests to me, an attempt to emend χύτραι consequent on the corruption of βολβῶν to βιβλίων, or (*b*) an accidental error of a copyist, helped subconsciously by the associated idea in βιβλίων. I confess this seems likelier to me; and I incline therefore to restore χύτραι here, but leave βιβλίων; jars of books are odd, indeed, but jars *can* contain ἄλλα χρήσιμα, and L might, I think, have believed in the text so constituted.

ὡς ... ἀντωθουμένους: 'that there were heaps so high that as people approached they thought at a distance that these were hills or ridges being pushed towards them.'

43. 3. ἐκ τῶν ὑψηλοτέρων: for the asyndeton—introducing comment on a passage just quoted—see 9. 5.

ὥσπερ γὰρ ... ἐγκατατατττόμενα: 'for just as if, amid the real pomp and show, someone had gone and put down some bags and sacks among the golden and jewelled bowls, the silver vessels, the gold tents and drinking cups, it would have been a very disagreeable sight, so words of this kind are disfigurements and blemishes, as it were, to style, if they are inserted out of season.' φέρων ... ἔθηκε: cf. 36. 2. ἐγκαταταττόμενα: cf. 10. 7.

43. 4. παρέκειτο ... ἡδύσματα: 'it was open to him, however, to describe in general terms the hills which he says were piled up, and (? having made this change) to proceed to the rest of the preparations, mentioning camels and a host of beasts of burden carrying all that is needed for luxury and pleasure of the table, or speaking of heaps of all kinds of seeds and everything that makes for fine cuisine and dainty living —or, if he wanted at all costs to make him as self-supporting (?) as all that, adding "all the refinements of *maîtres-d'hôtel* and chefs".'

L objects to ἄρτυμα, σάκκοι, and θύλακοι, and above all to κρέα τεϋριχευμένα: he wants both to get rid of these details and to put the general fact which they represent in a less conspicuous place than the point of climax. ἀλλάξας is grammatically quite satisfactory (παρέκειτο (αὐτῷ) = ἐδύνατο), though it is not clear whether it refers to the change of order or to the changes of expression, or whether οὕτως points forwards in sense or (as I take it) backwards. Toup's quite brilliant ἁμάξας is not grammatically necessary, involves adding καί, and should be honourably dismissed. Other points: (i) καὶ οὓς ... καὶ περί is illogical but perhaps natural here; Miss Hubbard's deletion of the first καί, however, makes the sentence neater. (ii) τραπεζῶν may go with χορηγήματα or, as I take it, with ἀπόλαυσιν. (iii) The idiom by which the article is put before a relative clause normally requires ὅσα not ἅ: but cf. Aristides 34 (50) (=κατὰ τῶν ἐξορχουμένων), 42 τῶν οὓς ⟨τοὺς⟩ πολλοὺς ὀνομάζομεν. (iv) αὐτάρκη οὕτως is very unexpected in sense and produces a harsh hiatus: Richards's αὐτὰ ῥητῶς οὕτως ('so very expressly') is perhaps on the right lines.

43. 5. τὴν δημιουργήσασαν ... κάλλος: a piece of popular teleology; when God made man, he put the shameful and dirty organs out of the way. L alludes to Xen. *mem.* 1. 4. 6 (see 32 for the influence of this passage): ἐπεὶ δὲ τὰ ἀποχωροῦντα δυσχερῆ, ἀποστρέψαι τοὺς τούτων ὀχετοὺς ᾗ δυνατὸν προσωτάτω ἀπὸ τῶν αἰσθήσεων.

Cf. Cic. *ND* 2. 141, *de officiis* 1. 126–7; Corp. Herm. 5. 6. The *locus* is exceedingly common. See in general, A. S. Pease, 'Caeli enarrant', *H. Th. Rev.* xxxiv (1941) 163 ff.

ἐν προσώπῳ: 'in front.'

ὄγκου περιηθήματα: 'drainings (purgings) of the mass.' ὄγκος is here used of the body in the derogatory tone of the moralist to whom the flesh is something inferior; so often σάρξ. Cf., for example, Philo, *quod deterius* 27: τὸν σωματικὸν ὄγκον.

ὡς ἐνῆν: 'as far as was possible.' So Xenophon (ᾗ δυνατόν). In Greek thought the creator is not omnipotent; he does the best he can with the ὕλη.

43. 6. ἐπ' εἴδους: 'in detail.' Cf. 13. 3.

ἐπείγει: 'is urgent.' For this impersonal use, cf. Aristides 36 (48) 10: εἴτ' οὖν ἐπείξαν εἴτε καὶ ἄλλως βουλομένους ἐπιδεῖξαι.

44. *Dialogue on the decline of literature and lack of really great writers.*

A philosopher advances the view that the decline is due to despotism; L counters with a moral explanation. This second account is meant to make the former appear superficial and to supersede it; L is more philosophical than his imagined philosopher, and in true Stoic fashion (cf. Philo, *quod omnis probus*) counts subjection to vices and desires, not political submission, the true servitude. Rostagni (*Introd.*, p. xxvii) is I think wrong in minimizing the difference between the two points of view and saying that L only 'in certo modo corregge, tempera, svia le precedenti affermazioni, ma non le annulla'.

It is a little surprising to find this elaborate piece at the conclusion of a stretch of writing (39–43) in which a certain haste and disorder are apparent. The theme, however, is intimately connected with the main theme of the book; L insisted from the start (1. 1) that an effort to develop one's nature was a prerequisite of great writing. It is made clear in this chapter than this effort is essentially a moral one. C. P. Segal (*Harvard Studies in Class. Philology* lxiv (1959) 121 ff.) makes the further point, which goes I think beyond what L actually says, that ὕψος, as something divine and eternal, is beyond the power of political malice, so that in striving after it a writer transcends the limitations of his age. He is right to emphasize the connexion of 44 with the rest of the book.

The topics of the chapter are also to be found in a number of writers of the first century A.D., from the elder Seneca to Tacitus. The fact that it is difficult to imagine their being handled in this spirit later than the age of Nerva and Trajan remains the crucial argument for dating L in the first century (Introd. xxv). L's explanations are in fact two of the three that were most canvassed in the early Empire. (The third was the inevitability of decline according to the cycles of destiny—'fato, cuius maligna perpetuaque in rebus omnibus lex est, ut ad summum perducta rursus ad infima, velocius quidem quam ascenderant, relabantur' (Sen. *contr.* 1, *praef.* 7; cf. Vell. Pat. 1. 16–17). This does not enter into L's discussion.)

Much of the material is collected in Norden, *AK* 245 ff. I give here only the salient things.

(i) The political explanation is the natural converse of the plausible and no doubt largely true theory sanctioned by Aristotle (cf. Cic. *Brutus* 46; Radermacher, *Artium Scriptores* 11 ff.), that the rise of rhetoric was due to the development of democracies in Sicily and the release of energy following the suppression of the early fifth-century tyrannies. At Rome, the age of Cicero had also been the age of greatest political turbulence; under the principate, political passions could not be so openly expressed, and the prizes of oratory were less glittering. See Seneca, l.c., and above all the speech of Maternus in Tacitus' *dialogus* 36–40, especially 36. 1: 'nam etsi horum quoque temporum oratores ea consecuti sunt quae composita et quieta et beata re publica tribui fas erat, tamen illa perturbatione ac licentia plura sibi adsequi videbantur, cum mixtis omnibus et moderatore uno carentibus tantum quisque orator saperet quantum erranti populo persuaderi poterat'; 37. 4: 'his accedebat splendor reorum et magnitudo causarum, quae et ipsa plurimum eloquentiae praestant. nam multum interest utrumne de furto aut formula et interdicto dicendum habeas, an de ambitu comitiorum, expilatis sociis et civibus trucidatis. quae mala sicut non accidere melius est isque optimus civitatis status habendus est in quo nihil tale patimur, ita cum acciderent, ingentem eloquentiae materiam subministrabant.'

(ii) It is to the moral explanation that the elder Seneca (l.c.) really inclines, though he gives weight also to the others: 'torpent ecce ingenia desidiosae iuventutis nec in unius honestae rei labore vigilatur; somnus languorque ac somno et languore turpior malarum rerum industria invasit animos.' The younger Seneca (*ep.* 114, see Summers's notes) gives a classic exposition of the reasons 'quare quibus temporibus provenerit corrupti generis oratio'. This, though a related question to the one his father tried to answer, is not the same: it does not concern the disappearance of the higher kinds of eloquence, but the appearance of new and inferior standards of taste in style. It does not, therefore, admit the historical explanation—except in the indirect sense that the loss of the field of public activity drove eloquence into the schools, where there was no contact with reality and verbal virtuosity won most applause. The key to Seneca's answer is the proverbial *talis hominibus oratio qualis vita* (on this and *le style, c'est l'homme même*, see Abrams, *The Mirror and the Lamp* 229–35). He simply extends it from individuals to societies: 'genus dicendi aliquando imitatur publicos mores, si disciplina civitatis laboravit et se in delicias dedit; argumentum est luxuriae publicae orationis lascivia.'

This way of looking at the problem, whether it concentrates on sterility or on bad taste, is not special to the case of eloquence. It will apply to any field wherein men find fault with the present—which, as L says, is ἴδιον ἀνθρώπου. Thus L's own discussion owes much to Pl. *Laws* 831–2, where the subject is the decline of physical culture and military training, and this is attributed (i) to selfish love of money, ἡ διὰ βίου ἄπληστος ζήτησις, (ii) to τὰς οὐ πολιτείας, i.e. existing democracy, oligarchy, and tyranny. And it is well worth comparing with this chapter the quite general remarks on moral decline and love of money in Philo, *quod omnis probus* 62–74.

44. 1. †ἐπιπροσθῆναι: the correction ἐπιπροσθεῖναι is generally accepted. But (i) the word is rare (add to the doubtful instance in LSJ Ammonius, *in categorias* 4 Busse), and (ii) the construction is difficult: Robortelli added καί before διασαφῆσαι, Wilamowitz read διασαφῆσαί ⟨τε⟩, and others have been driven to the expedient that the second infinitive explains the first (as with δρᾶν, πάσχειν, and the like). I find none of these agreeable, and think we should mark a corruption, but consider the possibility of ἐκ προσθήκης or the like (cf. ἐκ παρενθήκης 29. 2; προσθήκη, 'excursus', is common from Herod. 4. 30 onwards). The reading in P may be partly explained by assimilation to the ending of διασαφῆσαι.

τις τῶν φιλοσόφων: the phrase implies that the philosophers are a recognized class of whom L is not a member. Since the views expressed equate the principate with slavery, we naturally think of the association of certain Stoic groups in the first century with opposition to the principate. See, for example, G. Boissier, *L'Opposition sous les Césars*; J. M. C. Toynbee, 'Dictators and Philosophers', *Greece and Rome* xiii (1944) 43 ff.; C. Wirszubski, *Libertas as a Political Idea at Rome* 124 ff.

πρὸς ⟨ἔμ'⟩ ἔναγχος: I think Cobet was right. (i) προσέναγχος is not found elsewhere and seems an unlikely compound. (ii) πρὸς ἐμέ can perhaps be taken with ἐζήτησε, cf. ζητῶ πρὸς ἐμαυτὸν, Lucian, *Lexiphanes* 17. (iii) It seems more natural—though it is not essential—that it should be made clear early on that L himself participates in the conversation; without a mention here, we should have to wait till 44. 6.

ἐντρεχεῖς: 'skilful.' Cf. Pl. *Rep.* 537A.

πρὸς ἡδονὰς λόγων: 'for pleasant effects in literature.' For ἡδονή, see 29. 2 and note.

44. 2. δημοκρατία: here particularly the Republic as opposed to the Principate.

διεγείρειν: emendation is necessary, and Morus's suggestion is as good as any. We need a transitive verb meaning something like 'rouse'.

44. 3. οἷον ἐκτρίβεται ... συνεκλάμπει: 'are kindled by rubbing as it were and flare up, naturally enough, free in a free world.' An abrupt change of metaphor after ἀκονᾶται; but L has in mind Pl. *Rep.* 435A: τάχ' ἂν τρίβοντες ὥσπερ ἐκ πυρείων ἐκλάμψαι ποιήσαιμεν τὴν δικαιοσύνην. Or is L simply using the words which in Plato applied to kindling to work out his own different metaphor of highly polished, sharpened, and glittering weapons? (For this metaphor applied to oratory, cf. Quint. 10. 1. 30.)

οἱ δὲ νῦν ... μεγαλοφυεῖς: 'but we of the present day, he continued, would seem to have learned from infancy to live in justified slavery, virtually swathed round right from our first tender thoughts in the same habits and customs, never allowed to taste that fair and fecund spring of literature, freedom; so that we have turned out simply a set of magnificent toadies.'

παιδομαθεῖς, 'versed in from infancy'; cf., for example, Quint. 1. 12. 9.

Cf. in general Philo, *de ebrietate* 198: ἐγὼ δ' οὐ τεθαύμακα εἰ πεφορημένος καὶ μιγὰς ὄχλος, ἐθῶν καὶ νόμων τῶν ὁπωσοῦν εἰσηγμένων ἀκλεὴς δοῦλος, ἀπ' αὐτῶν ἔτι σπαργάνων [cf. *quod omnis probus* 98] ὑπακούειν ὡς ἂν δεσποτῶν ἢ τυράννων ἐκμαθών, κατακεκονδυλισμένος τὴν ψυχὴν καὶ μέγα καὶ νεανικὸν φρόνημα λαβεῖν μὴ δυνάμενος, πιστεύει τοῖς ἅπαξ παραδοθεῖσι.

The coincidences with L cover both expression and thought, and some connexion is probable, though, of course, this need not be the direct dependence of L on Philo, as Rostagni suggests. See Introd. xxix f. It is worth noting, too, the close verbal similarities between our passage and Heraclitus, *quaest. Hom.*, p. 2. 3 Oelmann: εὐθὺς γὰρ ἐκ πρώτης ἡλικίας τὰ νήπια τῶν ἀρτιμαθῶν παίδων διδασκαλίᾳ παρ' ἐκείνῳ (*scil.* Homer) τιτθεύεται, καὶ μόνον οὐκ ἐνεσπαργανωμένοι τοῖς ἔπεσιν αὐτοῦ.

δουλείας δικαίας: cf. δουλείαν, κἂν ᾖ δικαιοτάτη 44. 5. 'Justified' or 'justly exercised'? More probably the former; our moral degeneration deserves political subjection (cf. 44. 10).

τοῖς αὑτοῖς ἔθεσι: I follow Selb, who retains αὑτοῖς: with αὐτῆς neither order nor sense is wholly convincing.

ἐξ ἁπαλῶν ... φρονημάτων: the phrase is an adaptation of ἐξ ἁπαλῶν ὀνύχων, the Greek analogue of Horace's *de tenero ungui* (Porphyrio on *Odes* 3. 6. 24): cf. Apostolius 7. 51 a; Otto, *Sprichwörter* 356.

λόγων νάματος: based on Pl. *Tim.* 75E: τὸ δὲ λόγων νᾶμα ... κάλλιστον καὶ ἄριστον πάντων ναμάτων.

44. 4. τὰς μὲν ἄλλας ἕξεις ... ῥήτορα: slaves might be doctors, musicians, grammatici, even philosophers (like Epictetus). They were more rarely teachers of rhetoric (though note Ti. Claudius Hermes, *CIL* 6. 9857), for in this field Roman citizens competed strongly. They could hardly be *oratores*, pleaders in the courts, since this meant legal knowledge and engagement in public life. See in general *Economic Survey of Ancient Rome* i. 380; Duff, *Freedmen in the Early Roman Empire* 121 ff. (We must reckon all born slaves, whether manumitted or not, as relevant here.) By ῥήτορα L means, not a teacher of rhetoric but the Latin *orator* (for this compare—a random instance—Plu. *quaest. conv.* 743D). He is, of course, referring to actual facts: this is not the Stoic paradox, μόνον τὸν σοφὸν εἶναι ῥήτορα.

εὐθὺς ... κεκονδυλισμένον: 'the inability to speak freely and the consciousness of being a prisoner at once assert themselves, battered into him as they have been by the blows of habit.' For the indignity of κόνδυλοι see 20. 2.

ἀναζεῖ: literally 'boils up'. Cf. Plu. *quaest. conv.* 728B (of anger). It does not seem at all a natural word to use of a passive quality of submission. Should we consider the non-classical ἀναζῇ 'revives' (cf. Greg. Naz. 1. 415B: ἀναζῇ τὸ κακόν; and see Lampe, s.v.)? (Weiske's minute change into ἀναζεῖν assumes that *oratio obliqua* is likely to continue until the vicinity of the next φησί: but it is difficult to be sure of this.)

44. 5. γλωττόκομα: strictly, cases to keep the reeds or tongues of wind instruments.; but also used of any kind of cage or case. Not Attic according to Phrynichus.

οἱ Πυγμαῖοι, καλούμενοι δὲ νᾶνοι: if the text is right, L treats νᾶνοι as a current name which needs explanation or apology. This recalls the discussions in Aulus Gellius (16. 7, 19. 13) about whether *nanus* is a permissible word *in Latin*. Some thought it *sordidum et barbarum*: others pointed out that the early poets used it and that it was perfectly good classical Greek. It is difficult to avoid the conclusion that L feels about the word in Greek much as Gellius' Fronto (19. 13) does in Latin. In Arist. *Problem.* 10. 12, 892ᵃ6–22, both words occur: πυγμαῖοι are creatures (not necessarily human) dwarfed διὰ τὴν στενότητα τοῦ τόπου, their limbs being bent out of shape: e.g. puppies kept in quail-cages. The relation of νᾶνοι to πυγμαῖοι, *pace* Vahlen, is not made clear. The other cause of dwarfs is τροφῆς ἔνδεια: this sometimes yields miniatures with perfect limbs, like τὰ Μελιταῖα κυνίδια.

On dwarfs being kept as pets or curiosities, see Marquardt, *Privatleben* 152; Friedländer, *Sittengeschichte*⁹ (1920) ii 369. Medieval and Renaissance courts maintained the custom; there is a vivid reminder in the miniature apartments of the court dwarfs in the ducal palace at Mantua.

Casaubon (on Suet. *Aug.* 83) accepts L as evidence that 'mangones, ut efficerent nanos, conclusos alebant in arca pueros et fasciis revinctos'. It is at any rate in keeping with Roman ways to try to use some method of stunting growth, presumably to supplement the natural supply of Pygmies or other natural dwarfs. Cf. the revolting details about mutilating slaves to make them employable as deformed beggars, Cassius Severus *ap.* Sen. rhet. *contr.* 10. 4 (33).

†συνάροι: no wholly convincing conjecture: 'spoils', 'contracts', 'cripples'?

σώμασι: a necessary change—unless συνάροι by chance conceals a word for 'starve', which does not seem likely.

44. 6. ὑπολαβών: as Dr. Bühler points out to me, the aorist seems invariable in this use. For the corruption he compares Menander, *Dyscolus* 15: add the manuscript variants at Pl. *Meno* 85D6.

ἴδιον ... παρόντα: 'commonplace.' Cf. Tacitus, *dialogus* 18. 3:

'vitio autem malignitatis humanae vetera semper in laude, praesentia in fastidio esse.'

ὅρα ... πάθη: 'but consider—perhaps it is not the peace of the world which is the ruin of great natures, but rather this unlimited warfare which lays hold on our desires and all the passions which garrison and utterly lay waste to our modern life.'

πρὸς ἥν ... ἀπλήστως ... νοσοῦμεν: 'in regard to which we are morbidly insatiate.' See Vahlen, *Opuscula* i. 122 n.: νοσοῦμεν is a refinement for the colourless ἔχομεν. With Wilamowitz's περί we have the difficulty of attaching meaning to the expression 'being insatiably ill'. Or should we translate 'with which we are insatiably and morbidly enamoured', taking νοσοῦμεν as a refinement for πάσχομεν used as in Plu. *Eroticus* 749D: ἔπαθε πρὸς τὸ μειράκιον αὐτή ('she fell in love with the boy herself')?

καταβυθίζουσιν ... τοὺς βίους: 'sink the ship of life for us with all hands.' Cf. (though the point is a little different) Philo, *de ebrietate* 22: ἀμετρίᾳ τροφῶν ἐπικλύζοντες εἰς βυθὸν ἀναγκάζουσι δύεσθαι.

φιλαργυρία ... ἀγεννέστατον: either of Spengel's suggestions corrects the sentence adequately. Note that νόσημα is technically exact in Stoic terminology: according to Chrysippus (*SVF* iii. 102–3) φιλαργυρία is a νόσημα (i.e. an οἴησις τοῦ σφόδρα δοκοῦντος αἱρετοῦ), but φιληδονία a weakness (ἀρρώστημα, *aegrotatio*, defined as νόσημα μετ' ἀσθενείας). On this distinction, which is neither very clear nor very consistently observed, see especially Bonhöffer, *Epiktet und die Stoa* i. 275 f.

44. 7. οὐ δὴ ἔχω ... συνοικίζεται: 'I find it impossible to see how we can honour, or rather deify, unlimited wealth without admitting into our souls the evils which attach to it. When wealth is measureless and uncontrolled, extravagance comes with it, sticking close to it and as they say keeping step; the moment wealth opens the way into cities and houses, in comes extravagance and dwells therein too.'

The text at the end is uncertain, and none of the suggestions which have been made convinces.

ἴσα βαίνουσα is a classical reminiscence: cf. Dem. 19. 314: ἴσα βαίνων Πυθοκλεῖ.

The metaphor of opening the way into 'cities and houses' is something of a commonplace; cf. Eur. *Phoen.* 533: (φιλοτιμία) πολλοὺς ἐς οἴκους καὶ πόλεις εὐδαίμονας ἐσῆλθε.

In general compare Plu. *Agis* 3: ἐπεὶ παρεισέδυ πρῶτον εἰς τὴν πόλιν ἀργύρου καὶ χρυσοῦ ζῆλος καὶ συνηκολούθησε τοῦ πλούτου τῇ μὲν κτήσει πλεονεξία καὶ μικρολογία, τῇ δὲ χρήσει καὶ ἀπολαύσει τρυφὴ καὶ μαλακία καὶ πολυτέλεια.

For συνοικίζεται, compare also Plu. *SNV* 556B: ἀλλ' ὅπου φιλοπλουτία καὶ φιληδονία περιμανὴς καὶ φθόνος ἄκρατος ἐνοικίζεται μετὰ δυσμενείας ἢ κακοηθείας.

44. 9] COMMENTARY 191

κατὰ τοὺς σοφούς: i.e. according to Pl. *Rep.* 9. 573E: ἆρ' οὐκ ἀνάγκη μὲν τὰς ἐπιθυμίας βοᾶν πυκνάς τε καὶ σφοδρὰς ἐννενεοττευμένας; L's whole genealogical fantasy (that is all it is), in which extravagance and wealth are the parents of greed, vanity, and luxury, from which in turn spring insolence, lawlessness, and shamelessness, owes its general conception to the descriptions of democracy and tyranny in *Rep.* viii and ix: see especially 560C–D and 575A–B.

οὐ νόθα ... ἀλλὰ καὶ πάνυ γνήσια: a good example of the Greek idiom (polar expression) by which a word is emphasized by adding the opposite, negatived: cf. Soph. *OT* 58: γνωτὰ κοὐκ ἄγνωτα; and see Schwyzer ii. 704. For νόθος and γνήσιος, cf. the more elaborate phrase in 39. 3, which owes something to *Rep.* 382B.

τούτους ... τοῦ πλούτου: P's τούτου is probably due to the proximity of the other genitives: 'this wealth' could only mean 'unlimited wealth', and this seems forced.

44. 8. ἀναβλέπειν: 'open their eyes.' Cf. Philo, *quod omnis probus* 55–56: τοὺς δὲ πολλούς, οὐ συνορῶντας τὰς ψυχῆς βλάβας ... εἰ δὲ δυνηθεῖεν ἀναβλέψαι θεασάμενοι τὰς δι' ἀφροσύνης ἀπάτας . . . . For classical examples, see Dodds on Eur. *Bacchae* 1308. This seems better than assuming a reminiscence of Pl. *Rep.* 9. 586A (see 13. 1), or the occurrence of the commonplace thought that man, alone of animals, looks up to heaven (Dio Cassius, fr. 30. 2: ἄνω τε ὁρῶμεν καὶ τῷ οὐρανῷ ὁμιλοῦμεν; Manilius iv. 905 ff., &c.).

ὑστεροφημίας: Ruhnken's conjecture is at least very probable: cf. 14. 3.

ἀλλὰ ... τἀθάνατα: 'but the ruin of men's lives is gradually consummated in a cycle of such vices, and greatness of mind wanes, fades, and ceases to attract whenever men spend their admiration on their mortal parts and neglect to develop the immortal.'

Vahlen was almost certainly right to treat καπαηητα as a faulty repetition of -κα τὰ θνητά and delete it. If we take it instead as a corruption of, for example, κἀνόητα or κἀνόνητα, the sentence loses a certain balance, since τἀθάνατα has no accompanying adjective.

The thought that it is man's moral and rational being that is immortal is Platonic; cf. especially *Phaedo* 81B ff. Cf. also Philo, *de ebrietate* 110: θεοῦ τιμῆς ἀλογοῦσιν οἱ τὰ θνητὰ θειώσαντες. Similar wording in Plu. *Romulus* 28. 6.

44. 9. οὐ γὰρ ... ἐπιθυμίας: cf. 39. 2 for this type of long sentence. 'One who has been bribed to give a judgement will no longer be a free and sound judge of rightness and honour. The corrupt man inevitably thinks his own side's claims just and fair ⟨and his opponent's unfair and wrong⟩. Yet nowadays bribery is the arbiter of the life and fortunes of every one of us—that, and chasing after other people's deaths and lying in wait for wills—and we are all so enslaved ⟨by avarice⟩ that we buy the power of making profit out of everything at the price of our souls. Amid such a mortal plague in human life, how shall we expect any free uncorrupt judge of great things of permanent value to be left to us? How shall we hope not to be beaten by the corrupt practices of the love of gain?'

The text needs two small supplements, the exact wording of which is naturally uncertain: (i) e.g. δίκαια ⟨τὰ δ' ἀλλότρια ἄδικα καὶ κακά⟩ (οἰκεῖα μέν gives an unconvincing instance of μέν *solitarium*: precisely what is missing depends on the sense of οἰκεῖα; I follow the consensus of translators); (ii) e.g. τῆς ⟨φιλοχρηματίας⟩.

ἀλλοτρίων ... διαθηκῶν: the well-known *locus* on *captatio*, with a hint of murders of *orbi*. Mayor on Juvenal 3. 129 collects passages; see, for example, Sen. *ad Marciam* 19. 2, *de const. sap.* 6. 1; Petron. 116. 6; Plin. *ep.* 2. 20. Topical at any period in the first or second century.

τὸ δ' ἐκ τοῦ παντὸς κερδαίνειν: from Soph. *Antig.* 312: οὐκ ἐξ ἅπαντος δεῖ τὸ κερδαίνειν φιλεῖν.

ὠνούμεθα τῆς ψυχῆς: compare perhaps Heraclitus B 85: θυμῷ μάχεσθαι χαλεπόν· ὅτι γὰρ ἂν θέλῃ, ψυχῆς ὠνεῖται.

καταρχαιρεσιάζεσθαι: in Plu. *C. Gracchus* 11 καταρχαιρεσιάζειν means 'to defeat by corruption'; if it means the same here, there has been a change of subject, for which de Vries compares 13. 4. But perhaps it simply means 'corrupted', and applies to the *judge*.

44. 10. ὡς ἐξ εἱρκτῆς ἄφετοι: 'let out of prison, as it were.' Cf. Philo, *quod omnis probus* 18: τρόπων ... ὥσπερ ἐξ εἱρκτῆς προεληλυθότων καὶ δεσμῶν οἷς ἐπεσφίγγοντο διαφειμένων.

ἐπικλύσειαν: 'optime ut solet Marklandus noster', as Toup says. For the metaphor cf. Jos. *BJ* 2. 16. 372: τοῖς ἀγαθοῖς σχεδὸν ὅλην ἐπικλύζοντες τὴν οἰκουμένην; Philo, *de virtutibus* 14: (τὸ φρονοῦν) κινδυνεῦον ὑπὸ τῆς τῶν παθῶν φορᾶς κατακλύζεσθαι.

44. 11. δάπανον: Toll's suggestion is the best: (for δάπανος with genitive cf. Athen. p. 52E: ἡ τῆς πικρότητος δύναμις δάπανος ὑγρῶν οὖσα). Other possibilities are δαπάνην (Rothstein) and διὰ παντός (Spengel): 'In general I said that the characteristic of modern natures was ....' The possibility of deeper corruption is not to be excluded.

ἀναλαμβάνοντες: 'undertaking' (?).

44. 12. κράτιστον εἰκῆ ταῦτ' ἐᾶν: we expect a connexion: ⟨ἀλλὰ⟩ κράτιστον or κράτιστον ⟨δ'⟩ (scansion does not matter)?

τὰ πάθη: see Introd. xiii.

ἐν ἰδίῳ ... ὡς ἡμῖν: this passage is written in a later hand at the bottom of fo. 207ᵛ in P. There would be room for a few more words. As the construction is obviously incomplete, it seems unlikely that we have here a forged supplement, however seriously the sentence is corrupted. It seems most natural to conclude that the words were added when the next page was so badly damaged that nothing else on it was legible and it was about to be scrapped.

προηγουμένως: 'as my primary object.' Cf. Cleomedes 2. 2; Hermogenes *de ideis* 1. 1. 7 (Spengel ii. 269. 22).

ὃ τήν τε ... ⟨κρατίστην⟩: cf. 9. 1. 'Occupying as they do, as I have said, a very important place in literature in general and in ὕψος in particular ....' The supplement is, of course, *exempli gratia*.

We can be confident that very little of the book is missing at the end.

ADDENDA

p. 65 (on 2. 2). Pl. *Theaet.* 144 A is imitated by Hermogenes *de ideis* I *praef.* (ii. 275. 18 Spengel) in a context similar to L.'s.

p. 141 (on 23. 2). (i) αὐτίκα is more probably part of the hexameter than 'for example'. For the abrupt introduction of an instance cf., for example, 25, 26. 1, 27. 1. (ii) My colleague Mr. M. L. West suggests an attractive way of doing without the tunny, by reading: θινῶν ἠιόνεσσι ... 'on the shores of the sands'.

p. 146 (on 27. 3) εἶτα ... ἐπέστρεψεν: see now Blume (see p. 194) 27 ff. He retains P's text. Dem. turns away from his 'speech against Aristogiton' and apparently abandons it, while really intensifying it. I am not sure that this gives a possible sense to ἀποστρέψας, and it seems improbable that in this context τὸν πρὸς τὸν Ἀ. λόγον could be used in this wider meaning. If it can, I should prefer to take ἀποστρέψας intransitively ('turning aside' or 'using ἀποστροφή') and regard λόγον simply as the object of ἀπολιπεῖν, taking καί as emphasizing—unless indeed it should be deleted.

p. 168 (on 36. 2). Aion can be seen apparently crowning Homer in the Hellenistic relief from Bovillae illustrated in Wace–Stubbings, *Companion to Homer* (1962), Plate I.

p. 180 (on 42. 1). Blume (37) defends ἐπ' εὐθύ as an instance of brevity. Cf., anyway, Sex. Emp. *adv. rhet.* 23: σύντομον εὐθυρρημοσύνην.

APPENDIX

SOME REMARKS ON L'S LANGUAGE AND STYLE[1]

See also Index III (b), s.v. Style and Language

L's language and style are bound to seem strange to those whose reading has hitherto been confined to Greek of the classical period. Not only are there 'late' syntactical usages (e.g. of the optative), but the whole texture of the writing, with its rich mixture of classical ingredients forming a style very unlike that of any classical author, is striking and alien. To some extent, reading late Greek (Dionysius, Plutarch, Philo) removes this sense of unfamiliarity; nevertheless, some strangeness remains, hard to define and commonly regarded as the imprint of the writer's personality. This is a reasonable hypothesis, but we should not forget that we do not know very much about the literary fashions of late Greek, which were numerous and diverse; it is perfectly possible that we have before us not an individual idiosyncratic style, but an example of a manner taught and practised but not represented elsewhere in extant literature.

Apart from some apparently crabbed passages (e.g. 42) the whole book is written in elaborate formal prose (*Kunstprosa*), in which magnificent periods (e.g. 1–2, 34–36, 44) and weighty *sententiae* (e.g. 2. 1, 2. 3, 3. 5, 4. 7, 9. 2, 9. 14, 20. 3) both play a part; indeed, it is the interaction of these two contrasting elements which seems to give L's style its peculiar gravity and splendour. Something of the same effect is one of Demosthenes' secrets, and it is presumably from him that L learned the lesson, mastered on the whole by the Romans better than by the later Greeks, of the

[1] See now H. D. Blume, *Untersuchungen zu Sprache und Stil der Schrift περὶ ὕψους*, Göttingen, 1963.

APPENDIX 195

importance of variation in sentence-length and the effectiveness of an alternation between copiousness and shock-tactics.

An adequate general picture of L's vocabulary may be obtained from Rhys Roberts's word-lists (pp. 188–93); this material suffices to show L's debt to Plato and also the Hellenistic element in his vocabulary. But his list of ἅπαξ λεγόμενα is imperfect (Blume 1 ff.); e.g. εὐπίνεια, καταφέγγω, ὀνομάτιον occur elsewhere; εὐτελισμός, μαγεῖον, χρηστομαθέω are to be added; ἐποικονομία, μικροποιέω and προσέναγχος are probably ghosts: see on 11. 2, 41. 1, 44. 1. Richness of metaphor and a love of compound words are obvious features and do not need emphasis. Index III (Greek) should be consulted for particular words.

I deal here not with λέξις but with one or two matters of σύνθεσις.

(a) *Hiatus*. (See K–B i. 198; von Rohden; Ziegler, *Plutarchos* 295 ff.)

Isocrates, the first and greatest exponent of the notion that the clash of vowels should be avoided in formal prose, allowed himself in his epideictic speeches scarcely more freedom than the poets enjoy. Apart from places where elision or crasis is possible, the vowels of τί τι ὅτι περί εὖ πρό πολύ and καί may be left open, but not much else. Neither Isocrates himself in his forensic speeches nor any other orator obeyed such rigorous prescriptions. Demosthenes allows the article and ἤ εἰ ἐπεί μέντοι καίτοι also to remain open, and has no inhibitions at the end of cola. In Hellenistic and Roman times observance of some kind is natural and usual (many inscriptions are quite strictly composed in this respect) and neglect is often a sign of conscious effort, e.g. in the extreme Atticists and the ἀφελὴς λόγος of Aelian and his like. L's usage is moderate; he is rather less strict than Plutarch, himself no faddist. There are in L about thirty instances of a striking hiatus. Most are at the ends of cola: e.g. 2. 3 φύσει, οὐκ; 3. 5 πάθη, εἶτα; 9. 5 ἵπποι, οὐκέθ'; 9. 6 ταρτάρου, ἀνατροπήν; 9. 11 ἤδη, ἴδιον; 15. 7 τάφου, ἥν; 17. 1 διαλανθάνῃ, ὅτι; 20. 3 μεταβολῇ· οὕτως; 41. 2 βιάζεται, οὕτως. But there are enough besides to make one hesitate to emend *hiatus vitandi causa*, even within cola: see 23. 3 θατέρου 'Ιοκάστη; 38. 2 λόγου ὡς; 40. 3 τῇ πλάσει ἀναλογοῦν; 43. 5 πορρωτάτω ὀχετούς. The conjecture ἐπιβολῇ οὐδ' at 35. 3 need not then be ruled out on this ground. It is tempting, however, to think that the involved order πέτρους τε ἐκ βυθοῦ καὶ ὅλους ὄχθους ἀναφέρουσι (35. 4) is motivated by the desire to avoid the hiatus βυθοῦ ἀναφέρουσι. From Plato's later works onwards καθάπερ is often preferred to ὥσπερ for this reason; in L ὥσπερ would have caused hiatus at 7. 1, 8. 2, 10. 1, and 16. 2.

(*b*) *Rhythm.* (See notes on 39–42. Shewring's article on Prose-Rhythm in *OCD* provides a useful introduction and bibliography.)

Aristotle (*Rhet.* 3. 8) gives certain recommendations for the rhythmical patterns of sentence-beginnings and sentence-ends. His rules had not much future. Other precepts, which we find treated in many later rhetorical treatises (see note on 39), proved more influential, but even these give a very inadequate notion of the variety and subtlety of actual practice. Rhetorical teaching must have included a great deal of training of the ear, not to be reduced to written rule. L, like most later Greek writers, is rhythmical in the sense that he has a liking for certain forms at the ends of cola. Statistics are hard to construct: the following remarks are based on a study of main sentence-endings, just over 300 in number, so conducted that comparisons are possible with Plutarch's practice as analysed by F. H. Sandbach (*CQ* xxxiii (1939) 194 ff.).

(i) The so-called Asianic clausula, $-\cup-\cup$, occurs some forty-four times, or in about 14 per cent. of the sentence-ends. This figure is much lower than the corresponding one for Plutarch, about 29 per cent. in the *Lives*, and never as low as 14 per cent. in any genuine work. (If proof were ever needed that Vaucher was wrong in thinking that Plutarch wrote *de sublimitate*, it might be sought here.)

APPENDIX

(ii) The form $-\cup--\cup$ (cretic followed by spondee) accounts for some 11·8 per cent. of L's sentences; compare about 10 per cent. in Plutarch's *Lives*, and de Groot's figure of 9·35 per cent. for Thucydides, an author who does not pursue rhythmical effects. It is fair to say that L 'prefers' this, whereas Plutarch does not.

(iii) L also 'prefers' the double cretic, $-\cup--\cup\cup$ which accounts for 8 per cent. of his sentences. The comparable figure for Thucydides is 2·55 per cent.

(iv) The clausula $---\cup\cup$ occurs in about 10 per cent. of L's sentence-ends. As Thucydides has 5·7 per cent. and Plutarch nothing above 6 per cent., Plutarch may not be said to 'prefer' this, though, once again, L does. The pseudo-Plutarchean *de musica* happens to have almost the same proportion as L, though its style is in other ways quite unlike his.

(c) *Period-construction*.

It is perhaps worth while to illustrate, by means of a rather naïve analysis, the elaborate period-construction of which L is capable. Not only rhythm, but also balance and 'build-up' should be noted. I select 16. 1, a famous and much-admired passage:

(i) In the first subordinate clause ἐπειδὴ ... προκινδυνεύσαντας, note the two cola καθάπερ ... θεοῦ and καὶ οἱονεὶ ... γενόμενος, parallel in form and identical in meaning—a simple form of amplification.

(ii) In the main sentence φαίνεται ... φρονεῖν, note the set of four cola, (a) τοὺς ... παριστάνων, (b) τοῖς ... φρόνημα, (c) τὴν ... ἀξιοπιστίαν, and (d) καὶ ἅμα ... φρονεῖν. The first three deal respectively with (a) the ancestors to whom the appeal is made, (b) the audience, (c) the transformation of mere proof into 'conjuration'. The fourth, (d), is connected with what precedes differently (καὶ ἅμα instead of δέ) and thereby achieves some independence. Much the longest and most complex of the set, it returns to the all-important topic of audience-psychology, already touched upon in (*b*), and develops and explains this further.

(iii) Observe the clausulae:

ἐξεφώνησε – ∪ – – – (cretic+spondee)
προγόνους ἀποθεώσας – ∪ ∪ ∪ – – (cretic (resolved)+spondee)
ἐντιθεὶς φρόνημα – ∪ – – (double trochee)
ἀκουόντων καθιεὶς λόγον – ∪ – – ∪ – (double cretic)
-οις παρίστασθαι φρονεῖν – ∪ – – – ∪ – (cretic+long+cretic).

(iv) The trenchant conclusion οἷς . . . συναρπάσας ᾤχετο (double cretic) illustrates the effect of a smart blow after the splendid period. There is great emphasis on διὰ τοῦ σχηματισμοῦ; the point is that it is *the figure* which produces the effects.

Many other periods in the book deserve careful study. With 16. 1 compare especially 39. 2–3, where copiousness is again followed by a short conclusion (παντοίως . . . ἐπικρατοῦσαν). See also: 1. 1, 2. 2, 7. 1, 9. 13, 12. 4, 30. 1, 34. 2, 35. 4, 43. 4, 44. 9.

I. INDEX LOCORVM LAVDATORVM

Aeschylus, *Septem* 42 sqq.: 15. 5
fr. 58 N²: 15. 6
fr. 281 N²: 3. 1
Aratus, *Phaenomena* 287: 26. 1;
299: 10. 6
Archilochus, fr. 10 Diehl, 12
Diehl (?): 10. 7
Aristeas (*Arimaspea*), fr. 1 Kinkel: 10. 4
Aristoteles, fr. 131 Rose (?): 32. 3

Demosthenes, 4. 10, 44: 18. 1; 7.
45: 38. 1; 18. 18: 24. 1; 18.
169: 10. 7; 18. 188: 39. 4; 18.
208: 16. 2; 18. 296: 32. 2; 23.
113: 2. 3; 24. 208: 15. 9; 25.
27: 27. 3; dictum: 1. 2

Eupolis, fr. 90 Kock: 16. 3
Euripides, *Bacchae* 726: 15. 6
Electra 379: 44. 12
Hercules Furens 1245: 40. 3
Iphigenia in Tauris 291: 15. 2
Orestes 255-7: 15. 2; 264-5: 15. 8
fr. 221 N²: 40. 4
fr. 663 N²: 39. 2
fr. 779 N²: 15. 4
fr. 935 N²: 15. 4

Gorgias, fr. B 5 a Diels-Kranz: 3. 2

Hecataeus (*FGrHist*), F 30: 27. 2
Herodotus, 1. 105: 28. 4; 2. 29:
26. 2; 6. 11: 22. 1; 6. 21: 24. 1;
6. 75: 31. 2; 7. 181: 31. 2; 7.
188: 43. 1; 7. 225: 38. 4; 8. 13:
43. 1; locus incertus: 18. 2
Hesiodus, *Opera* 24: 13. 4
Scutum 267: 9. 5

Homerus, *Ilias* 1. 225: 4. 4; 4.
442: 9. 4; 5. 85: 26. 3; 5. 750:
9. 6; 5. 770-2: 9. 5; 13. 18-19:
9. 8; 13. 27-29: 9. 8; 15. 346-9:
27. 1; 15. 605-7: 9. 11; 15. 624:
10. 5; 15. 697: 26. 1; 17. 645-7:
9. 10; 20. 60: 9. 8; 20. 61-65:
9. 6; 20. 170-1: 15. 3; 21. 388:
9. 6
Odyssea 3. 109-11: 9. 12; 4. 681
sqq.: 27. 4; 10. 251-2: 19. 2; 11.
315-17: 8. 2; 11. 563: 9. 2; 17.
322-3: 44. 5
Variae *Odysseae* fabulae commemorantur: 9. 14
[Homerus], Epigramma Midae sepulchro inscriptum: 36. 2
Hyperides, fr. 27 Kenyon: 15. 10
pro Phryne, contra Athenogenem, Epitaphios: 34. 2-3

Isocrates, *Panegyricus* 8: 38. 2

Plato, *Leges* 5. 741C: 4. 6; 6. 773C:
32. 7; 6. 778D: 4. 6; 7. 801B:
29. 1
Menexenus 236D: 28. 2; 245D:
23. 4
Respublica 573E: 44. 7; 586A:
13. 1
Timaeus 65C-85E: 32. 5

Sappho, fr. 31 *Poet. Lesb. Fr.*,
Lobel-Page: 10. 1
Simonides, fr. 209 Bergk⁴: 15. 7
Sophocles, *OT* 1403 sqq.: 23. 3
OC 1586 sqq.: 15. 7
fr. 479 sqq. N² (?): 15. 7
fr. 701 N²: 3. 2

Theopompus (*FGrHist*), F 262:
31. 1

Theopompus (*FGrHist*), (*cont.*)
  F 263: 43. 2
Thucydides, 7. 84: 38. 3
Timaeus (*FGrHist*), F 102 a: 4. 1
  F 122: 4. 5
  F 139: 4. 1

Vetus Testamentum, *Genesis* 1. 3–9: 9. 9

Xenophon, *Cyropaedia* 1. 5. 12: 28. 3; 7. 1. 37: 25
  Hellenica 4. 3. 19 (= *Agesilaus* 2. 12): 19. 1

Memorabilia 1. 4. 5: 32. 5; 1. 4. 6: 43. 5
Resp. Lac. 3. 5: 4. 4

Zoilus (*FGrHist*), F 3: 9. 14

Scriptores incerti
  Comicus (cf. Strabo 1. 2. 30): 38. 5
  Poeta: 23. 2
  Poeta (?) (cf. Plu. *de garrulitate* 503F): 34. 4
  Tragicus (adesp., fr. 289 N^2): 23. 3

II. INDEX NOMINVM

Distinguuntur asterisco (*) quae in locis laudatis occurrunt, cruce (+) quae saepius in eodem invenies contextu

Ἀγαθοκλῆς 4. 5
Ἀθηναῖοι 4. 3, 16. 3, 23. 3, 38. 2
Ἀθηνογένης 34. 3
Αἴας 9. 2, 9. 10 +, *9. 12
Αἴγυπτος (rex) *23. 4
  (terra) 43. 2
Ἀϊδωνεύς *9. 6
Αἰσχίνης *16. 4
Αἰσχύλος 15. 5, 15. 6
Αἴτνη 35. 4
Ἀλέξανδρος 4. 2, *32. 2
Ἀλωάδαι 8. 2
Ἀμμώνιος 13. 3
Ἀμφικράτης 3. 2, 4. 4
Ἀνακρέων 31. 1
Ἀπολλώνιος (Rhodius) 33. 4+
Ἄρατος 10. 6, 26. 1
Ἀργοναῦται 33. 4
Ἄρης *9. 11, *15. 5
Ἀριμάσπεια 10. 4
Ἀριστογείτων 27. 3+
Ἀριστοτέλης 32. 3
Ἀριστοφάνης 40. 2
Ἀρτεμίσιον *16. 4
Ἀρχίλοχος 10. 7, 13. 3, 33. 5
Ἀσία *4. 2, *43. 2
οἱ Ἀττικοί 34. 2
Ἀχαιοί *9. 8, *9. 10
Ἀχιλλεύς *9. 12, 15. 7

Βακχυλίδης 33. 5
Βορέας 3. 1

Γοργίας 3. 2

Δαναός *23. 4
Διονύσιος (Φωκαεύς) 22. 1

Διονύσιος (Syracusarum tyrannus) 4. 3
Διόνυσος 15. 6
Δίρκη 40. 4
Δίων *4. 3

Ἑκαταῖος 27. 2
Ἕκτωρ *23. 3, *27. 1, 27. 1
Ἐλεφαντίνη *26. 2
Ἑλλάς 16. 2
Ἕλληνες 9. 10, 12. 4, 15. 7, *16. 2, *23. 4, *32. 2, 38. 2+
Ἑλληνικός 43. 2
Ἐνυώ *15. 5
Ἐρατοσθένης 33. 5
Ἐρινύες 15. 2, 15. 8, *15. 8
Ἔρις 9. 4
Ἑρμῆς *4. 3
Ἑρμοκράτης *4. 3
Ἕρμων *4. 3
Εὔπολις 16. 3
Εὐριπίδης 15. 3, 15. 5, 15. 6, 40. 3+
Εὐρύλοχος 19. 2

Ζεύς *3. 2, *4. 3, *9. 10, 9. 10, 9. 14+ [de νὴ Δία, v. Introd. xxx n. 2].
Ζωίλος 9. 14

Ἡγησίας 3. 2
Ἥλιος 15. 4
Ἡρακλεῖδαι (?) 27. 2
Ἡρακλείδης (Syracusanus) *4. 3
Ἡρακλῆς *4. 3, 40. 3
Ἠριγόνη 33. 5
Ἡρόδοτος 13. 3, 22. 1, 26. 2, 28. 4
-δότειος (adj.) 4. 7, 18. 2, 31. 2, 38. 4

Ἡσίοδος 13. 4
-όδειος (adj.) 9. 5

Θεόδωρος 3. 5
Θεόκριτος 33. 4
Θεόπομπος 31. 1, 43. 1+
Θεόφραστος 32. 3
Θερμοπύλαι 38. 4
Θῆβαι 15. 5
Θουκυδίδης 14. 1, 22. 3, 25, 38. 3
Θρηικίη *31. 1

Ἰλιακός 9. 7, 9. 12, 9. 13
Ἰλιάς 9. 12, 9. 13
Ἰοκάστη 23. 3
Ἰουδαῖοι 9. 9
Ἰσοκράτης *4. 2, 4. 2, 38. 2+
οἱ Ἰσοκράτειοι 21. 1
Ἴστρος 35. 4
Ἴων (Chius) 33. 5
Ἴωνες *22. 1+

Κάδμος *23. 4
Καικίλιος 1. 1+, 4. 2, 8. 1, 8. 4, 31. 1, 32. 1, 32. 8
Καλλισθένης 3. 2
Κασσάνδρα 15. 4
Κῆυξ *27. 2
Κικέρων 12. 4+
Κίρκη 9. 14
Κλείταρχος 3. 2
Κλεομένης *31. 2
Κύκλωψ 9. 14
Κῦρος *25+

Λακεδαιμόνιοι 4. 2, 4. 4, 38. 2+
Λακωνικός (ex coniectura) 38. 5
Λητώ 34. 2
Λιβυκός *15. 4
Λυκοῦργος (Aeschyleus) 15. 6
Λυσιακός 34. 2
Λυσίας 32. 8+, 35. 1

Μακεδονία *18. 1
Μακεδών 4. 2, *18. 1
Μαραθών *16. 2+, 17. 2

Μάτρις 3. 2
Μέγιλλος *4. 6
Μειδίας 20. 1
Μερόη *26. 2
Μεσσήνη 4. 2
Μίλητος *24. 1

Νεῖλος 35. 4

Ξενοφῶν 4. 4+, 4. 5, 8. 1, 19. 1, 25, 28. 3, 32. 5, 43. 5
Ξέρξης 3. 2

Ὀδύσσεια 9. 11, 9. 12+, 9. 13+ 9. 14+
Ὀδυσσεύς 9. 15, *19. 2, *27. 4+
Οἰδίπους 15. 7, 23. 3+, 33. 5
Ὅμηρος 9. 4, 9. 7, 9. 11, 9. 13+, 10. 5, 13. 4, 14. 1, 33. 4, 36. 2, 44. 5
Ὀρέστης 15. 8
Ὄσσα *8. 2
Οὔλυμπος *8. 2, *9. 6

Παρμενίων 9. 4
Πάτροκλος *9. 12
Πελοπόννησος *24. 1
Πέλοψ *23. 4
Πέρσης *43. 2, Πέρσαι *3. 2, 4. 2
Πήλιον *8. 2
Πηνελόπη 27. 4
Πίνδαρος 33. 5+
Πλαταιαί *16. 2+
Πλάτων 4. 4, 4. 6, 13. 1, 13. 3, 14. 1+, 28. 2, 29. 1, 32. 5, 32. 7, 32. 8+, 35. 1, 36. 2
Πλατωνικός 23. 3
Πλειάδες *15. 4
Πολύκλειτος 36. 3
Ποσειδῶν *9. 6, 9. 8, *9. 8
Πυγμαῖοι 44. 5
Πύθης *31. 2
Πυθία 13. 2

Ῥῆνος 35. 4

Σαλαμίς *16. 2+
Σαπφώ 10. 1
Σαρπηδών *23. 3
Σείριος *15. 4
Σικελία 4. 3, 38. 3
Σιμωνίδης 15. 7
Σκύθαι *28. 4
Σοφοκλῆς 3. 2, 15. 7, 23. 3, 33. 5 +
Σπάρτη *4. 6
Στησίχορος 13. 3
Συρακούσιοι (sic) *38. 3
Σωκράτης 4. 4

Τερεντιανός (Ποστούμιος) 1. 1, 1. 4, 4. 3, 12. 4, 29. 2, 44. 1

Τίμαιος 4. 1, 4. 2, 4. 4, 4. 5
Τρῶες *9. 8, *15. 4, *27. 1
Τυδείδης *26. 3

Ὑπερείδης 15. 10, 34. 1+

Φαέθων 15. 4
Φίλιππος 16. 2, *18. 1, *31. 1, *32. 2
Φίλιστος 40. 2
Φρύνη 34. 3
Φρύνιχος *24. 1

Χαιρώνεια *15. 10, 16. 4

Ὠκεανός 9. 13, 35. 4

III. SELECT INDEX TO INTRODUCTION AND NOTES

(a) Greek

ἀβλεμής 29. 1
ἀγανακτεῖν 17. 1
ἀγχίστροφος 9. 13, 27. 3
ἀγών xxxiii, 15. 1, 25
ἀδρεπήβολος 8. 1
ἁδρός xxx, 40. 4
ἀθροισμός 23. 1
ἀκριβής xxxiii
ἀλλά, in prayers 9. 10
ἄν omitted 9. 10, 13. 3, 27. 1
ἀναγκοφαγεῖν 31. 1
ἀναβλέπειν 44. 8
ἀνάγωγος 34. 2
ἀναζεῖν (?) 44. 4
ἀναθεωρεῖν 7. 3
ἀνακαλυπτήρια 4. 5
ἀνάστημα 7. 2
ἀναφορά 20. 1
ἀνειδωλοποιεῖσθαι 14. 2
ἀνερμάτιστος 2. 2
ἀνηθοποίητος 34. 3
ἀνήρ, ἀνήρ 3. 2
ἄνθος 10. 4
ἀντιμεταβολή 23. 1
ἀξιόνικος 13. 4
ἀξιοπιστία 16. 2
ἁπαλός 44. 3
ἀπαύξησις 7. 3
ἀπηνής 32. 7
ἀπήχημα 9. 2
ἀπό 12. 2
ἀποθεοῦν 16. 2
ἀποθηριοῦσθαι 17. 1
ἀποστρέφειν 27. 3
ἀποστροφή 16. 2
ἀπόψυχος 42
ἀρεταί 33. 1

ἀστεϊσμός 34. 2
ἀστήρικτος 2. 2
ἀσύνδετον 19
αὐλός 39. 2
αὔξησις 11–12. 2
αὐτός (τὴν αὐτὸς αὑτοῦ φύσιν) 15. 3
ἀφέλεια 34. 2
ἀψοφητί 13. 1

βάθος 2. 1
βάκχευμα 16. 4
βασανίζειν 10. 6
βασιλεύς 17. 1
βιολογεῖν 9. 15

γένος 23. 1
γλαφυρός 10. 6, 33. 5
γλωττόκομον 44. 5
γραφικὴ λέξις xxxiii
γῦπες ἔμψυχοι τάφοι 3. 2

δεινότης 12. 4
δείνωσις 11. 2
δημοκρατία 44. 2
διακληρονομεῖσθαι 12. 4
διασυρμός 34. 2
διατύπωσις 20. 1
διαφορεῖν 1. 4
διχόρειος 41. 1
δοξοκοπεῖν 23. 2
δουλεία 44. 3, 5
δύσκολος 7. 3

ἐγκαταλείπειν 7. 3
ἐγκωμιαστικός 8. 3
ἐθίζειν 9. 10
εἰδοποιία 18. 1

εἰδωλοποιία 15. 1
ἔκπληξις 1. 3, 15. 2
ἔκστασις 1. 4
ἐκτάδην 42
ἐκτραγῳδεῖν 15. 3
ἐμφέρεσθαι 10. 1
ἐν 8. 1, 12. 4, 24. 2
ἐνάλλαξις 23. 1
ἐνάργεια 15. 1, 26. 2
ἔνθεν ἑλών 34. 4
ἔνθουν 18. 1
ἐνθουσιᾶν 3. 2
ἐνσπαργανοῦσθαι 44. 3
ἐντάφιον 9. 10
ἐντρεχής 44. 1
ἐνύπνια (Διός) 9. 14
ἑξῆς xxv n. 1
ἐξοκέλλειν 3. 4
ἐπάνω 1. 4, 36. 1
ἐπαφρόδιτος 34. 2
ἐπείγει 43. 6
ἐπιβολή 35. 3
ἐπιμονή 12. 2
ἐπιπολάζειν 41. 1
ἐπιπροσθεῖν 32. 2
ἐπίρρωσις 11. 2
ἐπιστρέφειν 12. 3, 27. 3
ἐπίτασις (?) 11. 1
ἐπιφωνεῖν 4. 3
εὐγένεια 34. 2
εὐπίνεια 30. 1
εὔστοχος 34. 2
εὐτελισμός 11. 2

ζῆλος 1. 1, 7. 4
ζήλωσις 13. 2

ἡδονή 29. 2, 38. 5
ἦθος 9. 15, 29. 2
ἥρως 4. 4, 14. 2, 36. 2

θολοῦσθαι 3. 1

ἰδιώτης 31. 2
ἰδιωτισμός 31. 1

ἵνα (consec.) 10. 3
ἴσα βαίνειν 44. 7
ἱστορία 12. 5, 30. 2
ἰσχνός xxxi

καί 'intrusive' in text 3. 4, 8. 2, 34. 1; καί ... καί with one prepn. omitted, 3. 4
καί γε 13. 2
καὶ δή 16. 1
καίτοιγε 4. 4
κακόζηλος 3. 4
καταιγίς 20. 2
καταπυκνοῦν 9. 13
κατάρρυθμος etc. 41. 1–2
καταρχαιρεσιάζεσθαι 44. 9
κατασκελετεύεσθαι 2. 1
κατεξανάστασις 7. 3
κεκλασμένος 41. 1
κεκονδυλισμένος 44. 4
κλῖμαξ 23. 1
κλοπή 13. 4
κολοσσός 36. 3
κόρη 4. 4
κορυβαντιᾶν 5
κορυβαντιασμός 39. 2
κράτιστε 1. 1, 39. 1
κρίσις, κριτικός 6
κρίσις καὶ συγκατάθεσις 7. 4
κώδωνας ἐξάπτεσθαι 23. 4

λαλεῖν 26. 3, 34. 1
λαμβάνειν εἰς ... 17. 1
λείψανα 9. 12
λιτός 34. 2
λόγος 7. 4, 36. 3

μάχη 9. 10
μεγαλοψυχία 7. 1
μέγας etc. xxxi n. 7
μειρακιώδης 3. 4
μεταβολή 5, 20. 3, 23. 1
μεταξύ 32. 5
μετέωρος 3. 2
μικρότης ὀνομάτων 43

μίμησις 13. 2
μυκτήρ 34. 2

νᾶνοι 44. 5
νήφειν 16. 4
νοσεῖν 44. 6

ὄγκος 3. 1, 43. 5
οἰκονομία 1. 4
ὅρος 31. 1
οὐ μᾶλλον ... ἤ ... 9. 4, 34. 3

παιδομαθής 44. 3
παλαίστρα 4. 4
πάντως 1. 2
παράβασις 15. 8
παραβολή 37
παράβολος 22. 4
παράδειγμα 16. 2
παράστημα 9. 1
παρατράγῳδος 3. 1
παράφωνοι 28. 1
παρέκβασις 12. 5
παρένθυρσον 3. 5
παρορίζειν, 2. 2, 10. 6, 38. 1
πεποιημένος 8. 1
περί 10. 3, 34. 2
περίοδος 11. 1
περίστασις 38. 3
περιττός 2. 3
περίφρασις 28–29. 1
πίνος 30. 1
πλάσμα 15. 8
πλήν 4. 1, 9. 7
ὁ ποιητής (= Homer) 8. 2
πολιτικός x, xxix n. 1, 1. 2
πολὺ τό ... προστραγῳδούμενον 7. 1;
  cf. 12. 3, 12. 4, 22. 3
πολὺ ἔργον 16. 1
πολύπτωτον 23. 1
πολυσυνδετόν 21
πολύφωνος 34. 1
προεισβάλλειν 22. 1
προηγουμένως 44. 12

προσπίπτειν 14. 1
πρόσχρησις (ex coniectura) 27. 2
Πυγμαῖοι 44. 5
πυρρίχιος 41. 1
πύσμα 18

ῥοθίον 32. 4
ῥωπικός 3. 4

σκῆνος 32. 5
στόμφος 3. 1
συγγραφεύς 1. 3, 40. 2
συγκείμενος 41. 3
συγκίνησις 20. 1
σύγκρισις 12. 3
συνεδρεύειν 10. 1
συνιστάναι 34. 3
σύνθεσις 8. 1, 39–42, Appendix
συντομία 42
σύνοδος 20. 1
σύστασις 8. 1
σχῆμα 16–29
σχημάτιον 17. 1
σχολικός 3. 5, 10. 6
σωμάτιον 9. 13

τάξις ἄτακτος 20. 3
ταπεινός 35. 2
τεχνολογία 1. 1
τοπηγορία 11. 3
τραγῳδία &c. 15. 3
τροπικαί, scil. λέξεις? 32. 6
τρόπος 16–29
τροχαῖος 41. 1
τύπος 23. 1

ὑδρωπικός 3. 3
ὕπακρος 34. 1
ὑπέκ 10. 6
ὑπερβατόν 22
ὑπερβολή 5, 9. 5, 38
ὑπερέκπτωσις 15. 8
ὑπερήμερος 14. 3
ὑπεροχή 17. 1
ὑπολαβών (ex coniectura) 44. 6

INDEX III

ὑπόμνημα 1. 2
ὑπονοστεῖν 3. 1
ὑποφέρεσθαι 9. 11
ὑψαγόρης xxx
ὕψος xxx ff., Title

φαντασία 15
φέρων ἀπέδωκε 36. 2, cf. 43. 3
φησί 2. 1
φιλαργυρία 44. 6
φιληδονία 44. 6
φιλόνικος 13. 4
φλοιώδης 3. 2
φοιβόληπτος 16. 2
φορός (*ex coniectura*) 5
φρονηματίας 9. 4
φύσις, τέχνη, ἄσκησις 2. 1

φυσιολογία 12. 5
φωνεῖν 39. 4
φώριον 4. 5
φῶς νοῦ 30. 1

χαλινός 2. 2
χαρακτῆρες λόγου xxxiv ff.
χάρις 34. 2
χαῦνος 3. 4
χρηστομαθεῖν 2. 3
χρόνος 39. 4
χωρεῖν 9. 9

ψυχρός 4. 1

ὦ φίλος 6
ὥσπερ ... οὕτως concessive 2. 2

(b) English

Addison, J. xliv
Akenside, M. 35. 4
Allegory 9. 7
Arnold, M. xlvii
Asianism 3. 2
Attic salt 34. 2
Auerbach, E. 9. 15

Blair, H. xvi n. 1
Boyd, M. J. xxvi ff.
Boileau, N. xxxvii, xliv ff.

Criticism a duty of friendship 1. 2

Dennis J. xliv f.
Decline of literature 44

Exactness allied to meanness 33. 2
Eyes as sign of shamelessness 4. 4

Figures 8. 1, 16–29

Gibbon E. 9

Hall J. *Title*, 10. 2, 15. 4

Homer and the 'three styles':
    xxxvi n. 3
Homer's gods 9. 7
Homer: *Iliad* and *Odyssey* compared 9. 11–15

Imitation, plagiarism, &c. 13. 2–14
Inspiration, in poets and other writers 13. 2

John of Sicily, xxv–xxviii, 3. 1, 9. 9
Johnson, S. xlviii
Josephus 9. 9

Knox, V. xvi n. 1

Laughter 38. 5
Longinus, Cassius xxiii
Lowth, R. xlvi n. 3

Mean, Aristotelian doctrine of 3. 4
Menecrates 9. 11–15
Messenian wars 4. 2
'Midas' epigram 36. 2

Murray, G. G. A. 43. 2

Officia oratoris xxxvi, 1. 4

Painting, analogies with literature 17. 2
Pericles xxxix
Philo xxix, xli, 3. 4, 9. 9, 9. 11, 12. 4, 44. 3
Pity 8. 2
Plato 12. 2–5
Plato's debt to Homer 13. 3
Pliny xli, 9. 6, 22. 4
Pope, A. xlii, xliv

Quiller-Couch, Sir A. xlvii

Reynolds, Sir J. xliv, 14. 2, 34. 1

Sculpture and literature compared 36. 3
Smith, W. 4. 7
Spur and bridle 2. 2
Sterne, L. 9. 4
Style and language; see also Appendix:*
    dative ($αὐτῷ = apud\ eum$) 9. 10, 15. 4

diminutives 1. 1, 17. 1, 33. 5, 35. 4
hiatus 3. 5
negatives 26. 3, 28. 1
optatives 2. 2, 6, 7. 1, 10. 1, 10. 3, 21. 2, 29. 1, 35. 3
prepositions 3. 4, 12. 2, 16. 2
word-order (i) adv. separated from vb. by participle or phrase: 1. 1, 10. 7, 15. 6 (ii) position of πᾶς, πάντως: 1. 2, 1. 4, 9. 2, 36. 1 (iii) article or adj. separated from noun, often by verb: e.g. ἀθρόαν ἐνεδείξατο δύναμιν 1. 4: cf. 2. 3, 3. 5, 4. 4, 7, 9. 6, 9. 7, 13. 2, 14. 3, 16. 1, 20. 3, 22. 2, 28. 2, 33. 2, 35. 4, 40. 4, 44. 5. (iv) other points: 1. 4, 5 (cf. 43. 5), 10. 1, 10 end, 15. 8, 18. 2, 32. 5, 38. 1.
'Sublime', *Title*

Tate, A. 2. 3
Theodorus and Apollodorus 3. 5
'Three styles', doctrine of xxiv ff.
Tunny-fishing 23. 2

* Some examples are given here which are not discussed in the Commentary.